There is an Answer

Answer

Living in the Post-Apocalyptic World

Candace Frazee

Bunny House Books
Pasadena, California, USA

© 2008 There is an Answer: Living in the Post-Apocalyptic World by Candace Frazee
First Edition, Version 26
All rights reserved
Printed in the United States of America
Cover design and typesetting by Candace Frazee

Photo credits—front cover: Jerry Howard, drawing by Bridget Swinton, SILA August 1992; p. 1: Scott Streble; p. 5–7: Candace Frazee; p. 11: Candace Frazee; p. 17: Glendale News-Press; p. 19: Foothill Leader; p. 37: Swedenborg Foundation; p. 43: George Raabe; p. 48: Candace Frazee; p. 54: Swedenborg Foundation; p. 67: Candace Frazee; p. 69: Sweden Post Stamps; p. 72: Candace Frazee; p. 75: Jason B. Smith; p. 79: Candace Frazee; p. 93: Candace Frazee; p. 99: Candace Frazee; p. 106–107: Candace Frazee; p. 121: Candace Frazee; p. 141: Mila Zinkova; p. 147: Candace Frazee; p. 161: Candace Frazee; p. 169–170: Wikipedia.com; p. 173: Candace Frazee; p. 178–180: Candace Frazee; p. 198: Swedenborg Foundation; p. 201: Candace Frazee; p. 207: Candace Frazee; p. 209–210: Candace Frazee; p. 214: drawing by Bridget Swinton, SILA May 2000; p. 220: Scott Streble; p. 222–223: Scott Streble; p. 224: Richard Watson aka Crusader Rabbit; p. 232: LIFE magazine; p. 245: Candace Frazee; p. 274: Candace Frazee; p. 316: Steve Lubanski; p. 317: Spirituality & Health magazine; p. 318: Candace Frazee; p. 326: Candace Frazee; p. 328: Mary Nicholson, Conrad E. Iungerich; p. 334: Steve Lubanski; p. 335: Candace Frazee; p. 337–339: Ripley Entertainment, Inc.; p. 340: Henning Strandin; p. 341: Swedenborg Foundation; p. 354: The Royal Swedish Academy of Sciences; 368-369: New Church Life magazine; p. 373: Candace Frazee; p. 376: WXIA-NBCTV/11Alive; last page: Sweden Post Stamps; back cover: Scott Streble, Candace Frazee.

THANKS to
(in order of appearance in There is an Answer: Living in the Post-Apocalyptic World)
— Sweden Post Stamps for permission to reprint their 3 Emanuel Swedenborg stamps
— Ohio Historical Society for permission to quote from their website: www.ohiohistory.org
— Mary Roach for permission to quote from her books, Stiff: The Curious Lives of Human Cadavers. New York, NY: W. W. Norton & Co. (2003); Spook: Science Tackles the Afterlife. W. W. Norton & Co. (2005)
— John Wiley & Sons, Inc. for permission to quote from The Bible by Charles H. Patterson. Cliffs Notes, Revised Edition, 24 January 2003
— R. A. Gilbert for permission to quote from his article: "Chaos Out of Order: The Rise and Fall of the Swedenborgian Rite", Ars Quatuor Coronatorum, London, England: Quatuor Coronati Lodge No. 2076, Volume 108 (1995), pages 122–149
— LIFE magazine for permission to reprint page 137 from their Fall 1997 issue
— Ibrahim Kalin for permission to quote from his article: "Roots of Misconception, From the Middle Ages through the Modern Period: The European Discovery of Islam as a World Culture", Roots of Misconception: Euro-American Perceptions of Islam Before and After September 11th in Islam, Fundamentalism, and the Betrayal of Tradition. Edited by Joseph Lumbard. Bloomington, Indiana: World Wisdom (2004), pages 143–187
— Susan Cheever for permission to quote from her book My Name Is Bill: Bill Wilson— His Life and the Creation of Alcoholics Anonymous. New York, NY: Washington Square Press (2005)
— Hazelden Foundation, Center City, Minnesota for permission to quote from Not-God, A History of Alcoholics Anonymous by Ernest Kurtz (1979)
— Spirituality & Health magazine for permission to reprint their Nov/Dec 2007 cover
— Ripley Entertainment, Inc. for permission to reprint their 3 comics of Emanuel Swedenborg: #1934-09-16, #1948-01-25, #1988-08-02
— The Royal Swedish Academy of Sciences for permission to reprint their photo of Swedenborg's dream journal manuscript

For information about permission to reproduce selections from this book, write to Permissions, Bunny House Books: 1933 Jefferson Drive, Pasadena, CA 91104 U.S.A.
www.candacefrazee.com

ISBN 978-0-615-25275-9
1. Angels. 2. Spirituality. 3. Emanuel Swedenborg. I. Title.

ACKNOWLEDGEMENTS

Thanks to the Lord and Lennart O Alfelt Arvid J Ahlin Wasim Aziz Doris Barnett Reuben P Bell Edward C Bostock Jr Adriaan Braam Don Dennis Marian Elmont Richard and Adele Gladish Judy Glenn Ursula Groll Hor and Gutfeldt Jim and Kay Hauck Tuan Hauptmann Sarah Headsten Emma Heffernan Olle Hjern R L Howard Jane Howell Richard Hoyt Morna Hyatt Guus Janssen Neville Jarvis Carl Johnson Sally Johnson Mushir Khan Cedric King Vera Kitzelman Richard Lines George McCurdy R D Mote Jr Dan Negra Allison L Nicholson Pieter Noomen Judson Nyabuto Margaret Odhner Philip N Odhner Larry Peters John P Pitcairn Laren Pitcairn Louise Pollock George Raabe Bill Radcliffe Sylvia Rankin Leon Rhodes William T Rienstra N Bruce Rogers Don Rose Norman Ryder Erik E Sandstrom Ray Silverman David R Simons Rick Simons Trudy Soneson Bridget Swinton Doug Taylor Jean Treash Alan and Esther Uren Nancy Woodard Steve Honey Bunny Lubanski and the Lord

2008 is the 250th Anniversary
of the book

**Heaven and its Wonders
and Hell
From Things Heard and Seen**
by Emanuel Swedenborg

1st printing 1758
in Latin
1,000 copies

to date
Heaven and Hell
is Swedenborg's #1 bestseller
and has never been out of print

TABLE OF CONTENTS

ACKNOWLEDGEMENTS iii

PREFACE 1

INTRODUCTION 15

Chapter 1
MEET GOD'S GHOSTWRITER 20

Chapter 2
OTHER WORLDS 92

Chapter 3
WHO'S GOD? 123

Chapter 4
ANGELS 149

Chapter 5
CULTS 186

Chapter 6
IT'S NOT DIFFICULT TO GET INTO HEAVEN 195

Chapter 7
LOVE 211

Chapter 8
ERRORS AND MISTAKES 228

Chapter 9
REAL DEAD PEOPLE SWEDENBORG VISITED 264

Chapter 10
WHO'S WHO IN SWEDENBORGIANISM 281

BIBLIOGRAPHY 379

INDEX 383

REFACE

I won my school's public speaking contests when I was in grades 7, 8, 9. My speeches were about (7) humour, (8) fables, and (9) the twin advice columnists, Ann Landers and Dear Abby. That's everything you need to know about me!

I laugh all the time (sometimes to uncontrollable giggles), I love stories that teach lessons (especially the Word of God with its allegories), and I'm opinionated (enough said). Little did I know then, that I would grow up to be a Swedenborgian advice columnist running a museum about bunnies! Who could predict that?

Steve, my groom, surprised me at our wedding reception!

CANDACE FRAZEE

It just happened. Or more precisely, I was given the job by Divine Providence. There are no accidents. I was born and raised in Port Credit, Ontario, Canada. In my teens, my town was swallowed up (along with others) and Port Credit became the City of Mississauga. I was raised with my four sisters by *New Church* (Swedenborgian) parents—Keith Ivan (1923–2001), real estate broker: *Frazee Real Estate, Ltd.*; Joyce Margaret Carter (1926–1998), housewife.

I attended a *New Church* church every Sunday in Toronto, and went to a *New Church* college in Bryn Athyn, Pennsylvania. I didn't graduate. I set out to be a dancer and actress. I moved to "Hollywood North"—Edmonton, Alberta and got steady work for three seasons on the TV show *SCTV* (Second City) starring John Candy, Robin Duke, Joe Flaherty, Eugene Levy, Andrea Martin, Rick Moranis, Catherine O'Hara, Tony Rosato, Martin Short, and Dave Thomas. I also did TV commercials, radio dramas, bit parts in film, and extra work. In 1981, I became a member of ACTRA—Alliance of Canadian Cinema, Television, and Radio Artists.

In 1988, Swedenborgians around the world celebrated the 300th birthday of Emanuel Swedenborg (1688–1772). Two years prior to his Tricentenary, I joined the planning committee at my church and helped organize several events in Toronto. When I moved to Los Angeles in 1986 to "make it" in Hollywood, I found that the *La Crescenta New Church* wasn't planning any 300th celebration. So I formed a committee (called it *Information Swedenborg of Los Angeles* because Toronto called theirs *Information Swedenborg*) and got busy with plans. I rallied volunteers. With my show biz skills, I organized a big bash, SWEDENBORG: PAST & PRESENT. It was at the *Theodore Roosevelt Junior High School* in Glendale on 29 April 1988.

It was held the week Sweden's King Carl XVI and Queen Silvia visited Los Angeles. They came to the U.S. in 1988 because it was "The Year of New Sweden"—the 350th anniversary of the establishment of New Sweden in America.

About 300 people attended the Tricentenary, including The Mayor of Glendale, Carl Raggio and the Press Attaché of the Swedish Consulate, Claes Jernaeus. I hosted the event with (New Church) Rev. Cedric King of El Toro, CA. A slide presentation of Emanuel Swedenborg's life was shown; a panel of experts in psychology, science, and religion discussed his contributions to society; (New Church) Rev. Frank Rose of Tucson, Arizona costumed as a convincing Swedenborg answered questions from the audience; *Norwegian Imports & Bakery* in San Pedro donated Swedish cake and hot Swedish punch; we sang, "Happy Birthday, Emanuel"! It was a fun event.

Four searchlights lit up the sky. Guests entered under a 17-foot blue and yellow (Swedish colours) SWEDENBORG banner. The lobby was decorated with blue and yellow balloons, blue and yellow flowers. Every attendee received a blue and yellow souvenir bag of goodies including a book by Swedenborg and Swedish candy! Many companies donated to the Tricentenary. I don't do things small!

At church the following Sunday, I was handed a mailed letter from a stranger addressed to THE LADY IN THE RED DRESS with the church's address!

I attended the Tricentenary Party for Swedenborg's 300th birthday in Glendale. You were on stage. Please tell me more about the man.

L.P.
Glendora, California

I wrote back. A second letter was sent to me by another person! I answered it, too. A guest book had been set out at the Tricentenary. I figured others were probably thinking what these two newcomers were, so I wrote an Open Letter about Swedenborg and mailed it to all the 80 people that signed the guest book. I haven't stopped receiving and answering questions about Swedenborg since. That was 20 years ago.

SILA logo (drawing by Ed Redmond)
— first used July 1989

18th century caricature (stock graphic)
— reminding readers to donate money
to assist spreading the Writings of Swedenborg
— first used December 1996

My not-for-profit monthly newsletter *SILA (Swedenborg Information of Los Angeles)* is read worldwide. (*SILA* is pronounced S•eye•la not See•la.) *SILA's* motto: THERE IS AN ANSWER was adopted in November 2002.

In 1988, I crudely wrote *SILA* on a typewriter. Over the years its appearance has improved. It is usually 2-pages, but has been as large as 16 for special issues. But, my style has not changed. The answers have to be short. That is my thing. If I can't answer a question in one page, well…I have to. Swedenborgians are prolific writers. There are hundreds of excellent books and articles about Swedenborg out there already. Considered the best is *The Swedenborg Epic: The Life and Works of Emanuel Swedenborg* by Cyriel Odhner Sigstedt. I agree it's the best. Her book was published in 1952. What's been lacking are short articles.

As Ann Landers — Esther "Eppie" Pauline Friedman Lederer (1918–2002) — (my favourite) did, if I don't know the answer to a question, I contact a Swedenborgian expert to help me. What I bring as a layperson for newcomers to Swedenborg, is my enthusiastic curiosity. What people ask, I want to know the answers to, too!

September 1988
Dear *SILA* Readers,

The questions asked most often are: *Who is Emanuel Swedenborg? Why haven't I heard of him before?* My answer is: I don't know! I was born into a family of Swedenborgians. Both my grandfathers found Swedenborg's book, *Heaven and Hell*, in a public library, provinces apart in Canada [paternal in British Columbia; maternal in Ontario]. It changed their lives!

Thinking of you,
Candace

That's why I do what I do. Someone placed Swedenborg's most popular book in a library. (Actually, it was two different people!) I'm indebted to those individuals. So, since my teens, I've placed Swedenborg's books in libraries.

I answer all the letters I receive in my simple, straightforward manner, either in *SILA* or privately. I chose to use initials for published signatures because I found some that wrote *were* Swedenborgians and were embarrassed they didn't know the answers to their questions or were too shy to publicly support me when others were criticizing. Initials allow all letter writers to be equal. I do know the names and addresses of the "Anonymous" signed letter writers. I have never received a letter signed Anonymous. The moniker is used only if the writer asks to be anonymous.

I married Steve Lubanski in 1994. When we were dating, I called him my *Honey Bunny*. He liked that, so on our first Valentine's Day, he gave me a white, plush bunny holding a heart-shaped pillow that says, "I Love You This Much". For Easter, I gave him a white porcelain bunny. Before you know it, we were giving each other a bunny gift every day as a love token. And we still do that! Steve and I have acquired to date, over 23,000 bunnies and received in 1999—The Year of the Bunny—the *Guinness World Record* for the most bunny items in the world! (*Guinness World Records 2002*, page 131.) We opened our home to the public in 1998 as *The Bunny Museum* and over 14,000 have visited! That was 10 years ago!

For Swedenborg's 307th birthday, I organized an *Angel Festival* at the *La Crescenta New Church* because angels were becoming popular. Swedenborg has written more about angels (in detail) than any other author in history. So, who better to celebrate angels than Swedenborgians?! *The Angel Festival* was a success. People asked me when the next one was going to be. I thought it was a one-time event, but liked the idea of it being annual. I didn't want angels to be a fad, but a trend. *The 15th Angel Festival* is this year at the Memorial Park in Sierra Madre, CA. As you can see, I do things big every five years!!!!! (www.theangelfestival.com)

Huell Howser filmed an episode for his PBS-TV show *Visiting With Huell Howser* at our home. It aired the day after Easter, April 2007.

Nancy Rubin—Ambassador—
Head of the U.S. Delegation
to the *United Nations*
Commission on Human Rights
hopped over to *The Bunny Museum*,
12 February 2008.

Gayle Anderson
KTLA-TV News
live show 4 May 1998

Yeah Yeah Yeahs
Alternative rock band from New York
visited 15 March 2006

Katie Daryl
"Deadline" on HDNet-TV
taped 27 March 2007

Jane Velez-Mitchell with me and Steve
KCAL-TV News, taped 19 November 1999

I *attempted* to stop laughing for this photo with Adam Carolla. He was sooo funny! "Too Late with Adam Carolla" TV show, taped 22 September 2005

When I realized the 20th anniversary of *SILA* was approaching, I thought about publishing a book of "the best of *SILA*". But, all the questions are great, so that wasn't it. *There is an Answer* is more a permanent record of *SILA;* an introduction to Swedenborg available to a larger audience to raise public consciousness.

It has been a joy to read through the past *SILAs* to pick letters for reprinting. The ones selected are presented here in a different order than they were published. In the monthly newsletter, I answer questions as they come in. In *There is an Answer,* I can tell more of a story jumbling them up. However, I've included the letters original date of publication. I never made up any of the questions. Didn't need to. I always have a bundle on my desk waiting to be researched.

August 1988 was the first issue of *Swedenborg Information of Los Angeles* (note the name change from *Information Swedenborg*—I figured someone would look up "Swedenborg" in the phone book and not "Information").

When I began *SILA,* I received criticism from some New Church ministers and church members. *Who do you think you are?! You're not a minister!! A minister should check your answers before publishing them!!! You're making* SILA *too personal!!!! You shouldn't have your photo in* SILA*!!!!!*

In my young mind, I didn't know I needed to ask permission to evangelize. Naively, I thought Swedenborgians would be thrilled someone was doing it. Now, older and wiser, I can see that it is easier to read about a barefoot apple man walking around talking about Swedenborg in the past, than it is to see a contemporary pretty, buxom woman who only wears red doing it.

Dear Candace,

It took courage to begin to do what you are doing. You are doing it so well! The Lord has blessed you for taking the risk involved. You have my admiration and thanks. Please keep up the good work.

L.R.
Bryn Athyn, Pennsylvania
August 2003

Dear Candace,

I find your SILA *very interesting. I am glad you keep at it even though some people don't appreciate your efforts. I guess those who do more for the world have more enemies than those who do little.*

Anonymous
Bryn Athyn, Pennsylvania
August 2003

I persisted in writing *SILA* without "supervision" because the letters I received told me there was a need not being met. I can tell you that now there are many New Church ministers and church members appreciative of my efforts. However, I did not seek their approval because I know the Lord gave me this job.

I often think of *SILA* as the *National Enquirer* for the New Church. It's read by many in the church, but some won't admit it. It's a quick read, snappy, informative, and entertaining. It's often "quoted" in other publications without credit.

Drawing by Ed Redmond   SILA June 1990

Dear Candace,
  Have you suggested to your readers to get a loose-leaf notebook and a three hole punch to file the SILAs *for future reference?*

                                                        J.S.
                                              Iselin, New Jersey
                                                 December 1989

September 1988
Dear *SILA* Readers,
  I've decided to "personify" my monthly letter to you... I was asked by a reader to include my photo, so he could relate to a person. I find that a charitable thought. (Thanks for the suggestion!)

                                                 Thinking of you,
                                                         Candace

Dear Candace,
           You qualify!!

                                                     Anonymous
                                            New Church minister
                                         Bryn Athyn, Pennsylvania
                                                    August 1993

  One person can't make a difference. Growing up, I believed that. People said leaders need followers. But, over the years I've seen that one person can make a difference. One Valentine's Day, Steve and I set out for a romantic dinner at a restaurant. We couldn't get there because a guy was threatening to jump from an overpass, stopping traffic for miles around! Hundreds of couples couldn't get to their restaurant reservations. Gridlock. Chaos. Big news story. It turned out that it was this guy's fourth attempt at suicide on the freeway over the years; each time altering thousands of lives. I was stunned by the affect he—one person with one action—had on the city of Pasadena! It was oddly comforting to assimilate the thought. Despite the negative response I received doing *SILA* in the beginning, I knew I was making a difference in people's lives. One person can make a difference.

Dear Candace,
  Thank you for reaching out for a church that doesn't. If only we had more people like you!

                                                           A.B.
                                            Toronto, Ontario, Canada
                                                     March 2006
                                                (never published)

Dear Candace,

My feelings are that your enthusiasm and your publication is very valuable to the church.

Anonymous
Glenview, Illinois
December 2002
(never published)

Dear Candace,

One of the most enjoyable experiences last winter was meeting you. You were more than I expected. For one thing, you were much prettier than your pictures by camera. And you are so warm and friendly. I kinda expected to meet someone intellectual and aloof and cold. Thank goodness that's not you!

V.K.
Glenview, Illinois
April 2004
(never published)

Swedenborg was a rich man able to publish his books with his own money. He wrote, indexed, edited, and designed them. I wondered how *I* was going to find a publisher for such an obscure subject matter. Then it dawned on me that I could do as Swedenborg—self publish. I'm not rich, but technology now allows people to publish without a publisher!

In *There is an Answer,* I have added UPDATES to some answers and printed a few never before published letters. Both inclusions, no doubt, will delight *SILA* subscribers. For those of you new to *SILA*, you will notice that I don't answer every letter. Some don't need a response from me!

You will find throughout this book decorations or "ornaments" chosen (possibly drawn?) by Swedenborg in his first editions. Swedenborg generously used decorations in his books, so I have sprinkled them throughout mine in tribute. You can learn more about Swedenborg's ornaments at:

www.glencairnmuseum.org/ornaments/Ornaments.htm

Swedenborg used this ornament in *Secrets of Heaven*

Dear Candace,

When I read the last California Digest [church newsletter Candace Frazee edited from 2000-2005] *I got so excited I couldn't sit still. First I read your article about Johnny Appleseed and I was thrilled because I lived in Ohio (50 years) and I was so pleased to hear about the new* [Johnny Appleseed] *amphitheater.*

But when I read further and you said,

"Mark my words, the New Church will grow overnight
and explode in ways we can't imagine.
We must be ready to accept it in the form it comes",

I knew I had to tell you that I couldn't agree more.

Like you, I recognize the Ohio thing as a great breakthrough. Whatever the powers are that have been hiding the Swedenborg influences in our culture for so long, they are slowly losing power and beginning to dissipate.

Even now reading your words, I get goose bumps—because it is so true and its going to happen fast—pop. I'm sorry you weren't in Bryn Athyn when I was there. I know I would have enjoyed talking with you. Your words confirm everything I've been sensing and saying for the past 6 months.

I believe your words are truly prophetic and the time is not far off. It's already beginning to happen.

L.H.
Flagler Beach, Florida
August 2004
(never published)

Me at home, 2004

Dear Candace,

Just seeing your smiling picture over your letterhead brings back many good memories: when I met you personally, and when I admired your letters, or felt challenged, or perhaps also raised my eyebrows a little!

You do not have to be afraid: I am not critical of you, but admire your spunk, your ideas and dedication that you have upheld through so many obstacles and tribulations. Do I see a tiny little touch of mischief in your smile as well? I am not sure, but I sure hope that you keep a touch of humor in your eye in all your work!

You probably see that English is not my native tongue, and that I sometimes struggle with letters and sometimes feel that they do not fully express what I mean.

Let me take your hand and assure you my support, my genuine high estimation of what you are doing, and my wish that you will continue to find readers and supporters who will appreciate your unique combination of gifts and capacities. This letter is nothing but a warm expression of my regard for you, and my wish to bring you a little cheer, as much or a little as can be convey in a letter. Let me conclude with my deeply felt acknowledgment of your motives and style. Keep it up!

Love from,
Your Horand
Rev. Horand K. Gutfeldt, Ph.D.
New Church minister
Berkeley, California
November 1992

UPDATE
Horand K. Gutfeldt (1922–1997)

Dear Candace,
How did you end up publishing something on someone the rest of us plebeians consider so obscure?!?
N.R.
Del Mar, California
May 1993

Dear N.R.,
[After giving a brief description of my upbringing and the 300th birthday bash, I wrote the following.] I often wonder what I would think of Emanuel Swedenborg if I had discovered him on my own. I imagine I would have difficulty with his Writings. This is why I write *SILA*—to explain and exclaim—as Swedenborg has a wealth of info to offer.

In 20 years of *SILA,* 726 letters were published. I have reprinted 299 of them in *There is an Answer*. I've written 240 "Dear *SILA* Readers" columns. You will find 45 of them reprinted here. There are many, many questions that I have not been asked, but that I would like to answer. I see them everywhere. For instance, this was in the 19 May 2003 issue of *Us* magazine:

> "Our negativity collectively creates everything in the world: wars, hatred, famine, disease...Evil speech creates SARS. That's where all airborne diseases come from—evil speech about each other."
> ON HER UNUSUAL THEORY OF MICROBES,
> SANDRA BERNHARD

She is ALMOST right. Since the Second Coming happened—that's what Swedenborgians believe—there is a new consciousness that everyone is able to access from the spiritual world. All thoughts come from there. So, it doesn't surprise me that Sandra has tapped into a "new" universal truth from good spirits adjoined to her. Swedenborg wrote in *Conjugial Love* #62: **"Every universal truth is acknowledged as soon as heard. This is due to influx from the Lord and at the same time to confirmation by heaven."**

Swedenborg says in *Spiritual Experiences* #2127: **"Evil springs only from [humans] or spirits, who solely are the cause of evil."**

Secrets of Heaven #5712: **"The origins of diseases are, in general, intemperance, luxury of various kinds, mere bodily pleasures, as also feelings of envy, hatred, revenge, lewdness, and the like, which destroy [a person's] interiors; and when these are destroyed the exteriors suffer, and drag [people] into disease, and so into death."**

"Intemperance" is described as "excessive or immoderate indulgence in alcoholic beverages; excessive indulgence of appetite or passion; lack of moderation or due restraint, as in action or speech." (Dictionary.com Unabridged (v 1.1). Random House, Inc.)

Secrets of Heaven #5726: **"As death is from no other source than sin, and sin is all that which is contrary to Divine order, therefore evil closes the very smallest and most invisible vessels, of which are composed the next larger ones, also invisible; for the vessels which are smallest of all and wholly invisible are continued from [a person's] interiors. Hence comes the first and inmost obstruction, and hence the first and inmost vitiation into the blood. When this vitiation increases, it causes disease, and finally death. If, however, [a person] had lived a life of good, their interiors would be open into heaven, and through heaven to the Lord; and so too would the very least and most invisible little vessels (the traces of the first threads may be called little vessels, on account of the correspondence). In consequence [a person] would be without disease, and would merely decline to extreme old age, even until they became again a little child, but a wise one; and when the body could no longer minister to their internal person or spirit, they would pass without disease out of their earthly body into a body such as the angels have, thus out of the world directly into heaven."**

"Vitiation" is described as "to impair the quality of; make faulty; spoil; to impair or weaken the effectiveness of; to debase; corrupt; pervert; to make legally defective or invalid." (Dictionary.com; Unabridged (v 1.1). Random House, Inc.)

I am told by Swedenborgian scholars that Swedenborg would write "man" for "male"; "woman" for "female"; "people" for "people". The first MALE translators used "man" for all "humankind". You will notice that when I quote Swedenborg, I have changed "man" to "person" or "people" when that's what he means! Newer translations (done by male *and* female translators) of Swedenborg's theological books have gender-inclusive language. They're just not all re-translated, yet...

As we get older, we think less of our bodies and more of our spirits and where they are going after we die. It's supposed to happen that way. Forget the body and move on. But, modern fascination with our bodies being perfected with plastic surgery is unhealthy and keeps us living in the body and not in spirit. It's one thing to be physically fit, but physically obsessed is another thing. Materialism weighs one down. Our ancestors didn't live that long. We marvel now at how long we can on average live, even past 100! I think we are living longer not just because our food is fortified with vitamins and minerals, but providentially, so that we have more time to become spiritual!

I have written this book to share Swedenborg with the world because I know he can make life easier and more understandable. *There is an Answer: Living in the Post-Apocalyptic World* is the book I was looking for in my teens. Thanks to thousands of other curious individuals, this book has now materialized on earth; helped by thousands of angels and good spirits in the other world!

Many that write about Swedenborg get their facts wrong. When I started *SILA*, it was easy to write an author to inform them of their errors. Now with the Internet and bloggers repeating so many wrong facts, it's becoming an impossible task. I trust this book will put the truth out there and individuals will correct their own work.

If any questions arise as you read this book, please don't hesitate to ask me. I'll look up the answer for you.

People that know me because of *The Bunny Museum* may be surprised to discover I'm quite serious. People that know me because of Swedenborg may be surprised to discover I'm quite playful. It's amusing to me! Welcome to my heaven!

Thinking of you,

Candace Frazee

Candace Frazee
Madam Chair
Swedenborg Information of Los Angeles
1933 Jefferson Drive
Pasadena, California
91104, U.S.A.
www.candacefrazee.com

INTRODUCTION

Dear Candace,
I have been obliquely aware of your SILA *newsletter for a year or so, but I had never seen it and I knew nothing of its content or its editor. Now I do! Which leads me to comment on your rather unique entry into the world of Swedenborgian consciousness: More power to you! I particularly like your non-sectarian approach to your work. I like the informal and informative tone to your newsletter. I find it very engaging, and ideal for people new to the Writings of Swedenborg. Please keep it coming.*

Rev. Dr. Reuben P. Bell
New Church minister
Fryeburg, Maine
August 1990

Dear Rev. Bell,
How interesting that you have known about *SILA* for so long without seeing it! Amazing. I appreciate your compliments and encouragement more than you can know. Thank you!

Swedenborg used these astericks in many of his books

Dear Candace,
My goodness, a newsletter just on Swedenborg?

B.M.
Alvin, Texas
May 1990

Dear Candace,
You do a good job with such a specific topic. Keep up your diligence in putting forth your paper.

P.
Detroit, Michigan
May 1990

Dear B.M. & P.,
I was excited to receive your letters! Swedenborg, indeed, is worth a newsletter and more. You will discover he wrote on numerous topics. Continue to read *SILA* for information and share it with your friends.

Dear Candace,
I am a retired librarian of a Swedenborgian library. Who are you? You should talk more about yourself. I don't know if you can understand this, but I can only relate to something someone has written if I know who they are. Make [SILA] more personal.

Alice Spear
Los Angeles, California
February 1989

Dear Alice,
Thank you for asking. I am a 32-year-old, unmarried actress. I was brought up by strict Swedenborgian parents and attended the *Academy of the New Church College* in Bryn Athyn for a year and a term. I have always been interested in telling people about Swedenborg and what he wrote. The opportunity escalated in 1988 with his 300th birthday. I had spearheaded the international stamp petition to issue a new Swedenborg stamp in Canada, Great Britain, Sweden, and the United States—to no avail. That project showed me the large audience of Swedenborg readers.

After the 300th birthday party for Emanuel Swedenborg in Glendale last year [29 April 1988] which I organized—attended by the Mayor and the Swedish Consulate Attaché—I found myself answering letters about Swedenborg sent to me.

Thus the *SILA* newsletter.

Glendale turns out to honor Swedish legend

By SUSAN BROATCH
Correspondent

Religious philosopher, scientist and inventor, Emanuel Swedenborg, was remembered Saturday night, as people gathered at Roosevelt Junior High School to celebrate his 300th birthday.

Families, medical doctors, religious followers, dignitaries — such as the press representative for the Swedish Consulate — and those merely curious about this amazing man, came to learn and take part in the festivities.

"It has been said, 'You can measure a person's greatness by how he can transcend his/her own times,'" said the evening's host, Reverend Cedrick King. The rest of the evening proved how much Swedenborg had done this.

Mayor Carl Raggio opened the festivities with a brief welcome. Raggio's curiosity about Swedenborg stems from his own scientific background: The mayor was among those involved in the first U.S. space program.

After a slide presentation, the panel of guest speakers responded to questions from Reverend King. George Nash, a neurosurgeon and Medical Director at Sierra Tucson Center for Addictions, discussed how Swedenborg's wisdom benefitted the medical community today.

The highlight of the evening was the appearance of Reverend Frank Rose as Swedenborg himself, dressed in powdered wig and all, to answer questions from the audience.

Birthday cakes adorned with sparklers were transported down the aisles, as the guests sang "Happy Birthday", and then rose to eat and drink Swedish punch.

The evening officially over, many guests remained to talk to panelists, socialize and enjoy the displays.

Glendale News-Press
2 May 1988

SILA September 1988   *SILA* December 2004

January 2002
Dear *SILA* Readers,

The Bunny Museum took off because of *The Angel Festival*! When I was interviewed for *The 4th Angel Festival*, I was asked if I knew of anyone with an angel collection they could photograph for the story. I didn't, but suggested they could come over and photograph the bunny-angel section of our personal bunny collection. They did. [The photographer was real confused. He asked the reporter if this was a bunny story or an angel story.]

A year later, when Steve and I decided to share our collection at Easter with the public, I sent the *Foothill Leader* article with a press release to the media. Easter 1998 was a hopping success! Figuring we'd open up our home every Easter, we never imagined that it would become a year-round museum to satisfy the public's curiosity. We are now open daily by appointment, with an Open House on every holiday, when no appointment is necessary. (www.thebunnymuseum.com)

Thinking of you,
Candace

UPDATE

Now we receive media requests weekly from all over the world!

HEAVEN SENT

Candace Frazee holds three bunny angels, part of her collection totaling more than 6,000 bunnies.

MOVED BY THE SPIRIT

Angel Festival marks its fourth year this weekend, with collectibles, lectures and presentations in La Crescenta.

By Rodney Tanaka, *The Leader*

It must have been divine intervention.

Candace Frazee did not intend to start the Angel Festival, marking its fourth year this weekend and featuring vendors of angel collectibles and angel-themed lectures and presentations in La Crescenta.

Frazee celebrated the 307th birthday of Swedish philosopher Emanuel Swedenborg by lecturing in 1995 on the man who wrote extensively on angels during his career.

"Angels are religious and spiritual to me," Frazee said.

"I feel their influence. I know angels tell me the right thing to do."

She lectured to 100 invited guests and received calls from people who said they would have attended had they known about the event. The following year drew a crowd of 700 and last year the festival attracted 2,000 people to Atlanta.

Frazee said angel collections are a growing trend, and the festival will offer everything from angel clocks to angel screen savers for home computers.

Frazee owns a collection of rabbit figurines, with a small sub-section of rabbit angels.

ANGEL FESTIVAL

✧ **WHAT:** The Angel Festival, featuring angel crafts, collectibles and books for sale, along with speakers on near-death experiences for all religions and philosophies.
✧ **WHEN:** 10 a.m. to 6 p.m. Saturday and Sunday.
✧ **WHERE:** The New Church, 5027 New York Ave., La Crescenta.
✧ **HEAVENLY STUFF:** Door prizes, food and a free angel book to those named "Angel" who provide identification.
✧ **TELEPHONE:** 794-4458.

The festival will honor Princess Diana; Mother Teresa; the Amer-I-Can program, which rehabilitates gang members and ex-convicts into productive citizens; and Strive, an East Harlem employment service for young people who want to work but have had difficulty finding or keeping their jobs.

The festival awards are given to those that make the biggest impact during the year.

Darlene Jaman, president of the local chapter of the International Association of Near Death Study, will present a lecture regarding near-death experiences.

Jaman had such an experience in 1985 during a scuba diving accident.

She said she wants to meet others who have experienced similar circumstances.

"Many of the people who have had near-death experiences have angels that they have contacted and reached," Jaman said. "I want to show people that it's possible to have this kind of phenomenon in a person's life."

Frazee said the festival will present information on different views of angels, from Christianity to New Age to Native American beliefs.

She also said that the explosion of angel popularity, from collectibles to television shows such "Touched by an Angel," may be part of a passing fad sparked by the uncertainty of a new century. Yet she said she believes the spirituality behind the popularity of angels will continue.

"In three years, maybe the TV shows will be off the air," Frazee said.

"But there will be more people willing to talk about angels and spirituality and near death experiences."

Foothill Leader, 24 September 1997 (I didn't give a lecture as reported above!)

Chapter 1

MEET GOD'S GHOSTWRITER

Dear Candace,
  Who is Swedenborg and why should I read him?

J.A.
New York, New York
April 1992

Dear J.A.,

Emanuel Swedenborg was a wealthy scientist who went looking for the human soul in cadavers and ended up finding it in the Word of God. For a rich man he lived modestly, mostly in rooming houses in various countries. He wrote over 50 science books and pamphlets in chemistry, mining, physics, mathematics, mechanics, anatomy, geology, hydraulics, optics, botany, magnetics, mineralogy, astronomy, and acoustics. Swedenborg was an exceptional man of science who drafted many inventions such as the earliest model for an airplane—formerly accepted as by Leonardo da Vinci.

Interest in Swedenborg often stops at his scientific knowledge for he ventured into the science of "don't discuss" religion. When he was 56, in 1744, the Lord came to him and said that He had chosen him to explain to people the spiritual sense of biblical scripture. From that day on Swedenborg "talked" with angels and devils till the day he died in 1772—for 28 years!

Swedenborg asked his employer for early retirement when all this happened. He was offered a promotion instead, but turned it down in order to have time to write his spiritual "findings". He eventually wrote 30 books on Christianity. Swedenborg claimed that the Lord God Jesus Christ told him a "New Church" of Christianity would be formed, but he did not establish one. Swedenborg gave his books away for free—published at his own expense—to universities and the clergy of Europe. He was born in Sweden and died in England.

J.A., I think you would benefit by reading Swedenborg's theological books because they answer life's questions. Besides, the things he wrote about will blow you away—there is marriage (with sex) after death, God is love and wisdom, what angels' and devils' homes are like, the Bible is allegorical, the creation story is evolutional, and we will stay as teenagers for eternity!

He was a remarkable, prolific writer of psychology and religion which will serve as building blocks for future generations. Swedenborg's influence is enormous. The amazing blind and deaf Helen Keller—portrayed in *The Miracle Worker* (1962) by Patty Duke—was a Swedenborgian. Helen Keller wrote:

> When Swedenborg's message was revealed to me, it was another precious gift added to life. Heaven, as Swedenborg portrays it, is not a mere collection of radiant ideas, but a practical, livable world. I plunge my hands deep into my large Braille volumes containing Swedenborg's teachings, and withdraw them full of secrets of the spiritual world.

UPDATE

He's the "apocalyptic historiographer". That's what Swedish Professor Johan Hinric Lidén (1741–1793), in jest, liked to call Swedenborg. I like that!

Swedenborg used this engraving in *Divine Providence*

Look! Is that Swedenborg's summer house in Stockholm, where he wrote most of his Writings? Did Swedenborg draw this?

Dear Candace,
I would very much like to learn of this gentleman, Swedenborg, as I don't recall his name from high school or college. Thank you.

G.E.
Lodi, California
March 1995

Dear Candace,
I wanted to thank you for sending me the two newsletters. I think it's great that Swedenborg is finally being recognized for the things he did. I'm taking history right now in college and they don't even mention him.

B.C.
New York, New York
March 1995

Dear Candace,
I'm surprised I haven't heard of Swedenborg, since I was a philosophy major in college. Guess I concentrated more on Kant and modern existentialism.

L.P.
Philadelphia, Pennsylvania
March 1995

Dear G.E., B.C., and L.P.,
Emanuel Swedenborg was never mentioned in my high school classes either in Canada. He was mentioned in my college because I attended a Swedenborgian one—*Academy of the New Church College*—in Bryn Athyn, Pennsylvania. There are several Swedenborgian high schools and colleges around the world. Outside of these institutions Swedenborg, for the most part, is not included in educational curriculums.

I know, however, that at the *University of Hawaii*, Dr. Leon James, Professor of Psychology teaches about Swedenborg in his courses as does Dr. Andrei Vashestov at the *Moscow State University!* They are to be applauded.

It is a disgrace that Swedenborg is virtually ignored in the classroom. He certainly isn't ignored in encyclopedias. (Check him out.) To be ignored is the worst. I'd rather see Swedenborg mentioned and discussed as a kook than not at all. This may seem controversial, but if the aim is to arrive at the truth, no harm can come from the free expression of various opinions. Then at least there'd be a conversation and some might even open up a book by Swedenborg.

My suggestion to students is, if you would like your professors to teach you about Swedenborg, ask questions about him in class. *SILA* readers, you could write a letter to your local university or college (include a couple of *SILA* issues) and encourage them to teach about Emanuel Swedenborg, the Swedish philosopher.

Dear Candace,
  Were any of Swedenborg's siblings "Swedenborgians"?

H.L.
Pasadena, California
July 2000

Dear H.L.,
   No, not in the sense I think you mean—followers of his theological books. In October 1718, when he was 30, Swedenborg wrote to his brother-in-law, Erik Benzelius (1675–1743): **"Among all my brothers and relatives there is not one who has entertained a kind feeling towards me except yourself."** Swedenborg outlived all his 8 siblings.

   But, a friend of his, Major-General Christian Tuxen—chief customs inspector at the Danish port of Elsinore, and a secret agent for the King of Denmark—asked Swedenborg how many people in the world favoured his doctrines.

   "Perhaps 50," Swedenborg answered—**"50 in the natural world, and another 50 in the spiritual world."**

   As an adult, Swedenborg always spoke the truth. Saying only 50 people believed in the Second Coming as discussed in his books is certainly not the admission of a braggart!

UPDATE

   Lutheran Bishop Lars Benzelstjerna, Swedenborg's nephew, accepted his doctrines for the New Church. Swedenborg wrote in a letter to Count Anders Johan von Höpken (1712–1789): **"Bernzelstjerna is a rational man even in theology, and does not receive irrationalities from obedience to faith."**

Swedenborg used this ornament in *Secrets of Heaven*

Dear Candace,

I receive regularly your SILA. *Now I send you a report on two meetings between my friends and me. Now we prepare in Moscow an establishment of association for studying of Swedenborg's spiritual legacy in Russia. After that our first plan is to publish in Russian,* The New Jerusalem and its Heavenly Doctrine *[by Swedenborg]. I am very thankful to receive constantly your newsletter.*

Mikhail Rotschine
Moscow, Russia
February 1994

Dear Mr. Rotschine,

The report you sent is fascinating. It explains that you found Swedenborg through Wilson Van Dusen's book, *The Presence of Other Worlds,* and that you want to publish this book in Russian. Then you read Swedenborg's book, *Conjugial Love,* in Russian. Next you wrote Rev. Zacharias in Kitchener, Ontario, Canada in 1989. How did you come upon his name? Was it printed on a label in *Conjugial Love*? Rev. Zacharias directed you to Rev. Ian Franklin in California who sent you more literature. Then Rev. Franklin wrote me and asked that you be put on *SILA's* mailing list back in 1992. Currently:

- 80,000 copies of *Divine Love and the Divine Wisdom* by Swedenborg in Russian are now being distributed in Russia
- 200,000 copies of *Heaven and Hell* by Swedenborg in Russian are now being disturbed in Russia
- Professor Vashestov teaches a course called, "Swedenborg's World View" at *Moscow University*
- a Swedenborg Seminar with 6 speakers will be held at the *Moscow State University,* 5 March 1994, at which Swedenborg's books will be for sale

I have learned from others that you, Mr. Rotschine, are head of "Russia's Association for the Study of Swedenborg's Spiritual Legacy" and have been authorized to translate into Russian both of Wilson Van Dusen's books, *The Presence of Other Worlds* and *The Natural Depth in Man.* These books explain beautifully Swedenborg's spirituality and psychology.

Mr. Rotschine, I am thrilled you took the time to write me. In appreciation of your quest for Swedenborgian knowledge, dedication in translating his Writings into Russian, and the spirit of openness now felt in Russia, I am sending you a box of Swedenborg souvenirs—posters, T-shirts, bookmarkers, model airplanes, tea towels.

Swedenborg used these astericks in many of his books

November 1997
Dear *SILA* Readers,

AN EVENT OF HISTORIC PROPORTION HAPPENED

When: 6 April 1744.
What: Jesus Christ appeared to a man.
Who: Emanuel Swedenborg, 56.
Where: Hotel room in Delft, Holland.
How: Emanuel went to bed at 10:00 p.m. and was awakened at 10:30 p.m. by a roaring noise and wind; was thrown out of bed. He then felt the presence of holiness. He saw Jesus. Jesus held Emanuel in His arms.
Why: Jesus appeared to Emanuel to tell him he was chosen to tell the spiritual contents of Scripture and that he would be able to converse with spirits.
Appearance: Jesus wore a purple robe and radiated a majestic light that did not affect Emanuel's eyes.
Duration: Approximately fifteen minutes.
Dialogue: One thing Jesus said: **"Do you have a Certificate of Health?"**
—required certificate from authorities for passage aboard ship.
Source: Swedenborg wrote it in his *Journal of Dreams* #55, 6 April 1744 and Rev. Gabriel Andersson Beyer (professor of Greek at *Gothenburg University*) wrote to Carl Frederic Nordensköld in 1776 that Swedenborg told him this at a dinner party in 1765 at Rev. Johan Rosen's home when Beyer met Swedenborg for the first time.

Again?

When: 6 April 1745.
What: Jesus Christ appeared to a man.
Who: Emanuel Swedenborg, 57.
Where: Dining room in *Ye Olde Cheshire Cheese Inn,* 145 Fleet Street, London.
How: Emanuel was eating when the room darkened. He saw a vapour leave his body. When it fell on the carpet, it became worms and popped. He saw a male "angel" that wasn't there before, sitting in the corner. Frightened, Emanuel went upstairs to his hotel room. Later that evening, the same man appeared. This time, he was not frightened. He recognized Jesus Christ.
Why: Jesus appeared to Emanuel to tell him he was chosen to tell the spiritual contents of Scripture and that he would be able to converse with spirits.
Duration: Moments in dining room; unknown in hotel room.
Dialogue: One thing Jesus said: **"Eat not so much."** Swedenborg later realized He meant not only not to indulge in one's appetite, but also for him not to indulge in the natural sciences anymore, but to delve into the spiritual.

Source: Swedenborg wrote it in his *Spiritual Diary* #397 and Carl Robsahm (1735–1794) cashier at the *Swedish Central Bank* and member of the *Academy of Sciences* wrote in his memoir in 1782 that Swedenborg told him this.
Contemporary Conclusion: Some scholars suggest that the above two meetings with the Creator are one and the same. Nevertheless, Swedenborg wrote numerous times that he met Jesus Christ and was given the job of recording his visits to the spiritual world. Swedenborg wrote in a letter to Rev. Thomas Hartley in 1769: **"I have been called to a holy office by the Lord Himself who most mercifully appeared before me, His servant, in the year 1743, when He opened my sight into the spiritual world and enabled me to converse with spirits and angels, in which state I have continued up to the present day."**

Thinking of you,
Candace

UPDATE

For more information about Swedenborg's call to be a prophet, I suggest you read the article "Swedenborg's Alleged Insanity" by (New Church) Rev. Brian M. Talbot in the January–June, 1998 issue of *The New Philosophy*.
(www.thenewphilosophyonline.org/journal/article.php?issue=sanity&page=1095)
Please know the conclusion is that Swedenborg was not insane!

The world will grow to know

Drawing by Ed Redmond

Dear Candace,
  Since Swedenborg was Swedish, why did he write his books in Latin—a dead language—and not his native tongue?
                                                                Steve Lubanski
                                                                MY HUSBAND!
                                                                May 2001

Dearest Honey Bunny,
   I know Bishop Alfred Acton, II of Bryn Athyn, PA answered your question in person and told you, "Because a dead language doesn't change, the Writings for the New Church won't change; translations, yes, but not the original text." As your wife, knowing you would like some more information, I have found some for you.
   Swedenborg wrote in Neo-Latin. It was his second language having learned it around age five and used it all through school. His classroom textbooks were written in Latin, his teachers taught in Latin, his classmates spoke to each other in Latin. In his time, Latin was the language used internationally as English is for us today. His international letters were written in Latin.
   Swedenborg didn't jot down Swedish notes to himself for his books, only to translate them later into Latin. He wrote his thoughts down in Latin. Scholars today say that Swedenborg's Latin was not flowery or dull, but clear and simple. Translators have at times made Swedenborg's writing difficult to understand. That's why his theological books are now being translated, again, but this time, truer to his Latin.
   Emanuel Swedenborg said that in 1744, when he was 56-years-old, the Lord appeared to him and told him to write down truths which would be shown to him while reading the Word and on "trips" to the spiritual world.
   Immediately after his "call" Swedenborg began to keep a diary and an index to the Bible. In the book, *Emanuel Swedenborg: A Continuing Vision*, (New Church) Rev. George F. Dole talks about Swedenborg's diary and index in his article, "A Rationale for Swedenborg's Writing Sequence, 1745–1771":

> These were to serve as basic resources for his later writing; but the present issue is how they related to each other as he began to compile them. The [Bible] *Index* clearly relates to *Word Explained*, a major undertaking in its own right. He carried this work through the Pentateuch, and extended it by treating Isaiah and fifty of the fifty-two chapters of Jeremiah, at which point he apparently stopped. His intent was apparently to write a commentary on the whole of scripture.
>   The manuscript itself may have been intended for the printer. While the handwriting does vary, there is a minimum of deletion, and it was not in the two-column format that he later used for first drafts.
>   There is also evidence that the "diary" material was intended for publication. J. Durban Odhner has assembled some persuasive evidence that Swedenborg was thinking of a volume to be entitled *Spiritual Experiences*. There is also the

internal evidence, beginning early in the manuscript, of such **"addresses to the reader"** as **"To relate all the cases of experience would be prolix"** (*Spiritual Diary* #153), as well as the fact that Latin was Swedenborg's language for publication, while Swedish (cf *Journal of Dreams*) was his normal "diary language."

The format for the manuscript is, however, not up to his usual standard for submission to a printer, and his notes to himself (*Spiritual Diary* #153) indicate that he had in mind considerable editorial work. He eventually indexed it, and drew on it quite freely for other works.

[I made Swedenborg's words **bold** text.]

Oil painting of Emanuel Swedenborg
by Johann Martin Bernigeroth (German, 1713–1767)
This was the engraved frontispiece portrait Swedenborg published (1734) in his
Principia rerum naturalium (*The Principia*, or *The first principles of natural things*).
In other words, he approved of this likeness!

Dear Candace,
 What was Swedenborg's goal in writing his many books?
S.S.L.
Tahoe, California
December 2004

Dear S.S.L.,
   To write down as much as he could about the next life before he died. He didn't want money—he had lots of his own. He didn't want fame—he had had that as a young man and saw that it was fleeting. He didn't want power—he met the Lord and truly then knew who was in charge.

- He was permitted (by the Lord), starting in 1743, to see into the Spiritual World which consists of three places—1) Heaven; 2) The World of Spirits (between heaven and hell); 3) Hell.
- He learned the languages of Hebrew and Greek, so that he could read the Old and New Testaments in their original forms.
- He retired from his position on the Board of Mines in Sweden in 1747, so he could write down his spiritual experiences full-time.
- He witnessed the Last Judgment which took place in the Spiritual World in 1757—during the whole year.

Whether one believes Swedenborg saw Jesus and dead people in the next world or not, the fact remains that Swedenborg changed as a person after 1744 when he said that God visited him. He gave up his earthly belongings—job, self-importance, and vain pleasures—to follow his God-given mission in life, to write down what he experienced spiritually. This is what the Lord asked him to do.
   What would your goal be if the Lord visited you and asked you to follow Him and write books about Him? You'd write the books. Now, I'm being flip, the Lord doesn't work through fear, but imagine the power and love Swedenborg must have felt meeting the Lord! He accepted the invitation and now we have the Divinely inspired works of Swedenborg.
   In a 2 August 1769 letter, Swedenborg wrote his friend, Rev. Thomas Hartley—one of the first receivers of Swedenborg's doctrines in England: **"I rejoice at the friendship which you manifest in your letter; and I thank you sincerely for both, but especially for your friendship. The praises with which you overwhelm me, I receive simply as expressions of your love for the truths contained in my writings; and I refer them, as their source, to the Lord, our Savior, from whom is everything true, because He is the Truth Itself (John 4:6)."**
   Swedenborg wrote in *Spiritual Experiences* #803: **"The worst purpose of all is that of one whose goal is self."** It is known by the angels **"that the created universe is but a complex of means toward the goal of goals, which is the Lord, because He is Heaven."** (See *Spiritual Experiences* #798) The ultimate goal is to go to Heaven, to be with God.
   Swedenborg saw, first hand, what happens to those in the next life whose earthly goal had solely been fame and glory. It isn't pretty. An angel took him to see one such person and that devil-person was asked, if he were able to slay the whole

human race for the sake of the sole glory of his name, would he? He replied, yes, and would take the greatest pleasure in doing so. His self-love has given him a permanent home in hell, where he prefers to be. Angels once asked Swedenborg why he spoke with devils. He replied that **"it was permitted me"**. (*Spiritual Experiences* #5778) He was meant to see everything—the good, the bad, the newcomers.

Swedenborg wrote in a letter to another friend, Pastor Johannes Venator (1735–1798), 22 June 1771: **"...the Lord our Saviour leaves things which concern temporal (worldly) matters to my intelligence and judgment, and reveals to me only such things as treat of heaven and eternal life."** Swedenborg claims that he wrote **"those things which had to be written"**. (See *Spiritual Experiences* #5161) He had a useful purpose—to tell the world about what's to come and what has already happened. He, I believe, is an instrument for the Lord as the old prophets were. That's a noble goal.

Evil spirits incite evil thoughts into people's minds
In the light of heaven they appear as monsters

Drawing by Tuan Hauptmann

THERE IS AN ANSWER

Dear Candace,
  Do you know anything about Sadhu Sundar Singh?
                                                S.G.
                                   Durango, Colorado
                                     September 2004

Dear S.G.,
  No, never heard of him until you asked. Here's what I found.
  Sundar Singh (1889–1929) was raised a Sikh—a member of a monotheistic Hindu sect—in India. (Sadhu means holy man or monk.) Singh became a Christian at 15 after he saw Jesus Christ in a vision and heard His voice. He was a Christian for life, writing and evangelizing, though he was not a member of any denomination and did not try to begin one of his own.

Dear Candace,
  When a "psychic" has an almost identical appearance to a deceased "psychic" and was born under almost identical astrological signs to him, and says similar things (reincarnation, etc., evolving toward the Godhead and so on...), what gives? I'm referring to David Wilcox saying he is Edgar Cayce reincarnated.
                                                D.D.
                                   Sun Valley, California
                                     September 2004

Dear D.D.,
  Edgar Cayce (1877–1945) born in Kentucky, is often called "the sleeping prophet" because he would go into a trance and give readings for his clients who asked questions about their health. Cayce would also tell clients about their dreams, reincarnation, and prophecy.
  These psychic readings are claimed to constitute one of the largest and most impressive accounts of psychic perception to emanate from a single individual. They are housed at the Virginia Beach headquarters of the *Association for Research and Enlightenment* (A.R.E.), which Cayce founded in 1931. Edgar Cayce said he would "return" in 1998. David Wilcox claims he "is" Cayce—he uses similar photos of himself and Cayce as proof—and gives psychic readings for a living. The A.R.E. denies that Wilcox is Cayce and says that individuals claim to be Edgar Cayce on a regular basis.

Dear Candace,
  What is the difference between Ellen G. White and Swedenborg?
                                                J.N.
                                      Nairobi, Kenya
                                     September 2004

Dear J.N.,
  Never heard of her until you asked. Here's what I found.

Ellen Gould Harmon White (1827–1915) was born in Maine. She founded the Seventh-day Adventist religion writing more than 5,000 articles and 40 books. Seventh-day Adventists believe that Mrs. White was appointed by God as a special messenger to draw the world's attention to the Holy Scriptures and help prepare people for Christ's second advent. From the time she was 17-years-old until she died 70 years later, it is claimed that God gave her approximately 2,000 visions and dreams, varying in length from less than a minute to nearly four hours. White lived the last 15 years of her life in the rural town of St. Helena in northern California.

Dear S.G., D.D., and J.N.,

Swedenborg wrote many declarations; here are two.

Apocalypse Revealed #962: **"Since it has been given me by the Lord to see the wonderful things which are in the heavens and below the heavens, I must, from command, relate what has been seen."**

In a letter to the King of Sweden, 10 May 1770: **"That our Saviour visibly revealed Himself before me, and commanded me to do what I have done, and what I have still to do; and that there upon He permitted me to have communication with angels and spirits, I have declared before the whole of Christendom, as well in England, Holland, Germany, and Denmark, as in France and Spain."**

So what makes Emanuel Swedenborg's claims any different than Sadhu Sundar Singh's, Edgar Cayce's, or Ellen G. White's? Nothing. Anyone is able to have a vision and see the Lord. Many do. We are created to be able to do that. The first people on earth were regularly in contact with God. We are spiritual beings, made so that we can be connected with those in the spiritual world. Unfortunately, over time, our collective acceptance of evil loves have closed off an immediate connection with heaven and the whole spiritual world. But, occasionally, someone taps into the spiritual world and sees a vision of the Lord, or angels, or good spirits or the opposite from hell. However, Swedenborg's mystic experiences were different than other famous mystics, in that they were rational. All mysticism—the experience of God—can be called nonrational as it is deemed irrational to those outside of the experience. Similar to near-death or out-of-body experiences.

I would say that Sundar Singh's mystical experiences were genuine because of what he did with them—shared them and didn't form a denomination. I would say that Edgar Cayce's experiences were questionable—he profited from them and claimed to predict the future which as a Swedenborgian, I know is not possible, nor is reincarnation, which Cayce claimed he had done several times.

Swedenborg started by writing down his dreams. If he had stopped there, he would be similar to other mystics. But, he went on to write about the inner meanings of the Old and New Testaments. It may appear similar to what Ellen G. White did, but it wasn't. She was apparently not apprised in her visions that the Second Coming had already happened in the 18th century as Swedenborg claimed. And who wrote the inner sense of the Bible first? Swedenborg!

Who to believe then? Read any mystic's works and you will discover for yourself. Remove sentimentalism and emotionalism. Look for logic. Love is first, but without wisdom, love has no power.

Dear Candace,
 Thank you for your good words about Sadhu Sundar Singh [September]. I've translated 3 books about & by him. His tutor-Angel in the Heaven was E. Swedenborg. Please, look in the Internet article, www.baysidechurch.org/studia/studia.cfm?ArticleID=113&VolumeID=18&AuthorID=41&detail=1.

S.L.
Kherson, Ukraine
October 2004

Dear S.L.,
 Sundar Singh (1889–1929) "spoke with" Swedenborg (1688–1772)? I hadn't heard that before. I have heard of other people that have claimed to have "visited in spirit" with Swedenborg.
 It seems that every so often someone declares that they have been in contact with the venerable seer. It gives the "reporter" apparent credence. I would say, offhand, that they aren't in contact with Swedenborg, but either making it up for attention, or in contact with some spirit that claims to be Swedenborg which gives the spirit apparent credence.
 I say this because Swedenborg said that angels in heaven don't associate "directly" with people on earth. Good spirits—almost angels—do. It's noteworthy to point out that Swedenborg spoke with Mary, mother of Jesus, and he told her she was venerated. Mary said people shouldn't do that. She didn't like being given special favour in people's hearts and declared that only the Lord should be worshipped.
 Similarly, Swedenborg didn't like the term "Swedenborgian" when referring to someone that followed his Writings. He wrote to Dr. Gabriel Andersson Beyer in 1770: **"They call this doctrine Swedenborgianism, but I, for my part, call it *Genuine Christianity*."** He didn't want people to give him honours, but only to know that the Lord should be worshipped.
 The wiser—the greater one becomes—the more humble because the more you know how great the Lord is, the more you understand how small people are.
 I appreciated you directing me to the website of the *Bayside Swedenborgian Church* in Bayside, New York. They have put on their website the magazine, *Studia Swedenborgiana* article, "Sadhu Sundar Singh and the New Church" by Eric J. Sharpe, January, 1984.
 Born in Lancaster, England in 1933, Dr. Sharpe at the time his article was published was Professor of Religious Studies at the *University of Sydney* (since 1977) and President of the Australian Association for the Study of Religions. His 12-page study of the connection between Swedenborg and Singh is thorough and fascinating. I recommend it.
 Summarizing Sharpe's article, in 1920 when the Indian Christian went to Europe, America, and Australia to preach Christianity, Sundar Singh was interviewed in Oxford, England by A. J. Appasamy and B. H. Streeter. They published *The Sadhu* in 1921 and it is in that book that Swedenborg was first mentioned in connection with Singh. It is recorded that Singh prior to 1920 read Boehme, St. Theresa, St. John of the Cross, Swedenborg, and Madame Guyon.

In 1922, Singh toured the West again and in April of that year, he visited Uppsala, Sweden. During a day of sightseeing, he went to *Uppsala Cathedral* where Swedenborg is laid in honour. According to his tour guide, Archbishop Nathan Soderblom, Sundar Singh was impressed with Swedenborg's tomb and later Soderblom wrote: "For Swedenborg like him was a visionary."

How Singh first learned about Swedenborg is not certain. It is known that Swedenborg was introduced into India in 1850. (This is according to Sharpe's research; he doesn't give the evangelist's name.) In 1917, Rev. S. J. C. Goldsack, a Swedenborgian minister, gave about 40 lectures on Swedenborg in India, one in the city of Lahore where Singh had been a student a few years earlier. Goldsack gave books by Swedenborg to 10 public libraries.

When Singh was preaching in Sweden in 1922, members of the New Church contacted him. Rev. David Rundstrom gave Singh *Arcana Coelestia* (*Secrets of Heaven*) Volume 1 of 12. Singh thanked him for it in a letter. Eric von Born, another New Churchman, reported that Singh had earlier read *Heaven and Hell* by Swedenborg.

Singh then preached in Lausanne, Switzerland and it is recorded that several New Church members were in attendance. It is recorded that Singh taught in terms similar to Swedenborg.

An article by E. E. Iungerich about this public address by Sundar Singh was published in *New Church Life*, July 1922. (*New Church Life* is the monthly magazine for the largest Swedenborgian organization in the world, headquartered in Bryn Athyn, PA.) In April 1922, *New Church Life* published another article about Singh, this one by W. H. Alden. These men contended that Singh did have spiritual visions and did speak about Swedenborgian doctrines, but questioned whether Singh's visions of Jesus and the other world were given by "enthusiastic" spirits tricking him. They considered him more a spiritualist than a revelator. He wasn't revealing anything more than Swedenborg had and just a surface of what Swedenborg had done. Oddly though, not many, if any, in Singh's Christian Evangelical audiences knew about his other worldly visions. They would not have approved if he had conversed with the dead.

In 1926, Sundar Singh published his book, *Visions of the Spiritual World*. He does not mention Swedenborg in it. His book was reviewed in the monthlies, *The New Church Review,* October 1927 and *The New Church Messenger*, November 1927. It is said in both articles that Singh's and Swedenborg's descriptions of the other world were *so* similar. "Why?" was the question both asked.

In *Visions of the Spiritual World,* Singh tells about one time he was talking with angels and he asked their names. They didn't give them, saying, their spiritual names were different than their earthly names. Two years after his book was published, Singh wrote A. E. Penn, Secretary of the Indian *Swedenborg Society* that he had been in contact with "the angel of Swedenborg" for several years and wrote: "After I have finished touring I hope to write something about my conversation with Swedenborg in the Spiritual World." (He never did.) He wrote Rev. John Goddard of Newton, Massachusetts similar comments.

In 1929, Appasamy visited Singh again and he reported that Singh said: "I, too, see wonderful things in the spiritual world, but I cannot describe them with the accuracy and ability that Swedenborg has. He is a highly-gifted and well-trained soul. Having read his books and having come in contact with him in the spiritual world I can thoroughly recommend him as a great seer." In April of 1929, Sundar Singh travelled to Tibet and was never heard from again. His mysterious ending has created an aura of wonder about his life.

If Singh *did* see true spiritual visions, and *if* Singh *did* see the angel Swedenborg, the only conclusion is that that was wonderful and by his own admission, Swedenborg's books are to be read for a greater understanding of Jesus Christ and the spiritual world.

Dear Candace,

The answer to my question (September) was informative and at least has silenced my friends. However, when I told them that you had never heard of Ellen G. White before they were simply horrified. Why? Because they had been told that she is the byword for Christianity. That an American of Christian beliefs did not know her was mind-boggling to say the least!

J.N.
Nairobi, Kenya
December 2004

Dear J.N.,

I'm sorry your friends were misled. Saying something is true, when it is later seen as false, should lead one to question what else one was told...

UPDATE

Propaganda is usually associated with the negative. But, propaganda can be any message aimed at influencing others to your persuasion. It's not telling the "whole truth" or "withholding truth".

Ex-member Rev. Dudley Marvin Canright (1840–1919) said White plagiarized many writers including Swedenborg, in his book, *Life of Mrs. E. G. White, Seventh-day Adventist Prophet: Her False Claims Refuted* by D.M. Canright (1919). He was a preacher in the Seventh-day Adventist Church for 22 years.

Dear Candace,

I'm reading the Spiritual Diary, Volume IV, *which has illustrations, as you know. Too bad Swedenborg drew so few diagrams and pictures, which would serve to clarify difficult concepts such as are found in "heavier" works like* Divine Love and Wisdom. *I find the* Diary *fascinating and easy to grasp by contrast.*

P.R.
San Francisco, California
April 1997

Dear P.R.,

For scholars and the truly curious, the *Spiritual Diary* is a treasure trove. It is not for a newcomer to Swedenborg's books. It's best to have at least read his *Heaven and Hell* to give one a basis of comprehension of what he believes in. Because it was a private journal, not for publication, it is a collection of (almost daily) scenes he witnessed and facts he accumulated. Its appearance in manuscript form is much like someone's diary would appear today, unpolished for publication, with cross-outs, corrections, notes in the margins, and scribbly drawings.

Emanuel Swedenborg in his diary, not only jotted down seemingly random thoughts, but also drew 19 illustrations for his own reference. Much like someone would scribble down a map to a party's location, he drew maps of where he visited in the spiritual world, sometimes marking N, S, E, and W. Other times marking A, B, C, and D. And then he described what happened where in his spiritual journeys. Accompanying one sketch, he wrote the following in *Spiritual Experiences* #5249:

"At A was a precipice: the highest habitation, or city, was at BC; a second, at BD, a third, at DE; the shaft, made by windings, through which they descended, at FG; and the lower habitations, where were those of the greater consequence, was at IK."

In Volume V, he drew a map of Africa.

Swedenborg drew with words. He said that illustrations take place in the mind of a person according to their will and understanding. He obviously preferred to leave the reader in freedom to visualize for themselves spatial descriptions. He knew that each person would only see what their own enlightenment permitted them to see, no matter whether he drew them a great drawing of a heavenly scene or not.

Emanuel used his large personal diary as a reference book to refer back to as he wrote his other books. A Swedenborgian scholar can quickly find parts he used from his diary in his other books. Some paragraphs were used, sometimes condensed, sometimes expanded. Translators of Swedenborg's diary figured out that after Swedenborg had used a sentence in a book, he would cross-out that sentence in his diary! Some sentences have more than one line drawn through them. The translators also figured out that he would do that after putting it in the diary's index he kept! Swedenborg was a thorough man.

We are indebted to the translators of Swedenborg's diary (and his other books). This was not an easy task as the diary was in several folios. ("Folio" is described as "a large sheet of paper folded once in the middle, making two leaves or four pages of a book or manuscript." Dictionary.com; The American Heritage Dictionary of the English Language, Fourth Edition. Houghton Mifflin Company.)

He would be writing a book and put diary entries in it and then continue writing the book! Sometimes on his travels, his folios weren't available which had previous entries, so he would start another folio with daily entries. However, he did date every entry.

One translator of *The Spiritual Diary* (1883) has historical notoriety for being the great-great granduncle of the 41st American president, George Herbert Walker Bush. He was Professor George Bush, M.A. In 1845, Rev. Dr. Bush left Presbyterianism for Swedenborgianism and preached in Brooklyn, New York. In 1989, Dr. William R. Kintner, a Swedenborgian living in Bryn Athyn, an acquaintance of the former president, wrote Bush about his great-great granduncle. President Bush (41st, 1989–1993) wrote:

> Dear Dr. Kintner:
> Many thanks for your good letter sharing the works of theologian and scientist Emanuel Swedenborg. The passages you sent are most interesting, and I appreciate your thinking of me.
> With best wishes, in which Barbara joins.
> Sincerely, George Bush

UPDATE
As a student at the *Bryn Athyn College*, I housecleaned for Dr. and Mrs. (Xandree Marie Wyatt) Kintner. I wasn't aware of his distinguished history until recently. William Roscoe Kinter (1915–1997) retired from the Army in 1961 at the rank of colonel. He became Professor of Political Science at *University of Pennsylvania*; President Gerald Ford's Ambassador to Thailand (1973–1975); Deputy Director, then Director, then President of *Foreign Policy Research Institute* (1961–82). He authored many books including *Role of Ancient Israel, Written With the Finger of God: A Swedenborgian Perspective on the History of the Israelites from Abraham to Jesus* (1996). He is the father of Dr. Jane Kintner Williams-Hogan, Professor of Sociology and History at the *Bryn Athyn College*, a former teacher of mine. I didn't know then that I was cleaning the home of my teacher's parents!

www.newcenturytv.com/swedenborg

Dear Candace,
Do you know if the Bush family had any connections to the Swedenborg church? I seem to recall the name George Bush in connnection with Swedenborg's Writings sometime in the past and wondering if it might have been George W. Bush's great grandfather.

P.H.
Los Osos, California
March 2002

Dear P.H.,

Professor of Hebrew and Oriental Literature from 1831–1847, George Bush, M.A. (*New York University*), great-great-great granduncle of our current president, George W. Bush was a Swedenborgian. Some *SILA* readers may remember that I wrote about him ten years ago this month!

George Bush (1796–1860) published a pamphlet in 1846, *Statement of Reasons for Embracing the Doctrines and Disclosures of Swedenborg*. He went on to translate *The Spiritual Diary of Emanuel Swedenborg, Being the record during twenty years of his supernatural experience* (5-volumes) from Latin into English with Rev. John H. Smithson (1883). Excerpts from the Preface:

> The Diary, it is presumed, should be considered as a storehouse of spiritual facts, phenomena, and principles, which the author wrote down at the time he heard and saw the things he states and describes.
>
> ...it was not the author's intention to publish this work...
>
> That the author, however, thought his Diary of great importance, is evident from the fact of his having made a copious Index to its contents...
>
> The reader, being thus, as it were, introduced into the private company of Swedenborg, will receive a more vivid impression from the things described, and will be more thoroughly convinced of his extraordinary mission and office.

UPDATE

George Bush also wrote *The Life of Mohammed: Founder of the Religion of Islam, and of the Empire Saracens*, published in 1830. Imagine Rev. Bush's surprise when he began to read Swedenborg in 1845 and found that Swedenborg had written about Mohammed!

Dear Candace,

I'm embarrassed to say I never knew of Swedenborg. I'm of Swedish descent, too.

B.H.
Irving, Texas
May 1993

Dear B.H.,

You're not alone. I remember watching a TV game show (was it *Jeopardy*?) as a teenager in Canada. I jumped out of my chair when the question asked was: WHAT COUNTRY WAS EMANUEL SWEDENBORG FROM? Not one of the three contestants knew or guessed the obvious!

Unfortunately, Swedenborg is taught in Swedish schools as a mad scientist —a highly respected scientist that ended up in his twilight years seeing ghosts—or not at all. In time, this opinion will wane as acceptance of the reality of the other world strengthens.

North American bestsellers such as *Life After Life* by Raymond A. Moody, Jr., M.D. (1975) and *We Don't Die: George Anderson's Conversations with the Other Side* by Joel Martin and Patricia Romanowski (1988) credit Swedenborg with knowledge of the here-after—giving him his due.

After all, an occurrence at death, written about by Swedenborg over 200 years ago has become a common saying: I CAN SEE THE LIGHT AT THE END OF THE TUNNEL. Soon more catch phrases will be culled from Swedenborg.

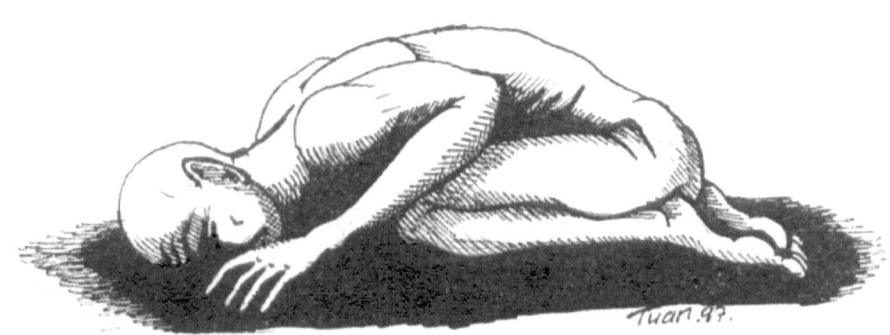

True humility is necessary for entrance into heaven

Drawing by Tuan Hauptmann

Dear Candace,
 How come Swedenborg never got credit for his inventions?

J.Z.
Huntington, New York
May 1992

Dear J.Z.,
 He did. You can read about Swedenborg's accomplishments in any encyclopedia—improvements to the hearing aid of his time, a musical machine that is a forerunner of our phonograph, a tank for testing ships that is similar to today's. He is on occasion mentioned in science classes and in philosophy books, but more often than not just among a list of other great thinkers without clarification.

Swedenborg and his finds are seldom discussed in detail because of his religious teachings. This is changing. For example, it is a fact that Swedenborg was the first to invent the airplane—the first rational design for heavier-than-air flight. It is a shame that schools are still teaching that Leonardo da Vinci (1452–1519) did. Da Vinci was the first to mechanically study flying in a scientific manner. He was a pioneer of aviation, but he did not invent a workable airplane. Swedenborg did.

In 1712, when Swedenborg was 24, he mailed to his father in several letters some inventions he had drawn, no doubt including his flying machine. The drawings were burned in a fire that destroyed his father's home! In 1714, Swedenborg shipped some of his books and documents (which included some sketches of his inventions) back home when he was abroad, and they were never delivered! The same year, he wrote his brother-in-law, Erik Benzelius and mentioned he had invented 14 machines of which were a flying machine and a submarine. This letter is preserved.

Swedenborg published his flying machine manuscript in his scientific magazine, *Daedalus Hyperboreus* (*The Nordic Daedalus*) in the October–December 1716 issue. The young inventor moved on to other inventions and other books to be written. He never took his invention of the airplane further. Attention on his airplane did not surface again until 1868 (almost a hundred years after Swedenborg's death), when a Swedenborg scholar discovered the brother-in-law's letter and the publication *Daedalus Hyperboreus* in Swedish libraries.

In 1909, Swedenborg's airplane manuscript was translated into English and published by another Swedenborgian scholar. In 1910, *The Journal of the Royal Aeronautical Society* (not a Swedenborgian organization) in London, printed Swedenborg's manuscript and drawing of the first flying machine.

Aviation was a hot issue at this time:
- first manned flight in North Carolina
 by Americans Orville and Wilbur Wright, 1903
- first flight in Europe in France
 by Brazilian Alberto Santos-Dumont, 1906
- first solo flight across the English Channel
 by Frenchman Louis Bleriot, 1910
- first public air passenger flights
 by the *Zeppelin's Delag Company*, Germany, 1910

Historical interest in aviation waned during the world wars as focus was on military aircraft. A 3–4 foot-wide model of Swedenborg's airplane was unveiled at the *Smithsonian Museum* in Washington, D.C, 29 January 1962. It is on display in the Early Flights Room. For a complete and excellent account of aviation history, I recommend *Swedenborg's 1714 Airplane: A Machine to Fly in the Air* by Henry Söderberg (published in 1988).

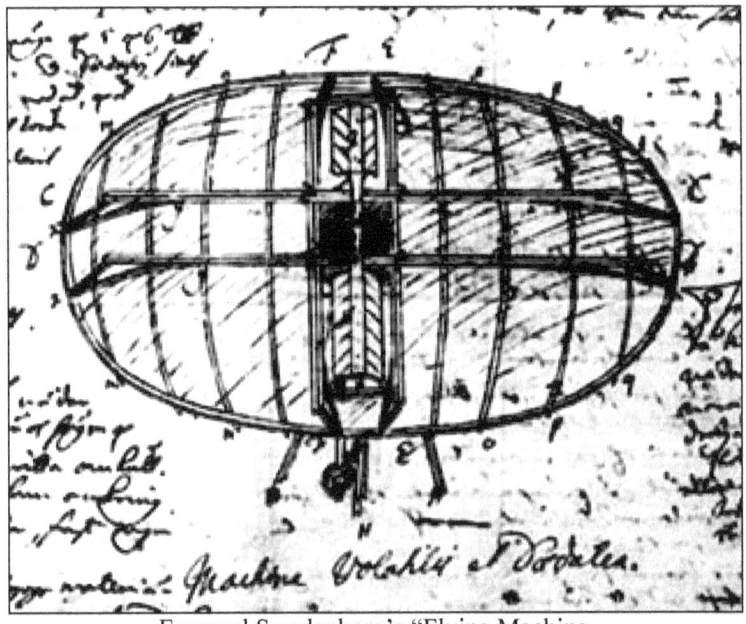

Emanuel Swedenborg's "Flying Machine, or the possibility of being sustained in the air, and being conveyed through it." Swedenborg was not copying a flying-saucer-shaped aircraft he saw!

Dear Candace,

I admire your missionary spirit. I am pretty sure that you have friends in your circle of recipients of the letters who really appreciate this sign of friendship and the well wishes from you, and, not only that, but who feel moved by your loyal and straight adherence to the interpretation of the Word of God through Emanuel Swedenborg. Even if I am not a Swedenborgian in the true sense of the word, I think...when I am checking out my beliefs and inner feelings with your writings and quotations, that I agree to most everything...thus, I must be not only a friend but a near relative of yours and my Swedenborgians friends in the USA and in other parts of the world. We are family, in a way. Affectionately yours,

Henry Söderberg
Stockholm, Sweden
April 1989

October 1997
Dear *SILA* Readers,

> In Loving Memory of
> Henry Söderberg
> 1916–1997

On Friday, 18 November 1988, I organized a lecture by Henry Söderberg, retired Vice President of *Scandinavian Airline Systems (SAS)* at the *La Crescenta New Church*. He spoke on Swedenborg's aircraft design. In America from Sweden on a book tour, sadly, his thoroughly researched book, *Swedenborg's 1714 Airplane: A Machine to Fly in the Air*, was not a bestseller.

School textbooks have not recorded correctly who designed the first airplane. Mr. Söderberg, after figuring out Swedenborg designed the first flyable aircraft wrote: "Even learned and intelligent friends of mine, experts in aeronautics, assured me, when I told them about my discovery, that it was Leonardo da Vinci who had invented the airplane—which is, of course, quite wrong."

I noted in the November 1988 *SILA* that when I called up the newspapers (because they hadn't responded to the press releases I sent out), I was laughed at! I couldn't convince a journalist to cover the lecture. I was told Leonard da Vinci had invented the airplane, period. When will this misconception end?

Mr. Söderberg was a delight to be with, strong and inquisitive. He wanted to tour *Wayfarers Chapel* (a Swedenborgian church) which overlooks the Pacific Ocean. I got a carload of friends and we took him there. His childlike wonder at seeing the beautiful famous chapel warmed my heart. It was a privilege to have given this remarkable Swede a treat he had been looking forward to for years.

Thinking of you,
Candace

UPDATE

When I met Henry Söderberg he gave me his biography, *The Welcome Swede* and autographed it for me:

> *To Candace Frazee with all good wishes from "The Swede" himself.*
> *I enjoyed meeting you. You have a great future in store with your talents and beauty which you are so humbly giving to a great cause.*
> *God bless—hope to see you again, on the screen, or, better, live!*
> *Henry Söderberg*
> *Nov. 18, 1988*

Me and Henry Söderberg inside (the walls are glass!) *Wayfarers Chapel* in Palos Verdes, CA. Mr. Söderberg told me that I was of the "salt of the earth, but, be careful. We need it, but not everyone wants it."

The Welcome Swede: The true story of a young man who brought hope to thousands of Nazi Germany's prisoners of war by J. Frank Diggs (1988) was written by one of those prisoners, J. Frank Diggs (1918–2004). He served 37 years (retiring in 1982) as senior editor at *U.S. News & World Report* magazine. Among Diggs's work is a 13-page interview with Navy Commander John McCain about his 5½ years as a prisoner of war in Vietnam.

Diggs appreciated visits from the friendly, Swedish lawyer who was only one of seven foreign nationals the Germans allowed to travel freely into the Nazi prison camps. (Sweden was a neutral nation.) Söderberg, as the *International YMCA* representative, visited all allied P.O.W. camps all over Germany.

Edward McMillan, 88 of Wenham, Massachusetts won the "What's Your YMCA Story?" contest. This was reported 22 April 2008 in the *Hamilton-Wenham Chronicle* newspaper (www.wickedlocal.com/hamilton/archive/x914614535):

"A P.O.W. had three main problems," McMillan wrote, "food, clothing and how to remain sane for 16 waking hours a day for no one knew how long." Soderberg visited their camp to see what they may need. Soon after he left, books arrived for the soldiers. McMillan recalls picking up a copy of Tolstoy's "War and Peace."

"All 935 pages. The thicker the book, the better," he wrote. After books, came sports equipment, like baseballs and bats. The soldiers cleared out one portion of the camp and created ball teams. A while later, musical instruments arrived and the soldiers created a jazz band.

"The Red Cross did a wonderful job in supplementing the food and clothing the Germans gave us, but nothing was done to preserve our sanity until Henry showed up," wrote McMillan. "It has always been my feeling that while the Red Cross's work was vital to our bodily health, the work the Y did was equally valuable for the health of our minds and they never really received any credit for the work they did."

Dear Candace,

If I had had your information on Swedenborg's airplane prior to my Smithsonian [Museum] visit it would have made the experience much richer.

F.G.
New York, New York
June 1992

Dear Candace,

I think I should read Emanuel Swedenborg. I did not know he played a big role in today's aviation. As you see, I work for Virgin Atlantic Airways here in New York. Sure, please send more information about Mr. Swedenborg.

E.H.
Brooklyn, New York
June 1992

Swedenborg used this ornament in the *New Jerusalem and its Heavenly Doctrine*

Dear Candace,
Emanuel Swedenborg helped me stop smoking and knows how much I appreciate that and him. Congratulations for your sincerity. Have fun—dear one—and never stop aiming for the larger picture.

M.E.B.
San Pedro, California
April 1994

Dear M.E.B.,
That's quite an accomplishment. You should be commended for quitting smoking. I'm glad Swedenborg helped you to achieve this goal. You, no doubt, were assisted by what he wrote on:
- self examination
- repentance
- prayer
- trust in Divine Providence
- abstinence

Swedenborg advised us to examine ourselves once or twice a year as to the evils we allow to stay within us and tells us to repent—to feel so contrite over one's sins as to change. Noteworthy is the once or twice a year instruction. True soul searching and self correction is difficult. A comforting truth we are told by Swedenborg is that once we *start* the process, the Lord will then *hold* us back from the evil.

M.E.B., I'm concerned that you may think that Swedenborg knows he helped you to quit smoking. He doesn't. Swedenborg is not omniscient. He is not a god, nor a saint. He was an intelligent man, but with no divine powers. In fact, not even our associate spirits (dead people who live in spirit around us that we attract) know who they are hanging around. If they did and if we did, we would both spiritually loose our freedom.

That is not to say we occasionally are aware of a dead relative near us, or may learn something about an associate spirit through déjà vu, but to know more than that would influence our individual freedom.

Dear Candace,
Must say that your SILA *leaflet is more essential than other big volumes.*

S.L.
Kherson, Ukraine
July 2006

Dear Candace,

I didn't know anything about Swedenborg, let alone the New Church, until about two years ago when I just happened upon an old book entitled Reasonable Religion *by E. Brayley Hodgetts, which made a profound effect on me. Since then, most all I've been reading these days are books by and about Swedenborg!*

The message of God's love and wisdom was something that I had always vaguely felt within me, but I had to discover the Writings to know *the truth of this Divine reality. It has all been an exciting adventure, following the Lord's appointed revelator of the internal sense of the Word into his descriptions of the three, 2-kingdomed heavens, the hells, and the world of spirits. We all now know something of what to expect when our time comes for the hereafter. Is it too grand a gesture to call Swedenborg the most amazing personality to have lived in this world in the last 2,000 years? I think not, though most of my friends still just brush him off. Of course, Swedenborg would have been the first to point out that all his brilliance came from the Lord, just as all love does.*

P.R.
San Francisco, California
January 1989

Dear Candace,

That Swedenborg was a gardener was one of many things I didn't know about him until I read it in SILA. *Your publication continues to please me and my brother.*

C.B.
Bryn Athyn, Pennsylvania
April 1992

Emanuel Swedenborg used this ornament in his book
The Infinite and Final Cause of Creation (1734)

He wrote this book before his "spiritual eyes" were opened in 1744,
so it's different theologically than his books after the Lord visited him.

Is that a self-portrait?

Dear Candace,

I just received your SILA *newsletter today. It's very interesting. I've never heard of him. This may be a silly question, but is Mr. Swedenborg still alive? From some of the things I read I get that impression.*

K.M.
Voorhees, New Jersey
September 1990

Dear K.M.,
No question is silly! I like your observation because it conveys two things: 1) what Swedenborg wrote over 200 years ago is still relevant today; 2) his humanity can jump off a page and make one talk about him as a friend: *Did you read what Swedenborg wrote?! Swedenborg said it! You've got to read Swedenborg!*

Swedenborg is not still alive. He died in 1772 in London, England. His Writings live on, however. They will awe you.

Dear Candace,
    How did Swedenborg die?

L.W.K.
Pasadena, California
September 1992

Dear L.W.K.,
Swedenborg took his last trip to London in 1771. He rented the 2nd floor apartment (parlour and bedroom) at 26 Great Bath Street, Wellclose Square for 5 shillings a week. The landlord was Richard Shearsmith, a wigmaker. Swedenborg had stayed there before.

He had a stroke just before Christmas, paralyzing one side. He was bedridden for three weeks, unconscious. Awakened, Dr. Messiter and Dr. Hampe (teacher to the Prince of Wales) prescribed some drops for their patient, but he refused to take them.

Two days before he died, a friend asked if he wanted to take Holy Supper. He did. Swedish Lutheran minister, Rev. Arvid Ferelius asked Swedenborg to deny completely or partly his new Christian books. He said Swedenborg must surely have written them to make a name for himself! Agitated, Swedenborg sat up and said: **"As truly as you see me before your eyes, so true is everything that I have written; and I could have said more had it been permitted. When you enter eternity you will see everything, and then you and I shall have much to talk about."**

In February 1772, Rev. John Wesley, a founder of the Methodist religion, received a letter from Emanuel Swedenborg: **"I have been informed in the World of Spirits that you have a strong desire to converse with me. I shall be happy to see you, if you will favour me with a visit. I am, Sir, your humble servant, Eman. Swedenborg."**

Wesley, astonished, admitted to his friends that he did indeed want to meet Swedenborg, but he had told no one that! He wrote Swedenborg back and said he could visit in six months, when he returned from a planned trip. Swedenborg replied, saying, that would be too late as he, Swedenborg, was to die on March 29th!

Sunday, the 29th of March, Mrs. Shearsmith (the landlord's wife) and Elizabeth Reynolds (their maid) were at Swedenborg's bedside. The clock struck. He asked what time it was. "Five o'clock," said Mrs. Shearsmith. **"That is good. I thank you. God bless you,"** said Swedenborg. He took his last breath.

I'm reading an original manuscript of Swedenborg's! It was breathtaking! On the shelves are all his original books (which he bound himself) in a sealed vault at *The Royal Swedish Academy of Sciences* in Stockholm, Sweden.

Depending on how much was available, he would use paper as wide as 8" or as small as 3". He used abbreviations. He would write a paragraph and then leave the rest of the page blank, in case he wanted to add more on the subject at another time. If he ran out of room on a page, he would insert a smaller sheet and write on that. [This was before post-it notes.] Swedenborg, the man, came to life for me when I saw a coffee cup stain in the centre of a page!

SILA October 1998

THERE IS AN ANSWER

Dear Candace,
What do you make of Sylvia Browne?

B.C.
Hollywood, California
February 2007

Dear B.C.,
    I have not met Sylvia Browne nor have I read any of her books. Well, I've read a few pages standing in a bookstore and online. (She has had 35 books published by *Hay House, Inc.,* headquartered in Carlsbad, CA.) But, over the years, I have watched many of her TV appearances on *Larry King Live* and *The Montel Williams Show*.
    While I am aware that "psychic" Sylvia Browne has sold over a million books and people are still hiring her for spiritual help, I personally don't understand why. I find her to be abrasive, unfriendly, arrogant, and a bully. She interrupts people and has an air of superiority that I find offensive.
    While many of her psychic predictions have proven NOT to be correct—by critics that follow such things—she came under the public microscope on 12 January 2007, the day Shawn Hornbeck was discovered alive after being kidnapped as an 11-year-old on 6 October 2002. Psychic critics alerted the press that Sylvia Browne had said on *The Montel Williams Show,* to Shawn's parents, that their missing Missouri child had been murdered. News shows replayed the 2003 clip of her saying it. *Montel Williams* didn't.
    This false prediction wasn't news to Robert S. Lancaster, a computer programmer living in Los Angeles County. (He doesn't reveal where he lives for his own safety.) Lancaster created a website, last year, to warn potential seekers that, in his opinion, Browne is a fraud, not a psychic medium. For more information go to: www.StopSylviaBrowne.com.
    Browne also had said, last year, on George Noory's live syndicated radio show, *Coast to Coast* (as it was breaking news) that the thirteen trapped West Virginia miners were alive. Twelve were later found dead.
    You can learn Browne's life story from www.Sylvia.org or by searching her name on the Internet. Her website states Sylvia has been a psychic since she was three. Her son, Chris Dufresne is also a psychic "from birth". Both are available for private, 20–30 minute, psychic phone readings. Sylvia charges $750; Chris, $450.
    Of note, news agencies had reported in 1992 that Browne had become a convicted felon having used her psychic abilities to defraud the public in a gold investment scheme in 1988. She claimed to psychically know that the mine would pay off. She pleaded no contest, plea bargained, and had to pay back the investors (or victims). Sylvia claims to her fans, it was her ex-husband's fault, and she had no knowledge of it.
    In my research, I found so many negative stories about Sylvia Browne, that in my opinion, they should outweigh her popularity. I find other psychic personalities to be much more kind and sincere than Browne. Not that I give credence to any psychic, but Browne always rubs me the wrong way.

I can only surmise that Sylvia Browne's popularity stems more from people's *need to know* about the spiritual world, than her knowledge *of* the spiritual world.

Most of her books are written with another author, ghost written, and/or plagiarized. Apparently, *Secrets & Mysteries of the World* by Sylvia Browne (2005) contains a lifted paragraph from Joe Nickell's article that was published in the July/August 1998 edition of *Skeptical Inquirer* magazine.

Browne has also written:
- *Father God: Co-creator to Mother God*
- *Mother God: The Feminine Principle to Our Creator*
- *The Mystical Life of Jesus: An Uncommon Perspective on the Life of Christ*

While many of her books have been #1 bestsellers, her "revelations" in them are not original or insightful. Sylvia Browne is marketed as "down to earth" with a "great sense of humor". I find Browne to possess neither trait. That people gravitate to her for glimpses into the spiritual world is totally understandable. People want answers!

Sylvia Browne does what is called "Cold Readings"—a method of investigation where a psychic calls out initials, names, colours, and objects until a match is met and the client lets the psychic know they understand what the psychic is "getting" from the spiritual world. Supposedly. Often, the psychic will "appear" to be right.

It's oddly interesting that Sylvia's son, Chris, is the only psychic recommended by her. Her website states he is "the best alternative to Sylvia". Does that mean that Sylvia Browne is the best source of all spiritual knowledge? Read this from www.sylvia.org:

> While Sylvia or Chris is doing a reading for you, they psychically reach into your soul, pull out your Chart, and then recite back to you those things you have already planned for yourself. There is nothing mysterious about this; it is simply their gift from God, one that they have perfected to a very high degree.

Sylvia is also famous for diagnosing physical illnesses and pregnancies. It shocks me that people will heed her medical advice! Keep in mind, this is a woman that recommends you put salt around your house to ward off spirits or negative energy! And I love this I heard her say on *Montel Williams*: "As I have stated many times, to many people, I simply cannot be psychic about myself." That's a convenient get-out-of-jail card to hold.

The truth is:
NO ONE CAN KNOW THE FUTURE!
Emanuel Swedenborg wrote that even angels don't know the future!

Divine Providence #179: "**As a foreknowledge of future events destroys the human itself, which is to act from freedom according to reason, therefore it is not granted to anyone to know the future; but everyone is permitted to form conclusions concerning future events from reason.**"

Part of a letter from Swedenborg to Pastor Venator in Germany, dated 22 June 1771: "**You may perhaps greatly wonder why I did not know from heaven that the letter was signed by his Serene Highness, the Landgrave's own hand. The reason is because angels do not know such things, and the Lord our Savior leaves things which concern temporal (worldly) matters to my intelligence and judgment, and reveals to me only such things as treat of heaven and eternal life; and, moreover, I have not ventured to ask the Lord Himself about these earthly matters.**"

Spiritual Experiences #206: "**Nor do the angels want to know what is going on on earth, because they are aware that everything has gone to corrupttion and ruin; wherefore they desire that the Kingdom of God the Messiah may come, hoping that communication may thus be opened up between them and [humankind].**"

I wouldn't be a Swedenborgian today, if it weren't for a psychic! I have never written about this before...but, my mother's father, Norman Augustus Carter, (a carpenter) was unhappy in his life and sought the guidance of a psychic. He had so many questions for her about the spiritual world that she told him he had to read *Heaven and Hell* by Swedenborg for the answers to his questions. He did. Here I am—third-generation Swedenborgian.

Dear Candace,
I am so happy to have met you. You are terrific. Keep up your research and clarifying writing.

L.P.
Bryn Athyn, Pennsylvania
December 2004

Dear Candace,
You do a wonderful piece of work! I enjoy your research.

V.K.
Glenview, Illinois
December 2004

Dear Candace,

You are doing a splendid job—somehow you have the "knack" of expressing things so well and explain things in an interesting manner—not everyone can do it!!

J.H.
Madison, Wisconsin
April 1992

Dear Candace,

My copy of SILA arrived today. Thanks. Kudos to you on this polished work. I'm sure Emanuel would be proud (unless he shunned pride). I appreciate your efforts to inform the public about a great mind who too often is overlooked.

N.G.
Los Angeles, California
May 1992

Dear N.G.,

No, I would have to say that Swedenborg would not be proud of *SILA*. He wrote that pride is to love one's self before others, to place one's self before others, and to exercise control over others.

Swedenborg called himself a **"Servant of the Lord"**. The last thing Swedenborg would want is to be remembered as a great man of science and theology. Yet, when he was a young man this was his aim—fame. He would, however, want his books to be printed, distributed, and read—period.

June 1994

Dear *SILA* Readers,

Did you know that on the 3rd of June 1994, a question on the American TV game show *Jeopardy* was...

Arcana Coelestia [Secrets of Heaven]
What two books of the Old Testament were explained by Swedenborg?

IT'S TRUE!

[Genesis and Exodus]

Thinking of you,
Candace

Dear Candace,

I was introduced to the New Church and Swedenborg about one and a half years ago by a family that were pen pals to my husband while he was in Saudi Arabia during Desert Storm.

Every now and then I think about the beliefs and teachings of Swedenborg, but I can never bring myself to understand them. I want to understand them, but I am afraid I will get so wrapped up in trying to comprehend what Swedenborg teaches that I won't be able to understand the "Basic Biblical Christianity" part.

My husband understands and agrees with the things Swedenborg teaches. He has tried to explain it to me many times, but I just didn't listen. Being a relatively new Christian, learning new things every day, can you help me?

E.C.
Hampton, Virginia
December 1993

Dear E.C.,
It took a great amount of courage to write to me as you have, to reach out for help. I am glad you did. First, let me assure you, you are not alone. There are other spouses out there that have, by virtue of marriage, been introduced to the teachings of Swedenborg, instantly and fervently. I contacted the New Church couple that wrote your husband and they replied:

Dear Candace,

I was very interested to hear that E.C. had corresponded with you. The story of our acquaintance is an interesting one!

During Operation Desert Storm our family sent a letter addressed to "Any Soldier". E.C.'s husband received it and we started a very intense correspondence during the course of the war. Our letters were full of religion and he became very interested in my Swedenborgian ideas.

I had written to E.C. a couple of times, and was surprised at how she had picked up his interest as well. I had given them many pamphlets and a couple of books. I put their name on your mailing list thinking that it would be a good way to keep them in touch. E.C.'s husband says they have read everything on Swedenborg they can find in their local libraries.

Thanks for what you had done for this very fine family. I admire the dedication you have to your newsletter.

Desert Storm Pen Pal
Huntingdon Valley, Pennsylvania

Dear E.C. (again),
I know that Swedenborg's teachings may at first appear hard to understand. Go slow and listen to your own feelings. If you trust your husband's judgment (in most things) trust his interest in Swedenborg. Please, be patient with yourself. You are not required to know everything about Swedenborg's Writings in, say, five years! There is not a test for you to take!

Swedenborg wrote that the mind consists of two parts: will and understanding. He stated this universal truth, that when the understanding is ruled by the will, they make up one mind. But, when the understanding is in disagreement from the will, they do not make up one mind, but a confused mind. It can also be stated that having the will for something is not enough, nor is the understanding alone enough. They both must be present for a contented mind.

It may be possible, even unconscious, that you are not willing to understand with an open mind what Swedenborg has to say. For, whatever a person does, they do from the will through the understanding.

Swedenborg is often quickly understood by people familiar with the Word of God because he explains difficult parts of the Word that have puzzled scholars. I can understand your reluctance to depart from the "Basic Biblical Christianity". Swedenborg says that that is the foundation to start with. He explains how in ALL the Biblical stories, they tell of the Lord and His relationship with us.

Another universal truth Swedenborg wrote about is the law of Divine Providence. Simply put, it means there are no accidents and God always provides good things. We are told by Swedenborg that we are asked to live in the Lord's Divine Providence. This means to trust that good will come to us today and tomorrow. Let go, let God, as 12-step groups put it (which are based on Swedenborgian principles).

E.C., it was no accident that you were introduced to the Writings of Swedenborg through a "Dear Any Soldier" letter. It is no accident that your husband has embraced the teachings of the New Church religion which is based on the Christian Word of God and the Writings of Swedenborg. I suggest you not worry about getting wrapped up in comprehension, but instead study how Swedenborg has affected other people's lives such as Helen Keller or your pen pals.

My Religion published in 1927 was revised and edited—in keeping with Helen Keller's wishes—by Ray Silverman as *Light in My Darkness* in 1994

Dear Candace,
 What do you find most interesting about this fellow?

J.Z.
Huntington, New York
August 1993

Dear J.Z.,
 That Emanuel Swedenborg lived a double life.
 Some people have claimed to "travel" into the spiritual world, but none have been as substantially documented as fact, by other people, as Swedenborg's experiences have. Some people have isolated themselves for years and "seen" spiritual visions. Swedenborg never insulated himself from his work or family life. Some people spend their whole life trying to convince others what they "heard" going on in the next world. Swedenborg left his readers to their own acceptance of the truth and never tried to persuade.
 It is truly amazing to me that Swedenborg functioned in the natural world and the spiritual world, at the same time. He "walked" around in heaven and in hell and then would write about it, but still go to dinner parties and attend sessions of parliament. And no one knew he was doing this. Only in his twilight years did a few people figure out he was the author of recent anonymously published books on the spiritual world. I also find it interesting that he:

- drank a lot of coffee (no doubt, assisting his long hours of writing)
- wrote 200 articles, pamphlets, and books from the age of 12 until his death at the age of 84 WITH A QUILL PEN (number is more when you consider that many of his books have several volumes, e.g. *Secrets of Heaven* is 12-volumes)
- wrote with both hands (this presumption on behalf of today's scholars must be true, for how else could he have written so many pages?)
- published anonymously at his own expense
- did not start a church or organization (one was started 15 years after his death)
- did not lecture (he stuttered)
- was egotistical as a youth and humble as an elder

Swedenborg used this ornament in *Secrets of Heaven*

Dear Candace,
I was reading Swedeberg's Readings the other day and was thinking about the Grand Man he talked about.

R.H.
San Marino, California
September 1988

Dear R.H.,
Accustomed to chuckling to myself as people mispronounce Swedenborg's name, of whom I'm an avid reader, I found myself laughing out loud when you referred to Swedenborg's books as the "Readings". Those that read Swedenborg religiously have named his 30 theological books, "The Writings". Indeed, The Writings should be renamed The Readings and read often for the insights into humanity they offer!

What a concept the Grand Human is! But then, the United States is called "Uncle Sam" or "Big Brother"; Canada "Little Sister". We personify everything!

Heaven and Hell #65: **"Since the whole heaven does reflect a single [person], even being the Divine Spiritual [Person] in greatest form (even in shape), heaven is divided into members and parts the way a [person] is, and these parts have similar names. Angels actually know what member one community or another is in. They say that this community is in some member or district of the head, that one is some member or district of the chest, that one is some member or district of the loins, and so on."**

Dear Candace,
What are the most appealing parts of Swedenborg's philosophy?

B.M.
Basking Ridge, New Jersey
April 1993

Dear B.M.,
It is most appealing that…
- there is sex after death
- one doesn't have to be of the Swedenborgian faith to get into heaven
- Divine Providence really provides
- life after death is explained in amazing detail
- we are living in the next world NOW
- Word of God—Old and New Testament—has a deeper meaning
- males and females are equal, but different
- God is a Divine Being of immense love and wisdom
- one's religion is a way of life, not church attendance

THERE IS AN ANSWER

Dear Candace,
What is Swedenborg all about? There is a whole bookshop with his name on it near my school. I've never stopped by to check on it. Can you give me more info?
A.J.
New York, New York
September 1990

Dear Candace,
I've passed the Swedenborg Library in Manhattan.
J.A.H.
New York, New York
September 1990

Dear Candace,
Tell me where to find out more about Swedenborg in the NYC area.
B.M.
Mt. Vernon, New York
September 1990

Dear A.J., J.A.H., and B.M.,
I'd be delighted to tell you all about the "bookshop" and "library" you saw, and where to find it. The *Swedenborg Foundation* is located at ~~139 E. 23rd Street, New York, NY 10010~~.* The *Foundation* is a nonprofit organization that translates, publishes, and distributes all Swedenborg's books. It began in 1849! The premise of the *Foundation* is that no religious education, Christian or non-Christian, can be considered well rounded without studying Swedenborg's theology. Hear, hear, I say!

UPDATE
  The Swedenborg Foundation moved to Pennsylvania in March, 1993.
  320 North Church Street, West Chester, Pennsylvania, 19380 U.S.A.
  1 (800) 355-3222   Philadelphia (610) 430-3222   Fax (610) 430-7982
  www.swedenborg.com

Swedenborg used this ornament in *Secrets of Heaven*

Dear Candace,

What is the role of the Writings? A reminder to be better Christians? Couldn't a well meaning Christian figure this all out on his own? Or am I missing something, like, that the Writings had to happen so that we could be told things?

C.I.
Glenview, Illinois
March 1998

Dear C.I.,

Emanuel Swedenborg (1688–1772) wrote books and articles about politics, science, philosophy, and theology. His theological books outnumber all his other works and are called, collectively, The Writings. The Writings are believed by his followers to be from God, given directly to Swedenborg.

One role The Writings were/are is to reveal to humankind the truths hidden in the Bible which had been lost through generations. His Biblical revelations go beyond traditional literalism and traditional allegorism. He wrote how the Bible is written in a correspondential language that the angels understand immediately, and how now we can understand it, too. Swedenborg elaborated further, saying, that as correspondences are the spiritual sense enveloped in the literal sense of the Bible, the human spirit is enveloped in the physical human body. When we die, the human body dies, and the human spirit lives on.

These two theological ideas were new in Swedenborg's time and are considered by some to be new today. It is believed by most Swedenborgians that a well meaning Christian will not figure out correspondences and spiritual matters of life after death on their own because we are living in a materialistic time. But, one can receive these ideas outside of The Writings through inspired books or from other enlightened people.

I and others believe The Writings did have to happen, as you say, so we could know spiritual things. Remember, Swedenborg saw and heard things in heaven and in hell and came back to tell us about them. No author has claimed this in the depth and volume Swedenborg has. He is worth a read.

Dear Candace,

I commend you on your decision to keep SILA *a quick read. Often I set a magazine aside, to read when I have the time or the mind to get into it. But with* SILA, *I always stop and read it right there on the spot as soon as I receive it.*

C.F.
Burbank, California
November 1990

Dear Candace,
I would love a copy of your newsletter. It sounds tremendously informative and I'm sure shall bring to my attention a very special historical figure who I apparently have overlooked.

L.K.
New York, New York
August 1990

Dear Candace,
The man sounds utterly fascinating. However did I miss him in the history books?

J.N.
Friendswood, Texas
August 1990

Dear Candace,
I find SILA *a bit bizarre, but interesting. It seems to be centered on someone almost totally overlooked in most western education...and yet, he seems to be a Renaissance man...enjoyed it, but still a bit skeptical and hesitant...why don't we know more about this guy?*

A.H.
Bedford, Texas
August 1990

Dear L.K., J.N., and A.H.,
I am not surprised at your bewilderment that you had not known about Emanuel Swedenborg. Many feel as all of you after learning about the 18th century scientist-theologian that changed the course of history in so many fields.

But, I can't say why you have never heard of him before. Swedenborg is in all encyclopedias, mentioned in thousands of research books, written into fictional and non-fictional literature, and reported about in newspapers. However, there are several historical factors that may explain, in a broad sense, why you weren't aware of Swedenborg until now.

- He often published his scientific books anonymously.
- He published most of his theological books anonymously for 20 years (without people knowing he was the author) for he didn't feel he deserved credit or fame.
- In 1768, when he signed his book, *Conjugial Love,* "**by Emanuel Swedenborg, a Swede**" it caused a heresy trial in Sweden which took years to be exonerated. And again a case involving this book went to the Pennsylvania Supreme Court in 1909, but, too, was exonerated.
- His theological books were banned in Sweden (his birthplace) as they didn't espouse Lutheran doctrine.
- He wrote in Latin, the language of scholars. (Some translations are faulty.)
- He wrote at least 20 scientific books; 5-volume diary; 30 theological books.
- He had a unique scientific writing style, unusual terminology, and new concepts.
- He did not start a church based on his theology. (Readers of his books did that in 1787, 15 years after his death.)

- Many believers of Swedenborg, fearing being tried and imprisoned or ridiculed, had/have difficulty sharing their convictions freely.
- Though he wrote that the *New Church of the New Jerusalem*, a new religion of a new Christian love and understanding (put forth in his books) will be among **"a few"** at first and then spread over the entire world, many followers of Swedenborg's theology are content to stay among **"a few"** and don't evangelize. (See *Secrets of Heaven* #547)

Dear Candace,

My trusty World Book Encyclopedia *shed a little light on Mr. Swedenborg. I'm sure that any familiarity with the name resulted from his work as a mathematician rather than as a philosopher or theologian. But, I'm always open to new ideas and knowledge, so I'd like to learn more.*

J.F.
Saratoga Springs, New York
September 1990

Dear Candace,

I was down in my local university library the other day, and I looked up Emanuel Swedenborg. WOW! He sure seems to have been a real well rounded person. I was particularly interested to see that he was (among many other things) a mathematician. This interests me, since I am a mathematician myself. I want to (when I find the time) look up some of his mathematics.

D.L.
Madison, Wisconsin
September 1990

Dear J.F. & D.L.,

Glad you two looked him up!

ALL encyclopedias have essays on Swedenborg (1688–1772). *Prodigy* (an online computer service) added *The Academic American Encyclopedia* to their features this month. Now *Prodigy* subscribers can read about Swedenborg without going to their libraries!

The *World Book Encyclopedia* says that Swedenborg was a "religious leader". He was NOT a leader. He led no one. Swedenborg was a religious writer. He wrote what he saw and heard in his dreams and visions and left his readers in freedom to believe or not.

In order to grasp Swedenborg's mathematical genius, one must understand his time. Rene Descartes (1596–1650) had developed his work in what is now called analytic geometry. Isaac Newton (1642–1727) and Gottfried Wilhelm Leibniz (1646–1716) were the central figures developing calculus.

Emanuel at 22, ventured from his home in Sweden to England. He studied Newton, algebra, and geometry. After two years, he went to Holland, daily visiting Swedish Ambassador Palmquist, a good mathematician and a great algebraist. Swedenborg put his mathematical and mechanical mind to work and drew 14 inventions. Among them were a hydraulic jack, submarine, musical instrument, and **"a method of ascertaining the wills and affections of people's minds by means of analysis"**.

Home after almost five years, Swedenborg started on his mathematical and ideas magazine, *The Northern Daedalus*. At the age of 28, he met King Charles XII of Sweden and gave him issues of his magazine. They hit it off, both loving math!

In 1718, Swedenborg wrote and published the first Swedish algebra textbook. He was 30. In his 50s, Swedenborg shifted his studying and writing from sciences to theology. He wrote that his early years prepared him to grasp the ideas he claimed later as revelation.

In *Heaven and Hell,* Swedenborg wrote that the Word of God is holy. Words and numbers correspond to spiritual things. But, there is a difference. Numbers involve generalities, whereas words details. Since generalities involve countless details, numerical writing enfolds more hidden things than alphabetic writing. Numbers in the Word mean real things:
- 7 means holy
- 10 means complete
- 12 means all things of faith

Swedenborg warns us as long as we confine ourselves to the historical sense of the Word, it will seem as though numbers do not hold inner meanings within them. But, they do!

Emanuel Swedenborg at 75, painted by Per Krafft, the Elder (Swedish, 1724–1793)
He holds his soon to be published book *Apocalypse Revealed.*
Painting hangs in *Gripsholm Castle*, Sweden.

Dear Candace,
Swedenborg is a new one on me. Does he talk about meditation?

J.P.
Mountain View, California
April 1990

Dear Candace,
What were Swedenborg's conclusions on life after death?

E.J.
Atlanta, Georgia
April 1990

Dear Candace,
By the way, can you recommend a good book by Emanuel Swedenborg to start off with?

D.B.
Glendale, California
April 1990

Dear Candace,
Dimly aware of Swedenborg, but never read anything of his. Do you have any favorite recommendations?

L.B.
Richmond, Texas
April 1990

Dear J.P., E.J., D.B., and L.B.,
Since childhood, Swedenborg studied the Word of God and meditated on it. (He tells us to do likewise.) As a boy, he discovered it was fun to slow his breathing. As an adult, his meditation developed into what we now know as the hypnagogic state—borderline of sleeping and waking. In this state a person is: 1) fully aware, 2) can remember, and 3) can talk in mind thought to other minds not on this plane.

Swedenborg conversed with people in the spiritual world through this hypnagogic state. He saw wondrous things and wrote about them in his most popular book, *Heaven and Hell*, published in London in 1758, when he was 70.

This book is the best introduction to Swedenborg because it contains in one book everything he expanded upon in 30 theological books. Swedenborg tells us that we will rise on the third day after death and enter the world of spirits. We will remain male or female. We will choose to live in heaven or hell by what we love to do most, no matter what our religion is. We will live in communities, in homes. There is government. There are books. We will have jobs that we love. There is marriage after death, and sex! And all children that die are immediately taken to heaven and brought up there.

Both my grandfathers found Swedenborg's *Heaven and Hell* in public libraries, provinces apart in Canada, and believed what they read. Naturally, this book would be my favourite! [I never knew my grandfathers.]

❄

Dear Candace,
I find it interesting to learn of a scientist who was also a theologian. This seems like a contradiction!

D.P.
Detroit, Michigan
May 1990

Dear D.P.,
Many scientists ARE religious. It does seem a contradiction, doesn't it? But, actually it isn't. Emanuel Swedenborg wrote that there are always two forces at work with everything. A force from the outside and a force from the inside. When these two forces come together something IS or exists.

First and foremost a scientist, Swedenborg wrote his nebular hypothesis theory in 1734 which stated that the origin of the planets was the solar mass. Immanuel Kant, the German philosopher, later acknowledged this theory as correct! Kant even wrote Swedenborg a letter after hearing of Swedenborg's ability to "see" into the next world. Not having received a reply, Kant asked a friend going to Sweden to visit Swedenborg to encourage him to write back. Swedenborg explained to the friend that he would have written, but for the fact that he was about to publish a new book titled, *Divine Love and Wisdom,* which he felt could answer Kant's letter! It was published in Amsterdam, Holland in 1763. In it, Swedenborg discusses the nature of spiritual substance. Throughout, he uses his vast knowledge in the physical sciences to illustrate his theological ideas.

He studied science religiously and then explained religion scientifically. Swedenborg wrote in a letter to Friedrich Christoph Oetinger (1702–1782), Lutheran pastor serving in Wurtemburg, Germany, 11 November 1766: **"I was first introduced by the Lord into the natural sciences and was thus prepared."**

Dear Candace,
Your newsletter is like a beacon of light in this world where so few have heard of Swedenborg and his revelations.

P.H.
Hawthorne, California
April 1992

September 1992
Dear *SILA* Readers,

The Nebular Hypothesis Theory

- In 1780, Sir William Herschel (1738–1822), the German-British astronomer hypothesized and later wrote that nebulae—clouds of interstellar gas; star clusters—are composed of individual stars in articles in the *Philosophical Transactions of the Royal Society of London* (1800-1843).
- In 1759, Ruggero Giuseppe Boscovich (1711–1787), the Dalmatian (region along the coast of Yugoslavia) scientist wrote his nebular hypothesis theory in his published work, *Constitution of the Universe.*
- In 1757, Johann Heinrich Lambert (1728–1777), the Swiss-German astronomer wrote his nebular hypothesis theory in his published work, *Letters on Cosmogony*.
- In 1755, Immanuel Kant (1724–1804), the German philosopher wrote his nebular hypothesis theory in his published work, *General History of Nature and Theory of the Heavens.*

BUT

- In 1734, Emanuel Swedenborg (1688–1772), the Swedish scientist wrote his nebular hypothesis theory in his published work, *The Principia* (chapter titled, "The Theory of the Sidereal Heavens").

Thinking of you,
Candace

Swedenborg at 14, painted in 1707
(According to Cyriel Odhner Sigstedt in her book, *The Swedenborg Epic*, this is "an unverified portrait". But, most accept it is him.)

THERE IS AN ANSWER

Dear Candace,
Does Swedenborg ever say why we should believe Him?

Anonymous
Pasadena, California
February 2008

Dear Anonymous,
What a great question! Yeah, he does quite often.
Spiritual Experiences #5: "**Yet who will believe it.**"
Spiritual Experiences #228: "**I testify to you that you may believe it, for it is true... Moreover, I also want you to believe this one thing that I know to be true because I observed it... I had a dream from which I awoke again and again, for evil spirits were attacking me from everywhere to the point where I was unable to continue sleeping... Then I realized the reason for it, namely that I was being let down to the unhappy in hell, in order to see their condition and then report to the world, especially to the incredulous or unbelieving person, that there is a hell—and not only that there is a hell, but also what their state is like, though I really cannot describe it satisfactorily.**"
Spiritual Experiences #5: "**But to the end that everyone may believe this, I can earnestly declare by God that I have experienced it so clearly that I am sure there could not be a clearer sensation in these matters.**"
A letter (2 August 1769) Swedenborg wrote to his friend—Rev. Thomas Hartley, a pastor of the Church of England—answers your question. Part of it:
"I have been called to a holy office by the Lord Himself, who most mercifully appeared before me, His servant, in the year 1743; when He opened my sight into the spiritual world, and granted me to speak with spirits and angels, in which state I have continued up to the present day. From that time I began to print and publish the various secrets that were seen by me and revealed to me, as the secrets concerning Heaven and Hell, the state of people after death, the true worship of God, the spiritual sense of the Word, besides many other most important matters conducive to salvation and wisdom.
The only reason of my journeys abroad has been the desire of making myself useful, and of making known the secrets that were entrusted to me. Moreover, I have as much of this world's wealth as I need, and I neither seek nor wish for more.
Your letter has induced me to write all these particulars, in order that as you say 'ill-conceived prejudices may be removed'.
Farewell; and from my heart I wish you all the happiness both in this world, and the next; which I have not the least doubt you will attain, if you look and pray to our Lord."
That letter was not published until after Swedenborg's death. But, the following was published in his lifetime.
Secrets of Heaven #448: "**I have spoken to many people whom I had known during their lifetime, and have done so for considerable lengths of time, for months or a year. I have spoken in as clear a voice, though an internal one, as when speaking to friends in the world.**

Conversation with them has included the subject of people's condition after death. They have been utterly amazed that nobody in the life of the body knows or believes that when one's bodily life ends they will be alive even as they are now. Yet there is a continuation of life such as involves passing from an obscure life into a clear life, and with people who have had faith in the Lord, passing into life that is more and more clear. They wished me to tell their friends that they were alive, and to write to them telling of their condition, just as I had reported to them also many things about the state of their friends.

I said however that if I did speak or write to their friends they would not believe me. They would call it sheer imagination, they would laugh me to scorn, they would ask for signs or miracles before believing, and so I would expose myself to their derision. And that these things are true, perchance but few will believe. For in their hearts they deny that spirits exist; and those who do not deny their existence nevertheless refuse to hear of anybody being able to talk to spirits.

In ancient times such disbelief concerning spirits never existed, but nowadays they wish to discover what spirits may be by a crack-brained reasoning involving definitions and presuppositions that deprives spirits of every one of the senses. And the more learned that people wish to be, the more they continue in this way."

As much as Swedenborg wanted people to know his secrets, he knew that forcing someone to read them or to believe them was folly. Freedom of acceptance is paramount. *Secrets of Heaven* #4422: "I received letters [informing me] that not more than four copies [of my books] had been sold in two months, and this was made known to the angels: they wondered indeed, but said that it should be left to the Providence of the Lord, which was such as to compel no one, though it might be done, but that it was not fitting that [any others] should read [my work] first, but those who were in faith; and that this might be known from [what happened at] the coming of the Lord into the world, who was able to compel [people] to receive His words and Himself, but [yet] compelled no one, as was also the case afterwards in regard to the apostles."

So, if the Lord can, but won't compel us to believe Him, Swedenborg will fare no better at it. *Secrets of Heaven* #322: "**Beware of the false notion that spirits do not possess far more exquisite sensations than during the life of the body. I know the contrary by experience repeated thousands of times. Should any be unwilling to believe this, in consequence of their preconceived ideas concerning the nature of spirit, let them learn it by their own experience when they come into the other life, where it will compel them to believe.**"

I will leave you with this terrific thought from Swedenborg. It's wonderful to read it in the 21st century as we now have a clearer universal picture of what constitutes a healthy relationship. *True Christianity* #163: "**If you are prepared to believe me, the idea everyone has of God determines one's place in the heavens.**"

Thinking of you,
Candace

In *Skansen*, an open-air museum in Stockholm, you will find Swedenborg's original yellow summer house. It was moved to the museum for preservation. Plaque reads:

> Part of the rose garden near the summer house is stocked with plants which are known to have grown in Swedenborg's garden, such as larkspur, sweet williams, flax, a sweet-scented white rose, bleeding heart, violets, tulips and hyacinths.

The house originally was joined on either side by a library and a garden tool shed. Here Swedenborg is known to have written most of his spiritual books.

SILA August 1998

Dear Candace,
Didn't Swedenborg start his own religion? I've never read a book by him. But, his religion sounds interesting.

P.B.
Garden Grove, California
March 1990

Dear P.B.,

No, Emanuel Swedenborg, the Swedish scientist-theologian did NOT start his own religion. One was fifteen years AFTER his death.

Swedenborg believed his mission was to communicate new ideas to the world by writing them down and leaving people in freedom to accept them or not. The religion based on the Old Testament, the New Testament, and the Writings of Swedenborg is called *The New Church of the New Jerusalem*. New Church for short. Or Swedenborgian. Swedenborg wrote his theological books in Latin (the language of his day) and published them anonymously in England and Holland as Sweden—a Lutheran country—did not have freedom of religion at that time.

In 1749, Stephen Penny of England has the distinction of being the first person to have accepted the Writings as Divine. Rev. Andersson Beyer, being the first convert to the new doctrines in Sweden, started to give Swedenborgian sermons in Swedish, a first. Rev. Johan Rosen, a Swedish newspaper editor and college teacher, also believing what Swedenborg wrote, held lectures about his teachings.

In 1769, books by Swedenborg gave rise to the most significant historical trial in history. Swedenborg said that this trial had been the most important and the most solemn brought before any council, up to that time, since it concerned the New Church which is predicted by the Lord in Daniel and in the Apocalypse, and agrees with what the Lord said in Matthew 24: 22.

This trial (for Swedenborg) was not over whether his doctrines were right or wrong, but over freedom of speech. Swedenborg's teachings were said to be corrupting, heretical, injurious, and objectionable. The Lutheran clergy of the day wanted Swedenborg to be committed to a lunatic asylum. There were assassination attempts. Beyer and Rosen were threatened with banishment from Sweden for teaching Swedenborgian ideas. Rev. Sven Schmidt was declared insane and put in prison for refusing to stop preaching the new doctrines.

Then on 26 April 1770, the Royal Council banned Swedenborg's Writings in Sweden. Rev. Beyer and Rev. Rosen were forbidden by law to preach Swedenborg's ideas publicly or privately. Swedenborg (82-years-old) heard of this ordeal while away in Amsterdam, Holland and wrote the King of Sweden, Adolf Frederic, for help. Later the King said to Swedenborg in person:

> The Consistories have kept silent on the subject of my letters and of our writings. We may conclude, then, that they have not found anything reprehensible in them and that you have written in conformity with the truth.

But, the trial dragged on for more than four years. The *Uppsala University* was asked to prove Swedenborg wrong, but eventually they declined to do so.

Swedenborg died in 1772. Rosen died in 1773 before the trial ended. The trial concluded quietly, however unresolved. In 1779, Rev. Beyer was granted permission to preach Swedenborg's theology again.

In 1782, the Marquis de Thome in Berlin said in defense: "The doctrine of Swedenborg is not his. If I thought it was his and not the Lord's, I should not adopt it, but reject it. I am a disciple of Christ, not of Swedenborg."

Swedenborg was commemorated on a Swedish stamp for his 250th birthday in 1938
(Emanuel Swedenborg: 29 January 1688 – 29 March 1772)
Actually, two stamps. Above, 10ö is violet! 100ö is green!

Swedenborg's summer house was commemorated on a Swedish stamp in 2003
(painting by Mikael Wahrby)

Dear Candace,
Do you hold true that Jesus Christ will come one day, but in spirit, rather than in person, and if so, how will He make Himself known?

S.M.
Phoenix, Arizona
June 1990

Dear Candace,
You say that your religion is based on the Old and New Testaments and the Writings of Swedenborg. The Bible is very clear in Revelations that nothing is to be added or taken away from the Bible. Do you see Swedenborg's teachings as subject to, equal to, or greater than the Bible's teachings? You state that your church is the church predicted in Daniel when the Bible says that the New Church came into being at Pentecost. We are in the days of Church now and will be until the Second Coming of Christ. I'm sure that you have good intentions, but no teaching of God will contradict His word in any way. In Christ.

C.C.
Richardson, Texas
June 1990

Dear S.M. and C.C.,
A "church" is not a building, but where God and His Word is loved and understood. A "church" can be with one individual or many.

It was prophesied in the Old Testament that the Messiah would come and a "new church" would be established called "Jerusalem". This prophecy came true approximately 1,990 years ago. A "new church" was established called Christianity.

It was prophesied in the New Testament that Christ would come a second time and a "new church" would be established called "New Jerusalem". This prophecy came true 220 years ago. A "new church" was established called the New Church of the New Jerusalem.

"Jerusalem" in the Bible signifies a "church" for Jerusalem, the city, was the metropolis in the land of Canaan where THE temple and THE altar were. "New Jerusalem" in the Bible signifies a "new church" in respect to doctrine. These are symbolic cities. It does not mean the physical city Jerusalem for it says in the Word that Jerusalem would be utterly lost and destroyed. But, Jerusalem with its almost a million occupants is still thriving!

It states in Revelations 22: 18: **"For I testify unto every one that heareth the words of the prophecy of this book, if any one shall add unto these things, God shall add unto him the plagues that are written in this book."** This refers clearly to the BOOK of Revelation.

For we read in John 16: 12, 13: **"I have yet many things to say unto you, but ye cannot bear them now. Howbeit when He, the spirit of truth, is come, He will guide you into all truth."** Each book of the Bible was printed separately and centuries later bound together.

Indeed, no teaching of the Lord's contradicts itself and in His Second Coming, He opened Emanuel Swedenborg's spiritual eyes to show him the deeper meanings of the Bible for everyone. The Writings of Swedenborg are equal to the Old and New Testaments.

On June 19th 1770, Swedenborg tells us the Lord told His twelve disciples that He had come again in spirit through Swedenborg's Writings! The Lord told them to go out and evangelize this news in the spiritual world! June 19th is celebrated as New Church Day by Swedenborgians worldwide.

UPDATE

From *California Digest* (New Church newsletter edited by me) June 2003:

Dear Californians,

Every June 19th we as a church are one year older. Are we wiser? Are we more settled? Are we growing? These things are asked on any birthday. A church is no different than a human being. Both go through infancy, toddlerhood, childhood, teen years, and maturity. I think we all agree that the New Church on earth is still in its infancy, though it is 233-years-old!

Or are we 246-years-old as some New Church scholars say? We are if one counts from 1757, being the year (written down by Swedenborg) the Lord reordered the spiritual world at the time of the Last Judgment. This reordering —sending evil people (that were just hanging around in the world of spirits) to hell, stopping them from corrupting newly deceased people—brought about spiritual freedom in the other world and in ours.

Before 1757, devils were leading people into "false" heavens. After the Last Judgment these were destroyed. New heavens were created. And the Lord provided a new revelation through Swedenborg to be given to everyone on earth. Everything starts in the spiritual world and "leaks" down to the earths. And that takes time.

Think of how the American slavery of Africans didn't get abolished until 1863. That's a long time since the Last Judgment in the spiritual world, in 1757, which freed people from bondage. Texans didn't free their slaves until two years later on June 19th 1865! That day is now celebrated in America as Juneteenth. THERE ARE NO COINCIDENCES. Juneteenth is freedom day for everyone. Now, let us all help the infant New Church with her potty training!

Until next month,
Candace

Swedenborg used this ornament in *Secrets of Heaven*

Dear Candace,

Swedenborg will always be one of my very favorite people. So I can readily understand your enthusiasm. I'm not writing to you to discuss Swedenborg's Writings, but just to assure you that his contribution to understanding and further growth is inestimable. Many wonderful humans have provided steps—but, in comparison, Swedenborg built a sturdy staircase. He did not plan on establishing another religion or church. Remember when Jesus said that some with ears won't hear and some with eyes won't see!

M.B.
San Pedro, California
December 1989

Dear M.B.,
 Your shared thoughts are treasured.

I met Lars Bergquist at the *Stockholm New Church* when I visited Sweden in 1998. Mr. Bergquist, a former Swedish Ambassador to Beijing and Vatican City, has authored many articles and books about Emanuel Swedenborg.

SILA November 1998

Dear Candace,
I have had a question for a long time. I think that the Writings of Swedenborg is difficult in general, so the female admirer are minority. Then, how about your country? Especially in Japan they are a few.

C.M.
Chuou-Ku, Chiba-shi, Japan
October 1999

Dear C.M.,
Emanuel Swedenborg's publisher in England was John Lewis. In 1749, Mr. Lewis advertised Swedenborg's book, *Arcana Coelestia* (*Secrets of Heaven*), Volume I in London and the first response was from a man in Dartmouth—Stephen Penny. He became a believer.

Ten years later, Mr. Penny converted his friend, a Quaker, Rev. William Cookworthy (1705–1780). Rev. Cookworthy then converted a Methodist, Rev. Thomas Hartley, of Winwick, Northamptonshire. Rev. Cookworthy and Rev. Hartley befriended Swedenborg. Rev. Hartley then converted Richard Houghton, Esquire. Mr. Houghton then converted an Anglican, Rev. John Clowes (1743–1831). Rev. Clowes befriended Swedenborg. And so on and so on.

By 1782, a Quaker man (name unknown) lent his copy of *Heaven and Hell* to his 19-year-old friend—Robert Hindmarsh (1759–1835)—printer and son of a Methodist minister. In his home in Clerkenwell Close, Mr. Hindmarsh started a reading group that studied Swedenborg's books. These men joined him:
1. Peter Provo—surgeon and apothecary
2. William Bonington—clock case maker
3. The Honourable John Augustus Tulk—wealthy patron

Then Mr. Hindmarsh placed an ad announcing the first public meeting of Swedenborg readers in the world. The meeting took place 5 December 1783 at the *London Coffee House* on Ludgate Hill, London, England. Besides the four above, one more man came—William Spence—surgeon. This group of five men adjourned to the *Queen's Arms Tavern.* And so on and so on.

It *appears* as though only men "got" the Writings of Swedenborg. It *appears* as though Swedenborg's books were too hard for women to understand— too intellectual. Even the *Swedenborg Foundation's* compiled list of 97 distinguished people that acknowledged the influence of Swedenborg includes only 11 women.

But, the truth is, more men than women have historically read Swedenborg because of cultural and economic restraints. Male children were preferred over female. (Even today in some countries.) Women were considered intellectually inferior to men. Women had fewer rights, fewer educational opportunities, and fewer career opportunities.

Women only obtained the right to vote in the United States in 1920. A woman in Canada was not considered a "person" until 1929. Women in Japan only obtained the right to vote in 1945. And divorce was not legal in Ireland until 1995.

Now nearing the 21st century, women (not all) around the world can read Swedenborg as they wish. One can even find excellent research and books about Swedenborg being written by women.

It can be said that Swedenborg's books are intellectual or scholarly, but both sexes can read them and understand them. If a book by Swedenborg is hard to get through, it probably is more the fault of the (male) translator than Swedenborg.

C.M., in my experience, I have seen more women at Swedenborgian churches and lectures than men. Statistically, the life span of a woman being longer than a man's can count for some of that. As for the books being more difficult for a woman to grasp than a man, I can't accept. Granted, for anyone, the sheer volume of books Swedenborg wrote may limit some from getting through his work.

I suspect that the more women in Japan become equal to men, interest in Swedenborg's books will rise which discuss in depth the equal-but-different qualities of the two sexes. Keep reading, dear woman!

UPDATE

I just learned that *Secrets of Heaven* by Swedenborg, while 12-volumes in English, it is 28-volumes in Japanese!

Drawing by Tuan Hauptmann

Dear Candace,
   Did you know there's a crystalline mineral called Swedenborgite? It occurs only in one skarn in Langban, Sweden. It would be so cool if you could get a sample.
                                                                                                    J. & K.H.
                                                                                              Chicago, Illinois
                                                                                                    May 2000

Dear J. & K.H.,
   No, I did not know that. Thanks for telling me. Since I received your letter prior to my going to Sweden in 1998, where I retraced Swedenborg's footsteps, I asked about Swedenborgite in several stores; especially in the city of Falun with its great mine and no one knew what I was talking about. Who in Sweden knows about Swedenborgite?
   I never print anything in *SILA* without verifying, so, not that I doubted you two, I had to substantiate your info before publishing it. I saved your letter for two years!
   When a new *SILA* reader contacted me and said he was just like Swedenborg, an assayer—an examiner or tester of the earth's minerals and analyzer of such—I asked him if there was a mineral named after Emanuel Swedenborg. Dr. Ralph E. Pray, 74, a metallurgical engineer in Monrovia, CA told me that he had never heard of one. But, he checked his big book, *A Text-book of Mineralogy with an Extended Treatise on Crystallography and Physical Mineralogy* by Edward Salisbury Dana (1906) and listed was SWEDENBORGITE! "Transparent, colorless to wine-yellow. Occurs in calcite or granular hematite with richterite, manganophyllite, etc., at Langbanshyttan, Vermland, Sweden." How exciting!

UPDATE
   "Swedenborgite is very, very rare and small," Jason B. Smith of Belmont, North Carolina wrote me. "The crystal itself [left] in calcite is less than 1.6mm across (long). It was only found one or two times in the *Langban Mine*, Varmland, Sweden and it has been closed for many years. The chemistry is very unusual and thus lends to the rarity. It is the clear, hexagonal shaped crystal you see in my picture. The mineral is also fluorescent and appears blue under a blacklight."

Swedenborgite specimen #5368
Photograph by Jason B. Smith

Dear Candace,
 Did Swedenborg predict the future?

S.B.B.
Pasadena, California
October 2004

Dear S.B.B.,
~~Only three times~~.*
Emanuel Swedenborg, born in Stockholm, 1688, predicted the day and time of his death at 84 years of age—Sunday, 29 March 1772, 5:00 p.m. in London.

Swedenborg, a famous scientist and renown religious author, predicted that staunch believers in faith alone wouldn't believe faith alone is wrong, even if angels visited and told them so.

He wrote in his small treatise, *Brief Exposition of the Doctrine of the New Church* #81: **"It is astonishing that the doctrine of justification by faith alone prevails at this day throughout the whole of Reformed Christianity that is, it reigns there as almost the one and only point of theology in the sacred Order. Wherefore I can predict that if divine truths concerning the union of charity and faith, concerning heaven, the Lord and eternal happiness, were sent down from heaven, written in letters of silver, they would not be thought worthy to be read by these upholders of justification by faith alone."**

Swedenborg predicted that there will be only one final spiritual dispensation and that it is happening now because the Last Judgment occurred in the year 1757, in the spiritual world. Swedenborg wrote in *Last Judgment* #280: **"Therefore it is predicted in the Apocalypse, that the New Jerusalem will descend from heaven after the Last Judgment, by which is meant the New Church."**

Last Judgment #270: **"Faith separate from charity is predicted in the Apocalypse, and is meant by the dragon and his two beasts."**

Swedenborg wrote that all the things which are predicted in the Apocalypse were fulfilled by the end of 1757! *Last Judgment* #45: **"This Last Judgment was commenced in the beginning of the year 1757, and was fully accomplished at the end of that year."**

It could be said that the latter prediction wasn't a prediction of his per se, but a revelation of something that had happened. As can be said of the famous three spiritual encounters that made Swedenborg a household name in his lifetime.

1) In 1759, Swedenborg "saw" a fire burning in another city than he was in. *The Stockholm Fire* incident was a clairvoyant occurrence and not a prediction.

Swedenborg was at a dinner party at the home of millionaire William Castel. He was upset and kept leaving the room. He told the guests that a huge fire was happening at that very moment in Stockholm. He was in Gothenburg, 300 miles away! The fire was burning close to his home. Then, he announced to his friends, **"Thank God! The fire is extinguished the third door from my house!"** His narrative was confirmed days later when news of the Stockholm fire reached Gothenburg. This incident made Swedenborg a celebrity.

2) In 1761, Swedenborg "spoke" with a deceased man on the request of his wife. *The Marteville Receipt* incident was a spiritual contact and not a prediction.

A year after Monsieur de Marteville—Dutch ambassador to Stockholm—had died, his wife was given a bill for a silver service her husband had purchased. Madam de Marteville was sure her husband had paid for it, but couldn't find the receipt. She visited Swedenborg and asked him if he had seen her husband in the spiritual world. Swedenborg said he had not, but if he did see him, he promised to ask about the receipt.

A few days later, he did happen upon the deceased ambassador and asked about the lost receipt. Monsieur de Marteville said he did pay for it and told Swedenborg that he would "go home" and tell his wife. Madam de Marteville reported that eight days after visiting Swedenborg, her deceased husband had appeared in a dream and told her the receipt was lodged behind a bureau drawer. And it was!

3) In 1761, Swedenborg "spoke" with deceased King August William of Prussia by request of his sister, Queen Louisa Ulrika of Sweden. *The Queen's Secret* incident was a spiritual contact and not a prediction.

A few days after the Queen met with Swedenborg, he returned to the palace and in private told her something from her brother. She exclaimed, "This no mortal could have told me!"

These three other-worldly incidents became famous throughout Europe mostly because Immanuel Kant (1724–1804) wrote about them in a letter to Fraulein von Knobloch in 1763.

Swedenborg, while in Holland, wrote to Ludwig IX (1719–1790), Duke and Landgrave of Hesse-Darmstadt, 13 July 1771:

"What is being said about me having predicted the death of the daughter of the Margrave of Schwedt is a fabrication coming from some gossiping newsmonger or other. I was not present there, nor did I know anything about that lady. What is being said about the brother of the Queen of Sweden however is true, yet this must not be regarded as some miracle but only as a noteworthy occurrence like those noteworthy occurrences concerning Luther, Melancthon, Calvin, and many others, which have been recounted and set out in [*True Christian Religion*]. For occurrences such as these are not miracles but only witnesses to the fact that I have been introduced by the Lord as to my spirit into the spiritual world and that I therefore speak with angels and spirits."

Swedenborg visited in spirit with thousands of deceased family members, friends, acquaintances, famous individuals, and strangers. He became famous for three that were viably documented. However, he didn't concern himself with spiritual contact for fun or profit. He believed his role was in documenting that we live on in spirit and that the Lord came again a second time.

Swedenborg wrote that knowing the future takes away freedom, so even the angels don't know it. My thinking is, Swedenborg was told the time of his death, so he could complete his important work for the Lord in time.

It should be pointed out that when Swedenborg contacted a deceased person, he didn't go into an immediate trance, or call upon a spirit guide, or "perform" in any bombastic style—as we are accustomed to seeing today by so-called channelers. Swedenborg was the real deal.

UPDATE

*I found another "prediction". Professor J. B. von Scherer told of the time when friends, after dining, were listening to Swedenborg talk about spirits. They decided to have some fun with him. They asked Swedenborg to prove his extraordinary abilities by telling which of them would die first.

After some silence, Swedenborg declared, **"Olof Olofsohn will die tomorrow morning at forty-five minutes past four o'clock."** Shocked, one man, a friend of Olof's, agreed to go to his home the next day. When he did, Olof's servant told him, Olof had just passed away.

These "parlour games" meant little to Swedenborg. In fact, the above story is an uncorroborated anecdote among other questionable rumours about Swedenborg's ability to forsee the future.

The few proven times Swedenborg gave accounts of spirit contact were so minor in Swedenborg's thinking as compared with the wonderous and earth shattering things he did see. He cared more about getting those down on paper than sitting around a fire telling ghost stories!

The Lord knew what He was doing putting Swedenborg in the time period He did. I believe that if Swedenborg was born in the 21st century, and had done all that he had done in his lifetime, our freedom would have been taken away. Millions may have believed his every word; he may have been worshipped. He would have been hounded by paparazzi. Others would not have believed him and he may have been assassinated. Afterall, people did try to assassinate him in his lifetime.

And another "prediction": Bishop Engelbert Halenius (1700–1767) was one day visiting Swedenborg in his Stockholm residence. His housekeeper, Maria was in the room when the men were discussing religion. Swedenborg told the Bishop: **"You spread falsity in yours."** Embarrassed, the Bishop told Maria to leave the room! Swedenborg said she could stay! They continued their debate. Finally, Swedenborg told him: **"There is already prepared for you a place in hell. But I predict that in a few months you will be attacked by a severe illness during which the Lord will seek to convert you. If then you will open your heart to His holy influences, your conversion will be accomplished. Write to me then and ask me for my theological writings, and I will send them to you."**

That's what happened. The Lutheran Bishop Halenius accepted the Writings of Swedenborg after his recovery and declared they were "the most precious treasures of humanity."

The more I research, the more I find that Swedenborg had many premonitions about people he knew. What's the big deal? He didn't write them down on paper and bring them out later to prove he was right. He said in a letter to Rev. Venator, 13 July 1771 that: **"these things are not miracles, but merely testimonies"**. *Divine Providence* #135: **"No spirit has dared, no angel has wished to say anything, still less to instruct me concerning anything in the Word or concerning any doctrine from the Word, but the Lord alone has taught me."**

THERE IS AN ANSWER

I dined with Rev. Olle Hjern (Swedenborgian who lives in Stockholm) in 1998 at the restaurant *Van der Nootska Palatset* (Van der Noot's Palace) in Stockholm which is the former home of Thomas Van der Noot. In 1759, southern Stockholm burned. This palatial home was not damaged, neither was Swedenborg's home, a few streets away. Swedenborg said he "saw" the fire raging in a vision and was relieved when it stopped three homes from his! The building on the left (below) is "modern". Only a few buildings in the area survived the 18th century fire.   *SILA* November 1998

Dear Candace,
    Swedenborg wrote so much. Do you know how many pages he wrote a day?
R.B.
Los Angeles, California
April 2001

Dear R.B.,
    No, I don't. So, I contacted an expert, my friend, Rev. Dr. Jonathan S. Rose of Bryn Athyn, PA. He told me the following:

> *Dear Candace,*
>   *There are a couple of statistics on Swedenborg's writing speed that I know of.*
>   *Alfred Acton writes in* An Introduction to the Word Explained *(Academy of the New Church, 1927) on pages 130-135, that Swedenborg wrote 5,000 folio manuscript pages (that is, large ones) in three-and-a-half years between 1745 and late 1748.*
>   *This comes out to four pages a day, year in year out, which is a pretty good clip considering that he was traveling and purchasing property and moving, and of course eating and sleeping now and then. He turned sixty toward the end of that period.*
>   *The other statistic is more astounding. In R. L. Tafel,* Documents Concerning the Life and Character of Emanuel Swedenborg, *Volume 3 (Swedenborg Society, 1890), page 1016, Swedenborg's friend, Cuno, reports that Swedenborg was writing* True Christian Religion *at what Cuno called an "astonishing and superhuman" rate of 128 manuscript pages per week that resulted in 32 quarto pages of printed copy with little words set in 10 point type on lines crammed together with no leading between. At the time that Cuno expressed astonishment, Swedenborg was about to turn 83.*
>   *I get a sense of urgency from this pace. There was a message to deliver, and time was running out!*
>   *Thanks for the question!*

    Thank YOU, Jonathan, for your fascinating, thorough answer. Your assessment that Swedenborg wrote with a sense of urgency rings true!

    As an example of what Swedenborg wrote about for so many pages, year after year, take a look at section #2954 in his *Spiritual Experiences* (formerly published as the *Spiritual Diary*): **"I was in a shop to buy cheese, and while I was buying, spirits poured into me a desire to buy this one or that one, to choose one above another, and to change my mind, which I did not notice. As usual I was in their company, without reflecting on the spirits. When it was finished, spirits were allowed to reflect on their state while they were making** me buy and change my mind, and they said that it was exactly as if they themselves were doing it, not knowing otherwise. **1748, 27 Aug."**

(New Church) Rev. William Ross Woofenden, wrote in his essay, "Swedenborg: The Man Who Had to Publish" in the book, *Emanuel Swedenborg: A Continuing Vision* edited by Robin Larsen (1988):

> Swedenborg seldom was without a pen in hand, busily writing away. Much of what he wrote he left unpublished. But the works that he did publish during his lifetime, translated for the most part into English and bound in standard-size volumes need about a six-foot shelf to hold them. If you add to that the posthumously published works, add another shelf!

Swedenborg did wonder how his writings would be received. Again, he wrote in his *Spiritual Diary* #2955: **"I spoke with spirits about how the writings concerning these matters, when they are published, seem to be received, for evil spirits had several times poured in the persuasion that no one would understand them, but that they would reject them. Speaking just now with spirits on the street, I was given to see that there are five kinds of reception.**

First, there are those who entirely reject them, who are of a different conviction, and are enemies of the faith. These reject them, for the things written cannot be received by them because they cannot penetrate into their minds.

The second kind are those who receive them as knowledge, and who take pleasure in them as knowledge, and also as curiosities.

The third kind are those who take them up with the understanding, receiving them quite enthusiastically, but still remain as they were before in life.

The fourth kind receive them with conviction, so that they penetrate and bring improvement to their life. They recall them in certain states, and put them to use.

The fifth kind are they who receive them with joy, and are confirmed in them. 1748, 27 Aug."

Dear Candace,
Why didn't Swedenborg have a secretary to help him with all that writing?
R.L.
Pasadena, California
July 2006

Dear R.L.,

Today, most of us couldn't imagine writing a letter, let alone a book, without a computer. Most professionals have secretaries or assistants to help them with their workloads. Even in Swedenborg's time, there were secretaries and professional human copiers. (The common way of teaching in the 18th century was by rote method: repetition—copying out a book, word for word. If you copied a book, you knew it better and once it was copied, it became yours. You didn't have to buy it!)

Yet, Swedenborg never hired anyone to help him write or organize his books. He did *all* his own research and handwriting (with a quill pen). And that was as unusual then as it is now. Why *did* he do it alone?

As a scientist, Swedenborg was trained to investigate and evaluate for himself the natural sciences. So, when his life changed course at the age of 55—with his new ability to see into the spiritual world—his working style was already set.

After the Lord visited Swedenborg and gave him the job of recording what he saw with his spiritual eyes, he got to work right away studying the Bible; for TWO YEARS. He ended up writing about the Bible in 3,000 folio pages (meaning 15 inches in height). Though born into a Lutheran home, he hadn't studied the Bible word for word.

He first started by reading a Latin translation of the Bible. (Later, he would switch to reading the Bible in Hebrew and Greek, once he mastered those languages.) As he read, he kept, at first, a list of passages about the Lord's First Coming to earth. That became the first of eight Indexes to the Bible he made for his own referencing! His indexing not only assisted his memory, but also opened up his spiritual mind to see what the Lord was telling him through the Bible. He got it!

This claim may seem farfetched in light of several infamous individuals of recent history who have claimed that God had spoken through them, too, only to have their followers commit murder, suicide, and child abuse—Shakers, Mormons, Jonestown, Branch Davidians. Swedenborg, however, unlike other self-proclaimed religious leaders, gravely realized his ego was getting in the way of receiving wisdom from the Lord. Recognizing that he had been motivated by future fame as a young scientist, he humbled himself. By doing so, he was "admitted" fully into the spiritual world.

If Swedenborg had left any of his research about the Bible to a secretary, he would have missed out on little comparatives and correlations he caught as he kept his lists.

Dear Candace,
I have heard that Emanuel Swedenborg is a prophet. Now where do we find him in Scripture? Can you show or prove me from the Bible?

G.O.
Kisii, Kenya
March 2001

Dear G.O.,
Your question has been asked by many. I checked with a Swedenborgian friend of mine in Tucson, Arizona. Rev. Frank Rose wrote:

> *Dear Candace,*
> *The question about where in the Bible does it prophecy a new prophet is a difficult one. For the most part, the Bible does not talk about prophets who will come in the future, with the exception of sending Elijah (Malachi 3:1, 4:5).*
>
> *We sometimes refer to John 16:12, 13:* **"I still have many things to say to you, but you cannot bear them now. However, when He, the Spirit of truth, has come, He will guide you into all truth."** *That is referring to the Lord, not Swedenborg. We see Swedenborg as a means whereby the Lord communicated His message.*
>
> *In Revelation 21:5 we have the words:* **"Behold, I make all things new."** *We see that as a kind of prophecy.*

Swedenborg was asked this question when he was alive. He answered that he was chosen by the Lord to be a spiritual fisherman, similar to the fishermen chosen by the Lord to be His apostles when He was on earth. The apostles were told that they would be fishers of people for Christ. Fish correspond to natural knowledges, wrote Swedenborg.

Swedenborg's role was to go one step further—write down the inner significance of the Bible. He said that from his early years, he had been a spiritual fisherman—one who investigates and teaches natural and spiritual truths in a rational way.

I may not have proved to your satisfaction, G.O., that Emanuel Swedenborg (1688–1772) was a prophet, but I suggest you read some books by him the same way you would read the Bible. Study them and see if Swedenborg's Writings speak to you. See for yourself if the things taught by Swedenborg are true—Divine truth—and thus that he was the prophet that gave them to you.

Dear Candace,
What is your prediction or guess on how long Swedenborg's works will be hidden from the public as foretold in Conjugial Love *#533 and/or* True Christian Religion *#848? In what way do you think his Writings will be brought to the public's view?*

S.G.
Durango, Colorado
November 2000

Dear S.G.,

I believe Swedenborg will become a household name, his books will be read by millions, and his teachings embraced into living action, in my lifetime.

The two numbers you mentioned are the same angel story. He often did that; put the same story into different books for emphasis. Swedenborg begins this story you mentioned with:

"I was once taken up as to my spirit into the angelic heaven and into a society there; and some of the wise ones there came to me and asked, 'What news from the earth?' I answered, 'The news is that the Lord has revealed mysteries, which in excellence surpass all the mysteries revealed from the beginning of the church even to the present time.' " (See *True Christian Religion* #846)

The angels asked Swedenborg what the mysteries were and he related many, such as correspondences, life after death, and true marriage love. The angels were surprised people on earth didn't know these things!

Seeing that Swedenborg was sad, the angels asked him why. Because people regarded these truths as of no value, he replied. The angels then asked the Lord to let them *see* down into earth and when they did, they saw just darkness. Then the angels were sad, too. Swedenborg and the angels were told by the Lord, that the mysteries would remain hidden, **"For a time, and times, and half a time (as foretold in Apocalypse 12:14)."**

I believe Swedenborg's books will be brought to the public's attention through pop culture via lay individuals. Scholars and ministers have their job—researching and preaching. But, Swedenborgian thinking will spread when it is portrayed in movies and books. When it is shared by word of mouth. And through role models. There are today famous Swedenborgians (actors, directors, writers) that haven't shared publicly what their religion is. If they did say that they *were* Swedenborgians...*well, then...*

Swedenborg was not a man of the cloth. He was a scientist. He was trained to investigate natural laws (truths) and later turned his methodology into investigating spiritual laws (truths). Emanuel Swedenborg's job as revelator was to make the doctrines public through the press. That's it! He didn't preach them. Occasionally, he gave his books away to his scientific and clergy friends, but he didn't start a religion or movement. His readers did that, 15 years after his death.

Contemporary thinking is that Swedenborg's books and his ideas should reach the masses and not just religious seekers and scholars in universities. His books should be bestsellers. I could name more than 100 lay people that are actively spreading Swedenborgianism by placing his books in libraries, mailing his books to the famous and those in prison, placing book ads, creating Swedenborgian novels, plays, songs, art, and making Swedenborg websites.

One tremendous undertaking towards making Swedenborg a household name is the new translation of *Heaven and Hell* by Emanuel Swedenborg, originally published by him in 1758. This 535-page hardback was published *this month* and cost $49.00. But, it is worth the money!

This new contemporary translation is easy to read. I recommend buying two copies—one for yourself and one to donate to your local library. To order in USA: *Swedenborg Foundation* 1 (800) 355-3222. In Canada: *Information Swedenborg*: 1 (877) 774-7775. In England: *Swedenborg Society*: 0207 405 7986.

Even though Swedenborgians agree that *Heaven and Hell* is the easiest book of Swedenborg's to read, earlier translations have sometimes stumped the eager. This new edition will not! It should be in every library in the world!

The new *Heaven and Hell* has contemporary and gender-inclusive language, Swedenborg's original prose styles and designs, and information about him.

Heaven and Hell is just the first book to be retranslated from its original Latin. All Swedenborg's theological books will be translated anew over the next 20 years! Book title changes to come:

- *Apocalypse Revealed* will be changed to *Revelation Unveiled*
- *Arcana Coelestia* will be changed to *Secrets of Heaven*
- *Earths in the Universe* will be changed to *Other Planets*
- *True Christian Religion* will be changed to *True Christianity*

Bernhard Lang wrote in the Introduction to the new *Heaven and Hell*:

> Emanuel Swedenborg (1688–1772) was a man of two careers: one in science and one in theology. The first career ended in 1747 when he retired from his position of the Royal Board of Mines in his home country, Sweden. With inherited resources augmented by a small salary, the fifty-nine-year-old scholar went abroad, spending much time in London and Amsterdam, cities he knew from earlier visits.

He had *two careers, inherited resources, and a small salary*. No one has said it that way before. Wow. You gotta get this book!!!!!!!!!!!

Dear Candace,
  Do you know when the New Church was founded?

                                                            G.G.
                                                    La Jolla, California
                                                    November 2001

Dear G.G.,
   I believe you are referring to the religion, New Church, or Church of the New Jerusalem, which follows the Old Testament, New Testament, and the Writings of Emanuel Swedenborg.
   Keep in mind that many people read and believed Swedenborg's books when he was living and corresponded with him about them. Keep in mind that many people read Swedenborg's books in different countries; his fame went beyond his Swedish borders. Keep in mind that Swedenborg died in 1772.
   It all began when a 19-year-old Englishman, Robert Hindmarsh was lent a copy of Swedenborg's book, *Heaven and Hell*, by a Quaker friend of his in 1782. Robert, convinced of the book's validity, saying it was "of heavenly origin" began to share it enthusiastically with his friends.
   Robert started a reading circle which consisted of four men meeting in his home. These men decided to place ads in their local London newspaper inviting readers of Swedenborg to meet.
   The first public meeting of receivers of the new doctrines written by Swedenborg took place at *The London Coffee House* on Ludgate Hill, 5 December 1783. One man answered the ad and joined the original four. However, since no private room was available (for they were bound to discuss and read aloud from the Writings), the five men moved over to *the Queen's Arm Tavern*, but only had tea.
   They advertised a second public meeting. It took place in a reserved room at *The Inner Temple* (part of *The Temple*) on Fleet Street, 12 December 1783. At this second meeting, it was decided they must have a permanent place to meet.
   The Theosophical Society, "instituted for the purpose of promoting the Heavenly Doctrines of the New Jerusalem, by translating and publishing the Theological Writings of the Hon. Emanuel Swedenborg" was formed at New Court, *Middle Temple*. (*The Temple*, named after Solomon's Temple in Jerusalem, is an office and apartment complex which still stands today.)
   By this time, Robert's father, James Hindmarsh, a Methodist minister, converted to the new doctrines, annoying his superior in the Methodist Church, Rev. John Wesley.
   By 1787, Robert Hindmarsh—now owner of a printing company with the distinction of being appointed as the Printer Extraordinary to H.R.H. the Prince of Wales—started to talk about forming a religion based on Swedenborg's Writings. The small group wrote a constitution saying that " 'introduction into the New Church is solely through the spiritual correspondent, Baptism, performed in the church' and that 'conjunction with the Lord, and consociation with the angels of the New Heavens, are effected by the Holy Supper, taken in the New Church, according to its heavenly and Divine correspondent.' "
   The first worship service of the New Church took place on Tuesday, 31 July 1787, at the home of Thomas Wright (watch maker to the King) at 6 Poultry Road in

London. Rev. James Hindmarsh was designated to administer baptism and Holy Supper. Of the five men baptised into this new religion, Robert Hindmarsh was the first. Eleven men took the Holy Supper.

The first public worship service of the New Church, led by Rev. James Hindmarsh, took place, 27 January 1788, at the *Great Eastcheap Chapel* in London. The Swedenborgians rented this chapel for 6 years.

Then there was Rev. John Clowes in Manchester, England who not only read Swedenborg's Writings (converted in 1773), he taught them from his Church of England pulpit. He believed that the New Church was to come about as a new spirituality *within* the established churches already on earth. Rev. Clowes was against a separatist movement and tried to dissuade Robert Hindmarsh from starting a new religion. This debate remains today.

James Glen of Scotland brought the New Church religion to the new world when he arrived in Philadelphia in 1784. He gave a lecture on Swedenborg at the *Green Dragon Tavern* in Boston, 1784. He had attended the second public meeting of Swedenborg readers, 12 December 1783. Glen, a rich sugar plantation owner in Demerara, British Guiana (now Guyana) in South America, first read *Heaven and Hell* in 1781. Aboard a ship, the captain had lent him the book. Glen was converted.

UPDATE

James Glen was an ardent Swedenborgian. He purposely went to the United States as a missionary. On 5 June 1784, at Robert Bell's auction room and bookstore, the *Universal Library*, on Third Street in Philadelphia, Glen gave the first public lecture about Swedenborg and the Writings in the new world. The *Universal Library* was "the" place to go to in Philly. He lectured three times there to crowds, but didn't convert many.

Some. Francis Bailey (1744–1817) editor of the *Freeman's Journal* and official printer to both the U.S. Congress and the Commonwealth of Pennsylvania was converted. (He was friends with Benjamin Franklin, who became a reader of the Writings after Bailey became the first printer to print in America the works of Swedenborg.) Robert Morris (1734–1806) became a reader. He was a wealthy merchant who helped finance the Revolutionary War, signed the Declaration of Independence, and served in the Continental Congress. (*Robert Morris University* in Pittsburgh, PA was founded in 1921.) John Young (1762–1840), presiding judge of Western Pennsylvania for thirty years, heard Glen's lecture and was converted. (John and Maria Young would later, living in Greensburg, PA, be a welcome stop for Johnny Appleseed on his travels.)

Glen went to Boston and lectured at the *Green Dragon Tavern,* 11 Marshall Street. It still stands today. Their website reports: "Hailed as 'Headquarters of the American Revolution' the *Green Dragon Tavern* was a favorite for Paul Revere and the Sons of Liberty. Hailed as a 'hotbed' meeting place by it's founding fathers, the *Green Dragon Tavern* continues that tradition today." Again some were converted, but not many. A few years after this lecture, Ralph Waldo Emerson would become a reader in Boston.

James Glen was very discouraged that he was not making thousands of converts, just a handful, and after more lectures in other parts of Pennsylvania, Virginia, and Kentucky, he returned home to Demerara, South America. But, as all

Swedenborgian missionaries eventually learn the hard way, it's the Lord that grows "the church" in a person. We humans can only plant the seeds. After Glen left America, an ordered box of Swedenborg books from Robert Hindmarsh finally arrived in Philadelphia. Unclaimed, they were sold at auction and went into the hands of eager readers making converts unbeknowest to James Glen.

One was Hetty Barclay who lived with the Francis Bailey family. Thomas Newport, a Quaker, read a copy of *Heaven and Hell* that Barclay had sent to her brother in Ohio in 1790! In a letter to W. C. Howells, 19 January 1840, Newport wrote he "read and received, on sight, the first doctrine of the Heavenly Jerusalem that *'the Lord is the God of heaven.'* " Many members of the New Church in the American West received their first knowledge of Swedenborg directly or indirectly from Hetty Barclay. More indirectly because of James Glen!

This tidbit is interesting. From *The Beginnings of the New Jerusalem Church in Ohio* by Ophia D. Smith, The Ohio State Archaeological and Historical Quarterly 61: pp. 235-261 (1952). (http://publications.ohiohistory.org/ohstemplate.cfm?action=detail&Page=0061248.html&StartPage=235&EndPage=261&volume=61&newtitle=volume%2061%20Page%20235):

> Hannah Holland Smith, had brought some of the works of Swedenborg from Holland to Woodstock, Vermont. She translated these writings on sheets of paper which she circulated among her neighbors even before James Glen gave the first Swedenborgian lectures in Philadelphia in 1784. Strictly speaking, Hannah Holland Smith was probably America's first active New Churchwoman. Since Benjamin Powers, brother of Hiram Powers the sculptor, was a prominent member of the Cincinnati society and came from Woodstock, Vermont, it is possible that the Powers family learned of Swedenborg from Hannah Smith's translations.

Is this the same Hannah Holland Smith "of England" who married Adam Hurdus (1760-1843) on 4 February 1783? They moved to America in 1804. While I'd like to say a woman was doing her bit for the Lord's Second Coming, I'm not sure how she managed to do it in America before James Glen in 1784. Scholarship is needed to investigate this further. (Could it have been Holland, Ohio?)

But, we do know that the founder of the California orange industry, Eliza Lovell Tibbets was a Swedenborgian missionary. Born in Cincinnati, Ohio, she moved to Riverside, CA in the 1870s with her family. She introduced seedless navel oranges from Bahia, Brazil into California. Just like Johnny Appleseed, she also planted spiritual seeds advocating abolition and women voting. Sadly, Eliza Tibbets is not even well known in Swedenborgian homes.

In 1792, the first established New Church (not a reading group) was in Baltimore, Maryland. When President George Washington (1743-1826) began his second term in office, the Baltimore New Church presented him with *True Christian Religion* by Swedenborg. In 1801, when Thomas Jefferson (1743-1826) became the 3rd president, they sent him the same 2-volume book. In 1802, President Jefferson invited Rev. John Hargrove of the Baltimore New Church to preach to Congress. In 1804, President Jefferson invited him to preach in the Capitol.

Dear Candace,
 What languages did Swedenborg speak?

S.R.
San Gabriel, California
September 2000

Dear S.R.,
 Swedenborg was fluent in Swedish, Latin, Hebrew, Greek, Dutch, French, Italian, German, and English.
 And he spoke the spiritual language—of ideas. He said that when we die everyone will speak the same spiritual language. At first, we will think we are speaking our earthly language, albeit English or Swahili, but we will be communicating with word ideas. He spoke the spiritual language with good spirits, bad spirits, angels, and devils. We are told this spiritual speech is perceived very rapidly, so that more can be expressed in a moment, than by human speech in hours!
 Swedenborg wrote in *Spiritual Experiences* #5102: **"This speech, also, can be written, I have seen papers and letters written in this language, which I was able to read, but not in the least to understand, unless I was in the spirit separate from the body. The letters were similar to those of natural language."**

Dear Candace,
 I want to know where you came up with the concept that Emanuel Swedenborg was the Second Coming of Jesus. I do want this question answered.

M.A.
Charleston, Missouri
November 2003

Dear M.A.,
 The Swedish, prolific author, Emanuel Swedenborg (1688–1772) **WAS NOT** the Second Coming of Jesus. What he wrote down on paper was! I know this because that is what he wrote in *True Christianity* #776: **"This, the Lord's second coming, is not in person, but in the Word, which is from Him and which He is.**
 We read in many passages that the Lord will come in the clouds of heaven; e.g. Matthew 17:5; 24:30, 26:64; Mark 14:62; Luke 9:34, 35; 21:27; Revelation 1:7; 14:14; Daniel 7:13.
 But no one up to the present has known what the clouds of heaven mean; they have thought that He would appear in them in person. It has so far been unknown that the clouds of heaven mean the Word in its literal sense, and that glory and power, with which He is to come at that time (Matthew 24:30), mean the spiritual sense of the Word.
 This is because no one has even guessed that there is a spiritual sense in the Word, as there is in essence in this example. Since the Lord has now

revealed to me that spiritual sense of the Word, and has allowed me to associate with angels and spirits in their world, as if I were one of them, it has been disclosed that the clouds of heaven means the Word in its natural sense, glory the Word in its spiritual sense, and power means the Lord's strength through the Word."

Swedenborg further explains in *True Christianity* #779: **"This, the Lord's second coming, is taking place by means of a man, to whom He has shown Himself in person, and whom He has filled with His spirit, so that he may teach the doctrines of the new church which come from the Lord through the Word.**

Since the Lord cannot show Himself in person, as has just been demonstrated, and yet He predicted that He would come and found a new church, which is the New Jerusalem, it follows that He will do this by means of a man, who can not only receive intellectually the doctrines of this church, but also publish them in print.

I bear true witness that the Lord has shown Himself in the presence of me, His servant, and sent me to perform this function. After this He opened the sight of my spirit, thus admitting me to the spiritual world, and allowed me to see the heavens and the hells, and also to talk with angels and spirits; and this I have now been doing for many years without a break."

Swedenborg mentions his role in the Second Coming in other books of his as well, but they all say the same thing—the new revelations he is writing about are what are referred to as the Second Coming of the Lord.

Emanuel Swedenborg was not, nor is now, holy or a saint, and is not to be worshipped. Only The Lord is!

What is noteworthy is that Swedenborg does not say that he was commissioned to establish a church or to preach the new doctrines as Jesus had asked of His twelve apostles. Swedenborg was just to make the new doctrines public through the printing press. That is why he paid for the publishing with his own money.

Swedenborg spoke with a stutter. He never, ever, gave a public speech. His skills were in his hands, both hands, writing day and night, the various secrets that were seen by him and revealed to him concerning heaven and hell, the state of people after death, the true worship of God, the spiritual sense of the Word, and matters of salvation and wisdom.

Dear Candace,

Why do you say Swedenborg was not charismatic? He had an enormous influence on others both in his lifetime and afterwards. Surely (that this is supposition) his goodness must have been shining out of him.

S.B.
Washington, D.C.
November 2003

Dear S.B.,
A charismatic leader is one that possesses an extraordinary ability to attract followers and is able to galvanize people into action because they have a magnetic personality; e.g. Winston Churchill, Adolph Hitler, Jim Jones, John F. Kennedy, Martin Luther King, Jr., David Kouresh, Abraham Lincoln, Charles Manson.

Charisma means "gift of grace" (from God) and was first coined by the German scholar, Max Weber (1864–1920), a political economist and sociologist. This modern phenomenon of a charismatic person is of one that has followers that confidently, emotionally, blindly, trust their leader's beliefs and obeys their whim.

I love Swedenborg, but I have to tell you, he had zip charisma. He was a Swede—reserved, quiet, formal, aloof. He spent more time writing than any other activity. Most of his family were jealous and disliked him. He never married. He was a genius—absentmindedly so. Kids laughed at his mismatched clothes. But, he had many friends. His friends said he had beautiful blue eyes and was a lovely gentleman. His goodness did shine out of him, but it mostly excited envy and hatred, not blind followers.

Dear Candace,

I'm impressed by your zing, speed, and staying powers. You seem to be the P.R. wizard of Swedenborg info! Your latest "tour de force", The Angel Festival, *seems full of good abilities.*

I went surfing on InterNet in our local town. My first attempt was to see what was under "Swedenborg"—but I found it very "bookish". The people who had put it in did it as though it was a book and not a new revolutionary medium that needs new layout to compete with all the other, "snap, crackle, pop" going on around it.

Anonymous
Jyllinge, Denmark
May 2001

Dear Anonymous,
I, too, have surfed for Swedenborg online. Encyclopedias do a good report. Individually placed websites about Swedenborg are bookish as you say. Time will tell, if they will improve or not.

Chapter 2

OTHER WORLDS

✣✣✣✣✣✣✣✣✣✣✣✣✣✣✣✣✣✣✣✣✣✣✣✣✣✣✣✣✣

Dear Candace,
    I hope that you don't mind a few questions. You mentioned that you can answer any question. Have you had any out-of-body experiences? Have you read many of Swedenborg's books? How long have you been involved with his teaching?
                                                                B.M.
                                                Los Angeles, California
                                                        January 1993

Dear B.M.,
    Here goes:
    No, I have not had any out-of-body or near-death experience. *However*, in Edmonton, Alberta in 1982, an angelic spirit sat on the end of my bed.
    I was tossing in disturbed sleep—worried about my boyfriend working on a dangerous oil rig up north—when I saw a female spirit (glowing white, no wings) sit on my bed. I will always remember how she was careful not to sit on my feet! I was comforted by her presence, at peace, not afraid, and fell back asleep.
    And, in Toronto, Ontario in 1984, I was working as an extra on the TV series, *Night Heat* starring Scott Hylands, Allan Royal, Jeff Wincott, and Sean McCaan. We were filming in an institution that was formerly a "home" for the mentally disturbed. This lakefront fortress was a series of sprawling buildings known decades ago as an "insane asylum". During filming breaks, it was common for the actors to go wandering around the grounds. I asked a co-worker to go searching with me and we ended up in areas we weren't supposed to be in. We located the "rubber room" with its 2x2" window. We saw the 4-foot wide cells, and a lunch room with long tables in neat rows. We found a large room with chairs strewn around and at one end was a cage! Next to its door was a desk and chair. I turned the doorknob and opened the cage.

Entering, I immediately heard people crying and wailing, and felt sadness. I turned to my fellow actor and said, "They're crying." He bolted and ran all the way back to the film location. Later, he told me he believed me, for the expression on my face changed, and he got spooked. No more "other worldly" experiences have happened to me since.

I have read many of Swedenborg's books, but not all, as they are numerous (if you add in his scientific ones and others published after his death). I AM trying to read them all.

I have been involved with Swedenborg's teachings since birth being born into a Swedenborgian family in Canada. I'm third-generation Swedenborgian.

Dear Candace,
I have had patients who, a day or two before they die, they see or talk to loved ones who have gone before. It's almost as if the loved one comes back to guide them on their way, or to make a different experience easier and more comfortable for them. Do you have any input on this theory?

L.S.
Philadelphia, Pennsylvania
March 1993

Dear L.S.,
My maternal grandmother—Mabel Georgina Langlois Carter (1889–1977)—talked to "dead" people she knew, days before she died, too. It is quite a common occurrence for those in your medical field to witness such communications. Swedenborg writes that this can happen.

I met Anders Hallengren (author of *Gallery of Mirrors: Reflections on Swedenborgian Thought*) at the *Stockholm New Church* when I visited Sweden in June. He is associate professor and research fellow in the Department of History of Literature and the History of Ideas at *Stockholm University*. He served as consulting editor for literature at Nobelprize.org. *SILA* November 1998

Dear Candace,
 Visionaries like Emanuel Swedenborg have provided the human race practical solutions to human needs—from the vast depository of their ... "dreams".
J.S.
Allentown, New Jersey
April 1996

Dear J.S.,
 I agree dreams can provide us with solutions to our needs, but we do not always heed our dreams because they aren't always understood.
 Swedenborg wrote about dreams in more than eight of his books. He said that the first people on earth conversed directly with God and angels, and were instructed by dreams and visions. Over time, people figured they knew more than God and the angels, and "pulled away" from them. Consequently, dreams were less believed and less understood. We can imagine where we are today, understanding this spiritual link to the other world!
 When Swedenborg wrote about his findings on dreams, over 200 years ago, he admitted he knew few people would believe that anyone can see things that exist in the other life because few believed in resurrection at all. Are we any different centuries later? Will people believe his findings now, with the current angel movement? I hope so.
 Swedenborg tells us there are three kinds of dreams:
 1. dreams from the Lord (as with the prophets)
 2. dreams through angels or devils
 3. dreams through good or evil spirits who are nearest us

 The fact is all dreams are from the spiritual world. Depending on which spirits are near us, dreams can be beautiful or terrifying.
 People have wondered why God does not sort of dictate through miracles, visions, and dreams. Truth is, if He did this, it would incite a reaction, and not an action of our own free choice.
 But, He still does try to reach us through our dreams. Many widows and widowers have said they *saw* their deceased partner and were comforted. This is one use of dreams.

Dear Candace,
   What does Swedenborg say about the spiritual world before the creation of man and his death?

                                                                W.A.
                                                        Tipton, Missouri
                                                        November 1996

Dear W.A.,
   Swedenborg wrote that this question bothered him a lot, until angels suggested to him that he think of it *not* from *time and space*. He tried that, and he could then see that God from eternity has no beginning nor ending.
   The world was not created out of nothing because the universe is created in the image of God. The Lord is the *sun,* in the spiritual world, from which spiritual things grow. He created the sun in the natural world, from which natural things grow.
   In Emanuel Swedenborg's *Spiritual Diary,* on 5 October 1748, he wrote that people can go mad from thinking about the time before creation. It is enough for us to think about God outside of *time and space* which are natural properties. Swedenborg says that first there was God. He created the spiritual world and then the natural world. When people were born, they inhabited the natural world. When people died, they inhabited the spiritual world.
   Heaven and Hell #167: "**I was once thinking about eternity, and was able, with the idea of time, to perceive what *to* eternity means, namely, without end, but not what *from* eternity means, thus not what God did from eternity before creation.**" (I added the italic underlings.)
   Emanuel Swedenborg wrote a magnitude about "before creation". Basically, the truth is that what God was before creation is the same as He is after creation. Or as He has been from eternity, will be as He is to eternity. God does not change. Eternity is an infinite state, not infinite time.
   If you think from time, this finite notion comes up—that there was some beginning to the existence of God, that He had an origin. It is impossible to think otherwise—from time. Similarly, concerning space outside of the universe, which, also, cannot be conceived in infinity—if from space. Time and space are those things which bound human ideas, and make them altogether natural.
   God created the natural world in time. God created people in time. When the first people died, they joined Him in the spiritual world which already existed.
   Angels, Swedenborg tells us, banish space and time from their idea of the Divine. But because human beings (before they become angels) are incapable of thinking except by means of ideas formed from spatial and temporal concepts, we cannot form any idea of the immensity of God before space existed or His eternity before time existed.
   Swedenborg warns his readers that if one persists in an attempt to penetrate these "mysteries", one can easily become deranged, and could even be led to deny the existence of God!

Dear Candace,
 My life reading showed I was a student of Swedenborg. My name was "Swenson" in that lifetime.

D.B.
Fort Lauderdale, Florida
June 1989

Dear D.B.,
 I believe you are referring to the act of reincarnation. You have experienced an interesting reading.
 The wonderful thing to me is the reality of the spiritual world—an actual, independent, separate world which we all enter at death and live on in as ourselves. The very thought of having to live again, until we get it right, would be an idea from a cruel God. We only need one lifetime to make our essential choice. For, to think of reincarnation, it negates the existence of hell. We all have spiritual freedom—to choose good or evil.
 Emanuel Swedenborg wrote that many in the Jewish faith believed in the absurd notion that the soul of one person passes into another. For example, that the soul of Elijah passed into the body of John the Baptist.
 The idea of reincarnation, Swedenborg tells us, masks as a spiritual philosophy when it actually is a materialistic philosophy—love of this world with a desire to come back!
 But, D.B., your reading tells me something different than you having lived before, as I doubt you did. Swedenborg had the privilege of seeing and hearing into the spiritual world for years, and was shown that there are spirits (previously lived humans) assigned to every living human being. Many refer to them as "guardian angels" or "the devil made me do it". Swedenborg calls them **"associate spirits"**. (Two good and two bad, in fact.)
 Sometimes, the departed know who they are with on earth, but <u>rarely</u>. And then, sometimes the spirit's earthly memory is triggered into the accompanying person's mind they are with, and the person experiences "déjà vu"—"already seen".
 I have encountered the feeling of déjà vu many times. I know I have not lived before, but my associate spirits have. One of your associate spirits, D.B., may have known Swedenborg. Or a bad associate spirit wanted to play with you and took your knowledge of Swedenborg from your mind and just fed it back to you, or possibly your psychic/spiritual reader knew you liked Swedenborg or saw you with a Swedenborg book and made up your life reading.
 I suggest you read Swedenborg's book, *True Christian Religion* (especially #171) and his, *Heaven and Hell* (especially #256).

Dear Candace,
 Do you think Swedenborg ever mentioned or dealed with the conception of reincarnation?

B.N.
Gothenburg, Sweden
December 2005

Dear B.N.,
 I answered this question back in June 1989, but will do it again... pun intended. Mary Roach, author of *Stiff: The Curious Lives of Human Cadavers* (2003), investigated reincarnation for her current book, *Spook: Science Tackles the Afterlife,* (released in October) by travelling to India for a week.

The first chapter of *Spook* is: "You Again. A visit to the reincarnation nation." Mary writes about the soul jumping concept with humour and healthy skepticism. She found it fascinating that most in India were reincarnated poor "ordinary people", whereas believers in reincarnation in the West "tend to spring from royalty and aristocracy".

Swedenborg doesn't use the word "reincarnation" when he writes about it, but talks about living again or returning to earth again. He tells us that while the idea is absurd, it is understandable how people can think that we may come back.

We are so close to the spiritual world that we sometimes tap into it vividly and imagine we have lived before because we remember something we didn't know before. That's commonly called the déjà vu experience.

Heaven and Hell #256: **"An angel or spirit is not permitted to speak with us from their own memory, but only from our memory. For angels and spirits have memory as well as us. If a spirit were to speak with us from their own memory, we would not know otherwise than that the thoughts then in our mind were our own, although they would be the spirit's thoughts.**

This would be like the recollection of something which we had never heard or seen. I have been allowed to learn this from experience. This is the source of the belief held by some of the ancients that after some thousands of years they were to return into their former life, and into everything they had done, and in fact, had returned. This they concluded because at times there came to them a sort of recollection of things that they had never seen or heard. This came from an influx from the memory of spirits into their ideas of thought."

We on earth are closest to those who have just died—good and bad spirits—who are not yet in heaven or hell. Furthest from us are angels and devils—that are living in heaven and hell. Under normal conditions, spirits who are spiritually connected with us—because we love the same things—can know our memories, but we cannot theirs. Under abnormal conditions, spirits can let us see their memories. (Know that all this is happening without either party knowing who the other is; yet, spiritually being connected.) So, for some, thoughts of reincarnation are very real because they've tapped into memories of spirits nearest them. It's not that we were that person, but are momentarily seeing with the same eyes.

Spiritual Experiences #1582: **"Moreover, that a spirit should be able to pass into the body of another, and live in that body, is at once absurd and** impossible, for the consequence would be that the form of one would be changed into that of another, the interior substances of the person would be entirely emptied out, and the substances of another applied, in their stead, to the fibers and vessels, while at the same time all that which had contracted a nature in the [life of] the body and been wrought into obedience to its proper form, would be assumed."

November 2002
Dear *SILA* Readers,

I was asked by a French TV show, a couple of weeks ago, if I believed in reincarnation; if I believed I was a bunny in a past life!

Interviewed weekly at *The Bunny Museum* (that Steve and I opened in 1998), I'm accustomed to odd questions, mostly the same ones. But, that was the first time I'd been asked if I believed in reincarnation.

When I answered, "No", the camera was stopped! The interviewer told me that the show they were doing was about individuals around the world that wear animal costumes on a semi-regular basis! The ones interviewed, so far, said they believed they were an animal in their past life and that is why they feel compelled to parade around as their birth-right animal.

The camera rolled again. Asked the same question, I answered, "No", but then went on to tell about my Swedenborgian belief in the afterlife—one life, marriage after death, my union to eternity with Steve, our still acquiring bunny items in the next world. The interviewer was satisfied with that answer. Can't wait to see the tape of that show! It will be airing in France, Germany, Switzerland, and other French speaking countries.

Thinking of you,
Candace

UPDATE
    We never were sent a copy of the show as requested.

Swedenborg used this ornament in *New Jerusalem and its Heavenly Doctrine*

December 2005
Dear *SILA* Readers,

    I am thrilled to tell you that Mary Roach wrote a page and a half about Swedenborg and Wilson Van Dusen (a Swedenborgian) in her new book, *Spook*, which is bound to be a bestseller as her first book, *Stiff*, was. Some of you may recall that I invited Mary to *The 10th Angel Festival* to sign her book.

    She didn't write about Swedenborg in *Stiff*, but I loved it and felt she grasped the sanctity of life with humour and wrote about the afterlife of a human body left on earth with hilarious honesty. That is what *The Angel Festival* is all about, having fun with what happens after we die.

    I was fully aware, at the time, that many thought I was crazy to have Mary Roach signing her *Stiff* book at the festival. *How can you make fun of life after death? It's serious. It's religious. How could you?* it was muttered.

    That pun's for Mary for she recently emailed me that her second favorite museum "(even though I have yet to make it to *The Bunny Museum*, it is my favorite, simply on principal!)" is *The Mutter Museum* (a collection of anatomical oddities) in Philadelphia. "The wonderful and wonderfully weird woman who founded it, Gretchen [Muff] Worden, is a Swedenborgian."

As it turned out, Mary at the time of the festival in 2003 was writing her second book on the soul, so I told her Swedenborg was looking for the soul in cadavers. Mary said she had come upon him in her research, but didn't have much on him. So, I gave her *Emanuel Swedenborg: A Continuing Vision* edited by Robin Larsen. Later, I put her in contact with (New Church) Rev. Dr. Reuben Bell and sent her a copy of *The New Philosophy* magazine with a great article full of biographical tidbits about Swedenborg.

The end result is Mary not only read about Swedenborg in "boring" research books, but met a few Swedenborgians, too, and discovered that we aren't archaic, but in her eyes, some of us are "wonderfully weird"!

From page 191 of *Spook: Science Tackles the Afterlife* by Mary Roach:

> Dr. Van Dusen is a Swedenborgian—a follower of the teachings of Emanuel Swedenborg, an eighteenth-century mining engineer/inventor/anatomist who began having religious visions in his forties. Swedenborg gained renown as a philosopher and wrote at length about the heaven of his visions, a dream realm inhabited by wingless angels and demons, which, he held, had once been mortal humans. Van Dusen began to notice that his patients' "others" fell into similar camps of good and evil, with the evil well outnumbering the good, and that they shared numerous traits with Swedenborg's opposing spirit entities.
>
> You might be thinking, and I could not blame you, that it is more plausible that Emanuel Swedenborg was having schizophrenic episodes than that the schizophrenics were having Swedenborgian episodes. However, by all measures, Swedenborg was not psychotic. He maintained a productive existence as a statesman and theologian, and enough people took — and take — him seriously for the Swedenborgian Church to have become, and to remain, a thriving international denomination.

Thinking of you,
Candace

"Mary Roach"
10ᵀᴴ Angel Festival℠
Saturday October 4, 2003

Dear Candace,
You are so great at answering questions about Swedenborg, I thought I would (at the risk of being called a "nit picker") ask you your comments on the following: The General Church teaches that the Writings are the "third Word". And, from my experience, the Writings are crammed full of truths. Then, I read Divine Love and Wisdom #401 *which states that the fetus is unable to move any part of its body. How, then, can the fetus kick and move its arms, which it truly does? It is extremely difficult for me to accept this as a truth, and consequently as part of the "third Word".*

Your comments would be appreciated. The best answer I have had to this one so far is, "Don't worry about it!"

Keep up your fantastic work of helping make more sense of a belief that already makes much sense!

J.T.T.
Glen Ellyn, Illinois
June 1993

Dear J.T.T.,

The *General Church of the New Jerusalem* is the name of one of the organizations that follows the Word of God—Old and New Testament—and the Writings of Emanuel Swedenborg. They believe that the Writings are as Divine as the first two Testaments, and therefore a third Testament as you indicated. The General Church is headquartered in Bryn Athyn, Pennsylvania and is worldwide.

Divine Love and Wisdom was written by Swedenborg and published in Amsterdam, Holland in 1763. Here's the numbered passage you referred to, #401: **"For in the fetus the blood does not flow from the heart into the lungs, giving it the ability to respire; but it flows through the foramen ovale in the left ventricle of the heart; consequently the fetus is unable to move any part of its body, but lies enswathed, neither has it sensation, for its organs of sense are closed. So is it with love or the will, from which the fetus lives indeed, though obscurely, that is, without sensation or action. But as soon as the lungs are opened, which is the case after birth, the baby begins to feel and act, and likewise to will and think. From all this it can be seen that love or the will is unable to affect anything by means of its human form without a marriage with wisdom or the understanding."**

That Swedenborg said, in the eighteenth century, that a fetus does not move, appears to us in the twentieth century to be untrue for we know it *is* true. At least it has the *appearance*. And that is what it is, an *appearance*; just as we say the sun sets, yet we know it never does. That is also an *appearance*.

A fetus refers to an unborn child from the third month of pregnancy until its birth when the mother's uterus can no longer hold the fetus and its forced to leave. Movement of the fetus begins generally around the third month and is extremely important. In fact, any long periods of time when the fetus isn't moving is considered abnormal and investigated.

An unborn child is called a fetus because it is incapable of independent life from its mother. A fetus does not act on its own, but reacts to stimulus, i.e. talking, music, smoking, hitting.

The respiratory and cardiovascular systems of the fetus are the ones most altered by the act of birth because of their spiritual correspondence.

Swedenborg used this example of a fetus not moving (on its own) to show us a spiritual truth. He was demonstrating that there is a correlation between a person's love and their wisdom. Even if there is a will (fetus with its own heartbeat) without some kind of wisdom of how to do it (a baby breathing on its own) nothing can be done. In other words, to will something is not enough.

That Swedenborg knew that fetuses did move in the womb is most definite, for being an avid Bible scholar, he knew what happened when Mary, pregnant with Jesus, visited her cousin, Elisabeth, who also was pregnant in her sixth month with John the Baptist. Elisabeth said: **"For, lo, as soon as the voice of thy salutation sounded in mine ears, the babe leaped in my womb for joy."** Luke 1:44

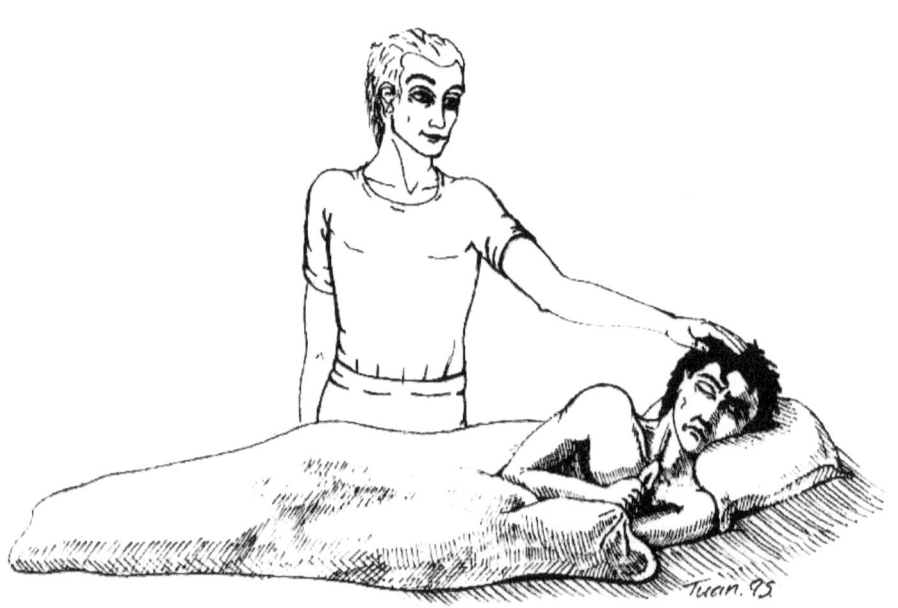

The spiritual world, being parallel to our world, allows people there to be near us

Drawing by Tuan Hauptmann   *SILA* November 1995

Dear Candace,

I was given a copy of Heaven and Hell *by a Swedenborgian in San Francisco. I found it to be an extremely fascinating book.*

The only thing that has kept me from investigating further into Swedenborg's literature has been something I read somewhere that the position of the Swedenborgian Church on abortion is not pro-life. Since Swedenborg himself remained a Lutheran, the position of the "Swedenborg Church" may not actually reflect his position. But in any case, I would like to hear from you whether fetuscide is in your view an immoral act.

B.M.
Salt Lake City, Utah
December 1989

Dear B.M.,

You are a thoughtful person to be considering such spiritual ideas and trying to apply them to your own life.

Swedenborg (born in 1688) was the son of a Lutheran Bishop, it is true, but he didn't remain a Lutheran as he disagreed with Luther's concept of faith alone. Swedenborg believed that life must consist of faith AND charity as the Bible states.

I am thrilled you found *Heaven and Hell* "an extremely fascinating book", but am sorry that you are kept from investigating Swedenborg's books further because you read somewhere of the church's position on abortion. I don't know what you read, but I have never read a Swedenborgian policy about abortion. I have read, however, discussions on doctrines written by Swedenborg in regards to life and abortion by New Church people.

The church, any church, should never dictate laws. (How can a committee's opinion reflect God's?) A church should lead people to the Lord and allow them to make their own choices from their own consciences.

Swedenborg wrote that life in the womb is the Lord's ALONE. He created it. It is a potential human being. Yet, it only becomes a person upon breathing its first breath, which spiritually corresponds to a person's rationality and freedom.

The Writings of Swedenborg further say that to end life is a disorder, and not what the Lord intends. It is also a disorder to have sex before marriage, to get a divorce, to eat meat, but these things do happen. The Lord does not will them, He allows them! For we are free spiritually to make our own choices. We are also told not to judge anyone.

Do we trust a woman to make her own choice when she is pregnant? It is her own individual state.

You ask what is my personal view on feticide (not fetuscide)—destroying a fetus or causing an abortion. This should not matter. I cannot tell you what to think. I'm not to judge others. The church cannot tell you what to think. Only you can know what you believe. I will tell you that I have accepted the Word and the Writings of Swedenborg as true and my guides, and therefore, I believe everything in them and live according to them.

Dear Candace,

I have seen and read lots of material from you to my Dad. It looks interesting. I have also heard him talk about Swedenborg and you. One time he told me that you are a genius or something.

In my school lots of kids were disappointed Sen. Kerry did not win the election. But why? I asked them. This man advocated for abortion to be allowed in law! I think it is because these people associate the Democratic Party with Africans, and why I don't know. What do you think?

M.M.
Nairobi, Kenya
January 2005

Dear M.M.,

I'm not into politics, so I asked my husband, Steve, to explain the difference between Democrats and Republicans. This is what he told me...

Yes, Democrats, who are also called Liberals, are associated with more freedoms, but this is only one issue of dozens which confront Americans in choosing a President. The Democratic Party is associated with African-Americans because that party is socially more willing to help blacks than the Republican Party. The main difference is the Democrats say: "We will help you." The Republicans say: "We will not stand in your way, if you help yourself." The end result can be the same, but the ways they are achieved are by totally different methods.

As for an answer to the abortion question, I go to the Lord in His Word which is the Old Testament, the New Testament, and the Writings of Emanuel Swedenborg and this is what I gather from them...

The ideal is for all babies to be born and not aborted. To "murder" a potential baby is abhorrent. But, the Lord is merciful and when an abortion happens, it is by permission—not something the Lord wants, but allows.

Senator John Kerry believes abortion is a woman's choice. President George W. Bush does not. He believes it is up to God who is born. According to Swedenborg, they are both "right"—as long as they are acting from their good conscience and not from selfish desires...thinking they can sway more votes. You see, we are "judged" by our motives.

Yet, one of the Ten Commandments is **"Thou Shalt Not Kill"**. Is a soldier wrong to kill? No, Swedenborg says, if the soldier acts out of love for country. Is it wrong to abort a baby? As hard as it may be to stomach, the answer is, not always. The aborter may be doing it out of love for the baby, not to bring it into an unbearable situation. Is the mother-to-be who aborts her baby a murderer? How can we judge her? We are told not to judge others. There is a difference between hatred of innocence (babies) which is excited in us from devils in hell and the preservation of the mother-to-be and the unborn child who is being protected by angels in heaven.

Swedenborg wrote that a person's life begins and ends with a breath. So, not until a fetus breathes air, is it a human that can potentionally grow up to be an angel. Swedenborg tells us that if a baby lives, even for a second (on earth) the baby will grow up in heaven and become an angel. But, miscarried, stillborn, or aborted fetuses do not grow up in heaven and become angels because they have not breathed—all human life begins with a breath. There is life in an embryo before birth, but the embryo is not conscious of it and consciousness is what makes a person a person.

Angelic Wisdom About Divine Love and Divine Wisdom #401: **"The human fetus lives because of its heart, but not because of its lungs... As soon as the lungs open, however, which happens after birth, it then begins to experience sensation and to act, and likewise to will and think."**

Swedenborg tells us that the soul of a new person comes from the father through his sperm. The body of a new person comes from the mother.

True Christian Religion #103: **"In the semen from which every person is conceived there exists a graft or offshoot of the father's soul in its fullness."**

If a pregnant woman aborts her fetus and is then labeled a murderer, then what of the other sperms that were active and "killed" by the father-to-be while, say, masturbating? Is he a murderer then, too? Fact is, Swedenborg tells us nothing can destroy a soul for a soul is actually life from God—a part of Him. Those souls that were spilled, aborted, miscarried, or stillborn "go to" the spiritual world and become a part of the soul of heaven. From the Lord's point of view, He sees all people together as one person, and that person—Swedenborg calls the "Grand Human" —has a soul.

Swedenborg explained in his book, *Secrets of Heaven* #1999: **"This internal is the very first form from which [a person] becomes and is a person, and by means of it the Lord is united to [a person]. The very heaven that is nearest the Lord is composed of these human internals; but this is above even the inmost angelic heaven, and therefore these internals belong to the Lord Himself. By this means the whole human race is most present under the Lord's eyes, for there is no distance in heaven, such as appears in the sublunary world, and still less is there any distance above heaven. These internals of people have no life in themselves, but are forms recipient of the Lord's life."**

If a fetus has a soul and is "killed", what happens to the soul? It just disappears. It didn't actuate into a person. Rev. Dan Goodenough, a New Church minister, wrote in the *Theta Alpha Journal* (1983):

> It disappears in the same way that a passing thought or affection disappears if we do not make use of it.

Rev. Erik Sandstrom, Sr., a New Church minister, wrote in the *Theta Alpha Journal* (1992):

> Nothing happens to the "fetal soul" if the fetus is lost, just as nothing happens to the sunshine when a flower withers. Is therefore Genesis 2:7 literally as well as spiritually true? **And the Lord God formed man dust of the ground, and breathed into his nostrils the breath of life; and man became a living soul.** Only the Lord knows why some fetuses are miscarried, stillborn, or aborted. As hard as it is for us to comprehend, some babies aren't born for good and eternal reasons, only known to God. Souls are not reincarnated or reused; they are of God. The Lord never makes mistakes and never changes His mind.

November 1998
Dear *SILA* Readers,

Uppsala University in Uppsala, Sweden houses three museums and one anatomical theatre. On the third floor is *Olof Rudbeck's Anatomical Theatre,* built in 1662. It is a standing-room only, theatre in the round for watching autopsies. Seven rows of four-foot high ledges to lean against are at an extreme angle for optimum viewing of the dissections below on the centre slab. The ledges are four-feet tall to stop fainting viewers from falling down into the show!

I asked the curator and she researched for me that there were only ten human dissections in this theatre: 1664, 1667, 1677, 1701, 1717, 1731, 1733, 1735, 1757, 1766.

Autopsies were frowned upon because it was believed that you had to have your whole body to enter heaven on judgment day. There were numerous animal dissections because it was believed animals didn't have souls. [Swedenborg says all animals have souls—life from God.] But, executed criminals were believed not to have souls (or at least not ones worth worrying about). Ignored by the Lutheran Church, they were sanctioned okay to cut up.

Human dissections were a spectacle. They lasted a week and tickets were sold. Programs were printed up. The first row around the slab, which held the dead body, has *benches*, exclusive for royalty, professors, and invited guests. But, they got blood splattered!

In 1701, Emanuel was a 13-year-old student at *Uppsala University.* Did he watch the human dissection at that age? Probably. In 1717, he was a 29-year-old employed engineer. He left school when he was 21. (This is important because later he went looking for the human soul in anatomy. He never did an autospy himself.)

Thinking of you,
Candace

Dear Candace,
Watching the Winter Olympics in Salt Lake City, Utah, I was wondering what Swedenborg thinks about sports?

S.B.
Los Angeles, California
February 2002

Dear S.B.,

In *Conjugial Love* #156, Swedenborg wrote that one day, he was leaving a **"Contest of Wisdom"** held in an auditorium, while he was *visiting* in the spiritual world. An angel dressed in blue came up to him and said, **"I perceive that you are not fully in this world, because you are at the same time in the natural world, so you do not know about our Olympic sports."** The angel told Swedenborg that wise men of antiquity (before the Middle Ages) would meet and learn from newcomers to the spiritual world what had gone on in our world!

Swedenborg writes about sports as spiritual exercises, mental trials of skill, or literacy activities. But, he also says there are physical activities such as dancing, footraces, and games with balls, e.g. tennis and racquetball. We can all look forward to the Olympics in the next world; not just Summer and Winter ones, but Mental ones as well. Just imagine!

This plaque hangs on a modern building showing
where Swedenborg's house used to be in Stockholm, Sweden

Dear Candace,
How do you know the difference between a dream where someone comes to you or you have a dream about that someone?

S.T.
Kitchener, Ontario, Canada
December 1997

Dear S.T.,
There is no difference. Swedenborg tells us that when we dream, we *are in* the spiritual world. When we dream of a deceased person that person *is* contacting us from the spiritual world. When we are dreaming of a living person, a *spiritual actor* is portraying that person.

There are different kinds of dreams. Dreams are induced by and from the Lord, angels, good spirits, evil spirits, and/or devils.

Emanuel Swedenborg, the Swedish scientist, was in the habit of keeping journals on his travels from Sweden to England, France, Germany, Holland, and Italy. He would record dates, places, and people he met. In 1743, at the age of 55, he started to add his dreams to these travel journals. He did this for one year. Keep in mind that dream study was not a science in Swedenborg's time. This was a revolutionary step on his part.

Today, we know through Rapid Eye Movement (REM) experiments that everyone dreams, on average, 8 dreams a night. Only a few of us can remember 2 dreams. Swedenborg recalled and recorded, on average, 6 dreams a night and analyzed them for his own spiritual growth.

During REM experiments, dream deprivation is performed on subjects. People are awakened just as they start to dream (evidenced by their rapid eye movements). They are then allowed to fall back asleep. This way they are given normal amounts of sleep, but no dream time. Those individuals became disturbed and psychotic during the day—even dreaming while awake! The conclusion? Dreams are necessary. To a Swedenborgian, these experiments demonstrate what the Writings say, that we *need* dreams not because they are fun, but because they are our connection with the spiritual world!

Dreams are experiences in the spiritual world. The Word is filled with dream stories. Through dreams, Swedenborg was introduced into the spiritual world, gradually. Eventually, he was able to be "awake" in the spiritual world, not only there in his dreams. He wrote his travel journals in Swedish, his native language. But, the last paragraph he wrote was in Latin—a language he would continue to use in his theological books. So, his recorded dreams were a stepping stone.

It is fascinating that his journal of dreams was "lost" to humanity for it was kept in the possession of Swedenborg's enemies until 1859! (They were trying to use it as evidence of his insanity, which backfired on them.)

In 1859, it was published in Swedish for all to read. The first English translation was not until 1869. The most current edition of Emanuel Swedenborg's *Journal of Dreams* was published in 1986 with commentary by Wilson Van Dusen.

Swedenborg's heirs tore out several pages of his journal that were to them scandalous! His sexual dreams. These have been lost to history and maybe rightfully so. This was Emanuel's personal journal, after all. We can read other dreams of his of a sexual nature, but those torn out pages must have been something else!

Swedenborg wrote that dreams are a natural, personal process that occurs with everyone. Dreams are presented in the language of correspondences, meaning symbolic. It is a spontaneous representation of our inner life, before our eyes, to assist us with our spiritual growth. (He told us this in the 18th century!)

Dreams are not an invasion of our privacy, but a real connection with our spiritual side. Dream interpretation is big business. But, our dreams cannot be analyzed by an outsider, only truly by ourselves for we know what lurks in our minds and hearts. And even if we don't want to admit it to ourselves, sometimes, Divine Providence can gift us with insight in our dreams. Or comfort us with a visit from a deceased loved one.

Personally, I get excited going to sleep, wondering what I will experience. I have been tormented by evil spirits, so terrible, that I have woken up in a sweat. I have been visited by many deceased people I knew and confused by some wild dreams. Sometimes, I wake up so tired from my spiritual travels that I am exhausted!

Dear Candace,
 I'm very interested...and chagrined to have never heard of Swedenborg. I'll look forward to learning more.
R.C.
Portland, Oregon
September 1995

Dear Candace,
 I've never heard of Swedenborg before. He sounds like an unheralded genius.
D.K.
San Diego, California
September 1995

Dear R.C. & D.K.,
Swedenborg was a genius. He is listed in *The Guinness World Book of Records* as the person with the highest IQ in history. He is in *The World Almanac: Book of The Strange* (1977). He made three pages in the "Strange Persons" chapter!

So glad you discovered Swedenborg. You'll be surprised at what he can teach you. Keep reading *SILA* for great info about him.

Dear Candace,
When I'm in the spiritual world can I talk to famous people from the past like Albert Einstein, Benjamin Franklin, and Abraham Lincoln? And can they in turn seek out people like their grandchildren or George W. Bush when he has passed on? Or would they even know about Bush? Can people from the past go forward in time? If they did, wouldn't they freak out to see people driving in cars, etc.?

Anonymous
Pasadena, California
March 2006

Dear Anonymous,
Yes, you will be able to talk with anyone you want. But—you suspected a *but,* didn't you?—with exceptions.

After a physical body has died, its spirit enters the spiritual world and continues living. If someone lived a truly "good" life, they would enter heaven, maybe within one month or a year. If someone lived a truly "evil" life, they would, enter hell fairly soon, too. However, the majority of people (Swedenborg tells us) take a longer process of sorting out who they really are—what they love—and live in the world of spirits ("the place" between heaven and hell) for awhile. Swedenborg wrote that even though time is irrelevant in the next world, some people live in the world of spirits for up to 30 earth years (not more than that—see *Heaven and Hell* #426) before choosing to live in either heaven or hell. Yes, we do the choosing!

Time travelling is mostly done during years spent in the world of spirits. Wanderlust and curiosity is strongest for newcomers to the spiritual world. They are still materialistic and want to stay attached to earthly things. (This isn't similar to what today's popular mediums call earthbound entities.) Newcomers can visit places in the spiritual world either by countries or centuries. My New Church friend, Rev. Dr. Erik E. Sandstrom of Bryn Athyn, PA wrote me:

> *Dear Candace,*
> *All eras of history can be located in heaven, since the highest heaven comes from those who lived on earth prior to the Flood (prehistoric calamity, but not of actual water, but falsities), the next heaven all those who lived from the flood down to the Advent [of Jesus], and the lowest or New Heaven, all who have lived since the Advent. These heavens are above and below each other, like layers. You can visit, but they don't normally consociate, except by constant communication signals received as images, etc.*

If a famous person died within your lifetime, you could most likely see them in the next world, in the world of spirits; if they wanted visitors. Some may still revel in public appearances and events. Others may not. But, if your desire was so great to meet a renowned scientist or movie star and they didn't want to, an impersonator would be provided for you to satisfy your curiosity. Sometimes you would know it was an impostor, other times not. As for past and ancient celebrities, you would be "permitted" to visit them, but again, only if they wanted to. But, once someone is in hell, they can't go travelling or be visited!

People can indeed meet their new relatives that were born after they had passed. They would know about the births, by the way, because others would have told them. Just as former living Americans would know that their current president was George W. Bush. People are the same after death, in every way. They would want to watch the news on TV and keep up with world affairs.

Time in the spiritual world is measured by states of happiness and sadness and not by increments of the sun's movements. So, people of long ago wouldn't have to go forward in time to visit newcomers in the next world, because it would be "now" to them. They would know about scientific, environmental, and emotional developments that had occurred on earth since they left it because newcomers there would have told them or they would have learned about them from a book.

Swedenborg said he visited libraries in the spiritual world. All the books ever written on earth (even from the lost *Royal Library of Alexandria*!) are available there. The libraries in heaven were so bright (glowing books!) Swedenborg said he could not see all the books because he was incapable of penetrating the depths of wisdom in them. Now that's deep, if Swedenborg couldn't understand them!

Swedenborg tells a story in his book, *Conjugial Love* #207, about three newcomers being amazed by all the books in the spiritual world. They asked, **"Are there also books in this world? Where do the parchment and paper come from? And the pens and ink?"**

They were answered by an angel: **"We perceive that in the former world you thought that this world was empty because spiritual; and that you so thought because the idea you entertained concerning the spiritual world was an idea abstracted from what is material, and to you, what is abstracted from the material appeared as nothing and thus as a vacuum. Yet in this world is a plenitude of all things. Here all things are SUBSTANTIAL not material; and material things derive their origin from things substantial. We who are here are spiritual people because substantial and not material. Hence all things which are found in the natural world are here in their perfection, even books and writings and much else."**

The deeper humankind explores the natural world, like scientists discovering the "mysterious particle" part of an atom: a neutrino—first theorized in 1930 and not actually observed until 1965—the deeper humankind should explore the spiritual world for an understanding of what the universe is made of and where it all came from. Swedenborg said angels often ask newcomers to heaven: **"What news from the earth?"** He was even asked that several times himself and told angels and spirits many things.

Swedenborg once witnessed a "conference" being organized because news had just arrived in the world of spirits from two newcomers about some people that had been found living in a forest on earth as beasts. Apparently, they had been lost or abandoned there from the age of two or three. They couldn't speak, nor be taught to speak when rescued as adults. They ate as animals, yet didn't know what they should eat (like a bird knows its proper diet and a tiger its). The newcomers said that scholars on earth concluded that human beings are similar to animals.

Swedenborg wrote in *Conjugial Love* #156 about his being at this conference with hundreds of other spirits listening to the newcomers tell this amazing news. Then angels discussed it. " **'What times are now on earth!'** they said. **'Alas, what changes has wisdom undergone! Is it not turned into fatuous ingenuity?'**

Who cannot see, from the example of those lost and found in the woods, that such is the nature of [humans] when not instructed? Is [s/he] not a [person] according as [s/he] is instructed? Is [s/he] not born in greater ignorance than beasts? Must [s/he] not learn to walk and to talk? If [s/he] did not learn to walk, would [s/he] stand erect upon [their] feet? And if [s/he] did not learn to talk, could [s/he] give utterance to any thought? Is not every one [a human] according as they are taught, insane from falsities, or wise from truths? And, when insane from falsities, is [s/he] not entirely possessed with the fantasy that they are wiser than one who is wise from truths? Are there not fatuous and insane people who are no more [human] than those found in the woods? Are not those who have lost their memory like them?

From all this, we conclude that, without instruction, [a human] is neither [human] nor beast, but is a form which can receive that which makes [a human]; thus, that one is not born [a human] but becomes [a human]."

Wow! That's why all the books! If we don't learn things from a relative, friend, or teacher, we can get them out of a book. But, we have to learn. (I trust those people raised in the forest by beasts were raised to be human by patient angels.)

Fourteenth-century angels wouldn't freak out seeing twenty-first-century angels in cars, since they would have been told about them. And yes, cars will be there. Swedenborg wrote: **"On the roads I saw some people riding horses, some in carriages, and some on foot."** (See *True Christian Religion* #459) That was in the 18th century. Remember, everything material derives its origin from things SUBSTANTIAL—substance is from the spiritual world. Everything is!

Swedenborg used this ornament in *Secrets of Heaven*

Dear Candace,

I feel something is truly special about the New Church, that it is the New Jerusalem described by John in the Revelation. With the guidance of the Writings of Swedenborg and the Word of God, I have a chance to regenerate a little before I pass into the spiritual world.

Candace, what are your views about Emanuel Swedenborg's description of physical inhabitants of Mercury, Jupiter, etc. from (his) Earths in the Universe?

P.R.
San Francisco, California
July 1989

Dear P.R.,
Thanks for writing with your heartfelt feelings. Many others who agree with you about the New Church are appreciative of your putting it into words. One of the most useful parts of *SILA* is hearing from people such as yourself.

I love Swedenborg's book, THE EARTHS IN OUR SOLAR SYSTEM WHICH ARE CALLED PLANETS AND THE EARTHS IN THE STARRY HEAVEN, AND THEIR INHABITANTS; ALSO THE SPIRITS AND ANGELS THERE, FROM THINGS HEARD AND SEEN, written in 1758.

Swedenborg was allowed by the Lord to see and speak with inhabitants that had died and were living in the spiritual world from Mercury, Jupiter, Mars, Saturn, Venus, our Moon, and five unnamed planets. (Uranus, Neptune, and Pluto were undiscovered at that time.)

Swedenborg tells us that if we desire to speak with people from other planets, we can do so, after death!

The Divine created the universe for no other reason than for the human race, and then a heaven from them. The bottom line is, where ever there is a planet, there are people. What would the human race from one planet be for the Infinite Creator?

Swedenborg recounts the spirits he saw from our moon; how they are dwarfs; that when they speak their voices are thunderous as they do not speak from their lungs like us, but from their abdomens from air collected in them because of the moon's atmosphere.

This month marks the 20th anniversary of the first men who walked on the moon. I can remember lying in a sleeping bag in front of the TV with my large extended family watching the astronauts land on the moon in 1969. We were anxious to see those dwarf moon men appear on the TV as a newspaper article predicted Swedenborgians would be watching for... But, time had passed since Swedenborg had talked to those dead people from our moon. Maybe they are no longer living on the moon. Maybe they are. But, I believe they were once!

To seek out contact with people from other planets will not confirm belief in the Lord. To seek out contact with people from the spiritual world will not confirm belief in life after death. Our beliefs must come from inward persuasion, not outward compulsions.

Dear Candace,
Emanuel Swedenborg's 1758 reference to aliens existing on other planets was truly intriguing. While Mercury, Venus, Mars, Jupiter, and Saturn were already known to science, 5 other unnamed bodies alluded to by him were not. Three of those planets were subsequently discerned: Uranus, Neptune, and Pluto.

One may have been a mysterious 10th planet beyond Pluto that many astronomers believe exists. With regard to the other missing planet, it should be noted that several candidates abide among the planetary moons. Indeed, Swedenborg in essence, suggested the possibility of life on planetary moons in general when he described homuncular beings on our Moon.

It is just a matter of time before we have a absolute scientific confirmation of Swedenborg's 18th century disclosures regarding ETs within our own solar family! May the Force be with You!

Franklin R. Ruehl, Jr., Ph.D.
Glendale, California
September 1989

Dear Candace,
Clearly Earths in the Universe *is Swedenborg's most puzzling work especially since we've landed on the moon and find it and apparently the rest of our solar system devoid of life.*

I studied everything bearing on this book and came to the conclusion it has an internal sense. Under the form of a journey thru the solar system he is describing entering into spiritual experience. It is remarkable to me that scholars haven't seen this long ago. But most miss it, so I don't recommend anyone read it. Swedenborg has many works more readily convertible into uses in one's life.

Wilson Van Dusen, Ph.D.
Ukiah, California
September 1989

Dear Doctors,
Thank you both for writing with your professional opinions. Science changes, truths don't.

One truth that Swedenborg's book, *Earths in the Universe,* teaches is that there is a universal God and He is Jesus Christ. Whether or not science proves to find people on other planets, in my lifetime, will not validate this book for me. I already believe its contents: planets are/were inhabited. (But, I'd be excited if it did!)

As to this book having a deeper meaning to it—maybe. Yet, Swedenborg made many references to this book in other books he wrote. In *Heaven and Hell* #417: "**Information on the planets in the universe, their inhabitants, and the spirits and angels who come from them may be found in the booklet [*Other Planets*, formerly *Earths in the Universe*] mentioned earlier. What you will find there has been revealed and shown to me to let people know that the Lord's heaven is vast and that it is all from the human race, and also that our Lord is recognized everywhere as the God of heaven and earth.**"

I recommend ALL books by Swedenborg! A good one to read first is his *Heaven and Hell*. In *Apocalypse Explained* #950, he states: **"That which one loves above all things is their god."**

June 2008
Dear *SILA* Readers,
Did you see Swedenborg mentioned on the TV show, *UFO Hunters,* on the History channel?! It originally aired on 26 March 2008, but has re-aired a couple of times. You can watch it online at: http://www.youtube.com/watch?v=3zdS92zlH4g. (Episode #109: Case #58105, *Alien Contact*.)

A portrait of Swedenborg is flashed quickly in the introduction. Later, the show discusses authors that have written about alien contact. I liked that the narrator pronounced Swedenborg's name correctly!

It's funny to hear that Swedenborg took "alien travels" and "journeyed throughout the entire solar system seeing beings on Saturn, Mars, and Venus." Swedenborgians don't think of it that way. It wasn't alien abduction. Several websites are discussing how Swedenborg did alien travel since he was featured on *UFO Hunters*. One thing that must be clear is that Swedenborg's physical body never left his bed or chair. It was his mind that went travelling. He didn't board any spaceship.

This subject makes many Swedenborgians uneasy and excites the UFO enthusiasts. Even if a being from another planet (which I believe there are) visited us, it's not going to make thousands read Swedenborg's Writings. The UFO enthusiasts have already read what Swedenborg wrote about other planets and for most of them, they aren't interested in reading his other books. Maybe I'm wrong and people will read Swedenborg if an alien contacted us...

Swedenborg tells us we are the most materialistic of all the planets in the universes. That's what we should take from all his alien travels. We gotta do better as earthlings! Clean up our own planet, clean up our own minds. We can meet our fellow universalians in the next world to our hearts content.

Ready for this? In Swedenborg's *Spiritual Experiences* #4741–4752, he writes about seeing King Charles XII of Sweden after he died. When Charles was living, everyone thought he was a pious man, but Swedenborg saw him in the spiritual world as a man with an insane love of glory and he had a wife from another planet that also loved glory! They cruelly dominated each other!!

Thinking of you,
Candace

Dear Candace,

I <u>do not</u> believe in a <u>Hell</u>! Let alone Hells, that Swedenborg believed in. I do not believe in many of the Bible verses either.

H.M.
Los Angeles, California
May 1989

Dear H.M.,

Sometimes, reading parts of the Bible, I can see how someone could think that God turns His back on us, gets angry, and sends us to hell. But, this not only does not happen, it cannot, as God is good, love, and mercy itself! And good is incapable of doing evil, and love and mercy are incapable of casting a person away from themselves.

If you look deeper into the Bible, you will see that evil and good are opposites and that everything good comes out of heaven, and everything evil comes out of hell.

So, it would follow that if a person does something evil, it is from hell, and if good, it is from the Lord. But, we all believe we do things from ourselves. So, the person choosing to do evil is responsible for making it their own. And the evil leads one into hell, not the Lord. We all go to either heaven or hell because of what we LOVE. *Heaven and Hell* #547: **"All of [a person's] will and love continues with [them] after death. [S/He] who wills and loves evil in the world wills and loves the same evil in the other life, but [s/he] no longer suffers [themself] to be withdrawn from it... Consequently, it is [the person] who casts [themself] into hell after death, and not the Lord."**

Swedenborg used this ornament in *Secrets of Heaven*

Dear Candace,

I've read Heaven and Hell *by Emanuel Swedenborg, but I don't have a copy with me now and I don't recall if he even mentioned such a thing as THE DEVIL.*

Isn't it true that Swedenborg made a real change in Christian thinking about evil by not having to personify evil forces into one being, or by not having to rely on THE DEVIL or THE SATAN to scare people?

R.H.
Corvallis, Oregon
June 1992

Dear R.H.,

Yes. Swedenborg tells us there is no such one person as The Devil or Satan. There was no king-devil born at creation. These are all-encompassing, descriptive words for evil people. A devil loves self only. A satan loves the world only.

Swedenborg says this because he saw devils and satans in hell, living and breathing. They were people who had lived on earth delighting in adulteries, hatred, and revenge. They appeared monstrous as corpses and mummies, black as soot. But, to each other they appeared as beautiful humans.

However, just as heaven as a whole appears to God as one "person", so does hell appear as one "person". Swedenborg did write about this in his most popular book, *Heaven and Hell* #553: **"The entire hell in one complex reflects a single devil, and might be exhibited in an image of a single devil."**

Dear Candace,

Greetings in the blessed name of our Lord Jesus. I am a born again Christian lady aged 25, married, and a mother of two children aged 4 years and 1 year, living in the country side. When I was visiting my husband's friend I received a SILA *from him. Reading it turned to be a true blessing. I desire to learn more about the New Church and especially Swedenborg. I write to you to request whether you may accept me as one to teach. Yours in Christ.*

G.K.O.
Nairobi, Kenya
November 2001

Dear Candace,

I'm so much impressed with SILA. *I always tell my friends to read* SILA *and they are most interested to read them. And they wish to receive more materials from your office's capacity. And this is because your materials teach us that in God-Man there are infinite things which appear in heaven and in people; because God-Man is not in space as other doctrines do teach people. Thanks.*

K.O.R.
Kisii, Kenya
November 2001

Dear Candace,
If God limits evil in the hells, does He limit evil on earth? Thanks for your response.

D.D.
Sun Valley, California
September 1989

Dear D.D.,
Yes, God limits evil on earth. Good people are led away from committing evil acts through their conscience. Evil people are led away from committing evil acts by fear of punishment. Yet, evil is tolerated because we are all in freedom to choose it or not. But, to say God permits evil does not mean He wills it.

Since you say, "God limits evil in the hells", I can tell you have read some of what Swedenborg reported he saw in hell. I find Swedenborg's book, *Divine Providence* helpful in understanding evil and how the Lord did not create it, but is always trying to lead us away from it.

Dear Candace,
I don't understand, if Swedenborg says people in hell are happy then why have hell?

Anonymous
Los Angeles, California
June 2000

Dear Anonymous,
Because the Lord God is merciful. He allows people to choose either hell or heaven. He does not send people to hell. They *want* to live in hell. Even though those in hell *appear* happy, if they had chosen heaven, they would be a thousand times happier. Swedenborg describes heaven as a state of wisdom and hell as a state of insanity. Which is which? Appearances can be deceiving.

Swedenborg wrote in *Heaven and Hell* that when a person dies, they simply cross from one world to another. All of their intentions and loves remain after death. One leaves nothing behind, except the physical body.

When you die, you are going on a trip to another country. And you take with you your passport—what you love. Your loves tell who you are. Not who you love, but what you love. People in hell are happy. But, their happiness is derived from self-love and self-intelligence which is empty. It's a tortured happiness.

Ex-gang members will tell you that they lived in constant fear. That they had to sleep with a gun under their pillow every night, look over their shoulder constantly, had to check every body movement, every word from their mouth. There was little time to live. But, some people still choose to live the life of a gang member. Some people choose the life of an adulterer. But, then they have to constantly look over their shoulder, check every word from their mouth. There's little time to enjoy the illicit sex. It's fleeting; the consequences linger.

States of heaven and hell happen here on earth. We are making choices every moment of our lives. But, when we die, we pick either heaven or hell for our future home. That's what Swedenborg tells us.

Dear Candace,
How could Swedenborg know for a fact that he was actually seeing into the spiritual world? I find this hard to believe because the devil has the power to deceive us into believing and also seeing what we want to see!!! The Bible clearly points out that it is a sin to associate one's self with "familiar spirits". I've come to the realization that intelligent minds are the easiest ones to be deceived into believing all kinds of abominable things.

B.B.
St. Andrew, Barbados, West Indies
August 1995

Dear Candace,
I have several intellectual, atheist, or pagan friends who believe the things of faith can be proven or disproven with their own logic. We know what Emanuel Swedenborg had to say about such "smart" doubting Thomases.

P.R.
San Francisco, California
August 1995

Dear B.B. & P.R.,

In Swedenborg's day, some people (once they discovered he was the author of some unusual anonymous books) doubted his claims, too, as do some today.

We can get a glimpse into Swedenborg's thinking about his unique claim from a journal he kept. He candidly wrote down his dreams and spiritual experiences with the knowledge they would never be published. (They were, however, decades *after* his death.) He wrote that he didn't know what to make of all his dreams and that he felt unprepared for his active dream-like-state visions. Gradually, he learned to accept that his spiritual eyes had been opened and consented that he was permitted to see into the spiritual world like no one else, before or since. Swedenborg knew for a fact that he was actually seeing into the spiritual world. His books attest to it, almost on every page. The real question is: *How do we know that Swedenborg did see into the spiritual world as he said?*

In written accounts by his peers (friends and foes), Emanuel Swedenborg was ethically impeccable. He had a famous reputation as a clairvoyant (seeing things happening miles away) and yet did not use his gift for fame or gain. Swedenborg did not organize people around him as followers. He lived modestly (although he was rich), paid his rent and bills on time, was kind, had a sense of humour, and was good with children.

Swedenborg did write that some intellectuals, of their own conceit, don't trust in God and His Divine providence. He demonstrated (in his books) that intelligence is not equal to wisdom. He also stated that seeking contact with spirits is not to be done. The belief in astrology, artificially induced near-death experiences, channeling, cryonics, magic, mystical experiences, new age practices, occult, psychics, reincarnation, UFOs, and witchcraft often lead people to believe in a supernatural existence that is horrific, striking terror for the future.

People obsessed with their own intelligence have an unhealthy approach to the spiritual world which is really governed by the Lord God Jesus Christ.

Miraculous happenings (e.g. sightings and healings) easily induce people to think they are miracles, but they are not.

In truth, the spiritual world is nearer than we imagine and every second we are being helped and affected by either good or evil spirits, without our knowledge. The belief that some people are more special for having had a spiritual experience is folly. We are all having ongoing spiritual experiences. I asked some friends of mine for their expertise on this subject. Here are their responses:

Dear Candace,

I have been fairly involved in the NDE [Near Death Experience] "community" for seven years now. It is one thing to receive communication that has not been sought. It is much more dangerous to seek communication.

Anonymous
New Church minister
Bryn Athyn, Pennsylvania
August 1995

Dear Candace,

It is an amazing fact that while Swedenborg is often called a spiritist, that he doesn't at any point encourage contacting spirits and even specifically warns his readers of the dangers that can accompany such attempts.

The context of his warnings seem to relate to people who want to know the future by contacting spirits or to gain other arcane knowledge. At times people have thought that they could get an "edge" on making the right decisions by contacting spirits. Angels and good spirits know that a person is not directed in his decisions by specific contact with the spiritual world. They won't give a person the direction they seek. The spiritual beings that will gladly give direction on specific decisions or try to convey future events do not wish well to us, though perhaps they might give a show of such beneficence in the short-run.

Furthermore, Swedenborg ensures us that such evil spirits cannot know more than we ourselves do, although they may give it a twist that makes it seem like new information. At best they will tell us what we already know, at worst they may seek to mislead us.

I do believe that sometimes the Lord allows contact between loved ones in this world and the next. But, He will choose when it is useful for both parties. My hope would be that people would put their energy into learning from the Lord, praying to Him, and receiving the loving care that He seeks to give us all.

Rev. Eric Carswell
New Church minister
Glenview, Illinois
August 1995

I'm standing next to Swedenborg's statue in Maria Square (park) in Stockholm in 1998. The building behind me is where Swedenborg's house once stood.

SILA October 1998

Dear Candace,
  Thank you for sending me SILA *which has had some very interesting presentation of New Church ideas. I am sure the informality, and yet the uncompromising presentation of new ideas will reach many people who otherwise might not have been interested. Thank you for your imaginative work of the Lord's new truth.*

C.H.
Southern-On-Sea, Essex, England
May 2001

Dear Candace,

Recently someone I loved died and at the funeral I could not stop crying. I realize this was not for the person because they are in the other world, but out of a sense of selfishness that I will no longer be able to see them from day to day. Does Swedenborg say anything about people that mourn at funerals?

S.R.
Pasadena, California
February 2001

Dear S.R.,

I don't believe you are being selfish for grieving the loss of your loved one. Self-love according to Swedenborg is wishing well to no one, but one's self. It's not a bad thing to grieve (unless you are indulging in grief). Every love contains fear and grief: fear of it being destroyed, and grief if it is. In joy, hours can seem as minutes. In grief, minutes can seem as hours. Time is only an "appearance" according to the state of affection. There is no time in the next life, only "states".

Swedenborg would sometimes "accompany" deceased people at their funerals, seeing their dead bodies, yet talking and walking with that risen spirit at the same time! He wrote that before death, most people are concerned about their own burial, about their tombstone or monument, the tributes paid to them, their reputation. But after death, finding that they are still the same, most people become more concerned that their relatives realize they are living.

Secrets of Heaven #4527: **"I have spoken on this subject with some on the very day their bodies were being entombed, who saw through my eyes their own corpse, the bier, and the funeral ceremony; and they said that they reject that body, which had served them for uses in the world in which they had been, and that they are now living in a body which serves them for uses in the world in which they are now.**

They also desired me to tell these things to their relatives who were mourning; but, it was given me to reply, that if I should do so they would scoff, because that which they could not see with their own eyes they would believe to be nothing, and would set down as delusive visions."

Swedenborg used this ornament in *True Christian Religion*

Chapter 3

WHO'S GOD?

Dear Candace,
  Does the Lord know the future or does He just help guide our free will?
  S.B.
  Altadena, California
  December 2005

Dear S.B.,
  Yes, the Lord knows the future. But, that doesn't mean He changes the future or causes bad things to happen. When thinking about the Lord one has to think outside of time and space and that's a challenge. He is omnipresent, omniscient, and omnipotent—present everywhere, all knowing, with unlimited power.
  The Lord doesn't guide our free will; He gives us our free will. And He gives it to all created things—animate and inanimate—in nature. I was amazed to read *that* in the Writings when I went looking for an answer to your question! I didn't know that the earth, plants, and animals have free will (only in natural matters, of course, but still...free will). I learned that because you asked the question. Thank YOU!
  Swedenborg wrote that if animals didn't have free will they could not select food suitable for themselves, nor could they reproduce, or look after their offspring. I think of the many stray cats that show up at our home. The "word" is obviously out that we will feed them, pet them, groom them—love them. They come to us of their own free will. That makes sense. And we've all seen plants spring up through concrete! The will to grow! Swedenborg tells us that without free will, no creation is possible.
  A human's (free will) purpose is to become spiritual. We are all given free will from our beginnings in the womb and will continue to receive it to eternity.

Our "job" on earth is to rid ourselves of evils. We can only do this by using our **"free will in spiritual matters correctly, that is, to focus the mind on thoughts of the conditions of life after death."** (*True Christian Religion* #498)

Keep in mind that it is **"the inward qualities that condemn in the other life, that is, what a person's intention is, or as they say, what [s/he] is of their own free will."** (See *Spiritual Experiences* #1397)

Swedenborg also says in his *True Christian Religion* #482: **"If [a person's] spiritual freedom were taken away from [them], it would be, to use a comparison, like taking the wheels away from a machine, the arms that catch the wind from a mill, or the sails from a ship. In fact, it would be like a [person] parting with [their] spirit when [they] die; for the life of a [person's] spirit consists in [their] free will in spiritual matters. The angels groan at the mere mention of the fact that this free will is denied by many ministers of the church at the present time; they call this denial madness on top of madness."**

Imagine, angels groaning! They probably sigh a lot, too, at what we on earth consider worth living for or debating about... *Silly people. Get your act together and think about eternity...* they, no doubt, are thinking.

Dear Candace,
  Can we make a contract with God that is binding to humans?

Anonymous
San Francisco, California
June 1997

Dear Anonymous,
   No. It doesn't work that way. But, God does have a bond with us and Swedenborg says it is charity (aka love and compassion). When we allow no charity/love in our lives or charity/love is ignored, then the bond with God is broken.

Bonds are internal and external. External bonds are the laws of God and the laws of the land. Internal bonds are our consciences—the plane into which the angels flow, keeping people in bounds, but still in freedom.

Swedenborg says that fear (of the law, loss of honour, gain, or reputation) is the only means by which evil is kept in check, for fear is the common bond of both the upright and the evil. As there can be no "contract with God that is binding", we cannot bind someone else to think as we do.

Love is the answer.

Dear Candace,
What do you think God is going to do to the Oklahoma bombers?
L.L.
El Monte, California
April 1995

Dear L.L.,

Nothing. God doesn't work that way. God is unchangeable. He is Divine Love and Divine Wisdom. He never punishes. It is an appearance that God punishes. Actually, it is the evil (opposite of God) that destroys or punishes itself.

At 9:04 a.m., Wednesday, 26 April 1995, one week after someone set off a 1,200 lb. bomb at the *Alfred P. Murrah Federal Building* in Oklahoma City, the nation observed a moment of silence. A National Day of Mourning was declared on Sunday, 23 April and was officially held at the Oklahoma State Fairground with American President Bill Clinton. This memorial service was televised live. At the time of this writing, the death total is 138. It will rise. Teddy bears are being given to the survivors of the Oklahoma bombing, symbolizing healing. Ribbons—purple and white—worn on lapels, tied around trees and mailboxes, pay homage to the memory of those lost in the tragedy.

This American bombing was felt around the world. Tears are being shed for the victims of this random act of violence. Answers are being sought by the afflicted. President Clinton said that the person or persons responsible for the bombing were evil. In our politically correct environment, this was an astounding statement to make. He is correct. The worst terrorist attack in American history was evil. And punishable. The perpetrators will be punished by the laws of society.

But, God is not going to send any natural disaster upon the evil doers. God permits evil to happen for the sake of free will. Without free will, we would be puppets. This truth appears to be harsh in light of the death of the kids innocently playing at the daycare centre in the *Murrah Building*.

Another truth Emanuel Swedenborg wrote in his Writings—after his peeks into the spiritual world—is that ALL children that die in childhood, grow up in heaven and become angels. Adults that die go to either heaven or hell, but not children. It was wonderful to hear a TV voice-over announcer say: "Next, a closer look at the newest angels in heaven."

The hundreds of rescuers that worked around the clock were selfless. Know that this had also happened in the spiritual world. Hundreds of good rescue spirits assisted those children and adults as they left this world and entered the next. Spiritual rescuers, just as earthly rescuers, had to calm the injured, comfort the shaken, and instruct the displaced as to what to do next. The newcomers to the world of spirits will need caring for. They will be grieving the separation from their loved ones left on earth. They will need to be shown how to live on in their new environment. Some will even doubt they have died.

Looking at the two famous photos of the police officer handing the lifeless body of one-year-old, Baylee Almon, to the firefighter, Chris Fields, I think of a spiritual rescue worker being handed Baylee shortly after the photos were taken.

It has been said Baylee will never play games, or fall in love, or go to college, or invent a cure for a rare disease. Swedenborg tells us this is not true.

Baylee and the other children will grow up in heaven into adulthood and will learn, love, and work. Swedenborg saw little children in the arms of female angels, others in school, more at play.

It is thought that this bombing could have been prevented through government intervention. Maybe it could have. But, we individually could have stopped it, too. At first, this evil act was suspected to have been done by international terrorists, but it was done by domestic terrorists. Evil comes from hell and enters our minds. We are not responsible for what comes in, but we are responsible for what we act upon. Often we suspect evil to be done by internationals (someone else) but, most often it is done domestically (inside ourselves).

It is only an "appearance" that we will not be able to stop the truly evil people roaming the earth with their terrorist desires. There have been numerous studies done by the Federal Bureau of Alcohol, Tobacco, and Firearms on how to stop violators, but suggested methods have not worked.

Evil can be prevented. We can stop the hate from hell by not housing it. God told us how to do this in His Ten Commandments. A spiritual life is acquired solely by a life lived according to them. When a person reads the Bible, with love, angels are brought closer to the reader. When a person stops doing an evil, angels come closer to them. The more we all stop evil from being entertained, the closer the Lord will send His angels around us ALL.

Dear Candace,

Thank you for your answer to the question of the Oklahoma City bombing (April). I am amazed at the clarity of your answer, and how succinctly you bring out the teachings of the New Church as found in the Writings of the Hon. Emanuel Swedenborg—yet without offense. Thank you for continuing this service, often showing us how to speak simply and in a relevant way about powerful true ideas now available for all of mankind.

Rev. Erik. E. Sandstrom
Head of Religion & Sacred Language Division
Academy of the New Church College
Bryn Athyn, Pennsylvania
October 1995

Dear Rev. Sandstrom,
  You're welcome. It's my pleasure.

Dear Candace,
I read the Oklahoma City article in SILA *again and noticed that you said that it is evil (opposite of God) that destroys or punishes itself. You know God created evil as well as good yet you later stated that God permitted evil to happen for the sake of free will. You know this could be termed as you contradicting yourself.*

I like your approach to stop violence, but you have to start at a governmental level and cure the greed of the government.

W.
Jefferson City Missouri
October 1995

Dear W.,
God is pure love and wisdom. There is no evil in Him. Evil cannot come from Him. Evil is the absence of good. And evil destroys itself. Love gives life. A good book to study is *Divine Love and Wisdom* by Emanuel Swedenborg. Stopping violence does not start at the government, but with the individual. Yet, government members can set a good example as *individuals* in society.

Dear Candace,
The real cause of violence is not the media or any external factors, but the desire to dominate, to control. All dictators love those who obey them, who flatter them and laugh at their jokes, but woe, if someone disagrees! So the evil is the desire to exercise influence over the thinking and behavior of others from self-love, self-importance and need for superiority.

This desire for power over others is the deeper cause of most divorces, of all wars and of violence in general. Especially a desire to retaliate, to make others suffer who stand in the way or where we feel that they have hurt us—to take vengeance and justice in our own hands is the danger.

This is a topic that I have much researched in the Writings, and was very impressed by Swedenborg's commentaries.

Rev. Horand K. Gutfeldt, Ph.D.
New Church minister
Berkeley, California
December 1995

Dear Rev. Gutfeldt,
I'm still getting letters about the April issue on violence. Thank you for a well thought out letter; goes right to the point.

Dear Candace,

The awful suffering of so many people in the aftermath of Hurricane Katrina raises that common New Church question when wars and natural disasters occur of: "Whatever is happening in the spiritual world to have caused this?"

In the last year we have seen the Beslan Massacre, the ongoing war in Iraq, the Boxing Day Tsunami, the July 7th London bombings, and now Hurricane Katrina. And that is to list only the major wars and natural disasters.

So what is happening in the spiritual world to inflict all this suffering on the natural world? Come on, spiritual world, we've had enough! Give us a break. If we think like this, are we missing out on the primary cause of natural disasters and wars? We are taught that the cause of wars is the conflict of falsity against truth and of truth against falsity (Apocalypse Revealed #52), *of the falsities of the former Church fighting against the truths of the New Church* (Apocaylpse Revealed #48), *and that these represent the states of the Church in heaven* (Divine Providence #251:3).

Although I am unaware of any passages that speak about natural disasters in general, we are told that such as earthquakes and storm winds relate to falsities, temptations, and the perversion of the Church through the falsification of truth.

From passages like these, it may be tempting to think that the causes of wars and natural disasters have little to do with earthly matters or with us as law-abiding individuals. They may seem beyond earthly influence, taking place in the spiritual world, or merely an attack by the falsities of a vastated Church against the New Church.

However, other passages put a different complexion on the picture. In Swedenborg's Arcana Coelestia *#1651 and #1659:3 we are told that the wars described in Genesis are descriptive of the Lord's temptations, and in Most Ancient times of the temptations of the Church and of those who belonged to the Church. Also we are repeatedly taught that the individual person is a Church in least form. Again, in an indirect way, that it is the regenerating person who makes the New Church. Also that our minds are in the spiritual world.*

So where does this fight of truths and falsities, of Old against New Churches, and of changes in the state of the Church take place? I suggest that while there is a general cause of wars and disasters, we as individual New Church members are also implicated. The combats of falsities against truths, and of Old Church falsities against New Church truths, representing the states of the Church in heaven, are actually descriptive of the combats that take place during the course of regeneration with us as individuals. These are the wars and disasters that are taking place in our minds; our minds being in the spiritual world even while we live on earth. How far is any individual on earth to blame for the natural disasters and wars that cause such misery as the current Hurricane Katrina? I suggest that as long as we are still combating the hells during our regeneration, we must take our share of the blame.

H.R.
Colchester, England
September 2005

Dear H.R.,
I agree with you.

However, with the possibility that some of what you are discussing is going over the heads of some *SILA* readers, let me start off by defining what Swedenborg means by the word "church" which I can tell you know.

A "church" is commonly understood to mean a building or location where people gather to worship God and enter into fellowship with like-minded worshippers. Sometimes that's what Swedenborg means, but more often "church" means the spiritual life in an institution or in an individual. This is a new, difficult concept for some to grasp. When Swedenborg writes about a new church at a specific time in history, he is talking about a new spiritual activity. When he talks about a new church after 1757 he is referring to the new spirituality that has happened since the Last Judgment, which consequently changed EVERYTHING. (So many are waiting for the Second Coming to happen, for the world to change, but are ignorant that it has, and did!)

Yes, H.R., we on earth ARE responsible, individually and as a group, for earthly disasters as well as ARE the people in the spiritual world. We are all connected. Swedenborg describes everyone collectively as a "Grand Human Being". And those of the "church" being like the heart (love) and lungs (wisdom) of the Grand Being. The best way to understand this Swedenborgian concept is to imagine the Lord seeing us all as one Big Person!

Add to your thought that the Lord is seeing this Great Big Person as made up of all people that have lived and died from ALL the planets in the universes!! Swedenborg says there aren't enough people from our earth to make up that Grand Being as there are relatively few of us from earth. There will need to be people from many other worlds!

Keep in mind, this so called Grand Being is not human in shape, but human from the use it performs. It is organic with organs and parts performing and interacting like uses in a human body. For example, those of the heart pump out love, those in the liver purify out falsities.

Here's a secret Swedenborg said he was revealing for the first time: The SOUL of the Grand Being is the Lord. The MIND of the Grand Being is made up of angels, recently deceased spirits, and the spiritual minds of people on all the earths.

The BODY is made up of all people living on all the earths in the universes. The WASTE EXCREMENT that exits the Grand Being are devils—deceased evil people—that rush out and make up hell. (See *Spiritual Experiences* #1742)

The Grand Being had an infancy. Think of humankind in time. The first beings on our earth were primitive, history reports. But, Swedenborg tells us that they weren't primitive, but intuitive and did not die from pain, disease, and murder! Their transition into the spiritual world from the natural world was peaceful. Only after "they fell" away from God's leading did they experience unnatural ways of dying. Evil was brought into this world (and other worlds) because of individuals pulling away from the Soul of the Grand Being—the Lord.

So, Hurricane Katrina was not an "Act of God" or a punishment of Biblical proportion, but a result of evil actions of people on earth AND evil actions of deceased people in the world of spirits. Swedenborg's theology explains that the Grand Being has a life, with stages of growth—that will erupt with pimples, upset stomach, menstrual cramps, and headaches.

I asked one of my Swedenborgian expert friends what age he thought the Grand Being was and Rev. Erik E. Sandstrom approximated it to be about 20-years-old. A person coming of age!

H.R., thanks for your thoughtful, thorough question. Yes, these awful earthly disasters of late are what we bring upon ourselves through evil loves, but they are permitted by a loving God for a purpose—so that good can result. Let's all change and grow up!

Dear Candace,
 Who created God according to Old Testament?

Y.G.
Seattle, Washington
May 1998

Dear Y.G.,
No one created God. God *is*. He is from eternity. The universe was not created out of nothing. Not even *Seinfeld* (TV show) is about nothing. Emanuel Swedenborg talks about this BIG subject in *Divine Love and Wisdom* (published in 1763). In the Old Testament, the Creator (God) of the universe was called *Jehovah*—a Hebrew verb meaning *to be*. When Jesus Christ (Jehovah) came on earth as recorded in the New Testament of the Bible, He commanded that His disciples call Him *Lord*. The Lord is called, **"the God of Israel, the God of Jacob."**

Swedenborg says that belief in an invisible God is belief in no God. Keeping in mind that God is neither in space nor time, from the beginning God was a Man. This can be difficult to comprehend by those who think of things from a sensuous mind. For one may think, if God were a Man, He would then be the same size as the universe.

God is one Man. He is not three Gods as some Christians believe. Swedenborg says that no one is admitted into Heaven who thinks of three Gods.

And being an expert on the Bible or an expert in any religion will not get you in Heaven, either. We are told by Swedenborg that no one can see the face of God, except *from* innocence in our hearts.

Dear Candace,
 Thank you for your publication, your honesty, and the humanness it brings to the content of SILA.

Anonymous
Tucson, Arizona
May 1996

Dear Candace,

Much food for thought in your September SILA. I did not know that the Grand Being or Man is not human in shape. I thought it was and is. I had never heard that the Grand Being was organic—having organs, yes—but not in the sense that it is organic or finite and perhaps that is what you actually meant. Just pondering...

I do not know what you mean when you say that the Grand Man is not "human". I think the Grand Man *is* human. I did a quick search [in the Writings] and came up with the following:

Swedenborg mapped the cosmos onto the glorified *human* body, a kind of alchemical cosmic Christ which he called the Grand Man.

"**That the universal heaven resembles one [person]**," he says, "**who is therefore called the GRAND MAN.**"

S.
Kitchener, Ontario, Canada
November 2005

Dear S.,

I so understand your thinking, for when I was a kid, being brought up as a Swedenborgian, I thought there was a Grand Man walking around in the sight of the Lord, too! I often wondered if this big guy had both male and female sex organs. I could never figure that one out. Now, having studied the Writings of Swedenborg for years, I've figured out what Swedenborg was actually teaching about the Universal Human (correctly translated from Latin as that) — it is the *appearance* of a human.

But, just to be sure, I checked my answer in the September *SILA* with two good friends of mine. Here are their responses:

Dear Candace,

The Lord is the Grand Man. Those who love Him can't fully comprehend what He is like. So the Grand Man is correspondingly the picture we are to have of Him. What the Writings call "the Grand Man" is a formation of uses. I resist the urge to "humanize" the Grand Man.

Picturing the Grand Man walking around is something that does not rest well with my mind. The Grand Man is a representation of Divine Uses. The angelic heaven is structured to manifest the ends and purposes of the Lord. Therefore heaven is the very likeness of the Lord. We are a form or likeness of the Lord. So when we leave this world the Lord incorporates us into His Heavenly Form according to our loves and uses.

Rev. George McCurdy
Bryn Athyn, Pennsylvania

Dear Candace,

The Grand Man concept is difficult because we don't have spiritual eyes (or at least the ones we have don't work all that well). Your answer is right on track, for reasons outlined in the attached document*. I hope this is what you are looking for.

Incidentally, I believe that the idea of the human form originating in the Lord, and then descending into Creation, is the seed of the answer to the Intelligent Design question. The "intelligence" in Creation is the human form, which comes from the order imposed on the universe; and the Lord is order itself. (Divine Love and Wisdom #29; True Christian Religion #52-55, #71:2, #73:2).

Rev. Dr. Reuben P. Bell
Fryeburg, Maine

Dear Candace,

Hello. Nice to hear from you. You are on the right track here, by sticking to a concept that is beyond the constraints of time and space, as heaven certainly is. The Lord in fact does see heaven as a "big person," but not in the way that our natural minds try to conceive it. He sees a collection of angels, in a collection of societies—parts of parts—all related in an interactive way that knows no limits, but that in the natural world become confined within a human body. Here is how I would explain it for SILA:

*The concept of the Grand Man of Heaven, or "Universal Human" is a very difficult idea to wrap our minds around because we are stuck in a universe of three dimensions and our minds are stuck in natural thoughts. But, given the power of the rational faculty, we can form an impression of it by carefully reading Swedenborg's experience of spiritual reality. The idea of creation in human form is not new — the Jewish Kabbalah teaches a creational scheme of ten steps, or "emanations," of the Divine descending into Creation. The collective mental image of these interwoven steps is the Adam Kadmon, or "primordial human," representing as it does the human nature of Jehovah Himself. The Writings [of Swedenborg] for the New Church expand on this elemental idea, explaining the purpose and function of Creation in human form.

Swedenborg came upon the idea slowly, as he was admitted into the spiritual world and began to see and experience the marvelous things there. What he gradually began to comprehend was that Creation proceeds from God into the heavens, through the world of spirits, and finally, in completion, comes to rest in the natural world. All components of these levels interact as do the individual parts of a human body.

True Christian Religion #119 *says that:* **"The whole heaven of the angels together with the church on earth forms in the Lord's sight a single person. The heaven of the angels makes up [the] internal, the church [the] external; or in more detail, the highest heaven makes up [the] head, the second and lowest heavens [the] chest and the middle region of [the] body, and the church on earth [the] loins, legs and feet. The Lord Himself is the soul and life of this whole person."**

And in, Invitation to the New Church #48 *we find that:* **"Whatever proceeds from God partakes of the human form, because God is Himself Man."**

The crucial concept is "form." The word is used here in its philosophical sense, meaning the relationships among parts in a whole, rather than the shape of a thing. Once we are beyond the three-dimensional limitations of shape, then the Grand Man becomes heaven in human form, or an infinite collection of distinct communities, each unique in its qualities, but all interactive in the same way that the parts of a human body interact. This human form is the Lord at work in Creation, imparting His form into the order of all things. Natural things owe their existence to the spiritual things to which they correspond, and the parts of a human body are no different. The marvelous mechanisms of anatomy and physiology, from the smallest of parts to whole systems in concert, all correspond to analogous regions of this Universal Human, that itself owes existence and form to the humanness of the Lord.

So the Grand Man, or Universal Human, is a rational concept that is "seen" by the mind's eye. The human form is the sum of all the workings of a body, be they the natural parts in yours, or the infinite mechanism of the heavens and all its parts, from which your body takes its existence. The Lord, who is Humanness itself, sees all of Creation as His own form going forth into the things of the spiritual and natural worlds, and hopes that His love, which is the soul of all, may descend into this Creation and then return to His abode above the heavens, in a loop of perfect veneration. This is the purpose of Creation and the origin of its human form.

Swedenborg used this ornament in *Secrets of Heaven*

Dear Candace,

I do know that Jesus himself stated that he didn't come to bring a new religion. Thus I'm at a loss for why Jesus is in fact worshipped. Also why the need to worship God in the name of Jesus or any other man and not worship God in God's name?

I'm also curious to know whether the Jews that E. Swedenborg spoke to about Moses was in heaven or hell? [April 2003] The other thing that totally loses me is why would dead Jews in the spirit world, heaven or hell, want a man to take the place of God? If E. Swedenborg elaborated on this any more please tell me.

W.A.
Charleston, Missouri
February 2005

Dear W.A.,

Not sure where you read that Jesus Christ said He "didn't come to bring a new religion." That's what these quotes are universally understood to mean:

"If anyone hears My words, yet does not believe, I do not judge him; for I did not come to judge the world but to save the world." John 12: 47. **"Do not think that I have come to bring peace on earth; I have not come to bring peace, but a sword."** Matthew 10:34. **"Those who are well have no need of a physician, but those who are sick. I did not come to call the righteous, but sinners to repentance."** Matthew 9: 12, 13. **"Whoever would be great among you must be your minister; and anyone who would be first among you must be the servant of all, even as the Son of Man did not come to be ministered to, but to minister."** Mark 10:43-45; Matthew 20:26-28. **"The Son of Man did not come to destroy people's souls, but to save them."** Luke 9:56. **"Do not think that I came to destroy the Law and the Prophets; I did not come to destroy, but to fulfill. Truly I say to you, Even until heaven and earth pass away, one jot or one little tittle [horn on a letter] will not pass away in the Law till all things are done."** Matthew 5:17, 18.

Jesus said to His twelve disciples: **"If anyone will come after Me let him deny himself, take up his cross, and follow Me."** Matthew 16:24; Mark 8:34; Luke 9:23. In these passages, Swedenborg wrote that **"take up his cross"** means temptations, and to **"follow Me"** means to acknowledge the Lord's Divinity and to do His commandments.

I believe you are referring to this paragraph from *SILA,* April 2003: "When Swedenborg 'spoke' with some deceased Jews from Jesus' time, they told him that they had wanted their leader, Moses, to be raised up above God the Messiah Himself! Yes, Swedenborg said there are Jews in the next world. Even some Jews in heaven."

History records that Jews were waiting for the Messiah to come as predicted in their books—the Old Testament—just as Christians are awaiting for His Second Coming as predicted in their books—the New Testament. Swedenborgians believe that the Second Coming has happened in the form of a new written testament—the Writings of Swedenborg.

Jesus is worshipped because He said He was God and demonstrated that He is the creator of the universe by performing healing miracles and rising up with His whole body after He had died. No other claimed Messiahs did that! Jesus Christ, our God, is a Man—with a capital "M" because He is holy—the original Man. We are all created in His image. God has had many names throughout history. It doesn't matter who you call God in your prayers. Only thing that matters is that you believe in Him, talk with Him, and do His Ten Commandments.

I tell our three Godchildren that God has many names—Jesus Christ, Lord, Father, Son, Holy Spirit, Messiah, Jehovah, Allah, etc.— just as I have many names —Daughter, Sister, Wife, Candace Louise, Honey Bunny, Aunt Candace, Aunt Bunny, Mrs. Bunny. Each name refers to the same person, but each represents a different relationship to different people.

Swedenborg spoke with Jews that were angels and some that were devils, and some spirits that had not entered heaven or hell, yet, but were still in the world of spirits—a "place" in between heaven and hell.

W.A., you wondered why some Jews in the next world would want Moses to take the place of God as Swedenborg said he witnessed. The answer is because they believed Moses was as God—big and powerful. Some Jews, awaiting the Messiah, believed he was Moses or wanted to believe he was Moses. (This elevating a-man-to-be-a-god idea is not unique to the Jews.)

Swedenborg did write in *Spiritual Experiences* that he witnessed some deceased Jews in hell thinking that **"by dreadful rebellious disturbances"** in the next world, they could raise Moses up above God the Messiah, and so gain control of Heaven. Swedenborg wrote that the thought was so wicked to him, he'd rather not think about it. (See *Spiritual Experiences* #75)

Swedenborg wrote that he did meet and talk in heaven with the historical Moses, who appeared to be about 50-years-old. (We grow younger in heaven.) Swedenborg noted that he was aware some people acted as though they were Moses. He saw it happen, very convincingly. But, angels reassured Swedenborg that he had met with the real Moses. (Obviously, those that want Moses to be their God won't be allowed to meet with the real Moses, so actors fill that role. Be careful who you idolize for we can "meet" our idols, too!)

Swedenborg used this onrmanment in *Conjugial Love*

Dear Candace,
  What does Swedenborg teach concerning the deity of Christ?

J.M.
Flagstaff, Arizona
November 1992

Dear J.M.,
  Any dictionary will explain deity as the state of being a god; divine.
  Throughout all Swedenborg's books, he states that Christ IS God, but never more clearly than in the last book he wrote, *True Christian Religion,* in 1771—one year before he died. Swedenborg makes it clear that there is a Divine Trinity —Father, Son, and Holy Spirit. These are, however, three essentials of ONE God (as a soul, a body, and its operation make a person), not three Gods.
  Swedenborg got all his answers from the Word. In it we read: **"For unto us a Child is born, unto us a Son is given: and the government shall be upon His shoulder: and His name shall be called Wonderful, Counselor, the mighty God, the everlasting Father, the Prince of Peace."** Isaiah 9:6. **"There is one God, and there is none other but He."** Mark 12:32. **"In Jesus Christ dwelleth all the fullness of the Godhead bodily."** Colossians 2:9.

Drawing by Ed Redmond

SILA May 1990

Dear Candace,
You always speak of "God" in your SILA. *In* Arcana Coelestia #14 *it is said that He should be called Lord, without other names. Perhaps you have some reason for saying God.*

P.O.
Bryn Athyn, Pennsylvania
November 1992

Dear P.O.,
Swedenborg wrote in *Secrets of Heaven* (*Arcana Coelestia*) #14: **"In all that follows the name THE LORD is used exclusively to mean the Saviour of the world, Jesus Christ, and He is called the Lord without the addition of the rest of His names. Throughout heaven He is acknowledged and worshipped as Lord, since He has all power in heaven and on earth. This He also commanded when He said, 'You call me Lord and you are right, for so I am.' John 13:13. Furthermore after the Resurrection the disciples called Him Lord."**
Yes, I often do (not always) call the Lord, "God". I do that because many *SILA* readers do not know who God is. Some are still searching for Him. But, they can understand a God that gives and guides us all; they just don't know Him by name. I think the operative words in the above passage are **"throughout heaven"** and **"He is acknowledged"**. On EARTH, the discovery of who God IS may take one a lifetime.

Dear Candace,
Your explanations of the various teachings in the Writings of Swedenborg are very interesting and thoughtful. Do you believe that the Second Coming of Jesus Christ has been completed in all aspects?

C.J.
Corona Del Mar, California
March 2007

Dear C.J.,
Yes. But, keep in mind that only some people will personally experience the First Coming in their hearts and minds while on earth. After death, the ignorant will be educated about both His Comings. But, everyone is a beneficiary of both events as they changed the spiritual and natural worlds.
I think you may be asking—*Has the new heaven or new earth been made?* Swedenborg wrote that **"the new heaven from which the New Jerusalem will descend is now almost completed."** (From his letter to Dr. Beyer, 30 April 1771) From that new heaven, we on earth are connected with the angels, more so, than before the Second Coming. Swedenborg said that those in the Universities of Christianity (outside heaven) were (then) receiving new instruction! The new earth will grow by gentle degrees. Remember, the Christian faith did not take its rise immediately, but increased gradually...

Dear Candace,

I arrived from visiting my grandmother's today upcountry. I found the TV showing the burial of the Pope LIVE through CNN. I heard them referring to Jesus as an independent person to God, the Father. And there was a time Mary, the God mother seemed to be referred for guidance and blessings. I have read a few books of Swedenborg's—True Christian Religion, *and* My Religion *by [Swedenborgian] Helen Keller—and in them, Jesus is Lord God. Or is He not? And if so, how do you explain that?*

M.N.
Nairobi, Kenya
May 2005

Dear M.N.,

CNN was reporting factually two things: 1) Pope John Paul II (born Karol Józef Wojtyla, 1920) died, 2 April 2005; and 2) the Catholic religion—which he was head of—believes that Mary, the mother of Jesus Christ, is Divine and therefore worshipped.

I, too, often hear the news report about two gods: the Father and the Son. I find it odd sounding at least and annoying at most.

Catholics are of the belief that if Jesus Christ ("son of God") was conceived immaculately—meaning to a virgin—and He was without sins, then how could He come from a mother with sins, so they claim she is without sins, born immaculate herself. Catholicism doesn't discuss how Mary became immaculate, if her mother had sins and so on. Catholics pray to Mary because she is perceived by them as more approachable, like a mother. Her son, to them, is a mystery. In Pope John Paul's *Last Will and Testament* (1979) he wrote: "I don't know when death will come but, like everything else, I entrust even that moment into the hands of the Mother of my Master."

Christianity has changed since Jesus Christ walked on earth because people have developed their own spin on "The Man". Swedenborg wrote quite a bit about Catholicism. He wrote that Catholic priests wrongly divided God into three persons: Father, Son, and Holy Spirit. Swedenborg says that God is only One Person with three aspects to Him as anyone has three aspects to them: soul, mind, body.

Emanuel Swedenborg wrote that he met Mary, the mother of Jesus, in heaven. She was horrified to learn that people prayed to her and she said that only prayers are answered that are sent to the Lord. Catholics aren't the only ones that think of God as more than one person. Most Protestants think of God and "His Son" as two separate deities. I read this in the *Los Angeles Times* article, "Bush Recalls a Spiritual Moment" by James Gerstenzang, 9 April 2005:

> As he did in his discussion of the pope's legacy, President [George W.] Bush later sought to make certain that he had been understood. "There is no doubt in my mind there is a living God," he said. "And no doubt in my mind that the Lord Christ was sent by the Almighty. No doubt in my mind about that."

Swedenborg says that Mary did have sins and that is *why* He was born of her, so that His Soul could be clothed with a human body that had hereditary evils within it. When the hells attacked the Lord through temptations, He could then overcome them by not giving in and then He was beating the hells at their own game.

I heard a lecture (27 March 2004) on this topic given by a New Church Bishop, Alfred Acton, II at "Eldergarten" held at *Asilomar Conference Grounds* in Monterey, CA. He explained it so simply. Here's my summary of his hour talk:—

Before Jesus came on earth, He was a God of pure energy—love and wisdom. You can't see energy. But, scientifically, energy can be changed into matter and then be visible. And matter can be changed into energy.

This is what happened: God bowed the heavens and came down into Mary. The angelic society, named Gabriel—not one angel—was the instrument that carried Jesus into Mary's womb. The heavens actually arced as the energy of God passed from heaven down to earth. (It is a fact that some turkeys and frogs have had virgin births! The process is called parthenogenesis.)

When Jesus was physically attacked, before He died, it was the devils of hell really attacking Him through the individuals on earth.

The process of dying, for Jesus, was similar to the process of birth for humans in that He was being birthed into heaven! And birth is pain and suffering, and bloody. It was the birth of Jesus as a Divine Human into heaven. When Jesus did rise with His whole body, His reentry into heaven created an earthquake on earth and the sun darkened, for His energy passed through matter again, but this time His energy had become matter and now He was, and is, a visible Divine Human-God.

Jesus Christ rose up into heaven with His whole body. But, when we die, we don't go up with our bodies, only in spirit. Jesus is no longer limited by the finite. He passed through it and entered heaven. God came down to earth and returned to heaven. The mystery of Jesus is solved because His true nature is now revealed in Swedenborg's Writings for the New Church.

Bishop Acton said that "the New Church has changed the meaning of the word *up* as much as Christopher Columbus changed the world's thinking that the world was flat."!

Dear Candace,
    Your short and careful answers in SILA *make it useful. I am glad you see this. You have a unique gift.*

J.A.
Richfield, Ohio
May 1996

Dear Candace,

So many Senators and politicians have declared openly that they don't believe in evolution. Now Lucy is touring the world. What does Swedenborg say about evolution?

S.H.R.
Altadena, California
August 2007

Dear S.H.R.,

He doesn't use the word evolution, but Swedenborg had much to say about "in the beginning". First, he tells us that Adam was not the first human.

True Christian Religion #466: **"I proved at length in the work called [SECRETS OF HEAVEN], which I published in London, that Adam and his wife mean the most ancient church on this earth. I also proved there that the Garden of Eden means the wisdom of the people in that church, the tree of life means the Lord being in [people] and [people] being in the Lord, and the tree of the knowledge of good and evil means [people] not being in the Lord, but immersed in [their] own self, as is everyone who believes that [s/he] does everything, even good, of [themself]. Eating from this tree means making evil one's own."**

This teaching (among others) makes Swedenborgians differ with other Christians. They say evolution did not happen. We say, it did. Creation took, and takes, a long time.

Swedenborg breaks down time into churches—five of them. A church meaning a group of people's true understanding of God. He calls the first group, **"The Most Ancient Church"**. Every member of that **"Most Ancient Church"**, without exception, is called Adam—male and female—in stories in the Word.

Swedenborg wrote that there was a genetic change from beast to human when celestial seeds were implanted in beasts from a celestial origin. Similar to God's virgin birth—He implanted Himself as a seed into Mary—to create the first humans He implanted human seeds into female apes! And they brought forth human offspring, female and male. Not surprising then, that scientists think of Lucy as the mother of humankind! Lucy is classified as an Australopithecus afarensis, who lived in Africa between 3–4 million years ago, and is the earliest known hominid. For Swedenborgians, it's not physical evolution that we accept and study, but spiritual devolution.

In 1974, "Lucy in the Sky with Diamonds" by the Beatles was playing in an Ethiopian archaeological camp when the partial skeleton of a 3½ foot-tall female adult was found. Thus she was named Lucy! Most scientists believe Australopithecus afarensis walked upright. Many, however, are still pondering whether they swung in trees. If they didn't, then Australopithecus afarensis may be the threshold of ape to human. Ethiopia is sending their Lucy on a 6-year-tour of the United States next year. First stop will be at the *Houston Museum of Natural Science* from 31 August–20 April, 2008.

What would Swedenborg make of Lucy? He may call her a Pre-Adamite. He writes that Pre-Adamites were beasts before human beings. Swedenborg teaches that creation happens because of discrete degrees (spiritual from God) and continuous degrees (natural from the sun). The soul is always from the father. The body is always from the mother. The miracle of sperm being implanted (celestially) in Australopithecus afarensis allowing for the creation of human beings may bother some scientists, but intrigue the spiritually minded ones.

Swedenborg teaches that humans as to their bodies are animals, and as to their minds are spirits. To be fully human, one has to overcome the body. God did not create the world and its inhabitants over a week and then leave us alone with our own plans, but created the universes with built-in perpetual re-creation. All in His likeness. God is a Man named Jesus with a face, arms, legs, etc. He wasn't an earthling in the beginning, but energy of love and wisdom—we can't even fathom—for Divinity is not in space. He came to earth through a virgin birth and upon His "death" became a Divine Human.

Jesus created everything in His likeness—mineral, vegetable, animal. All things in nature bear relation to the human form. Everything strives to become human because God is Human! The final end of creation is angels and angels are just evolved male and female human beings that lived in the natural world.

Have you seen on the news the tree that has developed an expansion of a seemingly human butt growing out of it? Or seen the squash that looks like Jay Leno? Or the rings of a tree that have the face of Mary or Elvis etched on it? These aren't freaks of nature, but evidence of Divine order. All creation—the human form being the highest—is from God and in His likeness.

There is no such thing as an accident. God created spiritual and physical laws for the universes which allow forms to receive influx from Him, first on the spiritual level, all the way down devolution to the natural level.

Have you seen the largest seed in the plant kingdom? It's the shape of the human female buttocks! The nut of the Coco de Mer Palm Tree weighs 15-30 kg. The Coco de Mer Palm actually has separate male and female trees.

The male Coco de Mer Palm Tree has flowers shaped like human penises! Coco de Mer is French for sea coconut. When first discovered floating on the sea and washed up on beaches, the nut was thought to have grown in the sea and not on a tree.

Elevating our minds back to the question... I am at once shocked and saddened when some of our elected officials declare they do not believe in evolution. How can that be? What ignorance. But, as Swedenborg teaches, thought has to evolve. And the finest minds in the world did not know the truths of evolution, spiritually speaking, until Swedenborg wrote about it.

A good book to start with for this subject is *Angelic Wisdom about Divine Love and about Divine Wisdom* by Swedenborg.

Dear Candace,

I do not know where to start from. Perhaps let me start by registering my outmost ceaseless thanks for sending me those two titles: The Four Doctrines *[by Swedenborg] and* The Natural Depth in Man *[by Wilson Van Dusen]. I will confess without hesitation that no book as yet has touched me so involvingly deeply as these two. I am even asking myself why it took so long in my life to "meet" Swedenborg.*

This man was amazing. Not by the larger picture of his life history, but by the depth and strength of his incisive mind that I experienced while reading his book, The Four Doctrines. *And yet this is just one of the more than 30 books he wrote. What will happen to me when I read more books by him?*

In fact, for the first time, even though I have been a follower of Jesus Christ for a long time, I came close to understanding His nature, personality, what the Bible is all about, about sin, and what sin can do to our relationship with God. In fact, when I read in your February edition that before purification from evils, prayers addressed to God are not heard, I understood perfectly.

Tell you what, I have developed an unsatiable interest in his works. I just have to let other people know about it so that I can enjoy the beauty of sharing these exciting and penetrating analysis of the Word. By the way, it is my considered opinon that Swedenborg's Writings are a must even for secular life! My children are fortunate because they will enjoy these knowledges early in their lives.

And Candace, rest assured that I really love your passion and show of depth in understanding of his Writings. Indeed, I have come to admire and respect the way you dissect readers' questions and systematically build up the answers in a way that leaves one not only satisfied, but also more informed.

You make me happy.

J.O.N.
Nairobi, Kenya
April 2002

THERE IS AN ANSWER

Dear Candace,
Did the Lord change after He was glorified? Did He have a different understanding experiencing the human condition? You would think that the hells attacking Him were a new experience for Him. Did He experience something He never experienced before? Does the Lord keep learning forever?

S.B.B.
Pasadena, California
October 2006

Dear S.B.B.,

Intelligent questions! However, ones that can't be answered fully. Swedenborg said that the things that happened to Jesus Christ while He was on earth (His human body from Mary turned into Divine matter), **"do not fall within the mental grasp of any [person], or indeed of any angel."** (*Secrets of Heaven* #4237)

Swedenborg explains that all human beings have a soul from their father (carried in the sperm) and a body from their mother (created in the womb). And so Jesus Christ's Soul was from Himself, Jehovah, and it entered Mary's womb and attached to one of her eggs. So the Lord's Soul was unlike the soul of any other human being, for His Inmost Self was Himself. As Jesus grew up, He gradually made all His body Divine, to be equal to His Soul. Some did, and do, find it hard to believe that God was anything but perfect, and therefore separated God into two beings—Father and Son. Yet, anyone who thinks of God from "person" only, Swedenborg said, and not from "essence" is thinking materially.

So, Jesus was born like any other baby and had to learn everything—how to suckle, how to crawl, how to walk, how to talk. He just did it faster than any other baby. By the time He was twelve, He knew spiritual things the local rabbis didn't. He was tempted to steal, murder, break all the Ten Commandments, but He didn't. This wasn't the first time God was attacked by the hells. That happened when the first people on earth, in the Most Ancient Times, broke away from God and thought they could do it alone without Him. But, did He *feel* it for the first time when He got to earth, since He actually became flesh and bones, and bled? Yes. And no.

Just as the birth of Jesus Christ is the greatest story ever told, it's also the greatest paradox ever! God, outside of time is eternal and God outside of place is infinite. So, while He can never be in one place only and can never change, He does change in the way He "accommodates" Himself to all humankind. It's only an "appearance" that God was walking and talking with His disciples. He was doing that, but He was also "helping" humans living in the Americas, Asia, and the whole universe at once, at that time in history!

Yes, Jesus experienced things that Jehovah had not experienced before. This is how He has became closer to us. But, God is not learning and growing in love and wisdom. He was already eternal and infinite. What He did do was accommodate His essence so that we could see, hear, and feel Him among us. How privileged were those few that lived in His time and recognized who He was. We all can know Him today through His Word and we can see Him, if we go to heaven.

Dear Candace,

What does the Lord want? Does He understand that the human race is trying to do what He wants? We overcomplicate things. We create a hierarchy. The Lord wants a simple religion. I acknowledge that this is all a contradiction. Free will indicates there is such a thing as free will, in the long term, but the Lord has stacked the deck in His favor. I don't think that is a BAD thing. It is His omnipotence at work. What do you think?

Anonymous
Los Angeles, California
November 2006

Dear Anonymous,

Humans are so imperfect that it is hard for us to grasp a perfect being—God. We put our humanness—limitations—on Him. Because God created the universe and everything in it, He wants for nothing. He wills. He wills good to all. He wills good for the sake of salvation, so that all can enter heaven and be with Him. He does not will evil to anyone because He can only do good. Of course the Lord understands us! God is Human, but with a capital "H".

While the Lord created all creation, He isn't sitting up in heaven judging everyone and keeping score as to who is doing what for Him. Opposite of what you're thinking, the Lord has stacked the deck in our favour, so to speak. He has given us spiritual freedom. Swedenborg writes in great detail about the equilibrium between heaven and hell and consequently the spheres emanating from both. This equilibrium is the source of a person's free will. He says that: **"In and through this equilibrium a person thinks and wills, so that [s/he] speaks and acts as if of [themself]."** (*Conjugial Love* #437)

When one turns to the Lord, their reason and freedom are guided by Him; but if one turns their back on the Lord, their reason and freedom are guided by hell.

Whatever a person does from love appears to that person as freedom. But, if what that person is doing breaks any of the Ten Commandments, then, they are not free. When a person is growing into a spiritual being, they learn to compel themselves to resist what is evil and false and to do what is good. That is heavenly love. (Don't quibble about what it means to be good; we all have knowledge of what is basically right and wrong.)

Here's the "stacking the deck in our favour" part—without the appearance that we are doing good ourselves, no one could be saved. It assures our participation in the act of becoming spiritual. For compulsion in things of a holy nature is dangerous unless it is received in freedom.

Note, we are talking about spiritual freedom, not natural freedom. Not everyone, unfortunately, has spiritual freedom as odd as that may sound. Those in extreme states of fear, misfortune, mental disorder, bodily disease, ignorance, and what Swedenborg called **"blindness of the understanding"** cannot make free and rational decisions that would affect their eternity. Swedenborg wrote: **"Since nothing can be appropriated to anyone except what is done from freedom of the will according to reason, it follows that no one is reformed in states that are not of liberty and rationality."** (For the former quote see *Divine Providence* #144; the latter see *Divine Providence* #138)

There is a difference between true wisdom given by the Lord and imaginary wisdom acquired by one's own effort.

Many believe that humans are basically good people. But, Swedenborg teaches us, there is nothing but evil in the human character. Goodness and mercy belong to the Lord only. Yikes! Swedenborg goes on to tell us that the human race is restrained by the Lord from falling completely into evil, although we don't know it. (WE DO NOW.) If the Lord let loose His spiritual restraints, we all would become as wild animals. Most of us have experienced a "taste of evil" that could lead us into hell at some point in our lives—abuses of power, alcohol, narcotics, gambling, sex.

Yes, the Lord created us. He created us as vessels to receive His love and wisdom, freely. He wants us to receive His gift of life and wills us to receive it, but on our "own" terms.

Dear Candace,

I have a question you may find worth discussing in SILA. *We in the New Church know that people are not saved by faith alone, but we are all a mixture of both good and evil impulses. What would you say is the minimum requirement for salvation?*

P.H.
Los Osos, California
November 2007

Dear P.H.,

The minimum requirement for getting into heaven is a belief in God, by any name—He's the same for everyone—and a willingness to follow your God. The main thing is to believe in someone bigger than one's self and outside self.

Many say they want to believe in God, but don't know who He is. Others say they're not sure if God exists. We cannot know what these individuals really believe deep in their minds away from peer or religious pressure, but most privately probably believe in God, they just don't know what to believe. They will be shown who God is when they die. So, Swedenborg says, even those people could go to heaven, if they want to be led by God.

We are all predestined to heaven, but are permitted to choose hell, if we want. That's a mind-bender! The more one loves the Lord and loves to live by His Ten Commandments, the "higher up" or "closer to Him" one will live in their heaven —there are three levels in heaven: celestial, spiritual, natural.

Martin Luther (1483–1546) taught that salvation is by grace through faith. He called his protesting (away from the Catholic faith) movement the Evangelical Church. Protestants today still postulate that the only requirement for salvation is accepting Jesus Christ as your personal Lord and Saviour; all others go to hell. Swedenborg said that was bunk. First know what the Lord said about it.

"Then Jesus went through the towns and villages, teaching as He made His way to Jerusalem. Someone asked Him, 'Lord, are only a few people going to be saved?'

He said to them, 'Make every effort to enter through the narrow door, because many, I tell you, will try to enter and will not be able to. Once the owner of the house gets up and closes the door, you will stand outside knocking and pleading, Sir, open the door for us.'

But He will answer, 'I don't know you or where you come from.' Then you will say, 'We ate and drank with you, and you taught in our streets.' But He will reply, 'I don't know you or where you come from. Away from me, all you evildoers!'

There will be weeping there, and gnashing of teeth, when you see Abraham, Isaac and Jacob and all the prophets in the kingdom of God, but you yourselves thrown out. People will come from east and west and north and south, and will take their places at the feast in the kingdom of God. Indeed there are those who are last who will be first, and first who will be last." Luke 13:22-30

Swedenborg explained that "Abraham, Isaac, and Jacob" means all people that dwell in love. Entrance into heaven was explained by Jesus in this dramatic fashion to wake people up. Instant salvation and deathbed conversion seem easy. Too easy. They don't work. One has to live a life of charity in order to enter heaven.

Who goes to heaven?
- All children that die go to heaven because they are innocent.
- All people born without all mental faculties—though they may live to adulthood—go to heaven because they are still children.
- All people who lived a life according to the doctrines of their religion—any religion—go to heaven because while they are ignorant, they are obedient.

Swedenborg says the act of repentance is definitely required for a person's salvation. A mere verbal confession that one is a sinner is not repentance, it's just lip service. What's your heart feeling? Okay in me-hood? What about doing for others? The Roman Catholic Church is trying to revive their traditional practice of confession to little success. From the 8 October 2007, *TIME* magazine article, "A Comeback for Confession" by Tim Padgett:

> Confession—telling your sins to a priest and receiving absolution—is one of her faith's seven sacraments...it now seems as anachronistic as prayer veils and meatless Fridays.

I find that interesting. Swedenborg tells us there is a **"church specific"** and a **"church universal"**. The stronger the specific, the stronger the universal. That more and more people in the **"church universal"** are not buying into "anonymous" confession to a priest in a box is encouraging. Turning from religiosity to spirituality is a good thing.

Dorothy Lee (above, right) and her art students portray Swedenborg in chalk at *The 10th Angel Festival*, 2003

Dear Candace,

If a creator God is centered in our grateful thinking, could we then abuse ourselves with addictive behaviors like work, sports, entertainment?

SILA, good stuff.

J.M.
La Jolla, California
October 1992

Dear J.M.,

No. Every person has two faculties—rationality and liberty. It is by these "vessels" that God conjoins Himself to a person and by which a person reciprocally is conjoined to Him. Animals do not have these faculties. A person needs both the faculties of rationality and liberty to function as a human being.

When these faculties are abused, that is the origin of evil. So, when we abuse our rationality or liberty, God is no longer centered in our thinking. If a person works excessively or participates in a sport excessively to the point it affects other aspects of their life, negatively, then it is an abuse. A person can abuse good things.

Rationality is the faculty to understand something. Liberty is the faculty to will something. Willing is not possible without understanding. Understanding is not possible without willing. If you take away willing from understanding, you understand nothing. An example is a person who does not "wish" (will) to understand something and says in retort that they cannot do it.

Drawing by Allan Meyer

Chapter 4

ANGELS

Dear Candace,
  Do you believe in angels?

V.D.
Los Angeles, California
January 1995

Dear V.D.,
  Yes! But, if you are asking me: *Do you believe in androgynous beings that have wings?* — no.
  Dictionaries define an angel as a messenger or attendant of God. That implies to me that God sits on a throne and has creatures attending His every whim. Nothing could be further from the truth.
  The Bible defines an angel as a fellow servant. That implies to me that angels are like you and me, and serve others. This makes sense, especially in light of current angelic anecdotal evidence.
  A fad is a craze or a passing fashion. A trend is a prevailing or probable tendency. Angels are a fad right now; but, I believe that they are a trend, and the belief in angels will eventually become the norm.
  In the 70s, the study of the near-death experience influenced people to talk more openly about their other worldly occurrences. The importance of NDEs has escalated for the past two decades into the current angel craze.
  The angel trend in America started in 1990 when Sophy Burnham published her book, *A Book of Angels*. It not only was a bestseller, but inspired others to write their angel stories. Sophy Burnham subsequently wrote five more angel books.
  Interest in angels is a reaction against traditional religion, which knows little to nothing about real angels. People seeking answers are buying angel books.

On 29 April 1993—the first anniversary of the civil unrest in Los Angeles —Jill D'Agnenica of LA started a personal angel project which she completed on 13 November 1994. Along with ten assistants and ninety volunteers, she placed ten bright-pink angel figurines per one square mile around Los Angeles to serve as unifying symbols for the city. The angels did not stay put long before they were stolen. Jill prefers to say her angels were adopted!

Millions of people watched the 1994 PBS-TV Special, *In Search of Angels* narrated by Debra Winger; millions more watched the 1994 NBC-TV Special, *Angels: The Mysterious Messengers* hosted by Patty Duke.

Premiere movie magazine dressed up Sharon Stone in an angel costume, complete with feather wings, for their cover. Now those wings are on exhibit at *The Angel Store* in Pasadena, CA! Another exclusive angel store is *Tara's Angels* in San Juan Capistrano, CA.

In light of the current angelic movement, who better to host *The Angel Festival* than *SILA (Swedenborg Information of Los Angeles)* for Emanuel Swedenborg (1688–1772), the eminent scientist and philosopher wrote more about angels than any other author in history and Los Angeles is literally a city of "The Angels"!

In over 30 books, Swedenborg wrote about angels 1,934 times, not counting the word angelic! Swedenborg wrote that he saw angels and that they were in human form—male and female. He noted that there were no angels with wings nor were there any angels that were created in heaven, but ALL had once lived on earth. (Current angelic visitations by deceased family members substantiate this.)

Swedenborg's most popular book is titled, *Heaven and Hell*. In it, he tells us he saw angels walking, talking, reading, writing, and holding down jobs.

The common belief that angels have wings and halos is based, partly, in fact. Angels are so wise that they radiate light and appear to earthlings as glowing and thus in art they were drawn with halos to depict the light surrounding them! Angels not only talk and walk, they communicate telepathically, and travel to other locations immediately, if they wish to. Thus the depiction that they fly! The symbols of the angel—wings and halo—are universal and descriptive. How else would you know you are looking at an angel? Maybe there is one developing in your mirror.

UPDATE

The Angel Store and *Tara's Angels* have closed.

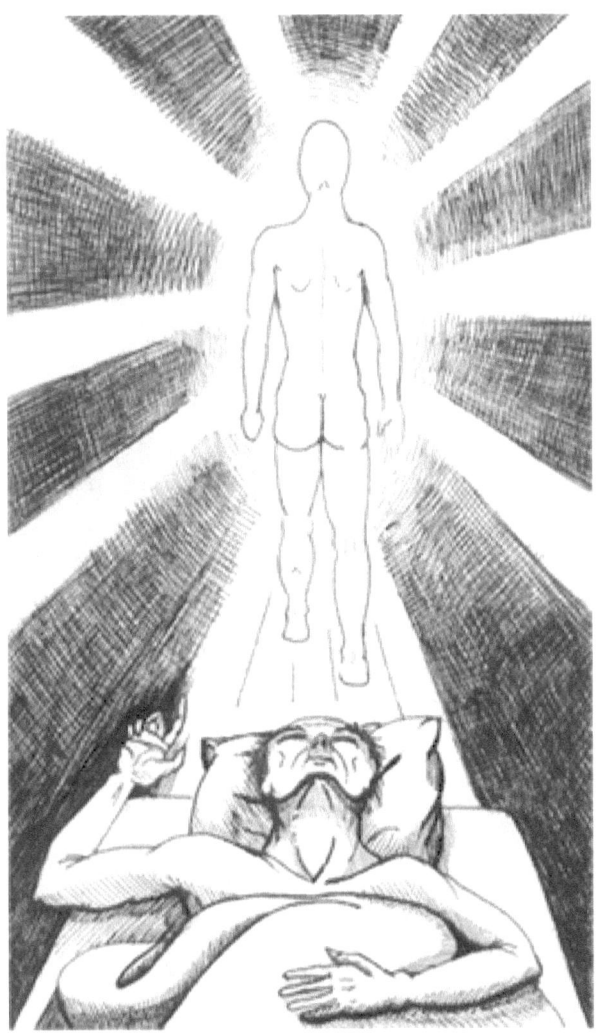

"I have heard from heaven that some people who die, while they are lying on the slab, before they have been revived [in the spiritual world], are still thinking in their cold bodies, and cannot help but feel that they are alive, but with the difference that they cannot move a single part of the matter that makes up their bodies."

From #433 in *Heaven and Hell* by Emanuel Swedenborg (1758)

Drawing by Tuan Hauptmann

Dear Candace,

Thus with the fact that ALL man came from Africa and the first man was Black then the true or say the first inhabitants of heaven would surely have to have been the Africans. Thus the truth would surely come out.

I just recently saw on the Discovery TV channel a show with a lot of details stating that all races came from the Black man. So what do you think about what I just said?

W.A.
Charleston, Missouri
September 2003

Dear W.A.

Yes, the first angels in heaven were Africans.

And they are what Swedenborg calls celestial angels living in the celestial kingdom in heaven. Heaven is divided into two kingdoms: celestial and spiritual.

Celestial angels act from love to the Lord, and therefore speak from wisdom. They are interior angels and are called by Swedenborg "higher angels". Spiritual angels act from love to the neighbour, and therefore speak from knowledge.

Swedenborg writes in *Last Judgment* #118: **"The African race can be in greater enlightenment than others on this earth, since they are such that they think more interiorly, and so receive truths and acknowledge them."**

When a person is interiorly infested with temptations
angels are sent by the Lord
to help assist the individual away from their torment

Drawing by Tuan Hauptmann
SILA August 1997

Dear Candace,
I'm afraid to ask, but what's the difference between spirits and angels?
Anonymous
South Pasadena, California
August 2000

Dear Anonymous,
Never be afraid to ask anything!
Some say that spirit is the breath of God or the energy that pours into all creation. Some believe that spirit is abstract thought and that it will vanish when death occurs. Swedenborg defines spirit as life. A human being is a spirit clothed with a physical body. When the physical body dies, the spirit moves on and continues to live in the spiritual world for whom it was created for in the first place. Each spirit is in the shape of a human body!
There is no spirit or angel or devil that was not first born a human being. And because everyone is a spirit (a life), it is impossible for one spirit to pass into another person's body and to live in it!
We are also told by Swedenborg that every person on earth is also in the spiritual world as to their spirit. For to be in spirit means a state of the mind separate from the body—when one is thinking abstractedly, interiorly. And to assist this connection with the spiritual world, there are at least two good spirits and at least two evil spirits near us through whom we can have communication with spirits in the other world.
When a person dies, they leave behind their physical body and their spirit body enters the world of spirits. After a time of sorting out one's thoughts and feelings about life and God, one chooses to live in heaven or hell.
Swedenborg goes into great detail about the different levels in the world of spirits. But, basically you will first be a good spirit, then an angelic spirit, then an angel (in heaven) or be an evil spirit, then a devilish spirit, then a devil (in hell). The difference between a spirit and an angel is not the Hollywood stereotypical scary spook versus the rewarded hero. A spirit is a deceased human newly arrived in the world of spirits. An angel is a deceased human spirit that chose to live in heaven.

Dear Candace,
I would love some more information about the idea of how the first angels came to be in heaven—also the evil spirits in hell.
In Genesis when the Lord says Let "Us" make man in our image, (meaning the angels would help)...how were there already angels to help if the man of the Most Ancient Church was not yet regenerated...he had to be made into a spiritual man from nearly a beast, right? Could it be that there were already angels from other earths in the universe? Am I making my question clear enough for you? Thanks for researching...
L.M.
Tujunga, California
August 2003

Dear L.M.,

In the Genesis story, it does not mention any creation of angels, but only the creation of human beings. Genesis 1:26, 27: **"And God said, Let us make man in our image, after our likeness. So God created man in His own image, in the image of God created He him; male and female created He them."**

Emanuel Swedenborg wrote that the first chapter of Genesis is allegorical and is talking about the new creation—regeneration—of a human being from a natural to a spiritual person.

Who is Swedenborg to say what Genesis means? Think of Shakespeare. Many (if not most) find the language of William Shakespeare's plays difficult to understand. Until *Cliffs Notes* were published. The company was founded by Cliff Hillegass in 1958 in Lincoln, Nebraska. Through his job as a college bookstore representative, Cliff met Jack Cole of Canada who owned *Coles Bookstore*. Jack Cole had created *Cole's Notes*—study guides. With the suggestion from Jack Cole that American students would no doubt appreciate study guides of their own, Cliff created *Cliffs Notes*—today the most widely used study guides in the world—which started with 16 Shakespeare titles. The authors of *Cliffs Notes* are Ph.D.s, professors, and experts in their respective fields writing on numerous subjects. There is even a *Cliffs Notes* for the Bible.

The Bible (*The Bible* by Charles H. Patterson, 2003) is summarized in just a few words by Presbyterian Rev. Dana Livesay of Wanganui, New Zealand.

> God made
> Adam bit
> Noah arked
> Abraham split
> Jacob ruled
> Bush talked
> Pharaoh plagued
> Sea divided
> Tablets guided
> Promise landed
> Judges led
> Saul freaked
> David peeked
> Kingdom divided
> Prophets warned
> People exiled
> Hope rose
> Jesus born
> God walked
> Anger crucified
> Love rose
> Spirit flamed
> Word spread
> God remained

Swedenborg gave us a complete study guide for the Bible in the 18th century, before Cliff Hillegass in the 20th century! Whether one believes the Lord instructed Swedenborg to write his interpretations (which I do) or not, it still remains that Emanuel Swedenborg wrote an extensive explanation of Genesis. It is agreed, however, by many (if not most) that Swedenborg needs his own study guide!

That said, here is what Swedenborg said regarding the first angels: **"And God said, Let us make man in our image, after our likeness."**

A person is a receiver of God—Love and Wisdom. A receiver of God is an *image of God* and becomes an *image of God* to the extent that s/he receives and acknowledges that the love and wisdom in one's self are not one's own, but are present only in God and therefore come from Him. A person is a *likeness of God* by virtue of the fact that s/he feels that what s/he received from God is one's own.

"Let us make man." The Lord regenerates people through angels. So, here in Genesis, He is referring to Himself *and angels* helping people to become an image of Him—loving and wise. The angels referred to as **"us"** applies to all time, not the beginning of time.

"So God created man in His own image." God didn't create any angels from the beginning, only human beings through evolution, on many planets, in many universes. Human beings can, however, grow into becoming an angel or digress into becoming a devil.

The first angels were from the first people born on earth called by Swedenborg as those of **"The Most Ancient Church"** and human beings from other planets. The first people on earth were already communicating with God on a daily basis and knew that all love and wisdom was of His authorship. They lived in peace, regenerated as young adults, didn't live very long lives, and then passed into the spiritual world. They all became angels.

Individuals who started to think that their love and wisdom came from themselves led to the destruction of the first society, spiritually and physically. They led themselves into hell as the first devils. This was the fall of **"The Most Ancient Church"**. Their descendents became part of an era or time Swedenborg called **"The Ancient Church"**.

Swedenborg used this ornament in *Divine Love and Wisdom*

Dear Candace,
Not all people retain what is in their spirit in this life when they go to the next. If this were true there wouldn't be a need for schools in the spirit world.
One thing you can say you do is let the reader think. I can't say that that is wrong. In fact, I agree with your method. You make your reader do what you have been doing.

W.A.
Tipton, Missouri
August 2000

Dear W.A.,
Swedenborg wrote that people *do* retain what is in their spirit into the next life. Because the spirit is the person—all that they love and have done. Nothing is lost. It may appear that one will lose some things which were learned, but one only retains things that are loved! We forget the rest. Think back on your school days. What did you retain?

There is a need for schools in the spiritual world because we are finite and couldn't possibly know everything. It would be arrogant to think we did. And often what we are taught about wisdom isn't really wise at all. Little children will need schools of instruction in all subjects. Newcomers to the spiritual world will need instruction about where they are. Spiritually sick people will need therapeutic instruction. Advanced schools of wisdom will teach to eternity. What we learn on earth isn't even at a spiritual kindergarten level.

UPDATE
Kindergarten means literally in German "children's garden".

> "The word 'Kindergarten', used where the care and education of very young children is involved, was coined by German translators of Swedenborg's Latin work *De Caelo et Ejus Mirabilibus, et de Inferno (Heaven and Its Wonders, and Hell)* regarding those who die in childhood being educated in paradisal gardens. Swedenborg's insistence that everyone is born into this world in a state of innocence, not full of sin and therefore to be dealt with harshly, transformed the way children were viewed and became a focal point for the pioneers of infant education in Europe 200 hundred years ago (such as James Buchanan, Johan Frederik Oberlin, Robert Owen, and Samuel Wilderspin) and since."

Swedenborg Association of Australia newsletter, April 2003
http://www.swedenborg.com.au/newsletter/anniversary.pdf

Secrets of Heaven #2309: "We can see what is the nature of the education of little children in heaven, namely, that by means of the intelligence of truth and the wisdom of good they are introduced into the angelic life, which is love to the Lord, and mutual love, in which loves there is innocence. But how contrary is the education of little children on earth, with many, has been evidenced from this one example.

I was in the street of a great city, and saw little boys fighting with one another. A crowd gathered and looked on with much pleasure; and I was informed that the parents themselves urge on their little boys to such fights.

The good spirits and angels who saw these things through my eyes were so averse to them that I perceived their horror, especially at the fact that the parents incite them to such things; saying that thus in their earliest age they extinguish all the mutual love and all the innocence which little children receive from the Lord, and initiate them into hatred and revenge; consequently that they deliberately shut out their children from heaven, where there is nothing but mutual love. Let parents therefore who wish well to their children beware of such things."

Secrets of Heaven #2296: "The manner in which all things are insinuated into the little ones of the other life by means of delightful and pleasant things suited to their genius, has also been shown me; for I have been permitted to see the little children most beautifully clothed, having their bosoms and tender arms encircled with garlands of flowers that were resplendent with the most pleasing and heavenly colors.

Once also I was permitted to see the little children with their maiden [teachers] in a paradisal garden, that consisted not so much of trees, as of laurel espaliers and of bowers thus formed; beautifully laid out with paths that led toward the more interior parts; and I also saw the little children themselves, clothed as above described; and when they entered the garden the flower arch above the entrance shone most joyously.

From this we can see the nature of their deliciousnesses, and also that by means of pleasant and delightful things they are introduced into the goods of innocence and charity, which are continually being insinuated by the Lord into those delightful and pleasant things."

Swedenborg used this ornament in *Secrets of Heaven*

Dear Candace,
I am interested in obtaining information that Swedenborg may have written about the dark angels in particular.

L.O.D.
Sun City, Arizona
December 1995

Dear L.O.D.,
I believe you are referring to Revelation 12: 7-9, 11. **"And there was war in heaven: Michael and his angels fought against the dragon; and the dragon fought and his angels. And prevailed not; neither was their place found any more in heaven. And the great dragon was cast out, that old serpent, called the Devil, and Satan, which deceiveth the whole world: he was cast out into the earth, and his angels were cast out with him... And they overcame him by the blood of the Lamb, and by the word of their testimony."**

The people in ancient times understood this as allegorical—a *story* with a deeper meaning. They didn't take it literally as they did not take the Adam and Eve story literally. Americans understand that *Uncle Sam* is an allegorical personification of their country operating as a friendly, but sometimes over-powering man.

Swedenborg says that Michael is actually a name for a society in heaven. Michael means to defend against those who "say" charity, but do not live by charity. Satan is actually a name for a society in hell. It's not one devil. Satan means falsity which destroys truth. The great dragon means naturalists who deny the Divine. Blood of the Lamb means the Lord's Divine truth. (He who drinks it has life.)

There are levels to this story that I can't relate here. (You gotta read *Apocalypse Explained*!) But, on one level the story is about you and me fighting a spiritual internal war. Look how much richer Revelation 12: 7-9, 11 reads with one of its inner senses revealed (my words):

> And there was an assault in a person. The person and its angels fought against the naturalist devils; and the naturalists fought back saying the Divine did not exist. And they lost and were removed out of the person. And the person overcame those devils that destroy truth, by the power of the Lord's Divine truth, and by the word of their own declaration.

The angels named Michael, Gabriel, and Raphael mentioned in the Word do not mean individual angels, but angelic societies. There are no dark angels. Angels of all races have a brightness emanating from them. The light of angels is their wisdom shining. Some angels are brighter than other angels. (Pun intended!)

UPDATE
Without Swedenborg, people are going to continue believing Michael is one guy, one angel. Even Moses who was a real person signifies something other than himself in Scripture. **"That Moses in the spiritual sense, signifies the law, thus the Word."** (See *Apocalypse Explained* #735)

Dear Candace,

I would appreciate information about Swedenborg. He and his teachings have briefly crossed my path on a number of occasions. I am an artist and now find myself painting angels with an increasing frequency. I am curious.

R.A.
Vista, California
May 1998

Dear Candace,

I would truly love to receive your monthly newsletter. Am an angel believer and want to receive all I can on them to enrich my life.

L.C.E.
Gainesville, Florida
May 1998

Dear R.A. and L.C.E.,

Swedenborg wrote that few Christians at his time understood where angels came from and what they did. It was believed that angels were created at the beginning of time. It was thought that the Devil or Satan was an Angel of Light who had become rebellious and was cast down with his crew and that this was the origin of hell. These ideas were taken from parts of the Bible as literal, yet other parts of the Bible dispute these claims.

Swedenborg spoke with angels and they told him that it is hypocrites who feign to be Angels of Light. Angels are forms of love and charity in human shape. All angels once lived on earth. He was also told that in heaven angels do not have anger, but zeal. Angels get indignant if anyone attributes anything of wisdom or intelligence to them, saying praise should go to the Lord. And the angels told Swedenborg they aren't to be adored or invoked.

Drawing by Bridget Swinton

SILA January 1995

Dear Candace,
> *This question is bothering my mind. Please help me.*
> *1) Can Emanuel Swedenborg's teachings save the lives of mankind?*
> *2) Do angels intercede for our sins?*
> *I would share this question with my group so give me much information.*
> *S.M.*
> *Mamprobi, Accra, Ghana*
> *February 1997*

Dear S.M.,

No, Swedenborg's teachings can't save lives. Only the Lord can. Angels can't even do it. Those facts can be found in the Writings of Swedenborg. What the Writings can do is educate about who the Lord really is and how He operates. For instance, the Lord has provided that in every religion there are two essentials of salvation: 1) acknowledgment of God; 2) do no evil because it's against God.

Swedenborg teaches, believe it or not, that as long as a person believes in a Supreme Being and shuns evil because of that Supreme Being and thus lives a life according to their faith and charity (not faith alone) that person can be saved. Swedenborg wrote that he knew few would scarcely believe this. But, he wrote down on paper what he saw and heard while in a long, near-death-experience-type state.

The knowledge that a loving God would not damn the unbaptised, unchurched, or someone from another religion is comforting. As is the knowledge that ALL kids go to heaven (if they die in infancy or childhood) and grow up to adulthood in heaven. No exceptions.

The teachings written down by Swedenborg can help humankind because they espouse an understanding of a visible God and show how we can rationally know Him, individually, and not be kept in obedience to some minister or priest or rabbi's concept of faith. People can only be saved in spiritual freedom.

This is why, though angels are near us, they can scarcely do anything to save us. Angels do not intercede for our sins. However, they can inspire, lead, and bend bad thoughts to good thoughts. They confessed to Swedenborg that they have no power, but that they act from the Lord. Human beings cannot possibly do what is good, except by the angels, and angels cannot possibly do what is good, except by the Lord. Keep in mind that angels (and devils) are humans souls living after the death of their earthly bodies. Angels cannot see into our world because the light of our world—the sun—is to them thick darkness. People cannot see into the spiritual world because the light of that world—the spiritual sun, being God—is to us clouded over by our materialism.

Angels care nothing for the material. Angels don't know the name of any person on earth that they're near. Names and words are like dust to them. Angels only perceive thoughts and affections of a person, i.e., what is within an idea, what is the affection in it, what is the origin of that affection, and what is its end goal.

Angels work for us by inflowing into our conscience. It is there that they operate. The ideal is communication between angels and earthlings. But, the consequence of people becoming so materialistic is we have closed heaven against ourselves. Angels indeed are near us, but stand, so to speak, outside our sphere. Yet, good spirits—deceased good people not yet in heaven, but living in the world of spirits—are in our sphere. They don't know who they are with just as we don't know who is near us. Furthermore, for a person to have communication with the spiritual world, the Lord has provided that at all times there are, at least, two good spirits and two evil spirits with everyone. This equilibrium between evil and good is so people can be in freedom.

Swedenborg teaches that if we knew who was with us, spiritually, we may want to attempt to interfere and then our freedom and the associate spirit's freedom would disappear. Though most are ignorant that we are governed by the Lord through angels, and that good spirits are led by the angels, and that human beings are stimulated by good spirits, it is true.

S.M., I am glad that you will be sharing these truths with your group. I am sending you several copies to pass out.

I'm standing in Swedenborg's doorway! That's his summer house in Sweden. Went there with a tour group organized by the *Bryn Athyn College*, 1998.

(l-r) Rev. Göran Appelgren, Ed Gyllenhaal, Rev. Frank Rose, Bill Radcliffe, Susan Asplundh, Marian Nelson, Devin Zuber, Dr. Jane Williams-Hogan, Nate Smith, Roger Landsbury, Nicole Hill, Joachim Ericksson, Jeremy Henry, Ruth Homber, Sue Odhner, Nicola Homber, me, Carolyn Heldon, Lamar Goodenough, Scott Frazier, Rev. Olle Hjern, Ethan McCardell, Rev. Jonathan Rose, Jennifer Kuhl.

SILA June 1998

Dear Candace,

Swedenborg's physical body required earthly foods and sleep. Does Swedenborg ever state he ate any food while visiting angels?

Anonymous
U.S.A.
April 1998

Dear Anonymous,

Good question! I've never come across any statement that Emanuel Swedenborg ever ate any "spiritual food" while visiting in the spiritual world. However, he did write about food he saw spirits eating. *Last Judgment* #292: **"Their house, clothing, and food are similar to those used in the world. I asked about wine, strong drink, beer, chocolate, tea, and the like, and was told that they had similar things."** He said, there are also table decorations which cannot be described in natural language!

Swedenborg says that spiritual food is given daily to angels and devils according to the labours they perform. If they don't work, they don't eat, but beg for food! Idleness is the root of all wickedness. For in idleness, the mind is open to evil ideas, but in work, it is held to useful things. Food in the spiritual world will not keep until the next day or worms will breed in it as they did in the manna God gave the sons of Israel in the wilderness. Wow! No leftovers in the next world!

You may recall that in the Lord's Prayer it says: **"Give us this day our daily bread."** Swedenborg always talks about natural things corresponding to spiritual things. He tells us food corresponds to knowledge or intelligence. In everyday language, it's common to say of someone that they are *hungry to know* or that something is *food for thought*.

We know from Swedenborg's diaries and letters he ate these natural foods:
- tea, coffee, wine, milk
- biscuits, bread, rolls, buns, butter
- almonds, raisins, pears
- cheese, pigeon pies, eels
- sugar, chocolate
- almond cakes, gingerbread nut cookies

We know he was not an overeater from contemporary paintings of him and anecdotes from colleagues. After all, he was too aware of spirits that were trying to induce him to overeat or make him feel guilty for eating some particular food. He knew food was to sustain the physical body only and not to be indulged to excess.

When he visited friends, he ate in moderation what was served. When he was "visiting in the next world", he sometimes would be sleeping on earth for longer than ten hours and therefore didn't need much food. Near the end of his life, he would mostly eat (or needed) bread, coffee, and sugar. He wrote in his *Journal of Dreams,* April 14-15: **"I had an extraordinary sleep for twelve hours."**

UPDATE
I found this tasty bite!

True Christian Religion #461: "Once when I was in the spirit I traveled deep into the southern region in the spiritual world, and came into a park there; and I saw that this one was better than the others I had so far visited. The reason was that a garden means intelligence; and it is to the south that all are sent who are especially intelligent. It was this that was meant by the Garden of Eden, where Adam lived with his wife; so their being driven out implies that they were deprived of intelligence, and thus also of uprightness of life. As I was walking in this southern park I noticed some people sitting under a laurel-bush eating figs.

I went up to them and asked them to give me some figs. They did so, and at once the figs in my hand turned into grapes. I was surprised by this, but an angelic spirit standing next to me said: 'The figs in your hand turned into grapes, because the meaning of figs by their correspondence is the kinds of good of charity and hence of faith in the natural or external man, and grape means the kinds of good of charity and hence of faith in the spiritual or internal man. As you love what is spiritual, so this happened to you. For in our world everything happens and comes into existence, and also undergoes change, in accordance with correspondences.' "

Swedenborg doesn't go on to say whether he ate the grapes. I like to think he did!

One day, there will be a diet book based on Swedenborg's Writings. I don't have the inclination to write it. Someone will. It would be fascinating to read!

Swedenborg did use these initials in his books, but he never spelt food with them!

Dear Candace,

I'm curious about the variations in the pigmentation of the skin of angels. You know since society has associated black with devil's food cake and anything of a low down or negative aspect this may not be noticed by a lot of white people. Plus most pictures and statues of such are of a European origin this can easily be understood.

W.A.
Moberly, Missouri
March 2000

Dear W.A.,

If you or others think white people named Devil's Food Cake for its colour, you and they are mistaken, and being overly sensitive. Devil's Food Cake is named, not for its black colour, but for its "sinfully chocolaty taste". Many foods are called devil's food:

- Deviled eggs—"the devil's best eggs"
- Devilled ham—"the devil's best ham"
- Devil Dog—"the devil's best hotdog"
- Devil's Juice—"hot as hell" (cranberry juice, tomato juice, Tabasco sauce, lemon juice, salt, pepper)
- Little Devil Cocktail—"a sin; you'll become a little devil after drinking it" (lemon juice, rum, gin, triple sec, ice)

The implication is that great food is so good, it must be a sin and the work of the devil. It is true, devils (dead evil people, of all races) attempt to enslave us to food. The Lord even told Emanuel Swedenborg when he first saw Him while eating in a restaurant: **"Eat not so much"**!

The colour black does commonly represent evil and the colour white good. We see it portrayed in movies—bad person wears black; good person wears white. Swedenborg says black represents falsity; white represents truth. Black absorbs; white reflects. Think of night and day. In the light of day, things are clear. In the dark of night, things are hidden. When evil is hidden, it flourishes and grows, but when the lights are turned on, evil is seen for what it is. The correspondences of white and black are states of mind. A black person is not evil because of their pigmentation. And a white person isn't good because of theirs. People are good or evil because of what's inside their skin—inside their minds.

Swedenborg tells us that he saw angels of all races (even some from other planets) and he said that ALL angels appeared bathed in a bright white light. Think of a person surrounded with sunlight. The whiteness emanating from them is their higher, purer wisdom glowing from their beings. Only ignorant people would label black people evil because of their skin colour. Emanuel Swedenborg wrote (in the 18th century!) that the African race can be in greater enlightenment than others on this earth, since they think more interiorly than other races, and so easily receive truths and acknowledge them. Missionaries that go to Africa attest to this.

Dear Candace,
  Tell about angels.

S.L.
Kherson, Ukraine
August 2006

Dear S.L.,
  Current Swedenborgian news is that seven 8x3' stained-glass windows—created in 1902–1903 by the New York artist, Louis Comfort Tiffany (1848–1933), creator of the Tiffany lamps—were rediscovered in 2001. They were originally made for a new sanctuary that was being built in 1903 by the Swedenborgian Church in Cincinnati, Ohio.
  The last book of the Word is Revelation. It opens with brief letters to "the angels" of seven early Christian churches.
  Tiffany designed angel windows based on his understanding of Swedenborg's interpretation of each letter. Swedenborg says that the seven angels correspond to a person's seven stages of regeneration—the process of becoming an angel. These angel windows are evidence of a Swedenborgian influence on Tiffany's work through his studies with landscape painter, George Inness (1825–1892), who was a Swedenborgian. Tiffany was a student of Inness's.
  They were displayed at the Cincinnati Swedenborgian Church until 1964 when the building came down to make way for Interstate 71. They were moved in crates to several locations, ending up at the Swedenborgian *Temenos Retreat Center* in West Chester, Pennsylvania, where they were found in storage a couple of years ago during spring cleaning. (Temenos is a Greek word for sacred-space.)
  The seven restored Tiffany stained-glass angel windows—worth about a million dollars—are now a touring exhibit called, *In Company with Angels*, travelling to churches and museums around the country. I was surprised to read this quote by Swedenborg on www.TemenosRetreat.org: "Inwardly, a person is in company with angels, though unaware of it."
  That's not true! Knowing that Emanuel Swedenborg didn't advocate such a doctrine, I sourced out the quote, since none was given on the website. Here is the COMPLETE quote from Swedenborg's *Heavenly Doctrine* #40: **"An <u>inwardly</u> spiritual <u>person is</u>, seen as they really are, an angel of heaven; and they are also, even while they live in their body, <u>in company with angels though</u> they are <u>unaware of it</u>; and after being released from their body they come to join the angels. However, a person who is inwardly only natural is, seen as they really are, a spirit and not an angel; and they are also, while they live in their body, in company with spirits, but with those spirits who are in hell; and after being released from their body, they come to join them."** [I added the underlining.]
  There is such a thing as "derived doctrine" in the Swedenborg movement, where one can deduce one thing that's not written in Swedenborg's books by comparing quotes on the same or similar subject. The quote on Temenos's website about angels is not derived doctrine, but spliced doctrine!!
  According to Swedenborg, we are "with" dead people that are like us. Period. We aren't associating with angels when we are breaking a Ten Command-

ment! Whether we are unaware of it or not. You can believe that if you like, and many do, but you can't say Swedenborg said it!

Angels are with infants. And angels are with the dying. But, Swedenborg says that as a person grows up or as a person wakes in the spiritual world, the angels withdraw and leave the person in freedom to choose either heaven or hell. Good spirits then welcome the deceased into the world of spirits.

No strong, beautiful, multi-coloured winged angel, like Tiffany's, will be standing in front of us compelling or enticing us to walk into heaven. That's pop culture. Unfortunately, while artists have depicted angels with wings and halos for the "other worldly" effect, millions today believe real angels are winged creatures and not human.

I've heard the argument that Swedenborg did mention that he saw an angel fly overhead that had two wings at his feet and two more at his temple. (See *True Christianity* #48 and *Conjugial Love* #136) Actual quote is: **"...appeared one as if were flying."** Appeared! And only one angel! Not millions of angels with bird-wings! Swedenborg also saw angels on horseback with **"on their arms what appeared to be wings."** (See *Conjugial Love* #103) Appeared!

Spiritual Experiences #5953: **"There appeared to me a single spirit with a little wing at the left side of the head; and [angels] said that [wings] sometimes appear thus who are sent by one to another, with letters or messages. Hence was evident whence the ancients derived their custom of representing a wing on the head of Mercury, who was the messenger between their gods."**

Swedenborg wrote wings "appeared" because "a wing", he says, represents spiritual truth. And spiritual truth has the power to soar your understanding to higher heights just as wings have the power to lift birds up. Ancient humans on earth knew that and put wings on angels or messengers of God when drawing them!

In Swedenborg's *Spiritual Experiences* #718, he wrote about those that, while living on earth who had desired to be the highest in heaven, when they got to the next world, they were then free to be who they wanted to be, and that was better than anyone else! **"When [spiritual freedoms] are permitted, [spirits] seem to themselves to fashion wings, and so to fly aloft."** It was an "appearance" that they were "angels", yet only in their egos; but they never entered heaven because they were selfish.

Nowhere in the Writings of Swedenborg does it say that humans are contacted by winged-angels. Angels are actually evolved humans on a higher plain of consciousness and we humans are remote from them, since we are so materialistic. Only a few people are regenerate—inwardly spiritual—enough to be in company with angels!

Jared Diamond in his book, *Guns, Germs, and Steel: The Fates of Human Societies* describes how the system of writing alphabets came about either by independent invention or idea diffusion. Almost all writing, he said, was through idea diffusion—when groups of people borrowed and adapted alphabets from visitors or prisoners of another geographic group. This is what has happened with the knowledge about angels. Swedenborg is recognized by non-Swedenborgian scholars as the father of spiritualism. He is quoted extensively in spiritual books. His ideas have been studied, and inspired, then sometimes diffused along the way, until hardly recognizable as a Swedenborgian thought.

For example, one Swedenborgian idea may start out as spirits are all around us. We are in communication with them at all times. Then it diffuses into we can see spirits in photographs—a big craze in the 19th century—or we can communicate with departed loved ones through mediums. Mary Roach writes in her book, *Spook: Science Tackles the Afterlife,* on page 201:

> What you need to know is that the heyday of spiritualism — with its séances and spirit communications zinging through the ether — coincided with the dawn of the electric age. The generation that so readily embraced spiritualism was the same generation that had been asked to accept such seeming witchery as electricity, telegraphy, radio waves, and telephonic communications — disembodied voices mysteriously traveling through space and emerging from a "receiver" hundreds of miles distant.

Swedenborg wrote in *Apocalypse Explained* #157: **"To this I will add a [secret] not yet known. After death, [a person's] spirit appears in a human form according to the life of [their] affection while in the world."** Careful what you love, I say! You'll look just like it!

What "burns" in a person on earth
will be reflected in their appearance and environment in the spiritual world

Drawing by Tuan Hauptmann   *SILA* September 1997

Dear Candace,
I've been reading a little Swedenborg. What's the difference between angels and good spirits?

Anonymous
San Diego, California
September 2002

Dear Anonymous,

Good question! Quick answer is: A good spirit is someone who has died and moved into the world of spirits—a place outside of heaven—and possesses attributes of love for the Lord and love for the neighbour. An angel is a good spirit that has moved into a heaven and become an angel after instruction of what it means to be an angel and after casting off any remaining lusts or evils that they had clung to from ignorance or practice.

Long answer is: Everybody is a spirit. Swedenborg wrote in *Conjugial Love* #44: **"I once saw three spirits newly arrived from the world, who were wandering about, gazing around and asking questions. They were surprised to find that they were still living as [human beings], and seeing familiar sights."**

While on earth, human being spirits are clothed with a natural body that is suited to the earthly atmosphere. At the same time, everyone, in regards to their spirit, is conjoined to some society, either hellish or heavenly. After the death of the natural body, the spirit is led to its society (future home) gradually, and at length enters it.

Swedenborg wrote in *Conjugial Love* #461: **"By newly arrived spirits are meant people who have recently died, who are called spirits because they are then spiritual people."**

There are three states a person goes through after death. The first is entrance into the world of spirits. The second state is when good spirits and evil spirits are separated. The third state is instruction. This state is only for those who enter heaven and become angels. It is not for those who enter hell because such are incapable of being taught because they don't want to learn.

When good spirits have been prepared for heaven by instruction which is effected in a short time on account of their being in spiritual ideas already, **"they are clothed with angelic garments, which are mostly glowing white."** (See *Heaven and Hell* #519)

Then the new angels are brought to the way that leads "upwards" towards heaven, and are delivered there to angel guards, and afterwards are received by other angels and introduced into societies. And as these are in conformity with the interiors of the angels who are in that society, the new angels are immediately recognized and received with joy.

Dear Candace,
My question is an art history one: when did angels first be painted with wings?
J.
High Point, North Carolina
March 2007

Dear J.,
Since humans began to draw.

 This Sumerian stone carving relief of a butterfly-winged human (angel?) in Iraq is from around 3,000 B.C. Sumer was a group of cities or states around the Lower Tigris and Euphrates Rivers.

This stone carving of a bird-winged human with a bird-head (angel?) was common in Mesopotamia (now Iraq, eastern Syria, southeastern Turkey, and southwestern Iran) around 2,000 B.C.

 The oldest drawing of a Christian angel is of the human wingless-angel Gabriel that appeared to Mary, telling her she will conceive and give birth to Jesus.

This fresco has been titled, "The Annunciation". Fresco is the art of painting on freshly-spread, moist, lime-plaster with water-based pigments. Fresco means "fresh" in Italian.

This Biblical event (and numerous others) was painted within the first 100 years after Jesus' birth, under the home of the noble Roman (Jewish) family of Manius Acilius and Priscilla Glabrio. Tradition says the apostle Peter used their home as his missionary headquarters. Manius Acilius was put to death for converting to Christianity. Their underground burial in Rome, Italy which interred martyrs and several popes, is now known as *The Catacombs of Priscilla*.

Professor H. S. Janson (1913–1982) — chairman of the Department of Fine Arts at *New York University* and Professor Emeritus from 1972–1982 — wrote that the human soul was depicted as a human-headed bird with wings as a visual representation by the ancient Egyptians. The Greeks and Romans then depicted a human soul as a young lady with butterfly wings. (See "Psyche in Stone: The Influence of Swedenborg on Funerary Art" by H. S. Janson, Ph.D. in *Emanuel Swedenborg: A Continuing Vision*, pp. 115-126)

Early Christians not wanting to associate their souls with pagan souls drew a departed soul as a bird-winged human baby.

These are all representations. Earlier than wings to depict a spiritual being or divinely inspired person was the halo—a ring of light around or above the head of a person. It has been found in the earliest Greek, Roman, Asian, and Christian art.

This cave painting located in the valley of Val Camonica, in the region of Lombardy, Italy is from around 10,000 B.C. I see a drawing of two humans (angels?) with light emanating from their faces. Some see "alien astronauts".

Angels with wings and halos or angels at all were seldom represented in art until the reign of Constantine (306–337 A.D.). He was the Roman Emperor who converted from sun worship to Christianity. Only after Christianity became the official state religion of the Roman Empire did winged-angels take flight in art.

Contrary to what you may think, angels aren't big in Christian literature and art. The New Age movement—20th century Western cultural approach to spiritual exploration in the occult, metaphysical, paranormal—has greatly embraced angels and marketed them.

Swedenborg wrote that everything in the Word signifies something spiritual, whether a story or an historical event. For instance, a seraphim (6-winged creature) and a cherubim (4-winged creature), represent Divine protective "guards". It's imagery of a sphere. They aren't angels!

Wings signify power. Flying signifies presence because a bird, when it flies, looks all about from on high and it can see seemingly everywhere. When flying is written about in reference to Jehovah/God/Jesus it signifies omnipresence—being present everywhere at the same time.

From a Swedenborgian perspective, the first humans on earth were in easy communication with heaven and its habitants (angels) who were their deceased relatives. For the beginning generations, angels would appear when needed or wanted, and then disappear. Angels glow from their celestial wisdom.

The first artists knew that wings signified power and presence. They put wings in their drawings of angels and God. They drew light around an angel's head. These pictorial representations for a spiritual being—halo and wings—have been passed down from the beginning of time.

But, people's understanding of angels have waned so far that most think angels are separate beings *with* halos and wings! Those appendages were for representation ONLY! Humans become angels, citizens of heaven, period.

It's important to know what past generations knew. They had a common code. We've lost their interpretations. We can't grasp their narrative from our cultural bias, like saying aliens visited 10,000 years ago. Swedenborg helps us to understand the past, in order to know our future.

Dear Candace,
While so many people do a lot of talking about spreading the good news of Swedenborg's Writings (including myself) you just go out and do it!

R.J.
Glenview, Illinois
October 1995

Swedenborg used this ornament in *Divine Love and Wisdom*

Dear Candace,

I have learnt that friends are made in strange ways and I consider you as my friend. So I shall keep you, my friend. A friend like you needs to be kept for eternity. Since Swedenborg talked to the spirits, why does he not want people to talk to the dead?

Anonymous
Dallas, Texas
September 1997

Dear Anonymous,

It isn't that Swedenborg doesn't want us to talk with angels, angels don't. But, devils would like to! Angels leave people in freedom; they lead through love. Devils persuade people in authoritative and domineering ways to choose as they direct; they control through hatred. This is why Swedenborg states in his book, *Heaven and Hell,* that it is *dangerous* to seek out contact with the dead. You don't know who you'll get!

Evil spirits hold hatred in their hearts for other people, and if given the chance, they would attempt to destroy a person body and soul. This may seem like an improbable scenario, but when you think about how some brutal criminals, here on earth, approach their potential victims—with charm and kindness—the methods are no different with deceased criminals approaching people in the natural world.

Swedenborg, the Swedish theologian, learned over years of study some pertinent facts about the spiritual world:

- people are created by God so that while they live in the body, they are capable of conversing with spirits and angels
- the first people on earth, during its most ancient period, did experience and enjoy unlimited angelic communication
- over time, as spiritual degeneration occurred during the ancient period, people generally lost the ability to receive angelic communication, because they focused more on material things, which cloud the way
- as thoughts of worldly things are removed from a person's mind, the way for angelic communication is again opened
- a spirit is a person who is temporarily in the first state of living after death, in a place called the world of spirits
- spirits, during a process of self examination and education, choose to be either angels or devils
- all angels (no exceptions) are people who have lived in the natural world and then after death, as spirits, enter heaven
- hell is the opposite of heaven
- people on earth cannot see people in the spiritual world with their natural eyes, only when their spiritual eyes are opened
- people in the spiritual world cannot see people on earth with their spiritual eyes, only through the natural eyes of someone on earth
- generally, people are unaware of spirits around them, and spirits are unaware that they are around earthlings

Swedenborg wrote that we are now in a new time period which promises communication again with the spiritual world like the most ancients enjoyed; that the more one puts off material things, the closer one can be in touch with the spiritual world, with its good spirits and its angels. It doesn't mean forsaking materialism altogether, but putting it in its place as servant, and not idol.

Even though it is advised not to contact spirits, sometimes they do contact us in the natural world, uninvited. Most times, it is pleasant, in the form of dreams or good feelings, or visitations from deceased relatives or loved ones. Contact with spirits, good or bad, can be useful leading to a spiritual change in our lifestyle. Messages from the deceased proves little more than their spirit lives on somewhere else, for they cannot reveal much information we don't already know. As with so-called miracles, spirit contacting is a temporary high, not permanent (criteria for authenticity). On the other hand, the near-death experience has been universally expressed by those who had one as life altering. This contact with the spiritual world has been useful and therefore the real thing.

Chalk art at *The 13th Angel Festival*, 2006

Dear Candace,
What do angels do? I'd like to know, because I don't know really what they do.
S.S.
Los Angeles, California
August 2001

Dear S.S.,
Angels perform uses in heaven. In other words, everyone has a job. (Even in hell, devils have jobs.) As heaven will never be closed, there is an unlimited amount of jobs to go around for everyone. No unemployment in the next world!

It's not hard to believe that **"to perform a use is the delight of everyone's life"** as Swedenborg tells us in *Heaven and Hell* #219. Most people on earth have a job that they wouldn't do to eternity. Not so in heaven. There angels pick a job they *love* to do and do it gladly.

Some jobs that angels can choose from are: therapist, child-care worker, sewer, preacher, teacher, librarian, writer, guide, government official, guard, and gardener. *Heaven and Hell* #391: **"But all these employments of angels are employments of the Lord through the angels, for the angels perform them from the Lord and not from themselves."**

Swedenborg tells a story about some newcomers to the next world in *Conjugial Love* #207: **"One of the older angels there greeted them and asked, 'What news do you have from earth?' They said, 'We have much that is new, but tell us, please, on what subject?'**

So the older man replied, 'What news do you have from earth regarding our world and heaven?'

They then answered, 'When we first came into this world, we learned that here and in heaven there are positions of responsibility, ministries, occupations, business dealings, scholarly studies in every field of learning, and wonderful kinds of employment. Yet we had believed that upon our departure or passage from the natural world into this spiritual one, we would come into everlasting rest from our labours. What are occupations, but labors?'

To this the older man replied, 'Did you think that eternal rest from labors meant eternal idleness, in which you would continually sit around or lie about, breathing in auras of delight with your breast and drinking in outpourings of joy with your mouth?'

Laughing gently at this, the three newcomers said that they had supposed something of the sort."

Dear Candace,
The SILA *which I usually discuss with my family and friends, more often than not keeps some of our evenings quite warm.* "No Unemployment for Angels in Heaven" *(August) so far made the most interesting discussion.*
J.O.N.
Nairobi, Kenya
October 2001

November 1993
Dear *SILA* Readers,

Sophy Burnham (no relation to Daniel H. Burnham that I am aware of) wrote, *A Book of Angels: Reflections on Angels Past and Present and True Stories of How They Touch Our Lives.* It was published by *Ballantine Books* in 1990. I was not aware of this book until a *SILA* reader lent it to me recently. Ms. Burnham devoted four pages to telling her readers about Swedenborg. I wrote her:

Dear Ms. Burnham,

Your book, *A Book of Angels* was brought to my attention by a reader of my monthly newsletter *SILA (Swedenborg Information of Los Angeles).* This monthly, not-for-profit newsletter is exclusively about Emanuel Swedenborg. People from around the world write me with questions about him or his Writings (theological and scientific). I research and find the answers for them. I have been doing this for 5 years. I am surprised by the errors regarding Swedenborg, passed off as facts, in your book. How could you or your researchers have been so sloppy?

You stated: Swedenborg was "the great theology professor at Uppsala, Sweden". Wrong—Swedenborg's father, Jesper Swedberg, was the professor of theology. Swedenborg NEVER taught religion!

You stated: Swedenborg was "bishop of Skara". Wrong—Again, this was his father, Jesper Swedberg. Swedenborg NEVER started a religion!

You stated: "In 1714 he was appointed to the Swedish Board of Mines." Wrong—It was in 1724!

You stated: Swedenborg said "we see angels either because the angel assumes a material body momentarily..." Wrong—Swedenborg wrote that angels have bodies, but of spiritual substance. NEVER does an angel assume a material body! If one sees an angel that is because the earthling's spiritual eyes have been opened and can see into the spiritual world.

You stated: that "he is not widely read today". Wrong—Tell that to my thousands of readers. *SILA* is read worldwide. Ghana and Kenya, alone, have thousands of Swedenborgian readers. Swedenborg is big there! I think you mustn't be aware of the famous Swedenborgian *Bryn Athyn Cathedral* in Bryn Athyn, Pennsylvania, nor of the famous Swedenborgian *Wayfarers Chapel* in Palos Verdes, California.

You stated: Swedenborg wrote the books, *Memorabilia*; *Larger Diary*; and *Spiritual Diary*. All three books are one and the same! The commonly used title is *Spiritual Diary.*

You wrote another book title as *Conjugal Love*. The correct spelling is conju<u>gi</u>al—unique word Swedenborg uses for marriage love.

Please feel free to contact me if you have any questions about Emanuel Swedenborg.

Dear Ms. Frazee,
   Thank you so much for the Swedenborg corrections you noticed in A Book of Angels *and for taking the time to pass them on. Now I have more to do! It is surprising and embarrassing to think all that research in the* Library of Congress *was wrong! In peace and love.*
                                                    Sophy Burnham
                                                    Washington, D.C.
                                                    30 August 1993

                                                    Thinking of you,
                                                    Candace

Dear Candace,
   I wanted to take a moment to thank you again for your letter of July 29, 1993, with the corrections to A Book of Angels. *I have gone back and re-checked at the library and was surprised and embarrassed at having confused Swedenborg with his father, misstated a date, and left out the "i" in that curious word "conjugial"—so many facts wrong. It is always a privilege to have them pointed out to me, in order to make corrections. And yes, in answer to your scolding "How could you or your researchers have been so sloppy?". I have no excuse: there was no researcher, only me, (writing a book is time consuming and expensive, when you work alone); and I guess the material got out of hand. At any rate the corrections have been sent to the publisher, as you requested, and in future printings I hope the information on Swedenborg to be correct.*
   The one note that I have not made concerns the titles of the books. I spent a lot of time considering what to do and finally decided to continue to list the several titles, rather than say that Swedenborg wrote only "Spiritual Diary"; first because in the Library of Congress each is listed (and bound) as a separate work, and each has been reprinted as a separate edition; and second because I thought it would be of interest to readers to have a taste of the various titles of his work, thus stimulating interest in such a fascinating mystic and high spirit, rather than to mention only that one title.
   Of course you are right that Swedenborg has followers worldwide! When I said that he is "not widely read today," I meant that if you go into a bookstore and ask for a Swedenborg book, the chances are the bookstore clerk will not have heard of him. Thousands, even hundreds and hundreds of thousands of readers, but many people do not know of him. And of course I have been to the Bryn Athyn Cathedral *and also several [Swedenborgian churches] around the United States.*
   I think the one dispute I have with your letter (apart from its puzzling aggressive tone, as if I were an enemy, instead of on your side) concerns the idea that angels NEVER assume a material body. The fact is, that more than one story has come to me in which the angel has manifested (or somehow created a human or a dog body) and physically saved a human being: a parachutist who suddenly appears and disappears...a man who comes to comfort a dying man...or even my own experience. But most of the time, yes—unquestionably—the reason one sees into the spiritual dimension is because the spiritual eyes have been opened, and this is the joyous good news of today. Do you think that we, as a species, are developing a

higher vibration, high enough so that more and more people are able to see into these other worlds, to see the form of angels?

And is this not what we are being led to? To open our hearts and fill our eyes with compassion, that we may be the living Christ and witnesses to the glory, and then to serve God with all our hearts and minds and souls and strength, which is to say, always to His service and the welfare of humankind.

This letter is longer than I had intended. I meant only to drop you a note to say that the corrections had been made, and to extend to you all the blessings, freedom, wisdom, and joy of God. In love and peace.

Sophy Burnham
Washington, D.C.
March 1994

Dear Sophy,

I am thrilled you wrote again! Your concern for correct info is appreciated and your affection for the truth, especially about life after death, is applauded.

I am sorry you perceived my letter as an attack. Its intent was not to be antagonistic. I want to explain that in doing my job—educating the public about Emanuel Swedenborg—it includes writing many letters to the media, authors, and publications correcting errors about him. Occasionally, I receive a reply. I honestly wasn't sure my letter to you would get by your publisher. I, therefore, wrote it with the thought in mind that someone else would be reading it before you and would be deeming whether it was worth showing to you or not. I purposely wanted to state facts strongly, so as not to have my letter ignored.

I'm pleased it reached you and has inspired you to study Swedenborg further! Thank you for notifying your publisher with the Swedenborg corrections for future printings. Bravo to you! What a superb human being you are for admitting your mistakes, correcting them, and telling me about it.

I can understand your dilemma about all the different titles published for Swedenborg's *Spiritual Diary*. I'm glad you feel it may inspire people to read more books by him.

The simple, but hard to grasp truth about the next life is that it will be identical to this life in all aspects. It is possible to see a dog in the spiritual world as there are all kinds of animals there. But, an angelic human being would not manifest or assume a dog body. Anything seen in the spiritual world is seen with spiritual eyes. We, as a species are not being led to see into the next world, but are asked to love our neighbour as ourselves.

Swedenborg used this ornament in *Secrets of Heaven*

Dear Candace,

It sounds promising that angels are "in" in the States—makes a nice change from Godzilla, King Kong and Judas Priest. They are not "in" here in Denmark (angels that is). But I hope that they one day will be.

T.H.
Himmelev, Denmark
May 1995

Dear T.H.,

I got a chuckle thinking that your short list is what Danes think of when they think of Americans! (What do they think of Canadians?) Maybe you can be part of an educational movement about angels in Denmark. Take Swedenborg's books to your local university library and copy your issues of *SILA* and mail them to your newspaper.

Dear Candace,

I think your plans for The Angel Festival *are terrific. I'm so glad you told me about what you are doing. I think that your work in* SILA *is the very best New Church Swedenborgian publicity that I've ever seen. You are terrific, not just beautiful (ha ha) but smart as well!*

Anonymous
USA
May 1995

Steve Dalby (right) of *The Spanish House Gallery* with his son Ronald Brittan was the first and only vendor at *The 1ˢᵗ Angel Festival*, 27 January 1995 held at the *La Crescenta New Church* in Southern California. They are not Swedenborgians.

Jill D'Agnenica spoke at *The 1ˢᵗ Angel Festival* about her angel project —placing 4,687 small, magenta, plaster angels all over Los Angeles

The Angel Festival moved to *Memorial Park* in Sierra Madre, CA for it's 10th anniversary

Dear Candace,
The City of Angels arranging an Angel Festival*! There is certainly an incredible amount of creativity in your area and in yourself as well! I am showing your flyer around in our church to show that there are entirely new ways to call attention to the land for which we all are heading. Strange that some people do not want to know about it or mistrust everything. But it is necessary to protect the freedom of anyone who wants to deny it. Congratulating you on your initiative.*

Anonymous
New Church minister
California
October 1995

The 14th Angel Festival, 2007 in Memorial Park, Sierra Madre, CA

Dear Candace,
No, never heard of Emanuel Swed— what does he write? (Mystery, historic, romance, etc.) I am a voracious reader and am always looking for new authors, so I will look him up.

N.R.
Little Rock, Arkansas
October 1995

Dear N.R.,
Once you start to read Swedenborg, I think you will find you may have read about him before in your travels with other authors. He is quoted often in historical nonfiction, in biographies, and in novels. At the past two *Angel Festivals,* at the Swedenborg booth, there was a fascinating display of 15 angel books by various bestselling authors of which had quotes by Swedenborg or pages about him. People who said they had never heard of Emanuel Swedenborg were astounded to find him in these angel books they were familiar with! Since *The 2nd Angel Festival* several have told me that they now see Swedenborg's name everywhere!

Dear Candace,
About angels...I know wings denote power, but as Swedenborg states, they are like us all, who have gone through their regeneration and are in the goods of love and the truths of faith, and far more superior in intelligence of wisdom and have gained Heaven, therefore about to help us, when called upon. But, Swedenborg does say angels have no wings. It is a falsity of the human mind. Wouldn't it be amazing if we got to Heaven and saw no beings with wings? I often think about this. In this light, why do you use an angel with wings for The Angel Festival *logo?*

E.H.
Emerson, New Jersey
April 1996

THERE IS AN ANSWER

First logo from stock graphic, b&w   New logo by Lora Lee (2004), colour

The Angel Festival is trademarked; registered 12 February 1996, approved 22 April.

Dear E.H.,
    I can understand and appreciate your concern. I personally believe Swedenborg and do not like angels depicted with wings, either. But…it is symbolic! Swedenborg, as you say, tells us wings do denote power, elevation, and protection. Similarly halos symbolize the light (wisdom) emanating from an angel. I find it interesting that in art, the halo isn't as prominent as it used to be.
    Please understand that I chose a winged-angel for *The Angel Festival* logo as a symbol that the public understands and accepts and not as a true depiction of an angel. After all, I have seen an angelic spirit and she didn't have wings.

January 1996
Dear *SILA* Readers,
    The 1st Angel Festival was held at a Swedenborgian church. For *The 2nd Angel Festival*, I invited other local churches to participate. (They didn't.) Opening up *The Angel Festival* to all religions—because Emanuel Swedenborg did say that people from any religion (if they lived by their religion) can go to heaven—was a good thing. However, some Swedenborgians expressed amazement and disapproval of me doing such a thing. But, I believe it is the right thing to do. I don't know of one faith that does not believe in angels—either created or born. All angel believers will continue to be invited to *The Angel Festival.*

I received this letter from a vendor:

> Dear Candace,
> I had checked Heaven and Hell *out of the library years ago. When I learned of your festival, I asked my friend about Swedenborgians, and she said the Swedenborg religion is the best religion in the whole world.*

Another vendor wrote:

> Dear Candace,
> *I looked up Swedenborg in the encyclopedia. And my husband is a psychologist, so he knew of him.*

Two other vendors told me in person that they had attended the *La Crescenta New Church* about ten years ago.

I was touched by these people's honest responses which showed they cared where they put their angel products and investigated what *The Angel Festival* stood for. An attendee, surprised to find Swedenborg's books for sale at *The Angel Festival* told me: *"I bought* Chrysalis *magazine [*Swedenborg Foundation *publication] last week in a bookstore. I had never heard of Swedenborg before."*

Thinking of you,
Candace

UPDATE
From *CALIFORNIA DIGEST,* October 2003:

Dear Californians,
The 10th *Angel Festival* happens on Saturday, October 4!
I got a call from a woman with a thousand questions about the festival. Finally she said, *"I don't know how to ask this without being politically incorrect."* I assured her, any question was okay with me. She wanted to know if *The Angel Festival* was *"weird like other New Age or spirituality events."*

Wow! Great question! The answer is: No, *The Angel Festival* is purposely a fun, family festival that is light in attitude.

I know what the lady meant. I, too, find some "spirituality events" can be heavy, mysterious, and not child friendly. I assured the caller that this festival was not like any other.

Come and see for yourself! See you at *The 10th Angel Festival*!

Until next month,
Candace

Dear Candace,

The Swedenborgian mysticism (and your own, apparently) is truly fascinating stuff. Should I question it, I would question the absolute, authoritative freedom Emanuel says a human being has.

D.D.
Van Nuys, California
May 1996

Dear D.D.,
There are many stories we all can tell of when our loved ones and innocent strangers appeared not to be in freedom. But, this is an appearance, a natural illusion. Swedenborg wrote about this in detail in his book, *Angelic Wisdom concerning the Divine Love and the Divine Wisdom* (published in Amsterdam, 1763). Recent printings are titled, *Divine Love and Wisdom*. Spiritually, all (good and evil) people are in freedom. Freedom is one of the two capacities given to all human beings (but, not animals) from the Lord. We are given from birth:
- rationality (ability to understand what is true and good)
- freedom (ability to do what is true and good)

People have these capacities that they may become spiritual beings. It is by knowing what evil is and what good is that one can become spiritual.

The origin of evil is from the abuse of these capacities. An evil person will abuse their freedom and rationality to confirm their evils. Yet, a good person will use their freedom and rationality to confirm their goods. Swedenborg further adds that people do not have the capacity to understand until one's natural mind reaches maturity. He says poetically in *Divine Love and Wisdom* #266: "**...until then it is like seed in unripe fruit, which cannot be opened in the soil and grow up into a shrub.**"

Swedenborg states that rationality and freedom is not with:
- children
- those whose natural body and mind has been injured by some accident (either in the womb, or by some disease or accident after birth)
- people who have gone insane (breaking down restraints)

People that grow to healthy maturity can use their capacities of rationality and freedom, but those that remain inert physically or mentally will not be able to use their capacities until they enter the spiritual world, where they can grow.
- The exercise of freedom to do what is evil is slavery.
- The exercise of freedom to do what is good is liberating.
- The exercise of reason to think what is false is irrational.
- The exercise of reason to think what is true is rational.

Dear Candace,
 The thing I appreciate most is your friendly and cheerful presentation of Swedenborg. So often we take everything so seriously—which is a comfort, yet it is nice to "smell the daisies" and to have fun along the way. Swedenborg's interpretation of the life hereafter makes it easier to tread the early path. I have met two of the angels that walk with me, and often go to the "heavenlies" to be with them.

J.T.
San Diego, California
May 1996

Dear J.T.,
 My goal is not only to educate, but also to spark a fun interest in the man called Swedenborg. He is fascinating. I'm glad you appreciate this format.
 I have no doubt you may have "seen" an angelic spirit. (I doubt it was an angel.) Are you aware that Swedenborg says that the spirits around us *change*? We attract good or evil spirits near us, according to the feelings and thoughts we project. You can read about spirits in his book, *Heaven and Hell*.

Dear Candace,
 I was so happy to see your notice in Angel Times *[magazine]. For several years I have been trying to get in touch with someone knowing about Swedenborg. Are there copies of his books in English?*

L.T.T.
Pingree, Idaho
October 1996

Dear L.T.T.,
 So glad you finally got in touch with a Swedenborgian!
 His books are published in many languages. You obviously are aware he wrote in Latin. Because it took you so long to find his books in English, I am sending you a copy of Swedenborg's *Heaven and Hell* as my gift. Enjoy! And write back with any questions you may have.

Dear Candace,
   What is the universal language and how can we tap into it?

E.R.
Syracuse, New York
October 1996

Dear E.R.,
   According to Swedenborg, thought is the universal language; not the language of words, but the language of ideas of thought. When we enter the spiritual world, we will be endowed with the gift of being able to understand all languages, for we will perceive with thought.

   At first, we will think we are speaking in English and the Italian talking with us will think they are speaking in Italian, but we both will be speaking in the universal language of thought. Even little children born on earth before learning a language will speak in the universal language as they grow up in heaven. We are already tapped into the universal language of thought; more so in our dreams, and will eventually chat in it, when our earthly bodies are no longer needed.

Dear Candace,
   First I will thank you for your nice information in your monthly newsletters! You learn us more about Swedenborg, his person and life, etc. than any Swede has done. May I ask you if you will publish some small short passages from the Writings of Swedenborg himself?!

A.L.
Gothenburg, Sweden
October 1999

Dear A.L.,
   You are most welcome! Leon C. Le Van of St. Petersburg, Florida wrote a book in 1987 called, *Poems from Swedenborg*. He took passages that Swedenborg wrote, verbatim, and structured them into poems. A.L., it is my pleasure to share this "poem" from Swedenborg with you. (*Secrets of Heaven* #1043)

> **Dense Clouds**
> **by Emanuel Swedenborg**
>
> There are with people
> Clouds so large and dense
> That were they aware of them
> They would wonder
> How rays of light
> From the Lord
> Could ever pass through them
> So that they could be
> Regenerated

Chapter 5

CULTS

Dear Candace,
   Thank you for your many letters. They have not fallen on deaf eyes. I have had no opportunity to gather any information on Swedenborg. I was about to direct an inquiry to Walter Martin but he recently died before I got a chance.
                                                                                    J.G.
                                                                    Westminster, California
                                                                            August 1989

Dear J.G.,
   I think you are referring to Walter Martin (1928–1989) who wrote *Kingdom of the Cults* (1965) which contains a listing of religions, in his opinion, that are cults. I have read it and heard him lecture. In the segment on "The Church of the New Jerusalem—Swedenborgianism", Martin tells of Emanuel Swedenborg's contributions as a scientist first and then of his beliefs as a theologian.
   Martin stated that Swedenborg's books were un-Christian, that Swedenborg was conceited, that Swedenborg was a spiritist (medium for fame), and that Swedenborg changed the Bible. All of these accusations are untrue. I recommend you read *True Christian Religion,* Volumes I and II by Swedenborg for some insight.
   Martin claimed that one does not have to read Swedenborg's books to determine that they are wrong; they are wrong because he said so! Even a man as extraordinary as Swedenborg was not as presumptuous as Martin, but encouraged people to make up their own minds about his books.
   Martin had termed any religion that was not fundamentalist Christianity, a cult. Swedenborgianism is NOT a fundamentalist religion. It is a faith that rationally explains the Word, life after death, and states that anyone can go to heaven as long as they live what they believe is right, in the sight of their God.

I am intrigued to know that some people have joined The Church of the New Jerusalem after reading *Kingdom of the Cults*, then researching and reading Swedenborg's books for themselves. J.G., if you want further information on Swedenborg or The Church of the New Jerusalem, I'd be glad to help you.

**"The human mind is like soil,
whose quality depends on its cultivation."**
Heaven and Hell #356

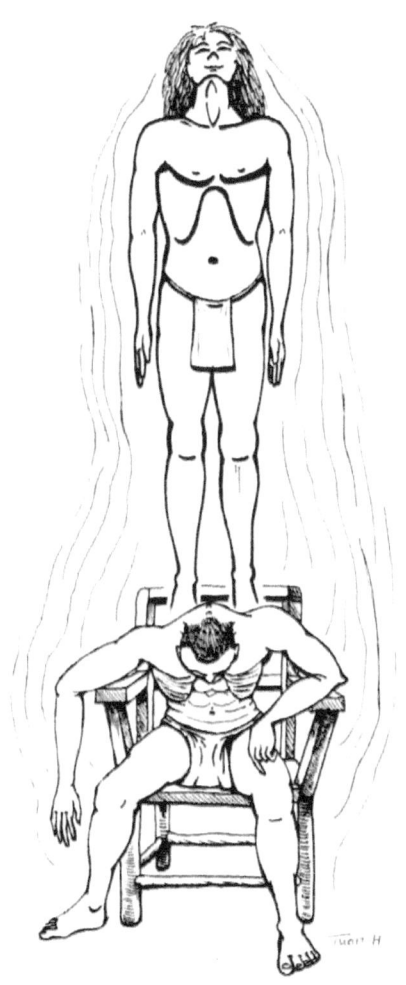

"When [a person's] body is separated from [their] spirit, which is called dying, they are still a [person], still alive." *Heaven and Hell* #433

Drawing by Tuan Hauptmann

SILA June 1994

Dear Candace,
Now it is hard for me to get books on Swedenborg because Swedenborg was a Mason. Being so the prison doesn't see reading about Masonry connected with Islam, so I can't persuade the chapel to buy any books on Swedenborg for the Muslims. Masonic Rites is very secretive and the Superintendent is, or some other on the board authorizing the buying of books, are Masons.

Anonymous Inmate
Correctional facility, Missouri
February 1998

Dear Anonymous,

I truly am sorry your prison library will not stock Emanuel Swedenborg's books. The book purchaser is incorrect. Swedenborg was NOT a Mason! Please show this *SILA* issue to your Superintendent and inform them.

Your letter was written in 1995. Actually, you did not ask a question, but made a statement: *"Swedenborg was a Mason".* Even though I've heard that "fact" before, I didn't want to write a snap answer to you, but have spent a great amount of time researching the subject.

Freemasonry is a fraternal order based on guild practices of medieval stonemasons. Here's what *Compton's Interactive Encyclopedia* (CD-ROM, 1998) states about "fraternal society":

> The word fraternal, like fraternities, is derived from the Latin word for brother. Fraternal societies are formed for social, economic, and benevolent purposes.
>
> The first Grand Lodge of Freemasonry, probably the best known of the secret orders, was found in London in 1717.
>
> Lodges and other secret orders are primarily men's organizations. Women may not join the Mason, Odd Fellow or Shriners.
>
> The secret orders have a great deal of ritual at their meetings. Once initiated, a member may advance within the society in a series of stages called degrees. In one rite of Freemasonry, there are 32 degrees.
>
> Many lodges are benevolent societies. The Shrine, to which one 32nd degree Masons may belong, operates more than 20 children's hospitals in the United States and Canada.

It is a fact that Masonic writers have repeated from book to book that Swedenborg was initiated as a Mason in 1706, in a Scottish Lodge in Lund, Sweden at the age of 18. It is a fact that many of Swedenborg's friends were Masons. He travelled in high societies of many countries. In 1710–12 at the age of 22, he visited London for the first time. War had broken out in Europe. Sweden and England were experiencing poor political relations. Many of his friends joined Freemasonry to obtain secret and trustworthy political friendships to conspire against their governments. It is a fact that there is a Rite of Swedenborg. It was created around 1760, but not officially called Rite of Swedenborg until 1783. Swedenborg died in 1772.

Despite Freemasonry's deliberate secrecy and destroyed documents, Swedenborg wrote down a great amount, keeping copious notes on the mundane and the sacred. He even wrote down his secret thoughts knowing they wouldn't be published. (But, they were after his death.) And not once did he mention Masons, yet he wrote about every religious and political group he knew about with praise or criticism. One theory says, he was being a good Mason by not writing about them. But, not one personal letter he wrote to a friend, who happened to be a Mason, even carried a hint of a Masonic meeting time or dialogue.

However, Swedenborg believed and wrote about how we are now permitted to enter into the mysteries of faith. He published books revealing secrets passed down through the ages. If he was a Mason, I doubt he would have written such revelations.

Thankfully, some scholars investigated the Masonic rites of the past. Arthur Edward Waite (1857–1942) in *A New Encyclopaedia of Freemasonry*, pp. 446:

> [Swedenborg] connects with Masonry only in a mythical sense. There is not the least reason to suppose that he belonged to the Order, but the kind of concern in his Writings produced by Masons like Abbe Pernety led, unwarrantable enough, to the belief that he was himself a member, while this in its turn offered an opportunity to Rites manufactured in his name. Findel was a victim of deceptions on this score, and Reghellini, who incorporated with his own reveries every fable which he met with, represents Swedenborg as instituting a Masonic reform.

The book's jacket reads: "*A New Encyclopaedia of Freemasonry* is a combined edition of two volumes in one, and includes: The true connection of Emanuel Swedenborg with Masonry."

According to *Freemasonry in the 21st Century* by Don Bradley, page 1: "Masonry has two primary functions. 1. To create, educate, and train disciples. 2. To aid life on our planet through the use of ceremonial White Magic."

For Bradley, being a Mason is a high use and therefore not to be taken lightly. He bemoans the fact that many Lodges today have degenerated into social clubs where degrees can be obtained by making a cash donation. He claims he has seen too many Masons receive rank for social climbing or because their father was a Mason.

Bradley is one (of a few) Mason that has written in detail about the secret initiations into Freemasonry. He describes waiting at a door, in a cloistered chamber "of reflection", not much bigger than a small closet. It is painted blue, because according to Masonry, that is "the Ray color of love in this universe—deep, electric blue." He writes that ceremonial aprons worn by Masons leading the initiation are still used today as they were "about 930,000 years ago on the continent of Atlantis." It is claimed that they know "how to magnetize these aprons so as to shut off influence from the lower centers, especially the sacral center and those minor and major centers related to regeneration."

And he claims: "It could be considered dangerous to work the ritual without an apron. It is a Masonic crime." He tells us what happens after the initiate knocks on the door for entrance into the secret society, after being left in the chamber room.

But, Don Bradley reveals Masonic rituals, in this labourious cryptic manner, in several chapters of his book (page 32):

> The ceremonial dress is generally to divest the person of all m..and v...; h...w...k their eyesight; s... s... the r... h...; make the l...t a..m, l...t b...t, and l...t k...e b...e; and finally to place a c... t... about the n..... Well, to repeat what has commonly been written upon this subject, the divestment is to induce in the candidate's mind that money, position, properties, etc. are of the mundane world and not of the world of spirit—they belong to a different place of manifestation.

I have viewed two films on Masonry—Toth and Parsons Production, *The Freemasons* (1995) and the A&E Production, *The Unexplained: Secret Societies* (1996). Both re-enacted out an initiation ceremony to the best of their research. It is a staid ritual full of symbolism.

Taking place in windowless temples, the rituals for each degree are secret. The men take binding oaths not to reveal the secrets they share. Throughout history, there has been presumed preferential treatment to other Masons, in society at large, and even between cops and criminals that were recognized as fellow Mason brothers.

Yale University in New Haven, Connecticut has a secret fraternity called, *Skull and Bones*. Founded in 1932, the university claims it is independent of them, yet its students are the ones initiated into it by blindfolded capture from their beds. It, too, is ritualistic and full of symbolism using candles, swords positioned at throats, and a skull claimed to be Geronimo's. Some say *Skull and Bones* is just a debating society of the best minds of the country. But clandestine plots for power were reported to have taken place at the Tomb where they gather. Members appear to be moneyed influential "soldiers" in a secret war for power.

The obsessive secrecy to form societies for spiritual or worldly power is the antithesis of Swedenborg's Writings. He tells us that nothing we think or do is hidden in the next world. All is revealed. And as we regenerate here on earth, our thoughts and actions mirror our true inner thoughts and desires.

Swedenborg tells us that we have no power, but from God alone, through His angels. There is a danger in claimed power over outsiders. Even if a secret society says they are doing secret work for God, it is imaginary power from their intellect. Swedenborg wrote in *Secrets of Heaven* #9809: **"All the power of good is through truth."** What good is hidden truth?

Sadly, I am aware of a secret fraternity of Swedenborgians. New Church Militant (NCM) is a fellowship dedicated to evangelization, founded about eight years ago. It is not officially recognized by any governmental branch of Swedenborgians, but by a group of people that profess their spiritual work is military work.

People who join NCM are imitated in a ceremony and pledge to do whatever it takes to spread the Writings of Swedenborg (within the context of the *Heavenly Doctrines* as a guide). Initiation ceremonies have included fire, swords, camouflage paint, and blindfolds. Members are given dog tags to wear and most, if not all, never take them off as symbols of their task.

I only became aware of this secret fraternity, five years ago, when I saw dog tags on someone and asked about them. NCM was explained to me in a hush-hush tone. I was told I could join, if I wanted. Over the years, I have asked people about NCM and it was always presented to me as conspiratory. I believe that this secret fraternity (one that is not written about in mainstream Swedenborgian publications) is elitist and detrimental to espousing what Swedenborg wrote about. Intentions may have been for good, but power shared openly is power from God.

Masonry is associated with Swedenborgianism because several Swedenborgians that became Masons took their understanding of his doctrines, especially correspondences, and added them to Masonic thought. Over time, people thought Swedenborg contributed them. As Masonry continues in secrecy, so does the truth that Swedenborg had nothing to do with the Masons. The public perceives that Emanuel Swedenborg was a Mason. This is one more reason why the Writings of Swedenborg are not better known by the masses. Some may figure that Swedenborgianism is a secret society, not to be understood. Wrong! It is up to Swedenborgians not to be secret, nor create secret fraternities, but to tell the world, they can learn truths, too.

UPDATE

To my knowledge, NCM was disbanded sometime after the publication of the February 1998 *SILA*.

Personal computers were in their infancy in 1998 (no Google) when I answered this question. I have since found a gem online by R. A. Gilbert. On 14 September 1995, Gilbert (at that time editor of the lodge's Transactions) presented his paper "Chaos Out of Order: The Rise and Fall of the Swedenborgian Rite" to the *Quatuor Coronati Lodge* in London, England. It was published in *Ars Quatuor Coronatorum*, the lodge's journal and posted online, with permission, by the Grand Lodge of British Columbia, Canada. (http://freemasonry.bcy.ca/aqc/swedenborg.html) Robert A. Gilbert is a British author of numerous masonic and rosicrucian books and articles, and editor of journals in these and related fields. Excerpt:

> One thing is certain: Swedenborg himself had nothing to do with [Freemasonry] — neither with the late 18th century Rite that has come to bear his name, nor with its bizarre successor that is the subject of this paper.
>
> It is unusual to find such diverse authorities as A.E. Waite, the Revd. A.F.A. Woodford, and H.W. Coil agreeing on matters of Masonic history, but on this issue they are at one. Woodford states bluntly, "we deny that Swedenborg was a Freemason"; while Coil is equally positive: "Swedenborg was not a Freemason and at no time, had any connection with or gave any attention to the Society". Waite, for once, is both clear and concise on the question: "[Swedenborg] connects with Masonry only in a mythical sense. There is not the least reason to suppose that he belonged to the Order". A detailed refutation of claims to the contrary is given by R. L. Tafel in his *Documents concerning the Life and Character of Emanuel Swedenborg*, (1875), Vol. 2, pp. 735-739, and the only contemporary scholar to argue in favour of Swedenborg having been a Freemason, Dr. Marsha Schuchard, has yet to produce any satisfactory evidence.

Dear Candace,

You know, The Writings are an easy pastime topic to bring up with first timers for discussion. I always thought so till one day in one of my upcountry visits someone alleged that I may be dealing with a devil-worshipping cult! You can imagine how terrible I felt!!!

J.N.
Nairobi, Kenya
August 2005

Dear J.N.,

I'm so sorry you and your religion were attacked. I do empathize with you because I've been there as most Swedenborgians have, at one time or another. Those of the New Church faith are often labeled by other Christians as belonging to a cult.

Once when I was dating a man (not my husband), his older sister called him away into his parents' kitchen for a chat without me. I thought it odd, but didn't follow them. Later, he told me, she informed him, I was in a cult and showed him copied pages from Walter Ralston Martin's book, *The Kingdom of the Cults*. She didn't scare him off dating me as she had hoped because he had already been to church with me and observed no cultism.

Now, saying New Church people are devil-worshippers as your accuser did is just laughable. S/he is not only ignorant of who we worship—Jesus Christ, the Lord—but, obviously only repeating what they were told! S/he's not thinking for themself and that is one sign of being in a cult. Now, isn't that a twist? Do you know that when someone points a finger at you, they are also pointing three fingers back at themselves?!!!

Cults are usually labeled from a traditional Christian definition—any group that deviates from their Biblical, orthodox, historical Christianity; e.g. one that denies the Deity of Christ, His physical resurrection, His personal and physical return to earth, and salvation by faith alone.

Cults can also be labeled universally—any group led by one individual considered to be extremist or false through psychological, commercial, or educational paths not necessarily Biblically based. The group will claim to be the only way to God or Paradise, using thought reform or mind control techniques to gain control and keep their members.

I find this statement by Leo Pfeffer (1910–1993) true: "...if you believe in it, it is a religion or perhaps 'the' religion; and if you do not care one way or another about it, it is a sect; but if you fear and hate it, it is a cult." Leo Pfeffer, the 20th century's leading legal proponent of separation of church and state, was born in Hungary and came to the United States at the age of two. The Fellowship of Reconciliation presents an annual Pfeffer Peace Prize to honour those around the world committed to working for peace with justice.

Swedenborg writes a little about cults, at least in the English translations— I don't know what word he used in Latin. He talks about the cult of Catholic saints, the cult of Mohammedans, the cult of idols, and the cult of self-love. So, basically Swedenborg is saying anyone or anything that is worshipped that is not Jesus Christ the Lord is a cult. Wow!

Now, this includes Christians who believe in God and His Son as two Gods! For it's not enough to say you believe in God. You have to say who your God is. Swedenborg wrote in *True Christian Religion* #634: **"But the truth must be told. When a belief in three Gods was introduced into Christian churches, which was done at the time of the Nicene Council, they banished every good of charity and every truth of faith, because these two are wholly inconsistent with a mental worship of three Gods and a simultaneous oral worship of one God; for the mind then denies what the mouth utters, and the mouth denies what the mind thinks; and the result is that there is neither a belief in three Gods nor a belief in one God."**

In a search on the Internet to see if Swedenborgians are listed as cultists, other than by Walter Martin, I came across these three sites:

1) Christian Apologetics & Research Ministry (www.carm.org) states Swedenborg: "Denies the Vicarious Atonement, the Trinity, and deity of the Holy Spirit. In 1744 he was stricken with a severe delirium which seems to have affected his mind for the rest of his life since many trance states were attributed to him as his life progressed. This is a dangerous mystical non-Christian religion. Its denial of the Trinity and the Holy Spirit, the vicarious atonement, and rejection of Acts and the Pauline epistles clearly set it outside of Christian orthodoxy."

2) Jude Ministries (www.judeministries.org) states Swedenborgians: "...believe in astral projection and automatic handwriting, that all religions lead to God (pluralism!), that one may sin in heaven, there is no physical resurrection, and there is marriage in heaven.

Here is a prime example of the dominant leadership of a cult founder. Not only did Swedenborg rule the cult when he was alive, but he still rules some 250 plus years later! This helps to explain the immense immorality of many cults. The morals of one person changes the view points of entire groups."

3) Troy Brooks (www3.telus.net/trbrooks/swedenborg.htm) states: "Emanuel Swedenborg was Definitely Unsaved. E. Swedenborg was NOT a Christian, therefore, he is going to hell. Apparently, he is considered as having the highest IQ of anyone in Christiandom (not everyone in Christiandom is saved), yet based on what he believes, there is no way he could be saved. It just goes to show you that spiritual knowledge (in your spirit) and regeneration is not related to human intelligence. The cult of Swedenborg's (new idea) teachings bear false witness against the Bible, misreading it, and altering it (Revelation 22.18, 19).

The general tactic of Swedenborg's unethical conduct is to claim a new idea that was already in the Bible for his own self-exaltation. He goes further to teach outright false teachings too like modalism. It is amazing how someone so smart could be so sinful, not entering new birth, nor able to overcome in life without entering that narrow gate. Now compare the writings of Watchman Nee, who also was considered as having an off-the-charts IQ. However, Nee was one of the uttermost spiritual Christians that ever lived. Compare their consciences."

I looked on the Internet and learned that Watchman Nee (1903–1972) born in China was a Christian Scientist.

The opinions above ARE mostly true—but Swedenborg never formed a church or group when he was alive; he didn't do automatic handwriting; and I doubt he's in hell! The doctrines listed above are fair summaries. Ironically, I have heard of people becoming Swedenborgians BECAUSE of similar said statements. Instead of scaring people away from the Writings of Swedenborg—learning that he says all religions lead to God, there is marriage in heaven, there won't be a physical Second Coming—the alarmists have interested people to seek more from Swedenborg!

There are genuine cults in the world that have selfish, cruel, brutal, sadistic, controlling, brilliant megalomaniacs at their helms. Unfortunately, we see them destroy themselves and others on the news all the time. Swedenborg wasn't one of them, nor are his followers worshipping him or the devil—only Jesus Christ.

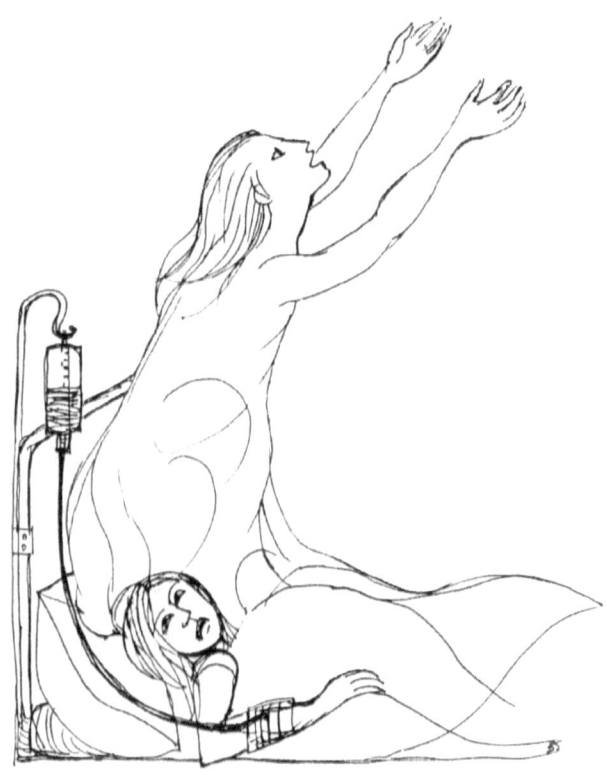

Drawing by Bridget Swinton

Chapter 6

IT'S NOT DIFFICULT TO GET INTO HEAVEN

Dear Candace,
What are you doing concerning the salvation message? It would be much appreciated if you could kindly furnish me with detailed information on your golden task and to also send to me related publications on the New Christianity.

T.Z.
Accra-North, Ghana
March 2001

Dear T.Z.,
Many religions focus on salvation as a conversion or a commitment—a definite assurance that one has been saved.
The Writings of Swedenborg teach that regeneration is a life-long process of looking to the Lord, shunning evils because they are sins against Him, and doing good acts because they are useful.
Swedenborg says that we cannot know if we are saved or not. We are to go to the Lord in daily prayer and have complete trust in Him. Remember, we chose either heaven or hell for our eternal home.

Dear Candace,

Enjoy your newsletter. Just finished my introduction to Swedenborg with Heaven and Hell. *Now I need more information. What are his reflections on suicide?*

G.T.
Sherman Oaks, California
January 1990

Dear G.T.,

We know Swedenborg "reflected" on suicide from his diary. He kept a 20-year diary, starting in 1746, to record his numerous spiritual experiences. Swedenborg saw things and events happening in the spiritual world and wrote them down. He never intended for these notes to be published, but many of his spiritual experiences recorded in his diary were used by him in books he did publish. His diary, called by his heirs, *"Memorabilia",* was not published until 1843 (he died in 1772) and was titled, *The Spiritual Diary.*

In *The Spiritual Diary* #1336, Swedenborg wrote how he saw a man in the world of spirits who had committed suicide by stabbing himself with a knife. The man had woken in the next life with the knife in his hand! He couldn't get rid of it, even though he desperately wanted to. At the same time, he wanted to stab himself to death again (spurred on by evil spirits). Swedenborg wrote that whatever happens in life, continues in the next life!

The Writings say that to kill is wrong as it is stated in the Ten Commandments. Suicide is killing one's self. It should not be done. But, since the Lord is all love and all mercy, and wills for everyone to live in heaven to eternity, He cannot damn anyone to hell, no matter what they do. (Only those that choose hell, go there.) If someone commits suicide from a good motive (only known by the Lord), they are forgiven, for the Lord sees a person's motive behind any act.

But, do we think we know better than God what's happening in our miserable lives?! Do we think, *All I have to do is pull this trigger and it's all over?* Can we play God? Swedenborg tells us, that if there is no longer a use being served by our living on earth, the Lord will take us from here SOMEHOW. Why don't we trust Him? On a higher level, to kill means to be rashly angry at the Lord.

How can one's self be destroyed by a misguided act such as suicide? Life isn't over after suicide. Whatever we were dealing with, which led to suicide, will still be with us when we live on in the afterlife. Suicide solves nothing as Swedenborg attested seeing that frustrated man carrying around his own murder weapon. Not until that man resolves his problems, will he be able to drop the knife and resume living healthfully.

Dear Candace,

As usual, I read your SILA *with interest. You are completely right (April) that Swedenborg says that repentance or self-examination should be done once or twice a year. However, in the* Doctrine of Life *Swedenborg says that a sincere effort to overcome or "resist" something negative in us* **"should be made once in a week, or twice in a month"** *(#97). This is practical advice that involves acting upon insights that have come through repentance, connected with a promise that one will "perceive a change" in oneself. I have definitely experienced this in my own journey. It is an important element towards spiritual advancement or regeneration, which we have to do as if of ourselves. It is not only the actions, but especially the deeper motivations that need to be examined with increasing sensitivity, especially our inclination to anger or resentment. Only then will we be able to really love.*

The goal of all this is a change in attitude and action, and only this is the real proof of its usefulness. This is an entirely different understanding of repentance than in wide traditions of religion. Not to feel self-pity or self-abasement (contrition) is the ideal, but to start courageously every time with beginning a new life, always asking for the help of the Lord. As it is in all the 12-step programs, we have to realize that of ourselves we can not accomplish anything, but we can increasingly develop a feeling of strength when we are close to God and receive some of His energy towards changing ourselves. Through this we can make important contributions to a change in the world. Any real change is hardly going to come by changes in our society, as Communism teaches. All progress has to begin in the individual, and this will radiate out into greater insight, responsibility, and capacity to love. Only then will the rates of criminality go down, and our frightening proneness to violence.

We cannot change others, but have to work first in line on ourselves, and all education has to begin with this main point—how easily this is forgotten! The help of the Lord is dependent upon, how much progress we make in genuine humility, in not taking any credit or merit for ourselves, but to attribute all power and strength to God alone.

Rev. Horand K. Gutfeldt, Ph.D.
New Church minister
Berkeley, California
June 1994

Dear Rev. Gutfeldt,

As you know, but to educate readers, *The Doctrine of Life* you refer to, is a dissertation that Swedenborg wrote in 1763. He published it in Amsterdam, Holland. It is only 67 pages long. In 1838, it was translated into English from its original Latin, along with three other doctrinal dissertations and bound together as one book, *The Four Doctrines,* which has gone through 51 printings. The four doctrines are:

- *Doctrine of the Lord for the New Jerusalem*
- *Doctrine of the Sacred Scripture for the New Jerusalem*
- *Doctrine of Life for the New Jerusalem*
- *Doctrine of Faith for the New Jerusalem*

It was Swedenborg's custom to number his paragraphs for cross referencing. (The age before computers.) *Doctrine of Life* has 114 numbered paragraphs. Keep in mind, Swedenborg wrote longgg paragraphs. (A common complaint of his readers.) He also numbered several paragraphs under one number for continuity.

Doctrine of Life #96: "A [person] who fights against evils cannot but do so as if from [oneself], for one who does not fight as if from [oneself] does not do so at all, but stands like an automation that sees nothing and does nothing; and from evil they are continually thinking in favor of evil, and not against it. But it is important to know that it is the Lord alone who fights in [a person] against their evils, and that it only appears to the [person] that they themselves are doing the fighting; and also that the Lord wills that it should so appear to them, because without this appearance no combat takes place and therefore no reformation."

Doctrine of Life #97: "This combat is not severe except in the case of those who have given free rein to their lusts, and have indulged them of set purpose; and also in the case of those who have stubbornly cast off the holy things of the Word and of the church. With others it isn't severe; let them even once in a week, or twice in a month, resist the evils they are inclined to, and they will perceive a change."

Rev. Gutfeldt, I am glad you pointed out that self examination alone is not enough. Self examination, once or twice a year, is the big picture. The resisting of evils, once a week, or twice a month, is the actual work that needs to be done. This explains why most can't keep their New Year's resolutions! Thanks for a great letter.

Emanuel Swedenborg's Masterpiece and Global Best-seller

Heaven *and* Hell

Continuously in print for 250 years!
Translated into twenty-three languages.

Heaven and Hell / Emanuel Swedenborg
George F. Dole, *translator* / *Introduction by* Bernhard Lang
978-0-87785-475-3, hc, 542 pp, $49.00
978-0-87785-476-0, pb, 542 pp, $15.00

Swedenborg Foundation • (800) 355-3222 ext. 10
customerservice@swedenborg.com • www.swedenborg.com

Dear Candace,

One of the babies in our group at work may not live much over 2 years old. This is so hard to accept and understand.

N.M.
Bridgewater, New Jersey
November 1990

Dear N.M.,

What a difficult process to witness. My heart goes out to you and the mother of the baby. You don't say what the baby is dying of—something the child ate, something passed on hereditarily, or some disease? It's not by Divine providence that this baby will die, but by Divine permission. The Lord does not want this human being to die prematurely, but He allows it.

God permits evil, so that people have freedom of choice. Someone, somewhere, somehow, exercised their freedom of choice (chose an evil) which led to a chain of events that will lead to this infant's possible death. Everything is interconnected. Unless evils were allowed to break out, people would not see them, not acknowledge them, and thus not be induced to resist them.

In 1771, Emanuel Swedenborg wrote in *True Christian Religion* #508: **"It is now allowed to enter with understanding into the mysteries of faith."** He dispelled many mysteries. Some unknown truths he wrote were:
- God can only do good
- all deceased baptised and unbaptised babies go to heaven
- all deceased kids grow up to young adulthood and become angels in heaven
- kids in heaven are not perfect

N.M., I agree this tragedy is hard to accept and understand, but it is lessened now that we know from Swedenborg's Writings what lies ahead for babies that die.

Dear Candace,

I continue to very much enjoy the SILA *newsletter. Over and over again I smile at the clear, uncluttered, but substantial answers you provide for the questions that you receive.*

Anonymous
New Church minister
Pittsburgh, Pennsylvania
August 1992

Dear Candace,

We appreciate the straightforward clarity and courage of SILA.

L.K.
Bryn Athyn, Pennsylvania
August 1992

Dear Candace,

Swedenborg's scientific accomplishments hold but little interest for me compared to his theological writings.

According to Emanuel Swedenborg, there are countless societies in heaven and when we go to heaven we go to the one in which we are happiest. He says it is our innermost or ruling love which determines where we fit in. This ruling love is derived from the life we lived while in this world.

Swedenborg says when we become an angel and go to heaven and arrive in our society of heaven we feel at home as if we were in the house where we were born. We are affiliated with the angels of that society and they are like ourselves.

P.H.
Hawthorne, California
January 1993

Dear P.H.,

Thanks for your beautiful explanation about **"ruling loves"**. The Writings of Swedenborg say the reverse is true when someone chooses an unangelic existence, by choice (not by birth or circumstances). They find their "home" in hell, and are (comparatively) "happy" there.

Dear Candace,

Greetings in Jesus' name. Well Candace Frazee, I'm reading through your [Swedenborg] books and have the belief that it can help me understand and apply the Emanuel Swedenborg teachings more.

I wish to inform you that your books which you have sent to me will become more blessing, because I will use your books to preach during a church service at my area and the message becomes powerful like a sword of God. Your books have been a spiritual lighthouse leading me.

Time and space would not permit me to share in detail what a wonderful blessing your ministry has been to me personally and also those who look to me for their spiritual guidance. My co-workers and members of our Christian fellowship groups throughout Ghana join me to say "Thank you for your ministry".

B.T.T.
Koforidua, Ghana
July 1997

THERE IS AN ANSWER

Dear Candace,

Your advice in SILA *today [June] was appropriate for me. I have read <u>very</u> little of Swedenborg, but I <u>have</u> read about Swedenborg instead. And I enjoy reading* SILA.

D.B.
Phoenix, Arizona
August 1997

Dear D.B.,

I'm glad you enjoy *SILA* and are learning about Swedenborg, the 18th century scientist and theologian (what a combo!) from *SILA* and other collateral works. You are not alone. Have you read *The Presence of Other Worlds: The Psychological / Spiritual Findings of Emanuel Swedenborg* by Wilson Van Dusen? It's thought provoking.

Dear Candace,

You are filling a need. All the letters in response to each issue of SILA *proves it. I also learn about different things from you I couldn't find out elsewhere. All Swedenborgians will attest to this. Even though I'm not Swedenborgian I know this from the knowledge I get. What do you think all your readers would do if you just stopped?*

W.A.
Jefferson City, Missouri
September 1999

Dear W.A.,

What a question! I can't answer it! It's curious. I am asked that question every year. All I can tell you, is that I plan on writing *SILA* until I reach the spiritual world. It delights me that you are getting much out of *SILA*. This is why I do it. One goal of *SILA* is to inspire a dialogue about Emanuel Swedenborg. If individuals asked their teachers, spiritual advisors, and friends, the questions they ask me, Swedenborg would be more discussed in society in general.

Chalk art by
Tiffany Vuong
at *The 12th Angel Festival*

Dear Candace,
  Look at June Reader's Digest *pg. 13 letter from atheist about prayer.*
                                                    Rev. Don Rose
                                                    New Church minister
                                                    Bryn Athyn, Pennsylvania
                                                    July 2005

Dear Rev. Rose,
  It's a good question! Here it is for all *SILA* readers to read. From the June 2005, *Reader's Digest,* Letters to the Editor section, about their April issue:

> YOU SAID IT
> Prayer Does Heal
> (Re: article, "New Proof Prayer Works")
>   Isn't prayer a paradox? As an atheist, I'd like to know how the religious think prayer works. Most Christians believe God is all-knowing and has a plan. So, if you pray to God to cure you of cancer, you're asking him to change his plan for you. When God hears your prayers and changes his plan, does that mean he was not all-knowing before?
>   NAME WITHHELD BY REQUEST

  This paradox isn't just one atheists have. It's one of those unanswered questions religious leaders say is just a mystery. But, Swedenborg has answered it for us because he was allowed to not only meet the Lord, but to also see into the spiritual world. He wrote that he saw some prayers reaching into heaven as foul stenches, rising up like incense. Wow! Think about it. Everything has a correspondence, as he says, and selfish prayers look like smoke and stink! (See *True Christian Religion* #108) Here's a big secret: God does not cure natural illness through prayer.
  First: God's plan is for everyone to live with Him in heaven and to be happy. That's it.
  Second: God is unchanging. He is love and wisdom and to the degree we accept Him, we get close to Him.
  Third: Prayers are for us to change our ways, not to change God's ways.
  An atheist is a person who denies God and blasphemes the holy things of His Word and of the Church. Many claiming to be atheists aren't atheists, only unwilling to accept by faith alone what current churches say who God is. For dogma only enters memory and not any understanding. Swedenborg says that non-believers are either foolish or atheist.
  True atheists don't believe in the existence of God—saying nature is the creator—and even hate **"especially those who acknowledge the Lord."** (See *Apocalypse Explained* #951*)*
  Swedenborg wrote in his 2-volume work, *True Christianity* #771: **"I have been allowed not only to talk with spirits and angels, with relations and friends, even with kings and princes, who have met their end in the natural world, but also to see the astonishing sights of heaven, and the pitiful sights of hell. So I have seen how people do not pass their time in some place deep in the earth, nor**

flit around blind and dumb in the air or in empty space, but live as human beings in a substantial body, in a much more perfect state, if they come among the blessed, than they experienced previously when living in material bodies.

So to prevent people from plunging yet deeper into erroneous ideas about the destruction of the sky we see and the earth we live on, and consequently about the spiritual world, as the result of ignorance, which leads to worshipping nature and this automatically to atheism—something which at the present time has begun to take root in the inner rational minds of the learned—to prevent then atheism from spreading more widely, like necrosis in the flesh, so as to affect as well the outer mind which controls speech, I have been commanded by the Lord to make known various things which I have seen and heard. These include heaven and hell, the Last Judgment, and the explanation of Revelation, which deals with the Lord's coming, the former heaven and the new heaven, and the holy Jerusalem. If my books on these subjects are read and understood, anyone can see what is meant there by the Lord's coming, a new heaven and the New Jerusalem."

Swedenborg used this ornament in *Doctrine of the Lord*

Dear Candace,
  Were the people wrong in the Lord's time to disbelieve He was the Savior? The Jews didn't believe Him and they were the ones waiting for Him. It's a miracle that Christianity survived in an era without the Internet or press where most communication was word of mouth. That is a miracle. And even that Islam survived.

S.R.
Truckee, California
December 2007

Dear S.R.,
  What a loaded question! No, some Jews weren't wrong for not accepting that Jesus was the long awaited Messiah, and yes, some Jews were wrong for not accepting Him. It's easy from our point in history to sentence them, but Jesus tells us not to judge...anyone. Are people today wrong to not accept that Jesus has come again as foretold?
  To expound upon your statements about how on earth religion survived, we have to look at earth history *and* heaven history.
  Here is the accepted earth history: The Roman Emperor, Constantine I or Constantine the Great (272–337 A.D.) was the first political leader to become a Christian. He was responsible for its continued existence.
  Though Constantine's mother, Helena, was a Christian, he did not declare himself a Christian until he was 40. When he was 41, in 313 A.D., Constantine made Christianity legal and returned confiscated church property to its rightful owners. He stopped institutionalized persecution of Christians in his Empire. They had been worshipping in secret before Constantine's conversion, for fear of death.
  Constantine changed the state religion from paganism to Christianity; it's more than likely he did it for political reasons. He made no distinction between church and state. However, to keep the masses content and to be popular with them, he kept aspects of paganism and combined them with Christianity. He kept gods portrayed on coins. The celebrated birthday of the Unconquered Sun God, on December 25, became the official birthday of Jesus Christ. However, the day of worship changed from Saturday to Sunday, to differentiate from the Jewish religion.
  It's argued that Constantine did not know what Christianity was, but that he only wanted and took power and wealth in the name of Christ.
  Arius (c.250–336 A.D.) from Libya was a popular Christian priest in Alexandria, Egypt. He began to espouse that the Son of God and God the Father were not equal; that the Son of God was a created being. His superior, Bishop Alexander of Alexandria excommunicated him (and his followers) for saying there were two Gods. Arius argued that that was what the Bishops were teaching already.
  In 318 A.D., Bishop Alexander advised Constantine to settle the dispute. The Council of Nicaea—all the Bishops in Asia, Africa, and Europe—convened in 325 A.D., in the Emperor's palace at Nicaea, to disprove Arius. That assembly reached the conclusion that three Divine Persons: Father, Son, and Holy Spirit, existed from eternity, equally. (Isn't that three Gods?)
  Here's what Swedenborg said about that time in history. It's when Christianity fell. It appears paradoxical that by the time Christianity was being accepted around the world, it was actually a dead religion. But, Christianity went from being

an Apostolic church where one God was worshipped—not a Son of God from eternity, but God born in time—to being a Bishop ruled church, the Roman Catholic Church. A church, where Jesus was only accepted, so that He would pity us humans and tell "His Father in heaven" to forgive us our sins.

Christianity, by the third century, had become externally rich and powerful, though, internally bankrupt and ineffectual. This is the faith that had been accepted by the Christian world from 325 A.D. until the 18th century.

Swedenborg tells us that heaven history records that after the Last Judgment, in 1757, spiritual freedom was restored. Now people can know Apostolic Christianity again. "The more" that Jesus promised He'd tell, he told Swedenborg.

The biggest thing to know is that there is only one God—Jesus Christ. Modern thinking cannot always be applied to old terms. Many words change their meaning over time, e.g. "nice" used to mean "foolish". The title, Son of God, meant a person who had a special relationship with God. Rulers used this title to denote their specialness or royal status. Even Constantine used it. Jesus was asked by some if He was the Son of God. He replied, He was the Son of Man. The common usage of Son of Man, at that time, meant "human". It was understood by the masses that He was saying, He was human and not royalty.

Swedenborg explains in great detail that correspondentially the term Son of God means His Divine Human—He came to earth through Mary and made that body rise and become Divine as it joined with His Soul (Father). The term Son of Man means The Holy Word—He allowed His body to be treated the same way His Word had been treated—trampled on, ignored, killed.

Swedenborg tells us Islam given through the prophet Muhammad (570–632 A.D.) was of Divine Providence in order to correct the then misunderstandings of God. Islamists were instructed to worship one God and were forbidden to worship saints and statues. But, the Islamist religion eventually fell, too, as it was not an internal religion for its accepted practice of polygamy. Swedenborg tells us that everyone in heaven is married—one male to one female.

Because the Lord wants everybody to go to heaven, He shows Himself to prophets, so that He will be understood. (He keeps trying to reach us!) God does not hate sinners as some would have you believe. He only loves.

The Book of Revelation is the last book of the Christian faith and because of that book Christianity survived. Not because of Constantine!

Here's why: John, an apostle of Jesus was the only apostle to live to old age. He was eventually banished to the Isle of Patmos in the Aegean Sea without any food. There, he saw the risen Jesus and recorded those visits or visions in the Book of Revelation. Because of John's second testimony, Christians knew that Jesus was now living in heaven and Christianity lived on.

Most of Revelation is unintelligible to Christians today, for prophecy is never understood until it is fulfilled. The Lord's Second Coming has happened revealing Revelation's meaning through another prophet, Emanuel Swedenborg.

Biblical scholars agree that John the apostle and John on Patmos were different people. Swedenborg tells us no, the same person! He spoke with John in the spiritual world!

I can see how, S.R., in our narcissistic global world today, that you would think that survival of any religion is a miracle. That's because we are burdened down with self-matters and choose not to see the Lord. But, the Lord has made sure that He stays in touch with us or else we would all perish! (He works through His angels.)

Swedenborg's Writings don't have any unexplained visions or mysteries, only explanations. Granted, some of it is hard stuff to grasp, and lots to read.

But, read what Swedenborg wrote in *Divine Providence* #330: "**The nature of heaven is to provide a place there for all who lead good lives, no matter what their religion may be.**"

Heaven is filled with more than Christians!!

Dear Candace,

God created man with a choice to do good or evil. In doing so He created evil. Yet the thing is that with man's own conception of the definition of evil it is easily construed to mean that God is evil.

Anonymous
Dallas, Texas
September 2000

Dear Anonymous,

You are in freedom to believe whatever you want to believe. But, if you want agreement from me, I can't give it as I believe what Swedenborg wrote—God is pure love and pure wisdom. He is not evil, nor did He create evil. Dictionaries define evil as morally bad or wrong. Swedenborg said, "**in evil there is not life.**" (See *New Jerusalem and its Heavenly Doctrine* #81)

It may *appear* that God originated evil because He *appears* in the Old Testament of the Bible to be angry and vengeful. But, His evil temperament is seen from the nature of the ancient Israelites' perspective and not from God's true qualities.

It also *appears* that we live from ourselves. We do not, we live from God alone. Swedenborg wrote in *True Christian Religion* #490: "**Unless freedom of choice in spiritual things had been given to people, not people, but God Himself, would have been the cause of evil, and thus God would have been the creator both of good and of evil. But to think God created evil is abominable.**"

I recommend, *Debates with Devils: What Swedenborg Heard in Hell,* edited by Donald L. Rose, translated by Lisa Hyatt Cooper (published 2000).

Dear Candace,

I'm glad to read that Emanuel Swedenborg sees that all people can go to heaven by following their religion and being good people. That is a major change in the thought plan than I've seen in the past books I've read.

W.A.
Moberly, Missouri
September 2000

Dear W.A.,

Swedenborg tells us that all are predestined to heaven and none to hell. The Lord has no other will for us than that we shall become angels in heaven. He gives us all salvation by means of faculties and abilities to receive it, and the power to choose to receive it or not. So, if a person does not choose salvation and thus enters hell, it is their own fault and not God's. He wants us all in heaven with Him!

The Lord's love and wisdom are given to everyone no matter what their religion. If a person lives according to "a" religion, the Lord looks at their love and obedience to that religion, their motives and intentions, not their membership and attendance. Religion is how you live. Swedenborg wrote in *Doctrine of Life* #1:

**"All religion is of life,
and the life of religion is to do what is good."**

Mihye Salazar and her assistant create a chalk masterpiece at *The 12th Angel Festival*

Dear Candace,

I'd like to ask if you could say a prayer for me. I read somewhere in Swedenborg's Writings that prayers aren't always heard, based on worthiness. Since I'm not sure if I'm being heard maybe a prayer from someone who does get heard would help.

Do you have a study course based on Swedenborg's works? Do you know of any? Thank you for your time!

Anonymous Inmate
Correctional facility, California
February 2002

Dear Anonymous,

I receive many prayer requests. The supposition that the Lord will listen to me and not you is ludicrous!

Not belittling your sincere request, but I am appalled that religions don't teach that everyone can talk with God directly. We don't have to go through Mary, the Saints, or any religious person to get to Him.

Swedenborg asks us in *True Christian Religion* #651: **"What sort of being the Lord would be, if He were to look upon the wicked from anger, and upon the good from mercy and were to save the good from a feeling of grace, and damn the evil from a feeling of revenge?"**

When God was on earth, He was asked how to pray. Jesus Christ answered, **"When you pray, pray like this: 'Our Father, who art in the heavens, hallowed be Thy name, Thy kingdom come.' Matthew 6:9."**

Swedenborg writes in *True Christian Religion* #112: **"Is this not an instruction to us to invoke God the Father?"**

You do not need anyone to intercede for you. Prayer is a conversation with God. Your relationship with Him, your Father, is different than my relationship with God, my Father. He listens to anyone, anytime—walking or kneeling.

As for some prayers not being heard because of their unworthiness, that's true, but not for reasons you may be thinking. We are taught in Isaiah that before purification from evils, prayers addressed to God are not heard. Jehovah says, **"Woe to the nation that sins, the people weighted down with iniquity. They have vanished themselves back again; from which place when you spread out your hands, I hide My eyes from you. Even though you pray time and again, I do not hear. Wash yourselves, put away the wickedness of your deeds from before My eyes; cease to do evil, learn to do good. And then your sins will be taken away and forgiven. Isaiah 1:4, 15-18."** In other words, keep the Ten Commandments!

Swedenborg wrote in *True Christian Religion* #459: **"Those who without repenting only pray to God to forgive them their sins, are like the citizens of a city smitten with plague, who go to the governor and say, 'Sir, heal us.' The governor will tell them, 'What do you mean, heal you? Go to the physician and find out the remedies, buy them from the chemist, use them, and you will be cured.' So the Lord will say [to those] who beg for their sins to be forgiven without really repenting, Open the Word, and read what I said in Isaiah: 'Woe to the nation that sins, weighed down with iniquity. When you spread out your hands, I hide my eyes from you; even though you pray time and again, I do not** hear. Wash yourselves, put away the wickedness of your deeds from before my eyes; cease to do evil, learn to do good. And then your sins will be taken away and forgiven.' Isaiah 1:4, 15-18."

And the Lord also says in Matthew, that if one prays, one is not to be a hypocrite and pray on street-corners or public places so that people can see us. It is to be a private conversation with God. Swedenborg does tell us that there is no need to list one's sins before the Lord or to pray to Him that they be forgiven because the Lord knows about them already! Duh! It's so obvious once you're told. And sins don't get wiped out. The Lord *takes them away* when one stops doing them and then embarks on a new path.

I'm glad you asked me if I know of any Swedenborg course. Yes, I do! If you can't take any of the accredited courses at the *Bryn Athyn College of the New Church* in Bryn Athyn, Pennsylvania (www.newchurch.edu/college) in person or via the Internet, I suggest you buy the book, *Rise Above It: Spiritual Development through the Ten Commandments* by Ray and Star Silverman (www.riseaboveit.org). This is the best spiritual workbook I've ever read. You can read the book and do the assignments at the end of each chapter, alone or with a group.

Swedenborg is entombed in the *Uppsala Cathedral* in Stockholm, Sweden

Dear Candace,
THANK YOU so much for continuing to see that I continue to get issues of SILA even though I am not able to pay for them. I very much enjoy your most informative newsletter on Swedenborg. You contribute tremendous knowledge to the world through your work.

I have been in prison for 13 years. I have <u>deeply appreciated SILA</u> for many years now. Leon [Rhodes] and I always have considered you as one of the most "useful" Swedenborgians here on earth. <u>I mean that Candace.</u> You have even been considered as a modern day "Johnny Appleseed" in the way you spread knowledge about the truths of "The Writings". My first encounter with your work began in 1988. You do it in such a very loving and special way. I thank you with all of my heart and there is no doubt in my mind that you will be richly rewarded in heaven for your "usefulness".

M.G.
Beaumont, Texas
May 2008
(never published)

Dear M.G.,

Leon S. Rhodes (1916–2006) was a great friend to you and me. Leon was not only the editor of *The Bryn Athyn Post* and a motion-picture writer, but he also wrote *Tunnel to Eternity: Swedenborgians Look Beyond the Near Death Experience* (1996). The second edition has a Forward by Kenneth Ring—co-founder and past president of the *International Association for Near-Death Studies (IANDS)*. Leon's doing greater work now in heaven!

Leon's book cover as chalk art at *The 13th Angel Festival*, 2006

Chapter 7

LOVE

Dear Candace,
  Do you believe opposites attract?

B.B.C.
Los Angeles, California
January 2008

Dear B.B.C.,
  No. While the saying is catchy and a common belief, no one knows the origin of it. Maybe it was a romantic scientist for it is true, two things with opposite charges—positive and negative—will pull toward each other. On the surface that is what is happening with male and female attraction and the subsequent joining together. But, "under the skin", it is the similarities that attract. Many scientific studies have been done and prove that with married couples, it is the similarities in personality, attitude, and religion that make for happily married partners.
  Swedenborg writes that opposites are not differentiated as relative, but as contrary. The opposite of light is darkness, of heat, cold; the opposites in times and seasons are day and night, summer and winter; the opposites in affection are joy and grief, gladness and sadness; the opposites in sensations are pleasure and distress; the opposites in perceptions are good and evil, truths and falsities.
  Swedenborg says two opposites cannot exist together. A married man and woman, each, are mutually and reciprocally the complement of the other.
  Think of when a "good" female teenager dates a dangerous "bad" boy. Some will say it's because opposites attract. Not so. Look deeper and you may find that she is dating someone like her father, or is dating someone that does not value her because she does not value herself, for she was sexually abused or experienced something else traumatic. Similarities attract in love. We choose our mates (and friends) that are our emotional equals. (Don't judge. Be open to listening!)

Dear Candace,
My own deep subjective gut feeling is that somewhere on the other side is one 4 letter word that fits all: LOVE. Isn't it odd how there is always someone who will say, airily, "Oh, you shouldn't discuss politics or religion." & I wonder if they watch anything beyond sports, sitcoms &/or x-rated movies. What is more stimulating than a free flow of ideas?

J.B.
San Francisco, California
October 1996

Dear J.B.,
Your gut feeling is correct. Not only will we experience Love, when we get to the spiritual world, but Love is with us now. **"The Lord is Love itself,"** wrote Emanuel Swedenborg in *Heaven and Hell* #318. The Lord's Love even enters hell. It is constant and only varies as to our reception of it. We either receive His Love or turn away from it.

Dear Candace,
I believe Swedenborg's lack of a true love with a woman had a definite impact on his story.

W.A.
Tipton, Missouri
December 2001

Dear W.A.,
Possibly on his life story, but not on his theological books as you may be thinking. Swedenborg was rich, but lived modestly. He lived alone. He travelled alone. He was a favourite dinner guest of many friends. He paid for his rent, goods, and employees on time. He took his employment and appointments seriously. He never married, though was engaged three times. Swedenborg was able to write about marriage love because he met wives in heaven and whores in hell and wrote what they told him, and what he witnessed.

Swedenborg used this ornament in *Secrets of Heaven*

THERE IS AN ANSWER

Dear Candace,
You recently wrote in the [December] SILA *news, and you told us that ... "everyone in heaven is married—one male to one female".* Heaven and Hell *teaches us that "true marriage love" is to be desired, but here on earth, there are many married couples (myself included) that do not have "true marriage love", as Swedenborg defines it.*

I very much want "true marriage love", but if I do not find it here, will I have another chance in heaven? Buddha taught that here on earth, if a married couple are happy all their married life together, and are of the same mind, then they can be together in heaven. I enjoy all that you do, very much.

B.M.
La Crescenta, California
January 2008

Dear B.M,
Yes. We have several choices. One can never have been married on earth and after death marry someone in the spiritual world. One can be married on earth and after death marry another in the spiritual world. One can be married several times on earth, stay with one of them to eternity, or marry someone else in the spiritual world. One can be married on earth and not remarry after the death of their spouse, waiting to rejoin their partner with a belief in eternal marriage.

While Swedenborg tells us that in his time, conjugial love (true marriage love of the minds) was rare, the more that the Second Coming is accepted, he states, the more conjugial love will be known and practiced.

I'm sorry that you feel you do not have a true marriage. But know this: the Lord is preparing you for your eternal home in heaven with the perfect person for you. That you love marriage and desire marriage is the first step. Live in the now. Please don't dream about heaven, but live here on earth and work on you. Why is your marriage not true? I could ask you all kinds of questions, but, they may come off as accusatory. Only you can examine your motives. Maybe separation is best for you and your partner.

Remember, it is what we love that we are. Conjugial love is heavenly love, which is without dominion. Not dominating, but mutual.

UPDATE

Conjugial Love #226: **"Conjugial love can be present in one of the partners and not at the same time in the other. ...for one may fervently vow for [themself] a chaste marriage, while the other does not know what chastity is. ...Because their minds are turned in opposite directions, they inwardly collide; and if this is not the case outwardly, still the one who is not in a state of conjugial love regards [their] companion by covenant as an insufferable old nuisance, and other like things."**

Dear Candace,

Love to receive your pages!! The last one [January] included a question regarding marriage and I think in today's world it would be such NEWS that in heaven are not only angels, but that one angel supposedly is the spiritual "unit" of one husband and one wife who did become one and are in conjugal love.

Regarding this, I've wondered how Swedenborg can describe a marriage in heaven? Are there 'half angels' walking around in heaven or was this really in the spiritual world (before entering heaven)?

A.B.
Toronto, Ontario, Canada
March 2008

Dear A.B.,

Half angels, indeed! What a brave question! I love your innocent observation—out of the mouths of babes—as you reach angel age.

While it is easier to get into heaven than most people think, it is a process. Only a really, really, really good person can walk into heaven immediately. One would have to have been "an angel" on earth in old age—regenerate, Swedenborg calls it—that had already gone through the stages of getting rid of evil thoughts and materialism before graduating to angel-level. Swedenborg was regenerate; not from birth, and not when his spiritual eyes were opened, but in old age.

Being half an angel is a universal truth most have heard: *My better half. My other half. I'm only half a person without so and so.* Truth is we all are half-angels on earth or half-devils! After death, we choose our eternal partners and *then* enter heaven. When a man and a woman become one angel, they are still two individual bodies and two individual souls, but act and perform uses as one mind.

This truism has upset many, especially women over the last few decades: *How unfair it is to think of a woman as incomplete without a man!* If only people would understand that we are ALL incomplete until we die. And one is not less-than for never marrying on earth.

I think you are asking how Swedenborg could have described a wedding in heaven, since only married people are in heaven. The weddings Swedenborg witnessed were no doubt of children that grew up in heaven. He says deceased children grow up to **"the first age of maturity"** (18?) and remain that age into eternity. They marry. Their wedding is **"celebrated in the heaven where the young man resides; and he shortly then follows his wife into her heaven or to her house if they are in the same society."** (See *Conjugial Love* #411)

What about happy single people? Will they not be allowed into heaven? Swedenborg asked some angels whether good nuns went to heaven. They did, he was told. But, the sphere of conjugial love eventually gets to them and upsets them, so they leave and live on the border of heaven with others like themselves. Not necessarily only nuns, but people who choose to be celibate.

Fact is, there is sex in heaven and hell. It's not hard to figure out which sex is better. Kids raised in heaven don't know what fornication is.

The reason the desire to have sex is sooo powerful
is because we are desiring to become an angel.
That's why we shouldn't "fool" with it.

THERE IS AN ANSWER

Dear Candace,
   Starting from the definition of <u>distance</u> as the space between two objects or the <u>measure of separation</u> in place "explain": <u>true</u> distances are based on similarity or dissimilarity of Love.

G.R.
Lakeview Terrace, California
July 1997

Dear G.R.,
   Distance, any dictionary will tell you, is being separated or removed in space or time. Swedenborg says in the spiritual world **"the truth is there is no distance, but the distance is an appearance."** (See *Divine Love and Wisdom* #109) To those in the other world, distance is not real. Distance is really states of mind—of thoughts and affections. States appear as spaces and their diversities as distances.

   We on earth can have a sense of this true distance. We can feel our loved ones near us when they are far away, and people who are distant from us in their thinking and emotions can be sitting right beside us.

   In the next world, Swedenborg tells us, when anyone is thought about, distance vanishes and the person becomes present in front of them!

   This idea can be hard to understand because we are so bogged down in time and space, but sometimes, here on earth this happens; e.g. when we think of someone and the phone rings and it's them calling; a letter arrives from them; they walk into our office or restaurant; bump into them on the street at the moment of thinking of them! We are shocked that it happened, and we say, *"I was just thinking about you!"* But, this is spiritual reality. Distance is just an appearance.

   We may think that God is at a distance from us. This is not true. The Lord appears to the angels as a sun, but He is still *in* their heaven as the soul is *in* a person.

   We can even know our own distance from heaven by examining our private thoughts and listening to our emotions—what we LOVE. That's who we are.

Swedenborg used this ornament in *Secrets of Heaven*
Is that Swedenborg?

Dear Candace,
 What do you make of the Law of Attraction?

B.C.
Los Angeles, California
June 2007

Dear B.C.,
 Like Attracts Like? I agree with that. I know it from personal experience. But, more so, I believe it because Swedenborg said it.
 You obviously are asking because of the bestseller film, *The Secret* (released 26 March 2006) and its follow-up bestseller book, *The Secret* (published 28 November 2006).
 The Secret comes to us from a woman in Australia. In 2004, Rhonda Byrne read *The Science of Getting Rich* by Wallace D. Wattles (published in 1910) and was, she said, spiritually changed by it. Being a filmmaker already, she decided to make a documentary about "the science of getting what you want" and sought out experts to talk about it. Even though her film and book are popular, many are criticizing them as being simplistic, not scientific, and dangerous.
 Rhonda Byrne's style of filmmaking gives her film a supposed credibility to the subject. I can't call it a documentary because it's more an infomercial or infotainment. Critics report that "the" secret is not a secret at all, but recycled from many religious faiths. "Birds of a feather, flock together. Whatever you want, wants you. What you sow, you reap. What you put out, you get back. What goes around, comes around. You create your own reality, with your mind."
 The film relates that this secret—Law of Attraction—"has travelled through centuries to reach you." First written on emerald tablets, we are "informed", it was buried next to the pyramids in Egypt. Then it was dug up and carried from hiding place to hiding place by the Knights Templar—Christian military in the Middle Ages. It was passed to the Roman Catholic Church. Then banned, suppressed, coveted, and only known by a few, 'til now!
 This slick film promises the viewer that they can obtain anything they want—wealth, physical healing, healthy relationships. You can have, do, or be anything you want, if you practice the secret, we are told.
 Byrne's Law of Attraction doesn't care if you perceive something is good or bad. It only responds to your thought. If you are in a car accident, debt, or bad situation, you brought it upon yourself, she says. The secret is that you become or attract what you think about most. I do not agree with Rhonda Byrne's interpretation of the Law of Attraction.
 Here's what Swedenborg wrote about it. It means being attracted to what you love. He says that angels actually feel they are being raised up and attracted to the centre of heaven. The centre being Jesus Christ—the Sun of Heaven. His love emanates warmth and His wisdom emanates light as a sun does. The reason the angels feel this pull is because love has the power of attraction. Who hasn't experienced the pulling power of loving someone?
 Most people understand and agree that Natural Laws govern the order of the natural world such as light, energy, gravity, motion, thermodynamics, and magnetism. And that Spiritual Laws govern the order of the spiritual world such as free

will, Divine Providence, and adherence to the Ten Commandments guarantees spiritual life. The Law of Attraction is another Spiritual Law.

Swedenborg says that whatever a person loves, that is what they will to do. What one loves, Swedenborg says in *Secrets of Heaven* #10124: **"...does not linger as a concept within the power of thought; rather it passes without delay into the will and becomes part of their life."**

$$\text{Thought} + \text{love} = \text{action}$$
$$\text{Thought} - \text{love} = \text{thought}$$
$$\text{Love} - \text{thought} = \text{impossible}$$
$$\text{Action} - \text{thought} = \text{compulsion}$$
$$\text{Action} - \text{love} = \text{compulsion}$$

Swedenborg had revealed the Law of Attraction in his 12-volume work, *Secrets of Heaven* (published in London, 1749 through 1756). You won't find it called the Law of Attraction, though, but **"Ruling Love."** *Heaven and Hell* #478: **"A person after death continues to eternity such as is their will or ruling love is."**

Swedenborg teaches in *Secrets of Heaven* #5288: **"...that every single thought flows in from the Lord by way of heaven."**

Now, you can read many volumes of Swedenborg to learn fully about this doctrine. In summary: All thought from the Lord is good and is received by angels in the highest heaven. They "pass it down" through three levels of heaven to people on earth. It's up to us to either receive or reject good thoughts from the Lord through His messengers. Hell also has three levels. The lowest devils excite other devils "all the way up" to us on earth, to love ourselves over others or to love wealth without a useful purpose. They want to stop us from thinking about heavenly things.

Another secret taught to us by Swedenborg is that we are only free when we acknowledge that all good comes from God/Jehovah/Jesus/Allah/Lord. It doesn't originate in us. It originates in the Creator.

To believe that by thinking about something hard enough you will achieve it, as *The Secret* claims, is folly. In the film, you see a boy gets a new bicycle he'd wanted and wished for. In the film, you see an adult gets his bicycle stolen (even though he double chained it) because he feared it would happen. What you think, *The Secret* states, will happen. Swedenborg tells us that as long as we imagine we are self-directed, and think from ourselves, and have knowledge, intelligence, and wisdom originating within ourselves, we cannot have any perception of heaven.

If you aren't aware of the secrets of heaven, Swedenborg writes, then your **"...conclusions are derived merely from self-love and love of the world, and the pleasures these give."** (*New Jerusalem and its Heavenly Doctrine* #269) Isn't that what *The Secret* teaches? How to obtain earthly material things?

The Secret also claims that one can self-cure diseases. It goes one step beyond rationality when it claims that anything that happens to you, albeit bad or good is because of your direct thinking about it. So, if one is being raped, kidnapped, murdered, or abused, they aren't victims, but culpable in their misfortune! Aaahh! Perish the thought!

Swedenborg explains in great detail another secret of heaven and that is affections and thoughts are measured by distance. The more you love and think about something or someone, the closer it will be to you. The more you hate and don't want to think about something or someone, the further it or they will be from you. Not quite *The Secret,* is it? Byrne just doesn't know the heavenly secret part of the Law of Attraction—one's **"Ruling Love"**.

Thought alone doesn't work. Action follows love. If you really love something, you will find a way to be conjoined with it! This isn't romanticism. It's truth. Examine yourself and ask, *"What do I love?"* Is it possessions or is it being useful? If you love material things over doing good for others, you may achieve them, but not spiritual happiness. Think eternity not immediacy.

God provides for each of us what we need for eternity. One chooses to receive that provision or not. Choose wisely. What love rules you? Your love is your life. You're not just what you eat, you are what you love! What's eating you?

Drawing by Bridget Swinton

March 2003
Dear *SILA* Readers,

Richard R. Gladish, former teacher and principal at the *Academy of the New Church Boys School* and professor at the *Bryn Athyn College* (both in Bryn Athyn, PA) passed into the spiritual world on Saturday, 1st of March. He was *my* teacher!

Mr. Gladish taught me English for one semester when I attended the college in 1976. His style of teaching was enthusiastic and intimate. He taught me how to be a better writer by asking me, one on one in his office, question after question why I wrote this or that, and then would lead me to see how to write more depth into my work. Mr. Gladish introduced me to the idea that the more I read, the better I would be as a writer. That took me years to understand!

I started to write *SILA* in 1988. I never sent any copies to Mr. Gladish, but somehow he discovered I was writing this newsletter and wrote to tell me I was doing a good job. Then he began returning issues to me with my errors corrected!! But, Mr. Gladish never once corrected the content. He would write:

- "*I enclose two pages from your December issue showing some minor changes that you perhaps have already caught.*"
- " '*Than she'*—*not 'her'* ".
- "*But, tut, tut...remember our illogical language! When 'its' is possessive it has <u>NO</u> apostrophe.*"

It gave me great satisfaction (and him pleasure, I'm sure) when, by 1996, Mr. Gladish stopped sending back corrected issues. I had finally "graduated"!!! But, he continued to write me:

- "*Enjoyed your very complete and informative write-up of homeopathy.*"
- "*Enjoyed your June issue of* SILA *with so much interesting information about the artists influenced by Swedenborg's Writings.*"
- "*Appreciate all that you are doing to spread the good word!*"
- "*Right on!*"
- "*Keep up the good work.*"

I will miss Mr. Gladish's letters. I look forward to seeing him again when I graduate into the next world. I'm sure he will have new things to teach me there!

UPDATE

Richard R. Gladish (1910–2003) is author of <u>*A History of the Academy of the New Church (from its beginnings to 1966)*</u>; <u>*A History of New Church Education*</u>; <u>*Bishop William Henry Benade: Founder and Reformer*</u>; <u>*Richard De Charms, Senior: New Church Champion*</u>; and <u>*John Pitcairn, Uncommon Entrepreneur: A Biography*</u>.

Steve Lubanski, 1994   Me, Steve, & Honey Bunny, our first bunny pet, 2004

Dear Candace,

Congratulations and best wishes for happiness to you and Steve. Quite a surprise! We wish you all the best in the years ahead. We'd be glad to learn more about Steve, but perhaps future mailings will help. Perhaps Steve learned about you from SILA*!*

Richard Gladish
Bryn Athyn, Pennsylvania
April 1994

Dear Mr. Gladish,

Thank you for your kind words! I am happy. Happier than I have ever been! Steve and I met at a Single's Group run by a marriage and family therapist. We were both actively looking for a lifetime partner. Steve Lubanski owns *Open Road Bicycle Shop* and is a cyclist that logs over 12,000 miles a year. At the Single's Group someone came up to me and asked if I wanted to meet a biker that was interested in me. I emphatically said, "No!" By the end of the evening, we did meet, and I was happy to learn he rode a *bicycle*. We dated for a bit before I told him I was a Swedenborgian. I'm a strong believer in introducing people to the Writings gradually. Steve explains:

Dear Mr. Gladish,

In meeting Candace, I had no idea of her feelings on religion. It was not brought up on our first dates and if I remember correctly, I broached the subject. I was talking about my vague Catholic upbringing. The idea of having crosses everywhere was so negative—remembering Jesus Christ's death, not His life. And Candace mentioned her church had no crosses. This was something that made me feel her church was headed in the right direction. It was after this that Candace showed me an issue of SILA. *Whenever I have had questions that she has already answered she pulls out a back issue and shows it to me. This has been helpful. Along with my betrothed, I thank you for your best wishes.*

Steve

Thinking of you,
Candace

May 1994
Dear *SILA* Readers,

Steve and I were married in the *Wayfarers Chapel* at 8 pm on 21 May 1994. We were married in the most famous Swedenborgian church on the west coast by Rev. John Odhner and Rev. Carl Yenetchi. And in Swedenborgian fashion, I was not given away by my father (although he and my mother attended), but walked down the aisle with Steve—representing that we are two adults making our own decisions.

The custom of the father or another male family representative giving the bride away goes back to the time marriages were arranged and the bride was given to the person who purchased her! Swedenborg saw a few weddings take place in the spiritual world. He wrote in *Conjugial Love* #20: **"Came the groom and bride holding each other by the hand, and leading each other."**

I wore a red Oleg Cassini dress! This may seem odd in North America where 90% of brides wear shades of white, but in China brides wear red as do brides in India. I wore red because Swedenborg saw a bride in the spiritual world wearing a red wedding dress. He wrote the groom wore a radiant purple robe and a tunic of shining linen. The bride wore a scarlet mantel and underneath it an embroidered dress that reached from her neck to her feet. (See *Conjugial Love* #21)

Swedenborg tells us that the colour red represents love. (A common knowledge since the beginning of time.) Steve whole-heartedly encouraged me to wear a red wedding dress, but couldn't see himself in purple! Other Swedenborgian brides have worn red and I've even heard of some Swedenborgian grooms wearing purple.

But, bridal customs are hard for some to break. Many Swedenborgian brides still prefer the white gown. But, white gowns are a fairly recent tradition. Anne of Brittany was the first to wear all white in her wedding to Louis XII of France in 1498. It was a sign of affluence. Not until the Victorian era did it symbolize purity. But, not everyone could afford it. Most married in yellow or blue in Early Greek and Roman times as well into the 19th century. Brides generally just wore their best dress. During the American Revolution, brides wore red as a sign of rebellion! Unfortunately, the commercial industry has marketed the white bride dress as the finest. Swedenborgian brides of the future, after much self study in the Writings of Swedenborg, may soon be all the fashion in their red wedding gowns.

Steve and I did not pledge to each other: "Till death do us part." Swedenborgians believe marriage is for eternity. (A good marriage is.)

We honeymooned in Niagara Falls, Canada—the honeymoon capital of the world! Then we visited Bryn Athyn—with its famous cathedral; the only Gothic cathedral built in the 20th century—the main centre for Swedenborgians around the world. We toured Bryn Athyn's museums, history archives, Swedenborg archives, library, college, and cathedral. I hadn't been back there in 16 years since college. Steve and I are happily husband and wife.

Thinking of you,
Candace

UPDATE

Steve suggested we go to Bryn Athyn for our honeymoon. The assumption is that I dragged him there, but no, he wanted to go!

Steve is now my first reader. I show him *SILA* before it's published and if he doesn't understand it, I have to rewrite it, 'cause Steve is a wise man. Guys come to his bike shop just to get his opinion, on any topic!

I love our wedding photos because he's so dressed up and *clean*. He's usually in bike shorts; his hands greasy from repairing bikes all day.

Dear Candace,
I didn't know that Swedenborg saw a bride in red in the other world. I read the Writings [of Swedenborg] every day. I'm always learning from you.
Anonymous
Bryn Athyn, Pennsylvania
September 1994

Rev. John Odhner, me & Steve, Rev. Carl Yenetchi, 1994

Steve's bike buddies surprised us and created a bicycle wheel arch for us!
(Steve has invented and patented several bicycle parts. He has reinvented the wheel!)
To see colour photographs go to www.thebunnymuseum.com/bm_love.html

Bryn Athyn, Pennsylvania is about an hour from Philadelphia
www.BrynAthynCathedral.org

January 1995
Dear *SILA* Readers,

We were awakened by the phone Christmas morning. Steve's bicycle shop had been burglarized. The following day, Steve was awakened at 2:58 a.m.

"I awoke out of a sound sleep," says Steve, "with a tremendous urge to go down and check my shop. I kept looking at the clock. 3:02, 3:03, 3:04. I slowly tried to quiet my pangs of anxiety and go back to sleep. At 3:08 a loud noise startled me and awoke Candace."

"What was that?" I asked him.

"I've got to go down to the shop. I gotta check something out."

"What happened?" I asked.

"Something fell," he said. "By 3:20 I was in my van approaching my bike shop. Upon turning my headlights on to a side door, I found three men trying to break in. Just think, twenty minutes earlier, they would not have been there; twenty minutes later, the deed would have been done."

Later that morning, we discovered that a brass trumpet—used in one of our Christmas displays—had fallen down from the top shelf of a five-foot high cabinet. Steve now believes a "guardian angel" woke him to tell him to protect his shop. When he didn't listen to his conscience the first time, or the second, or third time, the trumpet was knocked to the ground. This had never happened to him before.

Thinking of you,
Candace

June 1995
Dear *SILA* Readers,

Since the item about Steve, my husband, being awakened by a good spirit, appeared in the January *SILA*, many have written inquiring about what was the outcome. I want to share two letters with you:

Dear Candace,

Something similar as what happened to Steve when he was awakened by that brass trumpet happened to me some months ago. I was trying to sleep, when I suddenly thought about writing a letter to a girl I know. I said, "Nah, nonsense." I did not know her all that well. But I could not let go of that idear. So I had to get up and write on a piece of paper that I had to write to her. I did, explaining that I really had no idear what it was all about, but that I was "ordered" to do it. The reply was sad. Her mother had just told her that she (mother) had cancer, and the girl, on that night when I was trying to sleep, had been in a very sad mood. She was thankful for the letter, as she did not feel able to talk about it with her friends. It's a very strange feeling, because the thought or idear seems so much as our own...at first. Well, got to go. Please say "Hi" to Steve, and keep up the good work.

Anonymous
Europe
June 1995

Dear Anonymous,
    Spirits—people that have died—that are living in the spiritual world are all around us. Good spirits and bad spirits. They are always sending us thoughts. You obviously were receiving a good thought and acted on it. You are correct when you say that the thoughts coming in seem so much our own. This is also evident with those that think they have lived in a previous life. The truth is, Swedenborg wrote, all good thoughts come from God through good spirits and all bad thoughts come from hell through evil spirits. We do not own either good or bad thoughts, until we act on them.

Dear Candace,
  Steve was waked up in time to save his store. Hope he got police to jail the culprits.

Richard Gladish
Bryn Athyn, Pennsylvania
June 1995

Dear Mr. Gladish,
    In January, Steve didn't think it was important to tell the whole story, but wanted to focus on the "angelic" visitation he believed happened.
    Thank you all for caring about the outcome of Steve's robbery. He explains:

> *Dear SILA Readers,*
>
>   *On Christmas morning they did make off with some merchandise. And my alarm company notified the police. I repaired the door. The next day at 2:58 a.m. I was awakened with an urge to go down to my shop and then forced out of bed by our trumpet crashing to the floor. My car headlights startled the three robbers prying the back door open again. They fled.*
>
>   *At 5 a.m. I went back to my bike shop again, and found three suspicious characters hanging around the area. They were all riding bicycles in the dark—odd. And in the way they ignored me, made me believe they were the ones who broke in and were going to try it a third time. To this day no one has been apprehended.*
>
>   *But, to me it's no longer an issue. In a way, to of had the experience, it was worth the evil that I encountered. I now try to pay more attention to thoughts that come to me from apparently nowhere.*
>
> *Steve*

Thinking of you,
Candace

December 1999
Dear *SILA* Readers,

Steve has asked me to tell you this story:

About seven years ago, when we were dating, we attended a lecture at *The Theosophical Society* in Pasadena. Steve, at that time, wasn't fully aware of everything that I believed in. He just followed me to the lecture because he was falling in love with me. I wanted to attend because I had heard that theosophists were interested in Emanuel Swedenborg.

About fifteen people were in attendance and sat on chairs in a circle. The speaker did not rise from her chair, but spoke about "wisdom" from a seated position. Then a man spoke about "wisdom". Then another woman. It became apparent that the lecture was more of an open forum for people to espouse their theosophical and metaphysical leanings.

I was a little surprised. I was used to more structured lectures with a topic. Steve didn't have any previous experience with spiritual lectures and didn't see anything out of the norm. But, it seemed to me that each speaker tried to outdo the last with flourishing, detailed descriptions of "wisdom". They became more preposterous and fanciful to me. So much so, that I started to giggle to myself.

I thought of Swedenborg's description of people he saw in the spiritual world babbling on about "wisdom" thinking they were in heaven with the angels.

Aware of how silly they sounded, I feared that Steve would think that I, too, believed what these theosophists were saying. I found I couldn't suppress my giggles anymore and laughed out loud. I quickly coughed to cover it up. But, couldn't stop. I really got the giggles. My obvious coughing over my giggles was so often, and loud, that the speaker at one point stopped and asked me if I was alright. I said, I was, and apologized for my "cold".

Realizing I had to leave, I got up, excused myself, and ran laughing from the room. I figured Steve would follow me, but he didn't! I hung out in the next room, giggling, and "coughing". Steve told me later that my laughing was heard in the lecture room. A man brought me a glass of water. I felt so guilty interrupting what they truly believed was serious. Fifteen minutes later, Steve excused himself, figuring I wasn't returning, and found me.

Steve loves this story because it was the one time that I broke my personal philosophy of not being prejudicial, or condescending of others' religious beliefs, and just laughed in the faces of some true seekers. And the story shows how Steve was willing to do anything for me—to enter spiritual territory uncharted before. I love Steve!

Thinking of you,
Candace

Chapter 8

ERRORS AND MISTAKES

Dear Candace,
   I find Swedenborg long, tedious reading. Could he be wrong?
                                                            Anonymous
                                                    Altadena, California
                                                        September 1996

Dear Anonymous,
   No, I don't think so.
   It is true that Emanuel Swedenborg was a scientist in the 18th century working in the realm of his own Swedish culture and personal assumptions. But, when he became a theologian, he recognized that science and spirituality are both valid—different, but connected. This was a new idea. A paradigm shift. After all, in his century witches were still being burned alive!
   World views change when science, anthropology, psychology, and history demonstrate new discoveries. A paradigm shift occurs when new data challenges a fact that no longer seems to fit. But, people (scientists included) are slow to accept the new. Often an old paradigm is still embraced even with glaring new data.
   In his *Heaven and Hell* Swedenborg wrote about voices he heard and visions he saw. A paradigm shift is occurring now in the 20th century that declares visions are real as millions experience near-death and out-of-body experiences. Not everyone believes these are real. However, the documented accounts (bestseller books) closely emulate what Swedenborg recorded three centuries ago.
   It is important to keep in mind that details of Swedenborg's life are well documented, not just by himself, but by others of his day.
   What I find amazing in my amateur study of Swedenborg's Writings is that they are proven right time after time. Not as Nostradamus predictions, but as an understanding of science and spirituality. And I see Swedenborg's truths validated in my own life experiences.

THERE IS AN ANSWER

There are many, many things that Swedenborg states as fact that may appear hard to grasp. I believe in centuries to come, we will know what he was talking about. A paradigm shift will shape our thinking and the new generations may laugh at our earlier assessments of Swedenborg.

Even though I understand your questioning him, I'm pleased you are reading Swedenborg. Maybe one day, you will see it differently. I suggest you try a new translation of his books. (I agree some of his writing is long and tedious. I suggest blaming the translator and not the messenger.)

Dear Candace,

Greetings to you, and to all Swedenborgian church believers who fellowship with you in service and meditations.

From here in Kenya we as your brothers and sisters comradely at Swedenborgian church faith, us pray that this letter finds you all uses in both spiritual growth and physical health and God is blessing you.

Where you endeavor to execute His commissioned service at SILA *ministry, Sister Candace, the purpose to write this letter is to assure you that here, I and parties, we do always read* SILA *and use it. We get excited with the wisdom and knowledge that God has put in you. In wisdom you answer questions and questioners are satisfied.*

In June 2004 SILA *answer to Anonymous, we are ever pleased. Here we persist in standing firm for the truth and warn unwisely people and rally them earnestly to contend in teachings and doctrines of Swedenborg's Writings.*

We and other members at Swedenborgian Church in Kenya, we love Swedenborgian faith and it is where we belong always.

Our prayer is that God add more wisdom and understanding as you struggle writing SILA. *We are happy to receive it from you.*

A.K.
Kisii, Kenya
May 2005

Swedenborg used this ornament in *Secrets of Heaven*

Dear Candace,
Did Swedenborg ever write something or see something that he interpreted it the wrong way, wrote it down incorrectly?

Anonymous
La Crescenta, California
January 2008

Dear Anonymous,
　　A few would argue most of what he wrote was wrong. But, those that have studied all his works will tell you, no, he was consistent. Three fascinating examples do come to mind, though:

1) Swedenborg said when a black man and a white woman have a baby, it is black (and vice versa). That was shocking to early readers! *Isn't he wrong? When a white man and a black woman have a baby, s/he still is a shade of black, so how could it be called a white baby?* In its full context, Swedenborg was saying that the <u>soul</u> of the father determines the <u>soul</u> of the baby. (*Divine Providence* #277)

2) Swedenborg said there are people living on other planets. He named planets in our solar system. *But, we have not found people on the moon or on Mars. Isn't he wrong?* Well, he never said he visited the planets, he said he met angels and spirits that had died from those planets. Could they not have lived there once? Or maybe it was not our moon they were from, but another planet's moon?

3) As a wife, I'm touched by one conversation Swedenborg had with (our earth) angel wives. They were telling him how they have a power to perceive what their husbands are thinking and feeling not only by looking at them, but by touching them. It's not instinct, but innate. *Conjugial Love* #208: " **'Although we are eager to disclose deeper secrets, we must not. It may be that you are revealing to people what you have been told.'**
　　'Yes,' I replied; 'that is my intention. How can it hurt?' The wives had a private discussion about this, and then said, 'Reveal it, if you like. It does not escape us what power wives have to persuade; for they will tell their husbands, 'Don't take that man seriously; these are fictions, jokes based on appearances, and the usual sort of nonsense men talk. Don't believe it; believe us. We know that you are forms of love and we are forms of obedience.' So reveal this if you like, yet husbands will still not hang on your lips, but on those of the wives whom they kiss.
　　They are secrets and some of them so far surpass your wisdom that the power of understanding in your thought-processes is unable to grasp them. You brag to us about your wisdom, but we do not brag to you about ours."
　　(Reference was to all males, not just Emanuel Swedenborg.)

THERE IS AN ANSWER

Dear Candace,
 I am rushing to let you know of LIFE *magazine's special double full issue on Millennium. They say it is Linnaeus, but look at the photo!*

Rev. Don Rose
New Church minister
Bryn Athyn, Pennsylvania
October 1997

Dear Rev. Rose,
 Glad you wrote. I was aware of *LIFE's* Special Double Issue (Fall) which is titled, "The Millennium". Thanks for giving me an opportunity to talk about it.

In 172 pages, *LIFE* gives "a chronological guide to the 100 most important events of the millennium". In addition, *LIFE* listed the millennium's most important people. "To get on this team, a person had to change more than just a corner of the world—he or she had to divert the great stream of human history."

No, *SILA* readers, Emanuel Swedenborg did NOT make the list. Of course, I think he should have. But, on page 137, Swedenborg DID make the list, in a photo. *LIFE* magazine declared Carolus Linnaeus as the last—the 100th most important person this millennium. But, the photo of him was not Linnaeus, it was Emanuel Swedenborg!!! I like to think of this as not an accident (Swedenborg said there are no accidents) but, providential. Swedenborg SHOULD have been included in the list and someone else thought so, too...

If we go by *LIFE's* guidelines, Swedenborg not only changed his corner of the world, Sweden, he changed human history through science, art, psychology, and religion. Documents and letters record that Swedenborg did influence many people of whom diverted human history. (See page 281)

The Swedish botanist, Carl von Linne, known in English as Carolus Linnaeus (1707–1778) was called the "Flower King". He created the scientific system of classifying plants and animals that is still used today. Most notably, he coined the term "Homo Sapiens". In 1739, Linnaeus founded *The Royal Academy of Sciences* in Uppsala, Sweden. Linnaeus and Swedenborg were not only, each, pioneer scientists, but in 1740, Linnaeus as president, invited Swedenborg to be a member of his *Academy*. Swedenborg accepted. It is of interest to point out that Linnaeus not only married Swedenborg's cousin's daughter in 1739, but they married in the Swedenborg family home! He married Sara Elisabet, the daughter of Johan Moraeus—who was Emanuel's cousin and tutor when he was young.

Without any knowledge of what went down, I can imagine when *LIFE's* editors were sitting around a huge table debating who to include in the list of the 100 most important people for the millennium, Swedenborg may have been discussed. His photo and bio may have been on the table. When his fellow countryman, Linnaeus, was selected, Swedenborg's photo may have been picked up instead of his. But then again, the research department may not have done a thorough enough job, because this isn't the first time someone has mistaken Swedenborg for Linnaeus, which is quite laughable for they are so different in appearance! (Albeit, the same white wig.) But, hey, I'm thrilled Swedenborg was "included" in the list of the 100 most important people for the millennium!

LIFE magazine, Fall 1997, page 137

January 2000
Dear *SILA* Readers,

I'm disappointed no one asked me a millennium question! I was ready with a well researched answer.

Yet, I'm glad no one did because it tells me *SILA* readers weren't worried about the end of the world happening or apocalyptic events erupting as some were. Swedenborg assures us in his Writings that no such end of the world will happen. Then again, maybe you were asking yourself that question and were waiting for my answer...

Over Christmas, I met a *SILA* reader in La Crescenta, California and she asked me why I didn't write about "such and such" or "such and such". I told her because no one has asked me those questions.

Ask me anything!

There are many topics I'd like to tackle and discuss, but I won't until a *SILA* reader expresses interest in "such and such" a subject. All the questions I publish are real. Be assured. So, if you are wondering why I haven't touched on a topic you find fascinating, broach the subject with me. I'll answer you publicly or privately.

Happy New Millennium!

Thinking of you,
Candace

Dear Candace,

I enjoy what you are doing. I have a question. Did Swedenborg question what he was seeing? Did he believe or doubt he was seeing the Lord?

Anonymous
USA
March 2008

Dear Anonymous,

When Swedenborg first saw Jesus, he didn't know it was Him. Swedenborg was eating his dinner at *Ye Olde Cheshire Cheese Inn* in London. The room went dark (only for him) and when Swedenborg's eyes adjusted, he saw a vapour leaving his body. When it fell on the carpet, it became "worms". (See *Spiritual Experiences* #397) He then noticed a man sitting in a corner that wasn't there before.

The man spoke to him and told him not to eat too much. He disappeared. The room became normal again. Frightened, Swedenborg went straight to his room. Later that night, the same man appeared to him. Swedenborg was not frightened this time. *Journal of Dreams* #54: **"At that same moment I sat in His bosom, and saw Him face to face; it was a face of Holy mien, and in all it was indescribable, and**

He smiled so that I believe that His face had indeed been like this when He lived on earth."

Jesus told Swedenborg that he was going to be able to view the next life before he died. Swedenborg realized that the creepy worms on the floor signified earthly things. He was from then on not supposed to eat so much of the natural world, but feast on the spiritual world!

Readers may doubt that Swedenborg was telling the truth, but just making it up. That would be okay with him. He would want one to investigate his Writings, to come to their own conclusions. After his second meeting with the Lord, Swedenborg never doubted who he saw. He saw Him several times over the years. *Heaven and Hell* #159: **"I saw the Lord as a sun, at first glowing and brilliant with a splendor that cannot be described; and I was told that such is the appearance of the Lord as a sun to the angels in their first state."**

Isn't that what near-death experiencers say, that they see a bright light—that doesn't burn or hurt their eyes—at the end of a tunnel? Some have said that the light was loving and they wanted to go to it, but were told to go back.

Swedenborg did doubt many things he witnessed in the spiritual world. Who wouldn't? He would write that angels explained situations and things to him. (I know what some of you are thinking!) But, read this letter Swedenborg wrote to King Adolf Frederik of Sweden (1751–1771), 10 May 1770 (excerpt):

"Most Powerful and Most Gracious King,

I feel compelled at this juncture to have recourse to Your Majesty's protection; for I have been treated as no one has ever been treated before in Sweden since the introduction of Christianity, and still less since the establishment of freedom here.

Should they reply that the thing is inconceivable to them, I have nothing to gainsay, since I am unable to put the state of my sight and speech into their heads, in order to convince them; nor am I able to cause angels and spirits to converse with them; nor do miracles happen now; but their very reason will enable them to see this, when they thoughtfully read my writings, wherein much may be found which has never before been discovered, and which cannot be discovered except by real vision, and communication with those who are in the spiritual world.

If any doubt should still remain, I am ready to testify with the most solemn oath that may be prescribed to me, that this is the whole truth and a reality, without the least fallacy.

That our Saviour permits me to experience this, is not on my own account, but for the sake of a sublime interest which concerns the eternal welfare of all Christians.

Since such is the real state of things, it is wrong to declare it to be untruth and falsity; although it may be pronounced to be something that cannot be comprehended."

While reading something in the Writings, I have found myself sometimes thinking, *I don't understand this.* Because I have accepted the Divine authority of the Writings, I just put my incomprehensions aside, knowing that I will "get it" one day. And sometimes, I do!

Dear Candace,

I have a question. The phrase "man was made in the image of God" is a phrase that I see is taken in its literal sense with all who follow Christianity and the Bible. You ever think this statement, rather phrase, is taken wrong? I mean I see it as allegorical and the basis for most of the misconceptions about the spirit world and the soul. Not to mention this human body. To look at the phrase in the allegorical sense would change a lot of theories.

W.A.
Newton, Texas
August 1997

Dear W.A.,

Genesis 1:27 states: **"So God created people in His own image, in the image of God created He them; male and female created He them."**

Swedenborg wrote that this statement does indeed have an internal sense as well as being literal. He informs us that when it was written, the most ancient people understood its allegorical meaning—that in a spiritual person, the *understanding* is called *male*, the *will* is called *female*, and when they act as one, they are married. This applies to every individual. We have to conjoin or marry our own understanding and will within ourselves, to be a complete human being.

Our understanding and will can also be called our faith and love. Swedenborg tells us to think of faith as the Lord working through charity that is in a person. Because charity is only the form of love.

Unfortunately, we all have met people that say they have faith, but it appears they don't live a charitable life towards their spouses, children, neighbours, friends, or co-workers. Remember, charity is only the form of love.

Swedenborg used this ornament in *Apocalypse Revealed*

Dear Candace,

A book with an unfortunate paragraph on Swedenborg was just published and is selling very well. The book is Other Powers *by Barbara Goldsmith, published in 1998 by Alfred A. Knopf and getting much space in New York Times. On pages 33 and 34 we read:*

> Many spiritualists turned to the teachings of Emanuel Swedenborg, a highly influential philosopher. In 1750 while in a trance Swedenborg claimed to have seen the spirit world and recorded what he saw there. In the heavenly society, all foods and services were shared, and men were permitted both wives and concubines. Swedenborg's vision not only fulfilled male fantasies but also exploited the nascent interest in science. He wrote that "the Spirit World is derived from atoms…disintegrating chemical action of electricity and magnetism which throws out ethereal particles into a great ocean of individualized spirit." In a like manner, in the 1840's a French disciple of Swedenborg, Charles Fourier, propounded Fourier's theory of "passional attraction" advocating free sexual relationships based on "elective affinities".

Although we have quotation marks, there is no reference, and although the bibliography is huge, there is no reference to Swedenborg. I can't think of an avenue by which to show that this is grossly misleading.

Rev. Don Rose
New Church minister
Bryn Athyn, Pennsylvania
March 2000

Dear Rev. Rose,

Thank you for bringing this to my attention. I agree those quotes are unfounded and misleading. The summation is faulty.

Why Barbara Goldsmith picked 1750 is a mystery. Emanuel Swedenborg (1688–1772) started to "see" into the spiritual world around 1743, if you don't count his childhood experiences.

Men, he said in *Conjugial Love* #462 are **"permitted concubines"** (but, not in heaven) and that it is deplorable and not a good thing. ALL evils are permitted by the Lord, so that we can be in freedom to choose them or not.

Goldsmith apparently wrote about Charles Fourier (1772–1837) — failed leader of utopian socialism — because he makes odd copy.

Some authors do lousy research or none at all! (…sigh)

Dear Candace,
   I am interested in vegetarianism.

                                                         A.L.
                                            Gothenburg, Sweden
                                                 January 2000

Dear A.L.,
   Many Swedenborgians have been curious and/or zealous about vegetarianism since Swedenborg's time. He wrote in *Secrets of Heaven* #1002: "Regarded in itself eating animal flesh is something profane, for in most ancient times [people] never ate the flesh of any beast or bird, but only different kinds of grain, especially wheaten bread, also the fruit of trees, vegetables, milk and milk products such as butter. Slaughtering living creatures and eating their flesh was to them abominable, akin to the behavior of wild animals. Service and use alone was demanded of those creatures, as is clear from Genesis 1:29, 30.
   But, in the process of time when [humankind] began to be as savage as wild animals, indeed more savage, they first began to slaughter living creatures and eat their flesh. And because [people] had become such, they were permitted to do so and are still permitted today. And insofar as they do so from conscience, it is quite legitimate, for their conscience is given form from all those things they presume to be true and so legitimate. Consequently nobody nowadays stands in any sense condemned because [they] eat meat."
   John Wesley (1703–1791), founder of the Methodist Church, was a contemporary of Swedenborg. Some of Wesley's followers in England left his church to study Swedenborg. Some of them broke away in 1791 and formed a sect—*Bible Christians*. This group strictly adhered to no meat and no alcohol, claiming Swedenborg did that. Other Swedenborgians investigated those claims and discovered Swedenborg, in his later years, ate meat seldom, and never drank more than two glasses of wine. A group of 41 *Bible Christians* immigrated to America in 1817. They built a church in Philadelphia in 1823. They became obsessed with abstinence. They admitted they read Swedenborg for information, but not for authority, claiming there were many contradictions in his Writings. It became less a Swedenborgian Church and more as one of the earliest temperance propagandists in America.
   Swedenborg writes that spiritually, food corresponds to knowledges or intelligence. In common speech one says, *"I'm hungry to know."* The more we know, and act upon that knowledge, the more human we become. House pets become loved and then we don't want to eat them. We see them as God's creatures with a life, and we can't imagine killing them for dinner. Cows, sheep, chickens, and others are slaughtered every day for human consumption. When we learn that these farm animals are routinely killed with shockingly bizarre and cruel methods, we may think we should stop eating animals. When we learn about the health benefits of not eating "creatures with eyes" we may attempt to cut back on eating "red meat" or not as often.
   The Writings of Swedenborg describe conscience as being a **"new will"** received from the Lord through the act of regeneration—spiritual growth. Conscience is to do evil to no one and good to everyone. Good people can get a conscience. Evil people will never have a guilty conscience! Not all consciences are

equal. Some are natural and some are spiritual. Each religion has its own take on conscience and Swedenborg tells us none of them are "wrong" per se. If someone lives according to their religion with a clear conscience that they are doing the right thing, they are being a good person. And good people can go to heaven, no matter what their religion. It's worse to say one thing, and do another.

Emanuel Swedenborg tells his readers that New Church people are to get a New Church conscience based on new truths. Some have taken that to mean we are to be vegetarians. Some have tried, and failed. Some consciously attempt to limit their animal intake.

A new spiritual conscience or a **"new will"** is created this way: A person is moved to change their lifestyle. It can be frustrating when they can't live up to it. Pangs of conscience set in. A spiritual conscience is being born. When the truth about something affects the person so deeply, that they have to act on that change, true conscience has been formed. The Lord then gives the person a **"new will"** to live by. And it will go on being perfected for infinity. But, Swedenborg also says that it is not evil to eat animals, unless our conscience tells us it is.

It appeared the *Bible Christians* believed that they were better than everyone else by their chosen behaviours. But, morality is a by-product of spiritual growth, not its source. The ideal is vegetarianism. But, it is an individual's decision.

No Swedenborgian churches, today, have a "no eating meat or no drinking alcohol" decree, that I am aware of. Some Swedenborgians have, however, adopted vegetarianism. I have; since I was 16. Steve became a vegetarian after he met me. Some don't believe it's necessary.

Dear Candace,

New Church vegetarians like to quote Arcana Coelestia #1002, *as did you in the latest issue of your newsletter, in support of their choice of diet, but to be fair and present a balanced view, one ought to cite also the following from* Divine Love and Wisdom #331: **"Forms of use created for the nourishment of the body are all constituents of the plant kingdom which are serviceable for food and drink, such as fruits, grapes, seeds, vegetables, and herbs. So, too, all constituents of the animal kingdom which are eaten, such as steers, cows, calves, deer, sheep, male and female goats, lambs, and the milk obtained from them. And also fowl and fish of any kinds."**

You did say that Swedenborg says that it is not evil to eat animals, but I believe Divine Love and Wisdom #331 *goes further and speaks of the eating of meat as a useful service provided by the animal kingdom. In other words, eating meat is not only not evil, it is something useful to mankind.*

Anonymous
New Church minister
Huntingdon Valley, Pennsylvania
February 2000

Dear Candace,

In the millennium's first SILA *newsletter your thoughtful observations about carnivorous New Church people reminded me of the little boy who asked his mother, "If God didn't want us to eat animals, why did He make them out of meat?"*

I am tempted to go even further and to marvel that to me it is striking that God also knew when creating our universe that those little shrimp are not only delicious when sautéed in butter with a bit of white wine (allowable) and lemon juice, with just a dash of garlic. I believe that it is not simply dumb fortune that people can enjoy wonderful (healthy) meals with just the right "dash of this flavor", "teaspoonful of that condiment" and "a bit of honey" (which was stolen from those industrious bees).

I think He knew that food could be a blessing, even though some might abuse it, and ALL of the animals were going to die soon and be eaten by the predators which He also created.

L.
Bryn Athyn, Pennsylvania
February 2000

Dear Anonymous & L.,

This topic has generated almost as much mail as the subject of Alcoholics Anonymous. Your letter, Anonymous, was the most concise I received, and yours L., the most humourous. You both have expressed your personal choice. Obviously, your consciences tell you that it is not only okay to eat animals, you enjoy doing it. That is freedom of choice. Thanks for sharing.

Your decision to eat meat does not change the truth expressed in the Writings of Emanuel Swedenborg—the ideal is NOT to eat meat, but it is permitted. It's easier for some to accept it is "not evil" to eat animals than it is better "not to".

The question of whether animals are useful as food is debatable. Vegetarians do not eat any beast, fowl, or fish. Vegans do not eat any animal product —meat, dairy, eggs, or honey. Certainly at different times in history some cultures have relied heavily on meat to survive. But, in today's global awareness eating meat is often cruel, unsafe, and expensive. If people had to personally hunt for their food, I'm sure many couldn't. Did you know that...? (Fact Sheet, PETA.org):

- ducks have pipes shoved down their throats, so they can be force-fed with air-driven pumps, three times a day, to create "pate de foie gras"
- animals are killed by boiling, anal electrocution, clubbing, or neck braking, but, are not put to sleep, painlessly, by injection like family pets
- animals are kept in cramped, filthy wire-mesh cages and fed slops of raw slaughterhouse waste with chemicals and hormones
- horns, beaks, and tails are mutilated or cut off
- more than 40% of the world's grain is fed to animals going to slaughter, while humans go hungry
- meat production uses up water and raw materials causing soil erosion
- some cultures eat family pets: dogs, cats, horses, *rabbits*

We all must re-examine the teachings given by Swedenborg for ourselves and apply them to our own lives. We are invited to live up to the ideals of marriage, and civil, moral, and spiritual conduct. Some of us have second marriages, some of us break laws, some of us commit spiritual murder, but we all are asked to live up to a higher standard.

Let your conscience be your guide.

UPDATE

The Internet is clogged with vegetarian and vegan websites that have lists of famous vegetarians which include Emanuel Swedenborg. It's not true! While he wrote it was how the first people ate and that it is preferred, Swedenborg himself ate meat. Actually, after his spiritual eyes were opened, he ate little of anything. However, when invited to dine as a guest, he always ate what the hosts had prepared, including meat.

The Angel Festival is a no meat zone. I permit only vegetarian food vendors. I tell them that we won't be eating meat in heaven. So, since *The Angel Festival* is heaven on earth for one day, we'll act like the angels that day!

Dear Candace,

We have been enthusiastic readers of SILA *for several years. It is lively, caring, humorous (at times), thought provoking, and "to the point".*

You have a special talent for taking a question (sometimes simple, sometimes convoluted) or a somewhat off the wall comment about Swedenborg, or a teaching from the Writings, and responding in a clear, concise, simple, and understandable way. This editorial focus has made your newsletter a delight to read.

B.&N.
Glenview, Illinois
February 2000

Dear Candace,

I don't attend a Swedenborgian Church, because there is none in the area I reside. Also, I haven't heard of one around. I rather received SILA *surprisingly one day and it has continued to be among my mail ever since. As to who introduced my name to you, I am at a loss. I only suspect one vendor of books who has been coming around our offices. I managed to buy some few Swedenborg Writings from him, so I'm sure he saw my interest in Swedenborgian literature and he decided to send you my name.*

Anyway SILA *serves my purpose since I am a preacher at a local Spiritual Church. Although as much as I would like to have more of the Swedenborg books they are not easy to come by. So* SILA *becomes a substitute which helps with the explanation of some spiritual points to the congregation. I also learn a lot from Dear Swedenborg's spiritual revelations. God bless you.*

D.B.
Accra, Ghana
January 1998

Dear Candace,

In reading the December SILA *I came across something that I thought you might find interesting. I was reading the interpretation of the 4th commandment and it didn't seem to be as I remembered it. I went to the source material and found that in* True Christian Religion *the interpretation is exactly what you have indicated, but I kept on looking and found that in #67 of the* "Doctrine of the Holy Scripture" *(from* The Four Doctrines*) there is also an interpretation given of the various sense of that commandment.*

The natural and spiritual senses are described essentially the same as in True Christian Religion, *but the celestial sense is not. To quote from that number:* **"And a celestial angel understands the Lord's Divine love by 'father,' and His Divine wisdom by 'mother,' and by to 'honor' to do what is good from Him."**

It appears that Swedenborg came up with different interpretations at different times in his writings. It sure would be nice to have him on hand to ask about it. I think that I remembered the version that I quoted above because The Four Doctrines *was one of the first of Swedenborg's books that I read while* True Christian Religion *came very late in my reading of Swedenborg's work.* The Four Doctrines *was very important to me because the Biblical references given in it convinced me that the indicated doctrines were in accordance with and from the Word and hence that this was a new revelation from God.*

I believe that, spiritually speaking, one becomes a member of a church when he believes its teachings and lives according to them. I mark the time of my reading The Four Doctrines *and accepting them as true as the time of my entry into the Lord's New Church.*

R.R.
Yorba Linda, California
February 2001

Dear R.R.,

Your observation that Swedenborg "came up with different interpretations" is a common misconception. I asked my good friend, (New Church) Rev. George McCurdy, in Bryn Athyn, PA how to answer you.

> *Dear Candace,*
>
> *He asks a good question.*
>
> *Good in the sense that it offers us an opportunity to advise those who study the Writings of Swedenborg.*
>
> *I am amazed that Swedenborg was able to be so consistent in his role as a servant of the Lord. Thousands or myriad of ideas flowing in from the Lord. Angels expressing things in a few words that would take us paragraph after paragraph to explain. How could he stay so focused on the truth? How could he keep from being frustrated with things seen and heard that were beyond expression in human words?*
>
> *To do a thorough study of the Writings we need to collect as many passages on a given topic as possible before making a judg-*

ment. *A full study of any topic helps to avoid pulling something out of context. We are urged to love truth for truth's sake.*

The question posed offers a perfect example of our need to check all teachings before coming to any conclusion. The reader compares the Doctrine of Sacred Scriptures *with* True Christian Religion. *He tries to match the two side by side and he comes up with what he thinks is a possible inconsistency. A seemingly good observation for the moment.*

What about the Apocalypse Explained *reference to the fourth commandment?* Apocalypse Explained *#966:2 not only agrees with the* Doctrine of Sacred Scriptures, *but also offers us a possible insight as to why the* True Christian Religion *wording would differ.* **"The Lord gives life from Himself and through the Church He gives nourishment."**

What is life from the Lord? His Love. What is the nourishment the church receives? His Truth.

But, then that number goes on to explain what the Father represents and what the Mother represents. For me, the Apocalypse Explained *quote gives meaning and explanation as to why the* True Christian Religion *passage would have a slight "change" of wording.*

I'd also like to call the reader's attention to True Christian Religion *#88. There we read* **"By the Father the Divine good is meant."** *So* True Christian Religion *carries the same message as the* Doctrine of Sacred Scriptures.

One last note to your reader. Check out the wonderful references the Apocalypse Explained *number gives in the* Arcana Coelestia [Secrets of Heaven] *for the meaning of Father and Mother. Checking them out is of great importance so that consistency of the Writings can be seen and appreciated.*

THANK YOU George, for sharing your years of studying the Writings.

Swedenborg used this ornament in Secrets of Heaven

Dear Candace,
Do you happen to know where Swedenborg says the world will never end?
S.T.
Caryndale, Ontario, Canada
May 2007

Dear S.T.,
In his book, *Last Judgment*.
Full title is:
The Last Judgment
and
Babylon Destroyed
All the Predictions in
the Book of Revelation
Are at This Day Fulfilled
from Things Heard and Seen
by Emanuel Swedenborg
(published, in Latin, 1758)

Here are a few places he writes about it. The referenced numbers are much longer. *Last Judgment* #1: "**The destruction of the world is not meant by the day of the last judgment.**

Those who have not known the spiritual sense of the Word, have understood that everything in the visible world will be destroyed in the day of the Last Judgment; for it is said, that heaven and earth are then to perish, and that God will create a New Heaven and a New Earth.

...But since no one has hitherto known, that in the whole and in every part of the Word there is a spiritual sense, nor even what the spiritual sense is, therefore they who have embraced this opinion concerning the Last Judgment are excusable. But still they may now know, that neither the visible heaven nor the habitable earth will perish, but that both will endure."

Last Judgment #6: "**...the human race will endure, and that procreations will not cease.**"

Last Judgment #7: "**There are very many proofs that the reproduction of the human race will continue for ever; some of these were demonstrated in my book *HEAVEN AND HELL*, especially these:**
1. The human race is the foundation upon which heaven is built.
2. The human race is the seed-bed of heaven.
3. The extent of the heaven for the angels is so immense that it cannot be filled to all eternity.
4. The numbers in heaven so far are comparatively small.
5. The perfection of heaven increases as its numbers grow.
6. Every work of God reflects infinity and eternity."

Last Judgment #13: "**...the human race will never cease, for were it to cease, the Divine work would be limited to a certain number, and thus its looking to infinity would perish.**"

This "not ending stuff" flies in the opposite direction of current thinking. Media, books, and religious leaders are telling us the world will end soon! Well, they've been saying that for a long time. Here are the most famous *end* predictions:

- 1843—March 21 by William Miller, founder of *Millerite Movement*
- 1844—October 22 by William Miller
- 1850—by Ellen G. White, founder of *Seventh-day Adventist*
- 1856—by Ellen G. White
- 1890—by Joseph Smith, founder of *Church of Jesus Christ of Latter-day Saints*
- 1891—by Joseph Smith
- 1914—too numerous dates to list up to 2004 by *Jehovah's Witnesses*
- 1982—by Pat Robertson, *Southern Baptist* American Televangelist
- 1988—too numerous dates to list up to 2012 by Nostradamus
- 1998—2006 by Michael Drosnin, author of *The Bible Code*
- 2012—December 21 by the Mayan Calendar
- 2060—by Isaac Newton
- 2100—by Sylvia Browne

And we learn from horoscope columnist, Rob Brezsny that Emanuel Swedenborg was wrong when he predicted the world would end in 1757! Brezsny's "reporting" appeared in the news and arts weekly of the twin cities (Minneapolis and St. Paul, Minnesota) newspaper, *City Pages*, 11 April 2007:

> Free Will Astrology
> by Rob Brezsny
> LEO (July 23–Aug. 22):
>
> Swedish philosopher Emanuel Swedenborg predicted the world would end in 1757. American minister William Miller proclaimed the planet's "purification by fire" would occur in 1844. They're just two of history's many megalomaniacs disguised as moral guardians who've been shills for apocalyptic delusions. Our age has more of these wackos per capita, but the song is the same as it ever was. Your assignment, Leo, is to wash the taint of chronic doom-and-gloom propaganda out of your lovely brain. I'm not urging you to be a raving Pollyanna, merely suggesting that you exorcise the fear foisted on you by hysterical prophets of every stripe. That includes peak-oil fanatics, Luddites who preach the gospel of technocatastrophe, religious fundamentalists hyping Armageddon, and all the other nihilistic storytellers. You urgently need to declare your independence from our culture's professional scaremongers.

I wrote a letter to the editor refuting that ridiculous claim, but to my knowledge my letter was never published.

Last Judgment #46: **"This Last Judgment started at the beginning of the year 1757, and was fully accomplished by the end of that year."**

This year, 2007, is the 250th anniversary of the Last Judgment! It took place in the spiritual world! On the surface, the natural world stayed the same, and didn't end. It wasn't supposed to!

One reason many doubt that heaven and hell is made up of people from the human race, Swedenborg tells us, is that they believe that no one can go to heaven or hell until the end of the world! Swedenborg says, not true.

It's dangerous to think, Swedenborg said, that at the end-time Jews will be converted to Christianity and return to the land of Canaan. Evangelical and Fundamental Christians are not shy about their support for Israel. They are excited by the current political happenings in the Middle East, since they believe that when the nation of Israel is restored, the last days leading to the Second Coming of Christ will occur. Swedenborg says, not true. Swedenborg says this way of thinking demonstrates how far from the truth we have wandered. Taking the Bible literally is folly. Now we can learn our way back to God, thanks to Swedenborg. Life's not ending...

Swedenborg portrayed in chalk on the sidewalk at *The 12th Angel Festival*, 2005

Dear Candace,

Don't know what you think about the Swedenborgian Church. It's not necessary. He did not intend for there to be a church built. Emanuel Swedenborg said you don't need church. He said his Writings were a New Jerusalem movement. But, he still traditionally kept going to church. He contradicted himself.

And he made a prediction about the New Church being accepted all over the world. He gave a date. But he said there is no time in the next world. He contradicted himself.

P.N.
Los Angeles, California
July 2007

Dear P.N.,

Depends what you mean by the Swedenborgian Church. There are several branches of the Swedenborgian religion—organizations based on Swedenborg's Writings. I am a member of the largest branch, the most conservative, the *General Church of the New Jerusalem.*

If you meant "Church" as in a place to worship, it is true, Swedenborg said it was more important to live a good life than go off and pray all the time in a "church building". The real meaning of church, he said, is charity. You don't need a building or organization to perform charity. **"Worship of the Lord consists in a life of charity."** Problem has been, he continued, that **"every church begins from charity, and successively turns away from it to faith alone or to meritorious works."** (See *Apocalypse Explained* #104)

Swedenborg was born into a Lutheran family. As an adult, he rejected Martin Luther's teachings of the Trinity—3 Divine persons—and faith alone. After his spiritual eyes were opened and he met God—Jesus—Swedenborg rarely was seen in church. In 1768, Swedenborg, 80, was charged with heresy for refusing to accept the state religion. He was found guilty. The decision was reversed years later.

He wrote in *Secrets of Heaven* #7038: **"Anyone who thinks that serving the Lord consists solely in going to church regularly, listening to the preaching there, and saying prayers, and that that is sufficient, is much mistaken. True worship of the Lord consists in performing useful services; and such services during a person's life in the world."**

P.N., possibly you have read numbers such as that or this in *Secrets of Heaven* #8254: **"Worship of the Lord consists primarily in a charitable life, and not in a religious life without it. A religious life without the charitable life is no more than a selfish wish to look after oneself; there is no concern in it for one's neighbor."**

Now, what more can Swedenborg say? But, hear what some angels told him. *Heaven and Hell* #222: **"Divine worship in the heavens does not consist of going to church regularly and listening to sermons, but of a life of love, thoughtfulness, and faith in keeping with doctrine. The sermons in church serve only as means of instruction in how to live.**

I have talked about this with angels and have told them that people in this world believe that divine worship consists solely of going to church and listening to sermons, taking communion three or four times a year, and observing

other rituals according to the church's regulations, as well as making time for prayer and behaving devoutly. The angels have told me that these are outward matters that are worth doing, but that they are ineffective unless there is something within from which they flow, and that this something within is a life according to the principles that doctrine teaches."

Angels say they do worship in heaven. Therefore, so must we—in freedom. Don't go to church, if you don't want to. Worship God any way you want to, just worship someone greater than yourself!

Interestingly, Swedenborg tells us that in the highest heaven—the celestial—the churches or temples aren't that magnificent. However, in the lower heaven—the spiritual—they are magnificent. Now, isn't that something?! We all imagine heaven as this splendid place of beauty. But, we learn, the higher—closer to the Lord—we go in our love and wisdom, the less we need a magnificent house of worship. Actually, that makes sense.

But, we're not in heaven, yet...

Near the end of his life, people called Swedenborg "the New Jerusalem Gentleman". Swedenborg wrote in a letter to Friedrich Christoph Oetinger, 23 September 1766: **"Who cannot see that by the New Jerusalem is meant a New Church?"** He wrote volumes about a time when most would come to know the Lord for who He really is.

While Swedenborg, himself, did not start an organized church, he did know his Writings which reveal the Lord's Second Coming would be received all over the world one day. He knew a "church" would be formed.

True Christian Religion #113: **"At the present time a new church is being established by the Lord, which is meant by the New Jerusalem in Revelation. In this church, worship will be directed to the Lord alone, as it is in heaven, and thus all will be accomplished which the Lord's Prayer contains from beginning to end."**

Some Swedenborgians not comfortable with organized religion prefer to talk about a Swedenborg Movement. (Swedenborg didn't.) I don't doubt there is one, but a movement moves toward something greater.

Swedenborg says houses of worship are needed for a physical connection to the other world. Places that one God is taught and prayed to. Places that have a true understanding of His Word and the spiritual world. Doesn't matter what it looks like, just what is taught.

In his old age, Swedenborg not attending church shocked people. When one man commented on this to Swedenborg's landlord in London, Richard Shearsmith said, "To a good man like the Baron, every day of his life is a Sabbath."

Not sure what date you are referring to as a prediction Swedenborg made. He didn't make predictions. From the same letter quoted above to Friedrich Christoph Oetinger, 23 September 1766, Swedenborg wrote: **"These, my writings, concerning the New Jerusalem cannot be called Prophecies, but Revelations."** But, he did date journal entries and notes.

He wrote an epilogue in *True Christianity* #791: **"After this work was finished, the Lord called together His twelve disciples who followed Him in the world; and the next day He sent them all forth throughout the whole spiritual world to preach the Gospel that THE LORD GOD JESUS CHRIST reigns,** whose kingdom shall be for ages and ages, according to the prediction in Daniel (7:13, 14), and in Apocalypse (11:15). Also that blessed are those that come to the marriage supper of the Lamb (Apocalypse 19:9).

This took place on the nineteenth day of June, 1770. This is what is meant by these words of the Lord: — 'He shall send His angels and they shall gather together His elect, from the end of the heavens to the end thereof.' (Matthew 24:31)"

While there is no time in the next world, Swedenborg wrote down June 19th, 1770 as the day he witnessed Jesus together with His twelve disciples again.

Emanuel Swedenborg also gave us the year when the Last Judgment took place, 1757, in the spiritual world. Not an end time, but a "time" recorded by Swedenborg, so that we on earth would know what happened (ever the fine journalist) when the Lord rearranged or realigned the spiritual world. Earth history will celebrate those dates someday BIG TIME!

Dear Candace,

Greetings from Himalayan country, Nepal. Thanks for SILA. *From the first time I was reading it, I was blessed by reading them. May God bless you.*

I.K.
Kathmandu, Nepal
January 2002

Dear Candace,

Now I want an immediate answer as to why God deceives the devils into believing they aren't in hell.

W.A.
Charleston, Missouri
June 2004

Dear W.A.,

God doesn't deceive the devils, they deceive themselves! They think they are in a heaven. Their self-deception stops them from spiritually progressing into an actual heaven, but they don't know that. They think they are in a heaven because they are in the enjoyment of their evils. In the next world, we will be doing what we love. The more one loves to obey the Ten Commandments, the closer one will be to God, living in an actual heaven and not an imaginary one.

Dear Candace,

What do you think about Lilith? Adam and his first wife, Lilith. I read a short story recently in which Lilith came up again. It reminded me of the legend/myth and "Lilith Faire", a music festival started by women for women; keeps the word in my mind due to its origins.

B.C.
Hollywood, California
May 2008

Dear B.C.,
I'd never heard of Lilith before! Researching her, I found she is quite known in literature, among Jews and Christians alike.

The fabrication (not creation) of the woman Lilith shows how far humans have degenerated from understanding the story of creation. In the Jewish faith, Lilith came into existence to reconcile the (seemingly) different creation stories. In Genesis, Chapter 1, man and woman are created. In Genesis, Chapter 2, Adam is alone and God creates Eve from Adam's rib. According to rabbinical interpretation, Lilith had to have been the first woman created. She's in Isaiah 34:14. **"The tziim [wild beasts of the desert] shall also meet with the ijim [wild beasts of the island], and the satyr [wood demon] shall cry to his fellow; the screech owl [night monster] shall also rest there, and find for lilith [herself] a place of rest."**

The Hebrew word "lilith" is derived from the Babylonian-Assyrian word "lilitu" which means a female demon. Lilith since then has evolved from a hideous human creature with bird feet to a contemporary strong goddess of divorce and abortion. Keeping her myth alive is, I believe, more than not understanding Scripture; it's coming from a place of need. A need to have heroes. Female ones at that.

Lilith Fair was a music festival (1997–1999) founded by Canadian singer Sarah McLachlan at which only female musicians performed. It came to be because Sarah was told by concert promoters and radio stations that they wouldn't allow two female musicians in a row to perform! They chose Lilith as their symbolic leader.

Lilith magazine is for Jewish women. On www.lilith.org it states:

> According to myth and legend, Lilith was the first woman, created before Eve. She was Adam's absolute equal. In the Garden of Eden, long before the eating of the apple, the Holy One created the first human beings—a man named Adam, and a woman named Lilith. Lilith said, 'We are equal because we are created from the same earth.'— from the medieval text Alphabet of Ben Sira, 23a-b.

Before I tell you what Emanuel Swedenborg said about Lilith, first you need to read this from *True Christian Religion* #279: **"I am allowed to report this new piece of information about the ancient Word, which was in Asia before the Israelite Word existed. It is still preserved there among the peoples who live in Great Tartary. I have spoken with spirits and angels in the spiritual world who came from there. They said that they possess the Word, and have done so from ancient times; and they conduct their Divine worship in accordance with that Word. It is composed purely of correspondences. They said that it also contains** the book of Jashar mentioned in Joshua (10:12, 13), and in the Second Book of Samuel (1:17, 18); they also have the books called The Wars of Jehovah and The Utterances, which are mentioned by Moses (Numbers 21:14, 15 and 27-30). When I read in their presence the words which Moses took from this source, they looked to see whether they were there, and they found them. This made it clear to me that they still have the ancient Word. During our conversation they mentioned that they worship Jehovah, some of them as an invisible God, and some as visible.

They went on to say that they do not allow foreigners to enter their territory, except the Chinese, with whom they have peaceful relations, because the Chinese Emperor comes from there.* They added that they are so populous that they do not believe any region in all the world is more so. This too is plausible when one considers the wall so many miles long, which the Chinese in former times constructed as a defence against invasion by them.

Moreover I was told by angels that the first chapters of Genesis, dealing with creation, Adam and Eve, the Garden of Eden, their sons and descendants down to the flood, as well as Noah and his sons, are also found in that Word, and were copied from it by Moses. Angels and spirits from Great Tartary are to be seen in the southern quarter towards the east. They are separated from others by living on a higher level. They do not allow anyone from Christian countries to visit them, and if any do go up, they put them under guard to prevent them leaving. The reason for this isolation is that they possess a different Word."

    * [Translator's note] This may refer to the Yuan dynasty (13th–14th centuries) who were of Mongol origin; but perhaps the reference is to the non-Chinese Manchu dynasty who ruled China from 1644.

Swedenborg tells us the spiritual sense of the Genesis creation story is of how a person is created spiritually—regeneration of a person. *Apocalypse Explained* #586: "Here the subject treated of is the total devastation of the church [person] through corporeal and purely natural lusts from which flow forth evils and falsities of every kind; these lusts are signified by the tziim, and the ijim, and also by the bird of night and the wood demon, or satyr."

True Christianity #531: "Before repentance a person is like a desert which is the home of terrifying wild animals, dragons, horned owls, tawny owls, vipers and haemorrhoids [snakes], with thickets inhabited by ochim and tziim [howling creatures] where satyrs dance. When these creatures have been expelled by human labor and toil, the desert can be ploughed up and be brought into cultivation, the fields being planted first with oats, beans and flax, and later with barley and wheat."

Swedenborg has much to say about people that twist the Word to fit their thinking. *Spiritual Experiences* #1605: "So when a person just sticks in terms and reasons from them, and piles up meanings, so that there are nothing but scholarly expressions thus glued together, then all that they imagine to be involved is unknown, and more hidden from them than to those who do not know any such formula, and then [s/he] doubts about everything."

THERE IS AN ANSWER

Spiritual Experiences #1606: "**Moreover, philosophical matters that obscure human minds are also those forms of reasonings that are reduced to man-made rules, even if they are truths so lucid that anyone can see them clearly without such rules. These philosophers so limit and darken matters of understanding that even well understood truths are constantly called into question.**"

True Christianity #575: "**There is a further description of what the unregenerated person is like in the comparison and similes found in Isaiah: ... 'There shall meet there tziim and iyim, and the satyr shall encounter his partner; indeed lilith shall rest there. There the black-bird shall build its nest, lay eggs, gather food and hatch its young in its shadow.'** "

Apocalypse Revealed #458: "**That they should not adore demons, signifies that thus they are in the evils of their lusts, and make one with their like in hell. By 'demons' are signified the lusts of evil springing from the love of the world; the reason is, because in hell they are called demons who are in those lusts; and people also, who are in the same, become demons after death.**"

No judgment is made on those that think Lilith was a real woman; no less those that think Eve was a real woman. Ignorance is bliss. But, now we have more knowledge from Swedenborg to guide us.

On one level, Adam and Eve represented the **"Most Ancient Church"** in oral parabolical history. Noah and his wife represented the **"Ancient Church"**.

In the *Washington Post*, 30 October 2005, Michael Dirda reviewed *The Book of Imaginary Beings* by Jorge Luis Borges with Margarita Guerrero, Illustrated by Peter Sis, Translated from Spanish by Andrew Hurley (Viking Books, 2005):

> As one would expect, Borges is nothing if not a repository of every sort of antiquarian trivia. He tells us about Adam's first wife, Lilith; that the myrmecoleon, burdened with the head of a lion and the body of an ant, grew out of a translation error.

Borges, a Swedenborgian, wrote in *The Book of Imaginary Beings* (on page 128) that Lilith was a myth created because the Hebrew word "layil" translates as "night"—Lilith was said to be a creature of the night. In reality, she didn't exist.

It must be said, Genesis makes little sense without an interpreter. Swedenborg is my interpreter. In many volumes, he explains that Adam is us all. God creates people as animals and recreates us animals into angels. We think we're doing the regenerative stuff, but we're not. We are to think we have a part in it. In other words, we start the process and the Lord finishes it. So, in the creation story when God creates Eve from Adam's rib, He is taking out what is most precious to us, near our hearts, the belief we are in charge and creates a new person, the lovely Eve which is our **"new will"**. We only become a spiritual person when we regenerate and get a **"new will"** and a **"new understanding"** from the Lord.

Dear Candace,
We enjoyed the Genesis *series on PBS. Did you catch them? It was ground breaking religious discussion with lots of hooks for New Church ideas to attach to. Keep up the good work!*

K. & J.H.
Chicago, Illinois
December 1996

Dear K. & J.H.,
Your letter arrived as I was completing my research *on Genesis: A Living Conversation,* the 10-week TV series which ran on PBS stations in North America from October to December. I had anticipated *SILA* readers would be interested in a review of *Genesis* and your letter proved it, because every letter received represents how hundreds are thinking. Thank you.

Genesis, hosted by journalist Bill Moyers, cost $2 million. Its format was a weekly Bible study group. Moyers invited prominent professionals from different religions, and agnostics, to sit in a circle and discuss the first book of the Word; seven <u>experts</u> per show. Each segment started with Alfre Woodard or Mandy Patinkin telling the viewer a story from a chapter in Genesis. The segments were titled and presented in the following order:

>THE FIRST MURDER
>IN GOD'S IMAGE
>TEMPTATION
>APOCALYPSE
>CALL AND PROMISE
>A FAMILY AFFAIR
>THE TEST
>BLESSED DECEPTION
>GOD WRESTLING
>EXILE

The stories were discussed as to their popularity today and as to whether they were drama, opera, or novel in format. One <u>expert</u> commented, "I have a problem with this story." Apparently many others did, too, week after week. The <u>experts</u> changed story endings or added plot twists of their own to make the tales politically correct or more "comforting" as one <u>expert</u> said.

Each week some <u>expert</u> would ask if the story was narrative. *Did it really happen?* And suggest that it didn't add up. But, then conversation would return to a literal interpretation and the sequence of events would be debated as to why and what it was saying.

God was decidedly ambivalent and violent according to the <u>experts</u>. To them, He creates evil and punishes the good. He is the author of apocalypse. God destroys, condemns, regrets, reacts, terrifies, and makes mistakes. It was decided that God is an undeveloped god in Genesis. The Holocaust was brought up in almost all segments as an example of how God operates.

Watching *Genesis,* I quickly surmised that Emanuel Swedenborg was not going to be brought up in the conversations by any of the 39 learned experts. Yet, he should have been.

In *TIME* magazine, 28 October 1996, five new books published (not counting *Genesis: A Living Conversation*) were discussed in its cover story about *Genesis.* In this well researched article, Swedenborg was not mentioned. And yet, he has written books on the subject of Genesis! Scholars know that, even if the masses don't. Why do experts not discuss Swedenborg's interpretation of Genesis? (Obviously, they are not experts in their field!)

Even though (as evident in this series) a literal interpretation of Genesis is not favoured, it is accepted as literal because no one meaning of the whole book is understood and accepted.

The experts read the Bible from their own culture, race, and sex and slanted it in their favour. One expert went so far as to say, "Why not throw the Bible away?" Others said the Bible was over-detailed and over-written. Almost all the experts quoted the stories by heart, verse after verse.

Listening to the experts reminded me of what Swedenborg wrote in his *Spiritual Diary* #1604: **"But an abuse arises from the fact that philosophers abide in terms, and dispute concerning them without coming to an agreement, from which all idea of the thing itself perishes, and the comprehension of [the person] is rendered so limited that [s/he] at length ceases to know anything but terms.**

Accordingly when such [person] would master a subject by their terms they do nothing but heap them up, obscuring the whole matter, so that they can understand absolutely nothing of it, and even their natural lumen is extinguished.

Thus an unlearned [person] has much more extensive ideas and sees truth better than the philosopher; for such a one sticks in the mire like a swine.

When [a person], therefore, dwells solely in terms, and ratiocinates from them, heaping up senses, so that nothing remains but scholastic terms conglutinated together, an ignorance is induced of everything supposed to be involved (in the subject of inquiry), and it becomes more hidden to them than to others who have known nothing of any such formulas, and thus doubt arises concerning everything."

Genesis does make sense when you learn it is allegorical. Some people have figured that out on their own, but knowing it is a parable doesn't explain the inner meaning of it all. Emanuel Swedenborg painstakingly went through Genesis, verse by verse, and wrote down in six books its spiritual meaning.

With this in mind, I realized I had to invite a few Biblical experts myself to join the circle, if only on paper, to add the Swedenborgian perspective to the living conversation about Genesis.

May I introduce you to...?

Rev. Clark Echols, preacher at *The Sower's Chapel* in Sarver, Pennsylvania, 3 years; New Church minister, 18 years. He writes:

Dear Candace,
Thanks for the opportunity to join the circle. I am a bit disappointed that there isn't more historical/archeological/geographic stuff [in the series]. I was hoping it would be more like [a] Nova [TV series episode] and less like an interview show!
One of the men—which one I forget, made a passing reference, during the Cain and Abel discussion, to the story being allegorical. It seemed they all wanted to stay away from THAT subject and not talk about it. I would have consistently spoken about how the story is symbolic of all human emotion and is not actual history. I would emphasize how true the story is, and how Moses (or whoever) was Divinely inspired in writing it down, but that it is not actual history.
To consider it actual history destroys the points it is trying to make, for it leads us into trying to explain what such a fable does not need to explain—like what happened that God did not respect Cain's offering, etc.
It is not consistent to maintain that the Creator could be evil, cause evil or express it. The Infinite cannot contain opposites since it is infinitely One.
The book is Divinely inspired retelling of history, which retelling could only be told from the writer's perspective. Therefore it is going to be anthropomorphic and not descriptive of God Himself—but only what a simple, primate, and merely worldly person thinks God must be like.

Rev. John Odhner, preacher at the *New Church of La Crescenta* in California, 7 years; New Church minister, 16 years. He writes:

Dear Candace,
Jesus said that the whole Bible is about loving God and loving your neighbor. This is what Swedenborg shows us in Genesis. It is about our spiritual life, our relationship with God, and with our fellow human beings. It's not so much ancient history as it is the psychological, spiritual history of each one of us.
In the beginning, each of us is in the dark about God, but at some point God sends a ray of light into our minds, making us aware of our spiritual potential. God says, **"Let there be light"**! *This is the first step in a process of spiritual development. God is creating a whole new world for each one of us, and the process culminates with our becoming truly human—an image and likeness of God. That is why the creation story ends with God making human beings in His own image.*

The same is true for the story of Cain and Abel. Every religious person has the task of learning to love others. Religion doesn't do us much good if we treat our fellow human beings as enemies. That's where Cain was: he worshipped God, but hated his brother. The result was that he was isolated, exiled. There are a lot of Cain's around today, wherever people use religion as an excuse to grasp for power or go to war. When that happens, love dies, just like Abel died, and Christ died at the hands of people who cared more about religious power than about love.

There is ambivalence in the Bible when we look at it on a literal level. When we look at it on a deeper level, the contradictions disappear. For example, God is Love, and is always merciful, good, and loving. God could never condemn, punish or be angry with anyone. But the Bible speaks of God punishing. This is what Swedenborg calls an **"appearance of truth"**. *The sun appears to go around the earth, but in reality it is the earth that turns, not the sun that moves around. So the sun's rising and setting is an appearance.*

In the same way, God appears to be angry, but in reality people have their own anger that they project on God. God doesn't punish, but because evil carries its own punishment with it, it can appear as if the punishment were from God. As we learn to think more deeply about the sun rising, we get beyond the appearance that it moves. As we learn to think more deeply about the anger and punishment in the Bible, we get beyond the appearance that it is from God.

Rev. Erik Buss, preacher at the *Cascade New Church* in Seattle, Washington, 3 years; New Church minster, 6 years. He writes:

Dear Candace,

  All the inconsistencies in the stories are God's way of telling us that the literal story is not all there is. To make sense of the stories we have to look deeper. If these stories did not have an inner meaning, it seems that God chose a very inefficient way to communicate to us.

  Swedenborg says that all the depictions of God in Genesis really reflect how we feel about God when we are in the states described. A child who had done wrong may perceive the parent as angry when in fact the parent is simply being stern to make a strong point. It's the same in the Genesis stories with God. Only when we see the inner meaning do we see the story from the Lord's perspective, and in them He is always loving. In fact, Swedenborg says that God cannot even frown at us. Hope this helps.

THANK YOU Reverends Echols, Odhner, and Buss for your simple comments. Such terrific insights into how you may have held your own in the televised *Genesis* circle, if you had been invited.

Dear Candace,

I've been xeroxing the SILA *newsletter and sending it to certain people. Candace, what purpose did prehistoric animals serve in the grand scheme of Creation? Swedenborg didn't know about dinosaurs.*

P.R.
San Francisco, California
October 1989

Dear P.R.,

How wonderful it is that you are sharing *SILA* with others!

You are correct in saying that Swedenborg did not know about dinosaurs. They were "discovered" in 1822 and named as such in 1841. What Swedenborg did learn and subsequently wrote down is that everything in creation has a correlation with everything in a person—a person is a universe or heaven being created. There are six stages in the creation of a person (and humankind). From this viewpoint of creation we can surmise that the dinosaurs lived around the earth's development stage after childhood. They became extinct as our teenage will power and irrationality must become extinct in order for us to achieve the next level of development.

To understand how Emanuel Swedenborg knows all this about the creation story, it must be explained that at the age of 57 he came to a turning point in his life and stopped researching in science as he had (with recognition). After a period of symbolic dreams, he received a visit from the Lord on 6 April 1745 in a hotel in London, England. From that day on, he had regular glimpses (visits) into the spiritual dimension until his death in 1772. During these visits into the spiritual world, Swedenborg was shown the hows, whys, whats, and wheres of everything. For an in-depth study of creation, I recommend his *Arcana Coelestia [Secrets of Heaven]*, Volume 1 and *Divine Love and Wisdom*.

Swedenborg used this ornament in *Secrets of Heaven*

Dear Candace,
 My friend in the Philippines is seeking to be enlightened with "tree" and "perception". The True Christian Religion *book by Swedenborg states that "tree" signifies man (#467, 468), however, Swedenborg's* Arcana Coelestia *book says, "tree" signifies perception (#102). Can you explain this?*

M.R.
San Diego, California
March 2002

Dear M.R.,
 True Christian Religion #467 (excerpt): " **'The garden of Eden' in the Word does not mean a garden, but intelligence, nor does 'tree' mean any tree, but [a person].''**
 True Christian Religion #468 (excerpt): **"That 'tree' signifies [humans], can be seen from the following passages in the Word: 'And all the trees of the field shall know that I Jehovah humble the high tree, exalt the low tree, dry up the green tree, and make the dry tree to bud.' (Ezekiel 17:24)**
 'Blessed is the man whose delight is in the law. He shall be like a tree planted by the streams of waters, that bringeth forth its fruits in its season.' (Psalm 1:1-3; Jeremiah 17:3)"
 Arcana Coelestia (Secrets of Heaven) #102: " **'And Jehovah God caused to spring up out of the ground every tree desirable to the sight and good for food; and the tree of life in the middle of the garden, and the tree of the knowledge of good and evil.'**
 'Tree' means perception; 'tree desirable to the sight' means the perception of what is true; 'tree good for food' means the perception of what is good; 'tree of life' means love and faith deriving from love; and 'the tree of the knowledge of good and evil' means faith derived from sensory evidence, that is, from knowledge."
 A "tree" means a person with perception. Swedenborg says the allegorical Garden of Eden in Genesis is really the story of how a human being is made.
 The Garden of Eden represents intelligence. In the garden were placed two trees—one leading to life called **"the tree of life"** and the other leading to death, called **"the tree of the knowledge of good and evil"**. Having two trees to choose from represents our free will in spiritual matters.
 When God first created people, He "talked" with them directly. This direct communication with God is called perception. Swedenborg tells us in *Secrets of Heaven* #104: that **"perception is a certain internal sensation from the Lord alone, as to whether a thing is true and good"**. The Most Ancients, also, communicated with their deceased loved ones (angels) directly. The Most Ancients also were taught through visions and dreams.
 Angels have perception, too. But, a person on earth does not have perception. Swedenborg says, we can have conscience.
 Allegorically, Adam and Eve ate of the tree of the knowledge of good and evil. This means that the descendants of The Most Ancients turned away from God and believed they could be gods, too, from knowledges, from themselves alone, guiding their own lives without perception from God.

Swedenborg tells us in *True Christian Religion* that the heat of the sun is the only active principle in a tree, and it causes the tree to grow. From what we have learned above, we can say that people are represented as trees and the only active principle in us is God—Sun—specifically His Love and His Wisdom.

In the purest sense, a person had perception, leading directly from God, in the beginning, but can now only achieve perception by becoming an angel after death. Until then, a person is led by their conscience.

Dear Candace,
I like SILA. *While I agree Swedenborg says some things that seem right for some things you have to constantly read. This is much too tedious a task to find spiritualness. Everyone isn't incline to read that much.*

Anonymous Inmate
Correctional facility, Missouri
July 2004

Dear Anonymous,
I couldn't agree with you more! That's why He gave us The Ten Commandments. Can't get more simple, concise, and true than those. For people inclined to like reading, there is the Bible. For those that like back stories—the meaning behind words and events—there are the Writings of Swedenborg. For those that don't enjoy studying, but enjoy learning the truths of faith, there are Swedenborgian churches or lectures where they can listen to others that have studied.

Dear Candace,
SILA *is a wonderful, informative publication. I wouldn't miss a word of it. The letters are great—your responses even better. Just don't die and leave us without this monthly treat. Keep up the good work. I love it. In appreciation.*

L.E.
Bryn Athyn, Pennsylvania
November 1990

Dear L.E.,
I cried reading your letter...

June 1998
Dear *SILA* Readers,

    I'm back from Sweden!

    I went on the *Swedish Roots* trip sponsored by *Glencairn Museum* and *Bryn Athyn College*, 31 May–June 11. While the trip was part of an accredited course, it was open to non-students and I jumped at the opportunity.

    I had high expectations. It was a lifetime experience. It went beyond my expectations! I have returned with a new understanding and appreciation for Swedenborg. It will be impossible to relate, now, everything I learned. But, I know that my new knowledge of him will be conveyed in my writing for years to come.

    The first thing I came to discover about Swedenborg, the man, was that he wasn't as I had pictured him. I had known him as a friendly, courteous, honest, and warm individual. I wasn't aware that I had caricatured him as a smiley, chivalrous, upright, and huggy kind of guy, until I met his fellow Swedish citizens. The Swedes of the 20th century are surprisingly not that different than Swedes of the 18th century.

    We were pre-warned about Swedish characteristics before landing in Sweden. In our *Swedish Roots* trip book—a 3-ring binder full of maps, brochures, and photocopied pages from books—a printout of 28 pages from *Culture Shock! Sweden: A Survival Guide to Customs and Etiquette* by Charlotte Rosen Svensson (1996) was included.

    Chapter 3, "The Swedish People" outlined Swedish behaviours of the traders back in Viking times to Swedish citizens of today. What I read matched the people I met on Swedish streets, in stores, and at tourist attractions. Charlotte Rosen Svensson wrote:

> They are often seen as harder, colder, more efficient, and less relaxed when compared to their Scandinavian neighbors.

    I have reevaluated my conception of Emanuel Swedenborg. He's still a kind and honest gentleman, but more on the lines of a reserved, withdrawn, visibly unaffectionate man of few words. I can now easily comprehend him writing, alone, for days and weeks, and being okay with that. His Swedish temperament obviously allowed him to do what he had to do!

Thinking of you,
Candace

July 1998
Dear *SILA* Readers,

For ten years, I have written about Swedenborg's life and work. I hadn't studied the country of Sweden. I received a crash course on my trip to Sweden. Sweden is roughly the same size as California or Japan. Yet, Sweden's population is 8.8 million, California 33.4 million, and Japan 132.5 million! It was astounding to find that our tour group (22 people) was sometimes virtually alone at sites. No lines and no traffic!

Most Swedish people live in the southern half of the country; 1.5 million live in Stockholm. In Swedenborg's day about 75,000 people lived in Stockholm and 1.5 million in Sweden. It was a cold 45°F when we arrived in Stockholm—which is actually made up of 14 islands! (Sweden has 100,000 lakes.) It rained all our 12 days, but one! No wonder it was green everywhere!

We visited *The House of Nobles (Riddarhuset)* in Stockholm. In 1719, Queen Ulrica Eleonora ennobled her bishops in recognition of the good work they'd done. As is customary, Bishop Jesper Swedberg's family's name was changed, but not his. Emanuel Swedberg, at 31, became Emanuel Swedenborg.

Parliament took place in the Great Hall in *The House of Nobles*. Swedenborg, as the oldest surviving male of his ennobled family sat in parliament at age 31 until he died. Up until the 19th century, politicians were appointed, not elected. Sessions were not regular, but called whenever the monarchy felt one was needed.

Around 1,100 men sat in session in the Great Hall in Swedenborg's day. By today's fire regulation standards, only 400 people can be in there at one time! Because there were so many men present, most vied for attention in argumentative ways. A locked brass box with a slot was on the head table and monetary fines were issued to those men that got verbally or physically abusive. [Swear jars don't seem so new now, do they?] In 1769, a heated quarrel at session led to 10 duels.

It is fact that Swedenborg never gave a speech in public. It is commonly assumed it was because he stuttered. Instead, he wrote many political pamphlets and bills and submitted them in writing for pensive deliberation. After visiting *The House of Nobles* myself, I can see how Swedenborg may not have wanted to fight the other posturing politicians for floor time, with or without a stutter. He may just have seen the futility in yelling louder over the next guy's yelling. And he didn't have the ego he had had as a young man. He was more humble as an adult citizen.

Thinking of you,
Candace

August 2006
Dear *SILA* Readers,
   Doing research for this month's topic, I discovered the most amazing thing! While I had known that Swedenborg never gave a lecture in public or in his government job because he stuttered, I hadn't known he had given a lecture in heaven until I read, closely, #78 of *True Christian Religion*. While I had surmised that he wouldn't have a stutter after his earthly death, this number confirmed he truly didn't stutter in spirit. I've underlined the evidence.

   "The next day an angel came to me from another community in heaven and said, 'We have heard in our community that because of your thoughts about the creation of the universe you were sent for to a community near ours; <u>and there you gave a lecture on creation</u>, which they applauded and have since taken great pleasure in. Now I am going to show you how animals and plants of every kind were produced by God.' "

Thinking of you,
Candace

September 2005
Dear *SILA* Readers,
   Around this time, I am asked the same question year after year. And not just because of *The Angel Festival*, but because Halloween is coming up and spooks are on people's minds. I am asked, *What's the difference between ghosts, spirits, angels, the super-natural, hauntings, and apparitions?* Swedenborg tells us from his experiences seeing and hearing the departed, they are all the same species, no difference—all dead people—but, at different "levels" living in the spiritual world.
   Talking with my friend—a Swedenborgian authority—the other day about angels, Rev. Erik E. Sandstrom reminded me that even though we are born to be angels, the distance between us and them has so greatly increased over time (because evils of the human race have increased), this is why most people think angels are a separate species! We don't recognize angels as the same as us.
   It's only an appearance that angels are different than us, just as the sun setting is an appearance. "We don't say: *What a beautiful earth turning!*" Erik said. "We say: *What a beautiful sunset!*"

Thinking of you,
Candace

Dear Candace,
What can you tell us Swedenborg said about the Egyptians' mummies? Tut's tomb wasn't discovered until the 20th century and more important mummies later.

L. & S.
Tujunga, California
May 2003

Dear L. & S.,
It is true that Tutankhamen's tomb wasn't discovered until 1922 by Howard Carter. But, in the 18th century during Swedenborg's time, mummies were known about. More as curiosities than scientific wonders, however. Mummy-mania was around long before Tut's golden tomb was discovered.

Many mummies were brought back to Europe as souvenirs from tours to Egypt! The unwrapping of a mummy was frequently the entertainment for large gatherings of "fashionable" society. Con-artists took advantage of this craze and sometimes displayed fake mummies, artfully aged, often adorned with portions of genuine ancient wrappings.

Many people not only unwrapped the Egyptian cadavers, but also dissected, sniffed, and even ground them up into potions or medicines, then *ate* them! Even industry aided the destruction of Egyptian artifacts by using mummies' bandages to make paper or burned the bodies for fuel!

It is often assumed that mummification was only for royalty, but archeologists have proven that almost all Egyptians, who could afford to, became mummies when they died. Anthropologists estimate that there were 70 million mummies in 3,000 years!

By the 4th century A.D., many Egyptians had become Christians and no longer believed that mummification was necessary for life after death. Eventually, the Egyptians gave up the art and science of making mummies; and gave up guarding them which left them vunerable to thieves.

A.M. Mallet, a well-travelled French military engineer and geographer under King Louis XIV, wrote *Die Piramiden und Mumien-Pyramides et Momies* in 1719. I don't know whether Swedenborg read this book, but it was a popular book about what was known about mummies in the 18th century. (Napoleon's scientific mission to unveil Egypt's mysteries wasn't until 1798—Swedenborg died in 1772.)

Emanuel Swedenborg did write about mummies in his books—not as curiosities, but as a tool of demonstration for the misconceptions about death. He wrote in *True Christianity* #160: "**I was once walking in the company of angels in the world of spirits. This lies half-way between heaven and hell, and it is where everyone comes first after death; here the good are prepared for heaven, the wicked for hell. I discussed a number of topics with the angels.**

[The angels said,] 'Let us wait here a little while and talk with some of the newcomers.' We selected a dozen of those arriving; and since they had all just come from the natural world they did not know that they were not still there. We asked them their opinions about heaven and hell and life after death. ...The sixth [person], who stood opposite, said with a smile: 'How can a spirit which is just air return to a body which has been eaten by worms or to a skeleton burnt up by the sun and reduced to dust? And how can an Egyptian, who has been mummified, and then mixed by a druggist into his extracts, emulsions, potions and pills, come back and tell anything? So if that is your belief, go on waiting for that last day, but you will wait for ever and ever in vain.' "

So, here is Swedenborg telling a story about a recently deceased person that knew about mummies and how some people ate them. This deceased person figured it surely was an impossibility of returning to a body that had been consumed, and concluded, therefore, there was no life after death! And yet, he was in the spiritual world! (Swedenborg must have been smiling to himself when he witnessed that.)

In *Conjugial Love* by Swedenborg (published in 1768) we read in #182 about some wise men in heaven, who were from Greece, and their conversation with Swedenborg. They told him: **"Is there any more paradoxical belief than what is related about the Last Judgment: that then the universe will come to an end, the stars will fall from the sky onto the earth (which is smaller than the stars), and the bodies of [human beings] which are corpses or mummies consumed by [people] or reduced to shreds will be joined to their souls again?"**

That's an astounding statement from someone who lived in an age of prevailing wisdom that mummification was a vehicle to heaven!

True Christianity #595: **"An unregenerate person who pretends to be a respectable citizen and a Christian can be compared to a corpse wrapped in aromatic substances, but which still gives off a stench that spoils the aroma and penetrating the nose offends the brain. [S/He] can also be compared with a gilded mummy, or one laid in a silver coffin; but if one looks inside, the ugly black body comes into view."**

That's quite the imagery, **"gilded mummy"**. We, in the 21st century can now see the truth above—the splendor of Tut's gold casket with his shriveled black corpse inside—because through Divine providence, it is now on film.

Swedenborg wrote that satans in hell appeared in the light of heaven **"as corpses and some of them black like a mummy"**. But, in their own light in hell, which resembles **"the light of a coal fire"** (*Apocalypse Revealed* #153) they appear not as monsters, but as people.

How would we stand up in the light of heaven?

Swedenborg used this ornament in *Secrets of Heaven*

Chapter 9

REAL DEAD PEOPLE SWEDENBORG VISITED

Dear Candace,
 I don't see how one can readily accept what Emanuel Swedenborg says of what he was told when those he supposedly being told by are never given an identity.
 However, Swedenborg does have viable concepts. This is a total issue of blind faith. This further supports that the hierarchy accepted him because he is plausible and believable. Thus Emanuel Swedenborg catered to them and more than likely said things according to their psyche.
 As Emanuel Swedenborg stated in #533 of Heaven and Hell *that he had not been allowed into the whole of hell or better put was not allowed enough knowledge of hell. Then this shows that Emanuel Swedenborg is guessing and giving examples of people on earth instead of the spirit world.*
 This makes me discredit his supposed talks with so many dead and giving no names as to identity. Emanuel Swedenborg clearly states that he is guessing mostly in regards to the hells.
 His references to people of the Papal religion isn't defined much. Then I see you wrote [March] in regards to Pope Benedict XIV, (1675–1758) stating that the Lord had no power and holiness because He transferred it to Peter! Why do you feel he stated this in the spiritual world? This is the first time people dead were listed in SILA *as being spoken to Swedenborg by name. I want to know who else Swedenborg spoke to by name. Why doesn't Swedenborg give the name of any spirit he talks to?*
 W.A.
 Bowling Green, Missouri
 June 2003

Dear W.A.,

He does! Granted, you would need to read a lot of his books to find the names of his deceased family members, friends, royalty, and famous historical figures. But, for the most part, Swedenborg does not name spirits he talked to because in the long run, it doesn't matter what name they were called by on earth, but the message they give us.

Swedenborg wrote that blind faith is a faith in mysteries which are believed despite whether they are true or not, or whether they are reasonable or not. Swedenborg wrote volumes attempting to rationally explain what he saw in the spiritual world. He certainly didn't want people to blindly believe what he wrote. Quite the opposite. He repeats himself often and is always asking the reader to examine what he says is true or not for themselves.

His target audience wasn't the hierarchy, but everyone of a rational mind. As for the hierarchy accepting Swedenborg's books when he was alive and him writing with that audience in mind, that's absolutely not true! He gave away more of his books than were sold. When *Secrets of Heaven,* Volume 1 was published only 4 copies sold in two months! It took 20 years for all 12-volumes of *Secrets of Heaven* to sell out!

The section of *Heaven and Hell* #553 that you think says Swedenborg wasn't allowed in all of hell or not allowed enough knowledge about hell, reads: **"I have not been allowed to see what form hell itself is in overall. I have only been told that in the same way that all heaven as a single entity resembles a single [human being], so all hell as a single entity resembles a single devil and can be manifested as a likeness of a single devil."**

The only person that can see heaven as one person and hell as one person is the Lord! So, it's not that Swedenborg wasn't allowed to visit all of hell, he was, and it's not that Swedenborg didn't have enough knowledge about hell, he did. And what he didn't see or figure out on his own, angels told him, as for example, mentioned in the passage above.

Swedenborg never guessed about anything! He wrote facts as he saw them. Believe them or not. Or as Swedenborg would say, examine for yourself whether what he says is rational or not.

One mistake most newcomers to the Writings of Swedenborg make is to assume blanket statements about something Swedenborg wrote or didn't write about, after reading one or two books by him. I can see how you would think that Swedenborg didn't define his understanding of the Catholic religion well. Trust me, he does! Now, you ask me why did Pope Benedict XIV tell Swedenborg, in the spiritual world, that the Lord had given up His power and given it to Peter. I don't know why he said that! But, I do know that in the spiritual world nothing is hidden. Pope Benedict XIV obviously wants/thinks it to be true.

Swedenborg wrote that he was allowed **"to talk with almost all the people I had ever met during their physical lives...so that I could be convinced and could bear witness."** (*Heaven and Hell* #437) He does name many people (famous and not famous) he saw in vision after their deaths in most of his books. I have mentioned a few in past *SILA* issues such as the Lord, His twelve apostles, Mary, his two mothers, and his father. I do not know of any published "list" of individuals he met in spirit. (I'm gonna start a list of my own and add to it from time to time.)

UPDATE

Emanuel Swedenborg (1688–1772) wrote that he saw and spoke with the following real individuals after their natural deaths. This list is not complete.

Aaron (c.1400–c.1277 B.C.) — Hebrew, older brother of Moses
Abraham (c.1813–c.1638 B.C.) — Hebrew, founder of the Israelites
Gustavus Adolphus (1594–1632) — Swedish, king of Sweden
Andrew (?) — Hebrew, Simon Peter's brother, fisherman, chosen apostle of Jesus
Anthony of Padua (1195–1231) — Portuguese, *Catholic* saint
Aristotle (384–322 B.C.) — Greek, philosopher, writer
Peter Aulaevill (?18th c.) — Swedish, consul of justice
Brita Behm (1697–1755) — Swedish, Swedenborg's aunt, aka "Iron-Brita"
Benedict XIV (1675–1758) — Italian, pope, born Prospero Lorenzo Lambertini
Erik Benzelius (1675–1743) — Swedish, bishop, Swedenborg's brother-in-law
Jacob Benzelius (1683–1747) — Swedish, *Lutheran* archbishop
Lars Benzelstjerna (1680–1755) — Swedish, Swedenborg's brother-in-law
Johan Bergenstjerna (1668–1748) — Swedish, member Board of Mines
Mrs. Gabriel Andersson Beyer (?–1769) — Swedish, husband 1st Swedish convert
Hans Björck (?18th c.) — Swedish, member Board of Mines
Erik Brahe (1722–1756) — Swedish, count, politician, beheaded with Baron Horn
Carl Broman (?–1722) — Swedish, baron
Erland Broman (1704–1757) — Swedish, baron, president Board of Trade
John Calvin (1509–1564) — French, *Protestant* reformer
Carl XII (1682–1718) — Swedish, king of Sweden
Jonas Cederstedt (?18th c.) — Swedish, member Board of Mines
Jesus Christ (7/2 B.C.–26/36 A.D.) — Hebrew, The Lord, God incarnate
Christian VI (1699–1746) — Danish, king of Denmark
Christina (1626–1689) — Swedish, queen of Sweden
Marcus Tullius Cicero (106–43 B.C.) — Roman, philosopher
Clement XII (1652–1740) — Italian, *Catholic* pope, born Lorenzo Corsini
Johannes Cocceius (1603–1669) — Dutch, *Christian* theologian
David (c.1037–967 B.C.) — Hebrew, king of Israel
Magnus Gabriel de la Gardie (1622–1686) — Swedish, count, chancellor
Rene Descartes (1596–1650) — French, philosopher
R. Ekeblad (?–1771) — Swedish
Elizabeth (1709–1762) — Russian, empress of Russia
Johann August Ernesti (1707–1781) — German, *Lutheran* theologian
Esau (c.1653–c.1506 B.C.) — Hebrew, fraternal twin of Jacob
Martin Folkes (1690–1754) — English, scientist
Frederick I (1676–1751) — German, king of Sweden
Frederick V (1723–1766) — Danish, king of Denmark
Genevieve (419/422–512) — French, *Catholic* patron saint of Paris
George II (1683–1760) — German, king of England
Gustaf Frederick Gyllenborg (1731–1808) — Swedish, president Board of Mines
John Hart (?–1762) — English, printer of Swedenborg's books
Thomas Hartley (1709–1784) — English, *Anglican* minister
Sara Hesselia (172?–?) — Swedish, acquaintance of Swedenborg

Horn (?–1756) — Swedish, baron, beheaded with Erik Brahe
Ignatius of Loyola (1491–1556) — Spanish, founder of *Society of Jesuits*
Isaac (c.1713–1533 B.C.) — Hebrew, son of Abraham and Sarah
Jacob (c.1653–c.1506 B.C.) — Hebrew, 3rd OT patriarch, name changed to Israel
James (?) — Hebrew, Alphaeus's son, chosen apostle of Jesus, aka "James the Less"
James (?) — Hebrew, Zebedee's son, John's brother, chosen apostle of Jesus
John (?–100 A.D.) — Hebrew, Zebedee's son, James's brother, chosen apostle of Jesus
John the Baptist (2/6 B.C.–30 A.D.) — Hebrew, preacher, baptised Jesus Christ
Judas (?) — Hebrew, James's son, chosen apostle of Jesus, aka "Thaddeus"
Judas Iscariot (?) — Hebrew, Simon's son, political activist, chosen apostle of Jesus
Sven Lagerberg (1672–1757) — Swedish, ambassador, senator
Antony van Leeuwenhoek (1632–1723) — Dutch, scientist, microscope maker
Gottfried Wilhelm Leibniz (1646–1716) — German, philosopher
John Lewis (?18th c.) — English, printer of Swedenborg's books, Hart's partner
Adam Leyel (?–1744) — Swedish, member Board of Mines
Louis XIV (1638–1715) — French, king of France
Martin Luther (1483–1546) — German, founder of *Lutheran Church*
Monsieur de Marteville (?18th c.) — Dutch, ambassador
Mary (?) — Hebrew, mother of Jesus Christ
Matthew (?) — Hebrew, tax collector, chosen apostle of Jesus
Philipp Melanchton (1497–1560) — German, a ldr of *Protestant* reform movement
Johan Moraeus (1672–1742) — Swedish, Swedenborg's cousin
Moses (c.1520–1440 B.C.) — Hebrew, prophet
Muhammad (570–632) — Saudi Arabian, prophet, founder of *Islam*
Nathaniel (?) — Hebrew, Talemai's son, chosen apostle of Jesus, aka "Bartholomew"
Isaac Newton (1643–1727) — English, physicist, mathematician, astronomer
Jöran Nordberg (1677–1744) — Swedish, King Carl XII's military chaplain
Paul (3–64/67 A.D.) — Roman, *Christian* missionary
William Penn (1644–1718) — English, founder of Pennsylvania
Peter III (1728–1762) — Russian, emperor of Russia
Philip (?) — Hebrew, chosen apostle of Jesus
Christopher Polhem (1661–1751) — Swedish, scientist, inventor
Emerentia Polhem (1703–1760) — Swedish, Swedenborg's second fiancé
Maria Polhem (1698–?) — Swedish, Swedenborg's first fiancé
Nils Porath (1690–1753) — Swedish, member Board of Mines
Sextus Quintus (?–1592) — Italian, *Catholic* pope
Rebekah (?) — Hebrew, wife of Isaac
Anders Olafsson Rhydelius (1677–1761) — Swedish, *Lutheran* bishop
Conrad Ribbing (?18th c.) — Swedish, baron
Francois Eugene de Savoie-Carignon (1663–1736) — Austrian, prince of Savoy
Peter Schönström (1682–1746) — Swedish, military captain
Georg Johannes Silfverström (1701–1752) — Swedish, Swedenborg's relative
Simon (?) — Hebrew, Andrew's brother, chosen apostle of Jesus, aka "Peter"
Simon (?) — Hebrew, political activist, chosen apostle of Jesus, aka "the Zealot"
Sixtus V (1521–1590) —Italian, *Catholic* pope, born Felice Peretti di Montalto
Hans Sloane (1660–1753) — Irish, physician, his collection became *British Museum*
Solomon (970–928 B.C.) — Hebrew, king of Israel

Stanislaus I (1677–1766) — Polish, king of Poland
David Stjerncrona (?18th century) — Swedish, baron
Anders Swab (1681–1731) — Swedish, mining official
Sarah Behm Swedberg (1666–1696) — Swedish, Emanuel Swedenborg's mother
Sara Bergia Swedberg (1666–1719) — Swedish, Emanuel Swedenborg's stepmother
Eliezer Swedberg (1689–1716) — Swedish, Emanuel Swedenborg's brother
Jesper Swedberg (1653–1735) — Swedish, *Lutheran* bishop, Swedenborg's father
Thomas (?) — Hebrew, chosen apostle of Jesus
Ulrica Eleonora (1688–1741) — Swedish, queen of Sweden
Gustavus Vasa (1496–1560) — Swedish, king of Sweden
Wellingk (1651–1727) — Swedish
August William (1722–1758) — German, prince of Prussia
Christian Wolff (1679–1754) — German, philosopher
Frances Xavier (1506–1552) — Spanish, *Jesuit* saint, born Francisco Javier
Nikolaus Ludwig von Zinzendorf (1700–1760) — German, *Moravian* bishop

Add names of people to the list that you know Swedenborg spoke with in spirit. Be sure to tell me. If I can verify that he did, I'll add them to the next edition.

THERE IS AN ANSWER

Dear Candace,
I saw a bumper sticker the other day that said, "If you can't find Jesus, go find his mother." What do you think of that?

S.S.
Los Angeles, California
August 2001

Dear S.S.,

The bumper sticker you saw: "If you can't find Jesus, go find his mother," unfortunately, is a common practice in today's Christian churches—to call the Lord, our Saviour, the Son of Mary. Rarely is He called the Son of God. This is because the Roman Catholics have made Mary, His mother, greater than and above all the other saints, as if she were a goddess or queen. The truth is that when the Lord glorified His Human, He put off everything of His mother's. He "changed" His natural body and then was completely a Divine Body.

Swedenborg tells us he met Mary in the spiritual world. She appeared to him in white clothing. She told Swedenborg that she now worships Jesus as God. She admitted that He was born of her, but that He became God completely by putting off all the maternal human from her. Mary then relayed that she was utterly opposed to anyone acknowledging Him as her son! Because the Lord's Divine, not her!

You may recall that the Lord stopped calling Mary, His mother, and called her **"woman"** from the cross; and when **"His mother and His brethren stood without, desiring to speak with Him,"** (Matthew 12:46-50) He didn't call her His mother. Nowhere in the Bible, when Mary is called the Mother of God, did that title come out of the mouth of the Lord Himself!

The straight truth is that you don't need anyone to intercede between you and the Lord Jesus Christ. You can pray to or talk with Him directly. The bumper sticker you saw is wrong.

Drawing by Bridget Swinton

SILA May 1993

Dear Candace,

I know Emanuel Swedenborg was born a Lutheran. Since he knew so much about God and the afterlife, did he remain a Lutheran his whole life?

R.L.
Tahoe, California
July 2001

Dear R.L.,

No. Swedenborg's father was a Bishop in the Lutheran Church which was started by Martin Luther (1483–1546). Luther — a German Catholic priest and Biblical professor at *Wittenberg University* — dared to question his religion's practices which ultimately led to the Protestant Reformation.

In rebellion to Catholicism's practice of "selling of indulgences" where someone could be released from their sin's punishment by contributing money to a worthy cause, Martin Luther taught faith alone was the correct path to take.

He taught that people are made righteous in the eyes of God, solely through faith in Christ, apart from any works of their own. Luther was repulsed by seeing that "indulgences" were sometimes being abused as a means of raising money for the church. And parishioners were being told that they could release souls from purgatory by paying for "indulgences".

Not only did Luther criticize the practice of "indulgences", but other practices as well. He thought that the language of the people should be used in worship rather than Latin. He promoted congregational singing as part of worship. He posted his "Ninety-Five Theses" on the door of the *Wittenberg Castle Church* which was *Wittenberg University's* bulletin board.

Luther, teaching that the Bible should be the sole authority in the church, believed that people are saved by Christ dying for their salvation, based on his reading of the Gospels and the letters of Paul. Therefore, people are "not guilty" for Christ's sake, meaning God gives faith as a gift; people are justified by their faith.

In 1521, Martin Luther was expelled from the Catholic Church. In 1525, he married Katherina von Bora, a former nun, and they had five children. Luther spent the last twenty years of his life forming a new religion, protesting the Catholic stronghold on individuals.

Emanuel Swedenborg, in the 18th century, came to understand that the Word of God was written in a correspondential style which allows immediate communication with heaven. He said that the writings of Paul and the apostles were doctrinal writings—good books—but not written as the other books of the Word, e.g. Genesis, Exodus.

Swedenborg said he "met and spoke with" Martin Luther on several occasions. He said that Luther was (at that time) in a state of suffering in the other world for his having introduced the doctrine of faith alone. He added though, that Luther is not among the damned. Speaking to someone in the spiritual world, Swedenborg said: **"Do you know that Luther has risen, and has now renounced his erroneous ideas of justification by faith in three Divine persons from eternity, and therefore has been placed among the blessed in the new heaven, and sees and laughs at those who run mad after him?"** (*True Christianity* #137)

Swedenborg explains why faith and charity, together, are necessary for salvation. *True Christian Religion* #142: **"For faith is nothing but truth, and charity is nothing but good. It is by means of Divine truth acting from good, in other words by means of faith inspired by charity that a person's reformation and regeneration is effected, and by this means too [s/he] is renewed, quickened and made holy and righteous. As all these processes advance and increase, [s/he] is cleansed from evils, and this cleansing is what is meant by the forgiveness of sins."**

Days before Swedenborg died (29 March 1772), in London, England, friends suggested he take the Holy Supper. Rev. Arvid Ferelius, pastor of the Swedish Lutheran Church in London was brought to Swedenborg's deathbed to officiate. [Rev. Ferelius, though an affirmative reader of Swedenborg's theological Writings, he never openly acknowledged this and requested his name not be used in the newly formed proclamation for the New Church of the New Jerusalem. Yet, all his three daughters married Swedish Swedenborgians in the New Church!]

In preparation for the Holy Supper, Rev. Ferelius asked Swedenborg if he would deny anything that he had written, especially since some believed he had given his new theology for fame. Swedenborg replied: **"As truly as you see me before your eyes so true is everything that I have written; and I could have said more had it been permitted. When you enter eternity you will see everything, and then you and I shall have much to talk about."**

Then Swedenborg said that as a member of the other world, he didn't need to take the sacrament of Holy Supper, but that he would in order to show the correspondence between the church in the other world and the church here on earth.

Swedenborg used this ornament in *Secrets of Heaven*

Dear Candace,
The Bible Code predicts the future and Armageddon. The Old Testament has predictions that are controversial and hidden messages. Does Swedenborg agree with the Bible Code? Was it figured out independently of Swedenborg?

D.D.
Tujunga, California
January 2007

Dear D.D.,
Some think so. But, this idea of a cracking "the Bible code" is not new, just the marketing.

The first recorded person to say they figured out what the Bible "really" was saying was the Spanish rabbi, Bachya ben Asher (1255–c.1340). Knowing oral tradition said every word and every letter of the Bible was inspired by God, he found words made up of letters from each word per sentence.

Sir Isaac Newton (1642–1727) tried to prove the Bible true through science. He wrote about it, devoting more time to the Bible than the sciences. How many knew *that*?

Emanuel Swedenborg (1688–1772) published between 1749 and 1756 his longest theological work, *Secrets of Heaven (Arcana Coelestia)*. It is his "Bible code", but he called it the **"internal sense"**. *Secrets of Heaven* is twelve volumes covering Genesis 1–50 and Exodus 1–40, verse-by-verse.

Elijah ben Solomon Zalman (1720–1797) was a Jewish rabbi and scholar. He is often called "the Vilna Gaon" meaning "the saintly genius from Vilna". He was born in Vilnius, Lithuania. Vilnius is the capital of Lithuania and named after the Vilnia River. Zalman is said to have found the secrets of the universe in the Torah—Books of Moses: Genesis, Exodus, Leviticus, Numbers, Deuteronomy.

More explanations were recorded by the Slovakian rabbi, Michael Ber Weissmandl (1903–1957), but were not published until after his death.

In the 1980s, Eliyahu Rips (1950?–), a mathematician who was born in Latvia discovered in the *Hebrew University of Jerusalem* writings by a Israeli school teacher, Avraham Oren. Dr. Rips, Doron Witztum, Yoav Rosenberg, and several others attempted to continue what Oren had started. They used the computer to perfect their Bible decoding.

This quote is from *The Bible Code* (page 25): "Rips ExplAineD thaT eacH codE is a Case Of adDing Every fourth or twelfth or fiftieth letter to form a word. The hidden message — READ THE CODE."

D. Witztum, E. Rips, and Y. Rosenberg published their article, "Equidistant Letter Sequences in the Book of Genesis" in the *Statistical Science* journal in 1994.

The Bible Code by Michael Drosnin (1946–) was published in 1997. He began researching his Bible code in 1992 after meeting Dr. Rips in Israel. Drosnin was a reporter for the *Wall Street Journal*. He predicted Prime Minister of Israel, Yitzhak Rabin's (1922–1995) assassination a year before it happened through using his Bible code and told him about it. With the help of mathematicians, Drosnin found other predictions in the Torah: an earthquake in L.A. (2010), a meteor hitting the Earth (2006, 2010, 2012), and Armageddon (1998–2006). He also wrote about how Jerusalem will be destroyed by a nuclear bomb.

The Bible Code also implies that extraterrestrials delivered the message of the Bible. *The Bible Code II: The Countdown* was published in 2002. *The Bible Code III: The Quest* should come out April 2007.

So, who is right? The real question here should be: *Who is more known?* Currently, the more popular Bible code book is by Drosnin and not Swedenborg. It's obvious who had the better advertising and word of mouth! That aside, I'd say *The Bible Code* is more known than *Secrets of Heaven* because the former excites fear and voyeurism—naturalism.

Swedenborg's books ask the reader to examine their own life and to change it! His **"internal sense"** of the Word not only explains the stories from the Lord's view, but also demonstrates how we can apply those inner meanings to our own lives showing us how to become an angel in heaven—our potential eternal home.

Secrets of Heaven begins with this, #1: **"From the mere letter of the Word of the Old Testament no one would ever discern the fact that this part of the Word contains deep secrets of heaven, and that everything within it both in general and in particular bears reference to the Lord, to His heaven, to the church, to religious belief, and to all things connected therewith; for from the letter or sense of the letter all that anyone can see is that—to speak generally—everything therein has reference merely to the external rites and ordinances of the Jewish Church. Yet the truth is that everywhere in that Word there are internal things which never appear at all in the external things except a very few which the Lord revealed and explained to the Apostles; such as that the sacrifices signify the Lord; that the land of Canaan and Jerusalem signify heaven—on which account they are called the Heavenly Canaan and Jerusalem—and that Paradise has a similar signification."**

Secrets of Heaven #3: **"Without such a Life, the Word as to the letter is dead. The case in this respect is the same as it is with [a person], who—as is known in the Christian world—is both internal and external. When separated from the internal [person], the external [person] is the body, and is therefore dead; for it is the internal [person] that is alive and that causes the external [person] to be so, the internal [person] being the soul. So is it with the Word, which, in respect to the letter alone, is like the body without the soul."**

The Bible Code by Rips reminds me of the fun anagram game—the word "history" includes "hi", "his", "to", "story". There are even witty anagrams such as "A shoplifter = has to pilfer." (by Irene Fullarton of New Jersey, 1908).

Opponents of *The Bible Code* (and there are many) have put the 1851 novel *Moby Dick* by Herman Melville through a computer program to find codes and found death predictions for Princess Diana, President Kennedy, and Martin Luther King, Jr. (*Skeptical Inquirer* magazine, November/December, 1997.) Why would the Lord reveal these codes in *Moby Dick*? For what good purpose?

Swedenborg didn't predict anything about the physical world, but described the spiritual landscape of our inner beings and the next world. For instance, while reading the Word, he tells us to think the word "intelligence" when we read the word "garden"; think "false truths" when we read "serpent"; think "truth" when we read "sword"; think "self-love" when we read "dragon". It's much deeper than looking for individual letters.

A curious thing about Rips or Drosnin's Bible code is that anyone can look for whatever they want in the Bible. How does that make it Divine? For it to be Divine, the Bible must be consistent and applicable to all.

By the way, Swedenborg, who wanted to meet the famous Isaac Newton, never did. Yet, he wrote about meeting him in spirit in his book *Last Judgment* #289: **"I spoke with Newton concerning a vacuum, and concerning colors. I spoke with him several times. He is a thoroughly sincere man, and is among his own, and is beloved. He told me that he now knows that the Lord is the sun of the angelic heaven, and that all light, which in its essence is Divine Intelligence, and which gives intelligence to angels and also to people, is from Him; although people are ignorant that that light enlightens the understanding, and causes them to think intelligently."**

Students from *Marshall High School* of Los Angeles
drew Swedenborg in chalk at *The 9th Angel Festival*

Dear Candace,

I have around 12 Swedenborg books (everything but the set of the Arcana Coelestia*) and have read them many times. What gives the Writings authenticity (for me) is the fact that they come out of experience, which he reported objectively as a scientist. I am interested in spiritual experience of the type described by dear old Emanuel, because I believe that if one follows the path set down by him one will come into the same type of spiritual experience he did, though probably not as intense. What have you found Swedenborg says about Paul? I know he says his faith alone isn't correct.*

Z.M.
Los Angeles, California
February 2006

Dear Z.M.,

Swedenborg says a lot about Paul, a popular self-appointed apostle of Jesus Christ from present-day Turkey. Many Christian churches today—Anglican, Eastern Orthodox, Lutheran, Roman Catholic—follow St. Paul. Letters he wrote to newly formed Christian churches were responsible for the early spread of Christianity. These letters became books—Romans, Corinthians, Galatians, Philippians, Thessalonians, Philemon—in the New Testament and are called "Pauline Christianity". Modern scholars consider Paul the founder of Christianity (after Jesus).

One of the main tenets of the Pauline doctrine is that salvation—entrance into heaven—is achieved only by faith in Jesus Christ and not by any good acts by a Christian. Some Christian churches disagree with that doctrine, sighting James 2:24 that says: **"Man is justified by works and not by faith alone."**

What Swedenborg wrote in his books about Paul (3–64/67A.D.)—originally named Saul—will shock many Christians and turn them off to Swedenborg all together. He wrote: **"I have spoken with Paul for a whole year."** But, for those that this fact doesn't deter, episodes of Paul's afterlife which Swedenborg witnessed will bring amazement and confirmation of something they may have suspected all along. The best way for me to answer your question is to let Swedenborg tell you about Paul in his own words.

First, let me show you part of a letter (15 April 1766) he wrote to his friend, Dr. Gabriel Andersson Beyer in Sweden, while Swedenborg was in Holland: **"With reference to the writings of the Apostles and Paul I have not included these in *[Secrets of Heaven]*, and this for the reason that they are doctrinal writings, and so are not written in the style of the Word as are the Prophets, David, the Gospels, and the Revelation.**

The style of the Word wholly consists of correspondences, on which account it effects an immediate communication with heaven. In the doctrinal writings, however, there is another style which indeed communicates with heaven, but mediately. That they were so written by the Apostles was in order that the new Christian Church might commence through these, on which account doctrinal matters could not be written in the very style of the Word, but in a manner that might be more clearly and more directly understood. Nonetheless, the writings of the Apostles are good books for the Church, maintaining the doctrine of charity and its faith as strongly as ever did the Lord

Himself in the Gospels and in the Revelation, as can be clearly seen and observed if one attends to the matter while reading those writings.

That the words of Paul concerning justification by faith, Romans 3:28, have been completely misunderstood, is shown in the *Apocalypse Revealed* #417, as may be seen. It follows that the doctrine concerning faith alone as justifying, which constitutes the theology of our day in the Churches of the Reformed, is built on an entirely false foundation.

My most respectful greetings to you and to my friends. I remain, etc. Em. Swedenborg"

Many who delve deep into Swedenborg's books are surprised to discover that he not only spoke with the historical Paul, but that he saw Paul descend into hell. *Spiritual Experiences* #4321: "Hence it was made known to all that Paul is of such a nefarious character...and he is now among those companies which rove about, and approximate the place of the desert."

Spiritual Experiences #4412: "Paul is among the worst of the apostles, which has been made known to me by ample experience. The love of self, whereby he was ensnared before he preached the gospel, remained with him also afterwards, and because he was then, for the most part, in a like state, he was prompted by that love and by his nature to wish to be in scenes of tumult. He did all things from the end of being greatest in heaven, and of judging the tribes of Israel. That he remained such afterwards appears from very much experience, for I spoke with him more than with others; nay, he is such, that the rest of the apostles in the other life rejected him from their company, and no longer recognize him for one of them.

[I know it] also from the fact that he associated himself to one of the worst devils, who would feign rule all things, and pledged himself to this spirit to obtain for him his end; besides many other things, which it would be too tedious to relate.

If all the things which I know concerning Paul should be related, they would be enough to fill sheets. That he wrote epistles does not prove that he was such [as that would seem to imply], for even the impious can preach well and write epistles; it is one thing to be, and another to speak and to write, as was also said to him. Moreover he has not mentioned, in his epistles, the least word of what the Lord taught, nor cited one of his parables, so that he received nothing from the life and discourse of the Lord, as was also said to him, when yet in the Evangelists is the very Gospel itself."

Spiritual Experiences #4561: "Paul, while he was alive, thought, respecting the other life, only in a worldly manner. He supposed there would be worldly glory there, not knowing what heavenly glory was, or whether it was anything. And he therefore supposed that it was he who should introduce all into heaven, and that the Lord would accept them on his account.

Moreover, he imagined that he deserved better than others. On account of that glory, namely worldly glory, he underwent so many dangers and punishments, so that he might be greatest; consequently, from another motive than that the Lord taught, namely, that he who wished to be greatest should not enter, but he who [wished to be] least, and that the last will be first. Hence it is, that he associated himself, on several occasions, with evil spirits and devils, in order that he might make for himself an altogether infernal heaven; and hence it is, that he rejects the interiors of the Word, because they are opposed to worldly glory, and opposed to merit."

Spiritual Experiences #4562: "**At the last, Paul was given a habitation by himself above, on the left; but, still, he repeatedly wished to make a disturbance. At length, he was brought lower down, where he does not know that he had been Paul.**"

In *Newsweek* magazine, 30 August 2004, Jerry Adler and Anne Underwood wrote in their article, "Search for the Sacred":

> Scholars like John Dominic Crossan, a professor emeritus of religious studies at De-Paul University and former co-chair of the Jesus Seminar, can read volumes into a simple signpost in the Biblical town of Ephesus. "There's a gate to the market that Paul would have walked under," Crossan relates. "On top, it says Caesar is the son of God. When Paul applies that name to Jesus, it's not just a nice title. It's the title of Caesar. That is known as high treason."

Swedenborgians know that Jesus was God Himself that actually came down to earth! If Paul perpetuated that Jesus was God's kid, to slap Caesar in the face by saying Jesus was royalty equal to Caesar, that was more than treason, it was flat out wrong! As Swedenborg teaches us, Paul got several things wrong. But, a good use came from his inflated ego—the spread of Christianity.

Drawing by Tuan Hauptmann   *SILA* January 1998

Dear Candace,
What of Buddhism and some of the other major religions that don't follow Christ?
B.M.
Mt. Vernon, New York
July 1990

Dear B.M.,
    Swedenborg did not mention Buddha by name, but he did write about non-Christian faiths in many of his books which were written over 200 years ago.
    Swedenborg wrote that people before Jesus Christ's coming had religions that were representative. They understood the correspondences of spiritual things to natural things and used them in their daily lives and worship. The Egyptians understood correspondences and depicted them in their hieroglyphics. And the Jewish faith was a representative church as all of its judgments and statutes represented spiritual things.
    The ancients understood ideas such as the sun represents God's love (warmth) and wisdom (light) and many other ideas represented by lambs, birds, horses, etc. They sculpted these objects as reminders. But, after a time (centuries) the knowledge of these things corresponding to attributes of God were forgotten and the ancients' descendants, all over the world, began to worship the sculpted images as holy, unaware their forefathers saw nothing holy in them, but only what they represented.
    Buddha was born about 500 years before Christ in the country of Nepal. He taught inner peace and love to the neighbour, forgetting God in the process. Though this religion had remnants of good from the ancients' science of correspondences, it led some to worship Buddha, the man.
    Idolatrous worship spread over many kingdoms in the world.
    Then God came on earth revealing Himself. Christ was born. But, few took His ways and so, in His Divine Providence, the Lord (Swedenborg tells us) raised up a new religion, through Muhammad, which was adapted to the aptitude of the "Orientals" to **"blot out the idolatry of many nations"** (See *True Christian Religion* #833)
    Muhammad was born in Mecca, Saudi Arabia about 570 years after Christ's death. Muhammad wrote the Koran, a holy book, which has something from both the Old and New Testaments teaching Allah is God, and Jesus Christ is the Son of God. This religion was provided by the Lord, so people could have some knowledge of Him before entering the spiritual world. Still, some chose to worship Muhammad.
    Everyone will be shown after death that the Lord is the God of heaven and earth; that He came into the world; then His Divine and Human became one Person—united as soul and body.
    Some people believe that only Christians are saved. Swedenborg tells us this is an insane heresy! Fact is, there are more non-Christians in the world than Christians. There are today over a billion and a half Christians. But, there are over 300 million Buddhists, over 650 million Hindus, and almost 900 million Muslims.
    Swedenborg enlightens us that heaven cannot be made up of human beings from only one religion! Heaven consists of people from all religions for people have DIFFERENT characteristics.

Swedenborg rationally teaches that baptism does not save a person, only regeneration (term he uses often) does—being born anew through self examination.

Any person that 1) acknowledges God and 2) shuns evils by living a good life in keeping with their religion, will have a place in heaven for the Lord desires the salvation of ALL.

UPDATE

I found an interesting article, "Roots of Misconception, From the Middle Ages through the Modern Period: The European Discovery of Islam as a World Culture" by Ibrahim Kalin. He is Assistant Professor of Islamic Studies, at *College of the Holy Cross,* Worcester, Massachusetts. Full article can be found at http://www.theamericanmuslim.org/tam.php/features/articles/roots_of_misconceptio n_from_the_middle_ages_through_the_modern_period_the_e/. Here is an excerpt:

> Another very important exception of this period is the famous Swiss theologian and mystic Emanuel Swedenborg (1688-1772) and his historical theology of the rise of Islam. Swedenborg considered the spread of Islam to be part of the Divine Providence. For him, the true goal of Islam and its Prophet was to destroy the rampant paganism of pre-Islamic Arabs and their neighbors because the Church was too weak and dispersed to fight against paganism. It was as a response to this historic moment that the Lord sent a religion accommodated to the genius of the Orientals. Thus Swedenborg states
>
>> that the Mahometan religion acknowledges the Lord as the Son of God, as the wisest of men, and as the greatest prophet that religion was raised up by the Lord's Divine Providence to destroy the idolatries of many nations that all these idolatries might be extirpated, it was brought to pass, by the Divine Providence of the Lord, that a new religion should arise, accommodated to the genius of the Orientals, in which there should be something from both Testaments of the Word, and which should teach that the Lord came into the world, and that he was the greatest prophet, the wisest of all men, and the Son of God. This was accomplished through Mahomet.
>
> Although Swedenborg attributes the belief in the divinity of Jesus Christ to Muslims, which is unwarranted in the Islamic sources, he hastens to add that the reason why Islam accepted Jesus only as a prophet and not a divine being was because the Orientals acknowledged God the Creator of the universe, and could not comprehend that He came into the world and assumed the Human. So neither do Christians comprehend it. By combining his theology of history with anthropology of the Orientals, Swedenborg confronts Islam as a religion whose essential message is the same as that of Christianity. That such an inclusivist approach should be taken by a mystic theologian of the stature of Emanuel Sweden-

borg is extremely important considering the rising tide of conservative Christian attacks on Islam in recent decades and especially after 9/11. The example of Swedenborg together with Goethe and others evinces the reality of a peaceful co-existence between Christians and Muslims on both social and, more importantly, religious and theological grounds.

I wrote Professor Kalin to inform him Swedenborg was not Swiss.

I ask you to compare the Swedenborg quote above and the two quotes I found by Swedenborg which were most likely used to make that one quote.

Conjugial Love #342: "**The Mohammedan religion, however, is not a stumbling-block to those who believe that all things are of Divine Providence. These inquire wherein this Providence lies; moreover, they find it lies in this: That the Mohammedan religion acknowledges our Lord as the Son of God, as the wisest of men, and as the great prophet who came into the world that he might teach men. But because the Mohammedans make the Koran the only book of their religion, and Mohammed, who wrote it, is therefore inseated in their thoughts, they follow him with a kind of worship, and think little about our Lord. That it may be fully known that of the Lord's Divine Providence that religion was raised up for the wiping out of the idolatries of many nations, this shall be told in some order.**"

Divine Providence #255: "**In the course of time, when the science of correspondences had been lost, their posterity began to worship the graven images themselves, as being holy in themselves, not knowing that their forefathers had seen no holiness in those things, but only that they represented and consequently signified holy things according to correspondences. Hence arose the idolatries which filled the whole world, Asia with its neighboring islands, as well as Africa and Europe. In order that all these idolatries might be rooted out it was brought about by the Divine Providence of the Lord that a new religion should arise, adapted to the genius of Orientals, in which there should be something from both Testaments of the Word and which should teach that the Lord came into the world, and that He was a very great prophet, the wisest of all men, and the Son of God. This was effected by means of Mohammed, from whom that religion is called the Mohammedan religion.**"

Chapter 10

WHO'S WHO IN SWEDENBORGIANISM

Over the years, I've seen different lists of famous "Swedenborgians". But, never one list of "everyone". The following two lists were created by me. Some may quibble with the individuals included, but that's okay. I'd rather have dialogue than ignorance. Facts speak for themselves. The reason these lists exist at all is because Swedenborg is not a household name—the public at large don't know him. To learn that these famous and respected individuals knew/know about Swedenborg is significant and a testament to the power of his words. These lists are not complete. Most recently added was Rev. Dr. Martin Luther King, Jr. in February 2008.

THE SHAKERS

This list of movers and shakers did for a fact do one or some of these: owned Emanuel Swedenborg's books, wrote about Swedenborg, was/is a member of a Swedenborgian church or organization, used Swedenborgian doctrines to change the world. Many on this list would say they are Swedenborgian. All would say they had been influenced by Swedenborg in some way.

Mawutodzi Kodzo Abissath (?living) — Ghanaian, journalist
John Holmes Agnew (1804–1865) — American, *Presbyterian* minister
Alexander Aksakov (1832–1903) — Russian, philosopher, cnclr of state to Czar
Eddie Albert (1906–2005) — American, actor, born Edward Albert Heimberger
Bronson Alcott (1799–1888) — American, teacher, author
Carl Jonas Love Almqvist (1793–1866) — Swedish, poet, feminist, social critic
Joseph Andrews (1806–1873) — American, painter, engraver
Timothy Shay Arthur (1809–1885) — American, author, aka "T.S."
Per Daniel Amadeus Atterbom (1790–1855) — Swedish, literary critic, aka "P.D.A."
Honoré de Balzac (1799–1850) — French, novelist, playwright
Augustin de Barruel (1741–1820) — French, *Jesuit* priest

Clarence Walker Barren (1855–1928) — American, editor *Wall Street Journal*
Benjamin Fisk Barrett (1808–1892) — American, *Unitarian* minister, convtd 1840
Henry Bateman (1806–1880) — English, surgeon
Charles Pierre Baudelaire (1821–1867) — French, poet
Jonathan Bayley (1810–1886) — English, *New Church* minister
Daniel Carter Beard (1850–1941) —American, illustrator, author, aka "Uncle Dan"
Henry Ward Beecher (1813–1887) — American, brother of Harriet Beecher Stowe
Larry Beezer (1949–2000) — American, comic, born Thomas Lawrence Behlert
Saul Bellow (1915–2005) — Canadian-American, author, born Solomon Bellows
William Henry Benade (1816–1905) — American, *Moravian* minister, cnvtd 1843
Nikolai Berdyaev (1874–1948) — Russian, philosopher
Ingmar Bergman (1918– 2007) — Swedish, film and stage director
Oskar Bergman (1879–1963) — Swedish, painter
Lars Bergquist (1930–) — Swedish, ambassador, author
Louis Hector Berlioz (1802–1869) — French, composer, conductor, author, critic
Jean-Jacques Bernard (1791–1828) — French, captain under Napoleon
John Bigelow (1817–1911) — American, a founder of the *New York Public Library*
William Blake (1757–1827) — English, poet, artist
Ralph Albert Blakelock (1847–1919) — American, painter
Alexander Blok (1880–1921) — Russian, poet
Christen A. Blom-Dahl (?living) — Norwegian, consul general in Valencia, Spain
Jorge Luis Borges (1899–1986) — Argentinean, poet, author
Charles Carroll Bonney (1831–1903) — American, lawyer
William Booth (1829–1912) — English, *Methodist* preacher, fnder *Salvation Army*
Gabor S. Boritt (1940–) Hungarian-American, dir. *Civil War Inst. Gettysburg College*
Ted Bosley (?living) — American, director of *The Gamble House*, Pasadena, CA
Fredrika Bremer (1801–1865) — Swedish, writer, feminist activist
Arthur Otto Brickman (?–1886) — American, *N.C.* minister to Civil War soldiers
Albert Brisbane (1809–1890) — American, journalist at *New York Tribune*
Isaac S. Brittan (1826–?) — American, Illinois state superintendent of schools
Edward John Broadfield (1831–1913) — English, a founder of *Manchester Univ.*
Phillips Brooks (1835–1893) — American, *Episcopal* preacher
Arthur Page Brown (1859–1896) — American, architect
Charles Francis Browne (1859–1920) — American, painter
Elizabeth Barrett Browning (1806–1861) — English, poet, wife of Robert
Robert Browning (1812–1889) — English, poet, husband of Elizabeth
William Cullen Bryant (1794–1878) — American, editor of *New York Evening Post*
James Buchanan (1784–1858) — English, master of infant school
Joseph Rodes Buchanan (1814–1899) —American, scientist
Sergei Bulgakov (1871–1944) — Russian, philosopher
Edward Bulwer-Lytton (1803–1873) — English, novelist, politician
Luther Burbank (1849–1926) — American, botanist
Daniel Hudson Burnham (1846–1912) — American, architect, city planner
Sophy Burnham (1936–) — American, author
George Bush (1796–1860) — American, *Presbyterian* minister, converted 1845
Antonia Susan Byatt (1936–) — English, author, aka "A.S."

Leopold Enoch Calleja (1850–1930) — Mexican, doctor, advisor to pres. Madero
Thomas Carlyle (1795–1881) — Scottish, author
Andrew Carnegie (1835–1919) — Scottish-American, industrialist, philanthropist
Timothy Harrington Carter (1798–1894) — American, fndr *Old Corner Bookstore*
Robert Carter III (c.1727–1804) — American, plantation owner, abolitionist
Ebenezer Mattoon Chamberlain (1805–1861) — American, dem. Senator Indiana
Theophilus Parsons Chandler, Jr. (1845–1928) — American, architect
Jonathan Chapman (1774–1845) — American, nurseryman, aka "Johnny Appleseed"
Lydia Maria Child (1802–1880) — American, author, social activist, abolitionist
Zenon Chizhevzki (?living) — Polish, prof. of lit. at *Gdansk University* in Poland
Otis Clapp (1806–1886) — American, doctor, homeopath, a founder of *M.I.T.*
John Clowes (1743–1831) — English, *Anglican* minister
Thomas Cole (1801–1848) — English-American, painter
Samuel Taylor Coleridge (1772–1834) — English, poet, philosopher
James Bryant Conant (1893–1978) — American, chemist, president of *Harvard*
Pamela Colman Smith (1878–1951) — English, artist, aka "Pikie"
James Cook (1728–1779) — English, explorer
William Cookworthy (1705–1780) — English, *Quaker* rev., fndr Eng. porcelain ind.
John Calvin Coolidge, Jr. (1872–1933) — American, 30th president of the U.S.
Genevive Carosin (?living) — Mauritian, track athlete *Commonwealth Games,* 1970
Henry Corbin (1903–1978) — French, professor Islamic Studies at *Sorbonne*, Paris
Marie Corelli (1855–1924) — English, novelist
March Cost (191?–1973) — Scottish, author, born Margaret Mackie Morrison
Samuel Crompton (1753–1827) — English, inventor of the spinning mule
Vladimir I. Dal (1801–1872) — Russian, writer
Charles Anderson Dana (1819–1897) —American, journalist
Alfred Deakin (1856–1919) — Australian, 2nd, 5th, 7th prime minister of Australia
Carl Erik Deléen (1767–1850) — Swedish, author, printer, circuit court notary
Charles Dickens (1812–1870) — English, novelist
Herbert Dingle (1890–1978) — English, physicist
Fyodor Dostoevsky (1821–1881) — Russian, novelist
Arthur Conan Doyle (1859–1930) — English, author
Horatio Dresser (1866–1954) — American, philosopher, author
Henry Drummond (1851–1897) —Scottish, writer
Jacob Duché (1737–1798) — American, *Episcopal* minister
Margaretta Lammot Du Pont (1808–1903) — American, philanthropist
Glennyce S. Eckersley (?living) — English, author, broadcaster
Gunnar Ekelöf (1907–1968) — Swedish, poet
Vilhelm Ekelund (1880–1949) — Swedish, writer
George Eliot (1819–1880) — English, novelist, born Mary Ann "Marian" Evans
Ralph Waldo Emerson (1803–1882) — American, poet, philosopher
Warren Felt Evans (1817–1889) — American, *Methodist* minister, converted in 1863
Francis Oliver Finch (1802–1862) — English, painter, poet
John Flaxman (1755–1826) — English, sculptor
Théodore Flournoy (1854–1920) — Swiss, psychology professor at *Univ. of Geneva*
Emmet Fox (1886–1951) — Irish, leader in New Thought movement
Benjamin Franklin (1706–1790) — American, a founding father of the United States

Philip Freneau (1752–1832) — American, aka "poet of the American Revolution"
Friedrich Wilhelm August Froebel (1782–1852) — German, educator, psychologist
Robert Frost (1874–1963) — American, poet
Northrop Frye (1912–1991) — Canadian, literary critic
Margaret Fuller (1810–1850) — American, journalist, "Sarah Margaret Fuller Ossoli"
Albert Gabay (?living) — Australian, prof. History & Religion *La Trobe University*
Matilda Joslyn Gage (1826–1898) — American, suffragist, Native American activist
Jean-Jacques Gailliard (1890–1976) — Belgian, painter
Emiel van Galen (?living) — Dutch, homeopathic doctor
Amelita Galli-Curci (1882–1963) — Italian, operatic coloratura soprano
Paul Gauguin (1848–1903) — French, artist
Théophile Gautier (1811–1872) — French, author
Henri Gerard (1860–1925) — French, artist
Henry George (1839-1897) — American, political economist
Robert Andrew Gilbert (?living) — English, masonic and rosicrucian author
William Schwenck Gilbert (1836–1911) — English, dramatist, aka "W.S."
Lillian Gish (1893–1993) — American, actress
Scott Glenn (1941–) — American, actor
Johann Wolfgang von Goethe (1749–1832) — German, poet, novelist, playwright
Meir Goldschmidt (1819–1887) — Danish, writer
F. Golubinskiy (?19th c.) — Russian, prof. of Philosophy at *Moscow Academy*
Hans Burch Gram (1786–1840) — American, America's first homeopath
Nickolai Grech (1787–1867) — Russian, journalist, publisher
Horace Greeley (1811–1872) — American, editor *New York Tribune*
Wilfred Thomason Grenfell (1865–1940) — English, medical missionary to Canada
Jean-Francois-Étienne Le Bys des Guays (1794–1864) — French, soldier, judge
Edgar Albert Guest (1881–1959) — English-American, poet, aka "Eddie Guest"
Judith Guest (1936–) — American, novelist, great-niece of Eddie Guest
Anders Gyllenhaal (1951–) — American, executive editor of *Miami Herald*
Leonard Gyllenhaal (1752–1840) — Swedish, military officer, entomologist
Stephen Gyllenhaal (1949–) — American, film director, brother of Anders
Edward Everett Hale (1822–1909) — American, author, *Unitarian* minister
Anders Hallengren (1950–) — Swedish, history prof. *Stockholm University*, author
Lorenzo Hammarsköld (1785–1827) —Swedish, literary critic
Brooks Hansen (1965–) — American, author
John Martin-Harvey (1863–1944) — English, actor
Julian Hawthorne (1846–1934) — American, writer, journalist, son of Nathanial
Nathanial Hawthorne (1804–1864) — American, novelist, father of Julian
Sophia Peabody Hawthorne (1809–1871) — American, painter, wife of Nathanial
Henrich Heine (1797–1856) — German, journalist, poet
Henry John Heinz (1844–1919) — German-American, founder of *H J Heinz Co.*
Johann Gottfried von Herder (1744–1803) — German, poet
Alexander Herzen (1812–1870) — Russian, author
Ethan Allen Hitchcock (1835–1909) — American, U.S. secretary of the interior
Robert Hindmarsh (1759–1835) — English, son of *Methodist* preacher
John Hitz (c.1820–1864) — Swiss, consul-general for Switzerland in America
Francis Marcellus Hodson (?–1828) — English, *Methodist* minister

Anders Johan von Höpken (1712–1789) — Swedish, prime minister
Walter Marshall Horton (1895–1966) — American, *Baptist* minister *Oberlin College*
John Haynes Holmes (1879–1964) — American, *Unitarian* minister
Samuel Gridley Howe (1801–1876) — American, physician, abolitionist
Julia Ward Howe (1819–1910) — American, abolitionist, poet, wife of Samuel Howe
William Dean Howells (1837–1920) — American, author, literary critic
Elbert Hubbard (1856–1915) — American, writer, artist
Victor Hugo (1802–1885) — French, poet, novelist
Kenneth Hultgren (1915–1968) — American, animator of *Snow White, Bambi,* etc.
John Nelson Hyde (1865–1912) — American, *Presbyterian* missionary in India
George Inness (1825–1894) — American, painter
Henry James, Sr. (1811–1882) — American, *Christian* theologian, author
Henry James (1843–1916) — American, author, son of Henry James, Sr.
Leon James (1938–) — American, professor of psychology at *University of Hawaii*
William James (1842–1910) — American, psychologist, philosopher, brother of Henry
Thomas Jefferson (1743–1826) — American, 3rd president of the United States
Joseph Jefferson (1829–1905) — American, actor
Sarah Orne Jewett (1849–1909) — American, novelist
Inge Jonsson (1928–) — Swedish, professor at *Stockholm University*
Johannes Jørgensen (1866–1956) — Danish, poet
Ernst Josephson (1851–1906) — Jewish-Swedish, painter
Carl Gustav Jung (1875–1961) — Swiss, psychologist
Johann Heinrich Jung-Stilling (1740–1817) — German, writer
Toyohiko Kagawa (1888–1960) — Japanese, pacifist, *Christian* reformer
Solomon John Keal (1977–) — American, solo piano artist
William Keith (1839–1911) — Scottish-American, painter
Helen Keller (1880–1968) — American, author, 1st deaf-blind to graduate college
James Tyler Kent (1849–1916) — American, homeopathic physician
Hermann Alexander Keyserling (1880–1946) — Estonian, philosopher, author
Søren Kierkegaard (1813–1855) — Danish, philosopher, *Christian* theologian
Niels Andreas Vibe Kierulff (1796–1874) — Danish, judge
Basil King (1859–1928) — Canadian, *Episcopal* clergyman, novelist
Martin Luther King, Jr. (1929–1968) — American, a leader in civil rights movement
Stephen King (1947–) — American, author
William Roscoe Kinter (1915–1997) —American, colonel, ambassador to Thailand
Friedrich Gottlieb Klopstock (1724–1803) — German, poet
Gary Valentine Lachman (1955–) —American, inducted *Rock & Rock Hall of Fame*
Olof Lagercranz (?living) — Swedish, literary critic
Bernhard Lang (1957–) — Austrian, music composer, author
Alphonse de Lamartine (1790–1869) — French, author
Erik Larson (1954–) — American, author
Johann Kaspar Lavater (1741–1801) — Swiss, *Christian* theologian, physiognomist
Joseph Sheridan Le Fanu (1814–1873) — Anglo-Irish, novelist
Robert Lemm (?living) — Dutch, author
Gerald M. Lemole (?living) — American, MD, at 1st heart transplant in U.S., 1968
Clive Staples Lewis (1898–1963) — Irish, author, aka "C.S. Lewis" or "Jack"
Jacob Lindberg (1745–1791) — Swedish, supreme court judge on Virgin Islands

Abraham Lincoln (1809–1865) — American, 16th president of the United States
Nicholas Vachel Lindsay (1879–1931) — American, poet
Carlos Liscano (1949–) — Uruguayan, novelist, poet
Oliver Joseph Lodge (1851–1940) — English, physicist
Henry Wadsworth Longfellow (1807–1882) — American, teacher, poet
John Lowes, Jr. (?18th c.) — English, surgeon on 1st boat w/convicts to Australia
Malcolm Lowry (1909–1957) — English, poet, novelist
Fitz Hugh Ludlow (1836–1870) — American, author, journalist
Lucius Lyon (1800–1851) — American, democrat senator for Michigan
George MacDonald (1824–1905) — Scottish, novelist, poet
James Ramsay MacDonald (1866–1937) — Scottish, a founder of Brit. Labour Party
Maurice Maeterlinck (1862–1949) — Belgian-French, poet, playwright
Kristine Mann (?–1945) — American, psychoanalyst
Horace Mann (1796–1859) — American, educ. reformer, republican senator for Mass.
Mary Tyler Peabody Mann (1807–1840)— American, teacher, wife of Horace Mann
Margaret Rose Armstrong-Jones (1930–2002) — English, princess, countess
Edwin Markham (1852–1940) — American, poet
William Rainey Marshall (1825–1896) — American, repub. 5th gov. of Minnesota
Raquel Martin (?living) — American, author
Richard Matheson (1926–) — American, author, screenwriter
Stefanie Matteson (?living) — American, author
Bernard Maybeck (1862–1957) — American, architect in CA *Arts & Crafts* mvmt
Suetonius McGowan (1775–1798) — Anglo-Indian, district judge in India
Africanus Mensah (1875–1942) — Ghanaian, *Methodist* missionary, converted 1915
Dmitri Merezhkovski (1865–1941) — Russian, novelist, poet
James Albert Michener (1907–1997) — American, author
Adam Bernard Mickiewicz (1798–1855) — Polish-Lithuanian, poet
Cleopatra Mikhailovna Shakhovskaya (1809–1883) — Russian, princess
Frances Davis Millet (1846–1912) — American, painter, died in sinking of *Titanic*
Czeslaw Milosz (1911–2004) — Polish-Lithuanian, author
Oscar Vladislas de Lubicz Milosz (1877–1939)— Lithuanian-French, diplomat, poet
Jean Pierre Moet (1721–c.1806) — French, royal librarian at Versailles
James Moffatt (1870–1944) — Scottish, *Christian* theologian
Raymond Avery Moody, Jr. (1944–) — American, MD, coined *near-death experience*
David William Mooki (1876–1927) — S. African, *Catholic* minister, convtd 1909
Robert Morris (1734–1806) — American, helped finance the Revolutionary War
Peter Eberhard Mullensiefen (1766–1847) — German, industrialist
Alexander Nikolayevitch Mouravieff (1792–1863) — Russian, general
Frederic William Henry Myers (1843–1901) — English, writer
John Muir (1838–1914) — Scottish-American, preservationist, author
Gérard de Nerval (1805–1855) — French, author
Joseph Fort Newton (1880–1950) — American, *Protestant* minister
Richard Heber Newton (1840–1914) — American, *Episcopal* minister
Malcolm Edwin Nichols (1876–1951) — American, republican, 44th mayor Boston
Victor Alfred Nilsson (1867–1942) — Swedish, historian
John Frederick Oberlin (1740–1826) — German, *Lutheran* minister, philanthropist
Jonas Pehrson Odhner (1744–1830) — Swedish, *Lutheran* minister, converted

Vladimir Fëdorovich Odoyevskiy (1804–1869) — Russian, prince
Friedrich Christoph Oetinger (1702–1782) — German, *Lutheran* minister
Molara Ogundipe (?living) — Nigerian, prof. *University of Leeds*, England, author
Robert Dale Owen (1801–1877) — Scottish-American, socialist author
Lisa Lemole Oz (?living) — American, producer, writer, actress, wife of Mehmet
Mehmet C. Oz (1960–) — American, cardiothoracic surgeon, author
William Page (1811–1885) — American, painter
Theodore Parker (1810–1860) — American, *Unitarian* minister
Theophilus Parsons (1797–1882) — American, dean of *Harvard Law School*
Walter Pater (1839–1894) — English, essayist, art and literary critic
Coventry Patmore (1823–1896) — English, poet
Elizabeth Palmer Peabody (1804–1894) — American, opened 1st Eng. kindergarten
Norman Vincent Peale (1898–1993) — American, *Protestant* preacher
Charles Sanders Peirce (1839–1914) — American, scientist, founder of pragmatism
Charles Rittenhouse Pendleton (1850–1914) — American, democrat senator for GA
Antoine Joseph Pernety (1716–1801) — French, *Benedictine* monk
William Lyon Phelps (1865–1943) — American, author
Elizabeth Stuart Phelps (1844–1911) — American, author
Hovhaness I. Pilikian (?living) — Armenian-English, prof., film producer, composer
John Pitcairn (1841–1916) — Scottish-American, co-founder *Pittsburgh Plate Glass*
Raymond Pitcairn (1885–1966) — American, architect of *BA Cathedral*, son of John
Harold Frederick Pitcairn (1897–1960) — American, aviation inventor, son of John
Theodore Pitcairn (1893–1973) — American, *New Church* minister, son of John
Feodor Pitcairn (1935–) — American, underwater filmmaker, son of Harold
Elizabeth Pitcairn (1973–) — American, class. violinist, great-granddaughter of John
Isaac Pitman (1813–1897) — English, inventor of shorthand
Edgar Allan Poe (1809–1849) — American, author
Louis Freeland Post (1849–1928) — American, writer, reformer, asst. sec. of labor
Ezra Pound (1885–1972) — American, poet
Hiram Powers (1805–1873) — American, sculptor
Penny Price (?living) — American, film producer, director, writer
Alexander Pushkin (1799–1837) — Russian, poet
Alice Putnam (1841–1919) — American, leader in U.S. kindergarten movement
Howard Pyle (1853–1911) — American, painter
Salomon Mauritz von Rajalin (1757–1825) — Swedish, governor of Gotland
Ernst von der Recke (1848–1933) — Danish, poet, dramatist
Sampson Reed (1800–1880) — American, w/s druggist, mentor to R.W. Emerson
Edouard Richer (1792–1834 — French, writer
William Rienstra (?living) — American, father of John in *National Football League*
Kenneth Ring (1935–) — American, author, fndr *Int. Assn. for Near-Death Studies*
Robert LeRoy Ripley (1890–1949) — American, creator *Ripley's Believe It or Not!*®
George Ripley (1802–1880) — American, social reformer, journalist
Mary Roach (?living) — American, author
John Roebling (1806–1869) — German, civil engineer, designed *Brooklyn Bridge*
Franklin Delano Roosevelt (1882–1945) — American, 32nd president United States
John Welborn Root (1850–1891) — American, architect
Dante Gabriel Rossetti (1828–1882) — English, artist, poet

Robert I. Rotberg (1935–) — American, prof. *Harvard*, president *World Peace Fdtn*
Mikhail Rotschine (?living) — Russian, professor at *Moscow University*
Josiah Royce (1855–1916) — American, philosopher
Johan Ludvig Runebert (1840–1877) — Finnish, writer
John Ruskin (1819–1900) — English, art critic, author
Maciej Rybinski (1784–1874) — Polish, general
Louis-Claude de Sanit-Martin (1743–1802) — French, philosopher
George Sand (1804–1876) — French, novelist, born Amandine Aurore Lucile Dupin
Jean-Paul Sartre (1905–1980) — French, philosopher, author, screenwriter
Jonathan Young Scammon (1812–1890) — American, fndr Chicago's 1st newspaper
Kristin Schaffer (?living) — American, prof. architectural hist. *N. Carolina St. Univ.*
Friedrich Wilhelm Joseph von Schelling (1775–1854) — German, philosopher
John Metz Schneider (1859–1942) — Canadian, founder *Schneider Corp* meat firm
Arnold Schöenberg (1874–1951) — Austrian, composer
Stephen Alonzo Schoff (1818–1904) — American, artist, engraver
Arthur Schopenhauer (1788–1860) — German, philosopher
Loreto Scocia (1836–1902) — Italian, political activist, *Methodist* minister
Anna Sewell (1820–1878) — British, writer
Arthur Sewall (1835–1900) — American, dem. candidate for U.S. vice pres., 1896
George Bernard Shaw (1856–1950) — Irish, playwright
Robert William Shields (1918–2007) — American, *Protestant* minister, diarist
Robert Rakes Shrock (1904–1993) — American, prof. at *Mass. Inst. of Technology*
Sundar Singh (1889–1929) — Indian, *Christian* missionary
Juliusz Slowacki (1809–1849) — Polish, poet
Jessie Wilcox Smith (1863–1935) — American, painter
Henry Söderberg (1916–1997) — Swedish, lawyer, vice president *SAS*, author
Vladimir Solovyov (1853–1900) — Russian, philosopher, poet
Emma Dorothy Eliza Nevitte Southworth (1819–1899) — American, author
Erik Johan Stagnelius (1793–1823) — Swedish, dramatist
John Steinbeck (1902–1968) — American, author
Rudolph Steiner (1861–1925) — Austrian, philosopher
Harriet Beecher Stowe (1811–1896) – American, author, abolitionist
Richard Georg Strauss (1864–1949) — German, composer
August Strindberg (1849–1912) — Swedish, dramatist
Louis Henri Sullivan (1856–1924) — American, architect
Henry Septimus Sutton (1825–1901) — English, author, owner *Nottingham Review*
Daisetsu Teitarō Suzuki (1870–1966) — Japanese, *Zen Buddhist,* scholar, aka "D.T."
Johann Friedrich Immanuel Tafel (1796–1863) — German, librn *Univ of Tübingen*
Alfred Lord Tennyson (1809–1892) — English, poet
Ian J. Thompson (?living) — New Zealander-American, professor of physics
Henry David Thoreau (1817–1862) — American, author
Thomas Thorild (1759–1808) — Swedish, poet, feminist
Eliza Lovell Tibbets (1825–1898) — American, founder California citrus industry
Louis Comfort Tiffany (1848–1933) — American, stained glass artist
Alexsey Tolstoy (1817–1875) — Russian, poet
Leo Tolstoy (1828–1910) — Russian, novelist
Andrzej Towianski (1799–1879) — Polish-Lithuanian, philosopher

Ernest George Trobridge (1884–1942) — English, architect
Charles Augustus Tulk (1786–1849) — English, William Blake's patron
Fyodor Tyutchev (1803–1873) — Russian, poet
Paul Valery (1871–1945) — French, poet, author
Narcissa Cox Vanderlip (1879–1966) — American, a fndr *League of Women Voters*
Wilson Van Dusen (1923–2005) — American, psychologist, author
Carl Bernhard Wadström (1746–1799) — Swedish, abolitionist, author, aka "Charles"
Alfred Russel Wallace (1823–1913) — Scottish, naturalist, explorer, geographer
George Washington (1732–1799) — American, 1st president of the United States
Anton Webern (1883–1945) — Austrian, composer, conductor
George James Webb (1803–1887) — English, co-founder *Boston Academy of Music*
Herbert George Wells (1866–1946) — English, writer, aka "H.G."
Gustav Albert Werner (1809–1887) — German, fndr *Gustav Werner Foundation*
Walter Lucius Whitehead (1891–1969) — American, prof. at *Mass. Inst. Technology*
Walt Whitman (1819–1892) — American, poet
John Greenleaf Whittier (1807–1892) — American, *Quaker*, poet, abolitionist
Lars-Erik Wiberg (?living) — American, prof. at *Mass. Inst. of Technology*
Samuel Wilderspin (1792–1866) — English, founder of infant school system
James John Garth Wilkinson (1812–1899) — English, homoeopathic physician
Colin Wilson (1931–) — English, author
William Wilson (1895–1971) — American, cofounder of *Alcoholics Anonymous*
Lois Wilson (1891–1988) — American, cofounder of *Al-Anon,* wife of Bill Wilson
Mary Wollstonecraft (1759–1797) — English, author, feminist
Benjamin Worcester (1783–1849) — American, author
Joseph Worcester (1836–1913) — American, a founder of CA *Arts & Crafts* mvmt
Gretchen Muff Worden (1945–2002) — director of *The Mütter Museum,* Phila, PA
Frank Lloyd Wright (1867–1959) — American, architect
Frank Lloyd Wright, Jr. (1890–1978) — American, architect
Eric Lloyd Wright (1929–) — American, architect, grandson of Frank Lloyd Wright
Newell Convers Wyeth (1882–1945) — American, artist, aka "N.C."
Richard Yardumian (1917–1985) — American, composer
William Butler Yeats (1865–1939) — Irish, poet, winner 1923 *Nobel Prize*
John Young (1762–1840) — American, presiding judge for Western Pennsylvania

Add names that you know about to this list. Be sure to tell me. If I can verify the individual's affiliation with Swedenborg, I'll add them to the next edition.

THE TAKERS

The following movers and takers did for a fact do one or some of these: plagiarized Emanuel Swedenborg, used Swedenborg's terminology in their work without giving credit, twisted Swedenborg's words to advantage, misinterpreted Swedenborg's doctrines, attacked Swedenborg in print.

G. Beaumont (?19th c.) — English, wrote *The Anti-Swedenborg,* London, 1824
Andrew Jackson Davis (1826–1910) — American, spiritualist, author
Mary Baker Eddy (1821–1910) — American, founder of *Church of Christ, Scientist*
Helena Petrovna Blavatsky (1831–1891) — Russian, a founder of *Theosophical Society*
Charles Fourier (1772–1837) — French, utopian socialist
Gerald Gardner (1884–1964) — English, a founder of *Wicca*
Thomas Lake Harris (1823–1906) — English, spiritualist, author
Immanuel Kant (1724–1804) — German, philosopher
Walter Ralston Martin (1928–1989) — American, *Evangelical* minister, "cult expert"
Sun Myung Moon (1920–) — Korean, founder of *Unification Church*
Joseph Priestley (1733–1804) — English, chemist, a founder of *Unitarianism*
Thomas de Quincey (1785–1859) — English, author
James Randi (1928–) — Canadian-American, magician, aka "The Amazing Randi"
Joseph Smith (1805–1844) — American, fdr *Church of Jesus Christ of Latter-day Saints*
Robert Southey (1774–1843) — English, poet
Herman Vetterling (1949–1931) — editor of *The Buddhist Ray,* aka "Philangi Dasa"
John Wesley (1703–1791) — English, a founder of *Methodist Church*
Ellen Gould Harmon White (1827–1915) — founder of *Seventh-day Adventist*

Add names that you know about to this list. Be sure to tell me. If I can verify the individual's link with Swedenborg, I'll add them to the next edition.

Dear Candace,

I've always wondered about the people who write books taken from Swedenborg's Writings, which the Lord Himself dictated to him. What makes them think their words are more enlightening than our "Lord's"? I think when people are ready for the real truth, they will find it in Swedenborg's books.

Do you think these writers are just making a name for themselves? Do these writers think their wisdom, or intelligence, or knowledge are greater than our Lord's? I just can't find an answer to this.

E.H.
Emerson, New Jersey
November 1995

Dear E.H.,

Plagiarizing Swedenborg is a common occurrence. It has been going on for hundreds of years. It can be seen in the long list of current angel or spirituality books. A few authors do list books by Swedenborg in their bibliographies. Others don't say where their "knowledge" came from, but Swedenborgians can recognize if a passage has been lifted almost word for word from Swedenborg. Sometimes personal "documents" (surfaced after death) have revealed that an author did read Swedenborg and was influenced by him.

You zeroed in on two reasons why writers steal from Swedenborg: personal fame and ego. Emanuel Swedenborg wrote so much that unless you are a regular reader or a student of his, much of what he wrote could be claimed by another and go unrecognized as to who was the original writer. Apparently, you E.H., can spot a Swedenborgian thought in someone's work, as can I. Good for you!

It is sad that a person would consciously take an idea from Swedenborg and say they thought of it. But, sometimes a person isn't aware they have taken one of his ideas. It is possible to prove that someone was influenced by Swedenborg, indirectly, through other authors who *did* read and write about him such as Balzac, Blake, Coleridge, Emerson, Goethe, Herder, Hugo, James, and Milosz.

Swedenborg said that he received all that he wrote from the Lord. It was NOT dictated to him, nor was it automatic writing. Swedenborg means that as he read the Word, he could see what it meant. The Lord was leading Him.

He wrote that every single person on the planet, as to their spirit, is in spiritual light. This light enlightens the interiors of our understanding, and as it were, *dictates*. With this light, we can think analytically, form conclusions, and see truths.

It can be shown that Swedenborg's books are not dictation for he wrote notes in the margins; he did a great deal of editorial work; he indexed his works so he could use parts in other books; and with his high standards, he reworked many pages before they were published.

He was permitted to see and hear into the next world and to record what he witnessed. Today, many authors are making this claim. Some are genuine. Some are short glimpses stretched into a book. But, no author can claim a deeper, more concise body of work than Emanuel Swedenborg!

UPDATE

Secrets of Heaven #9094:
"**Inspiration is not dictation, but is influx from the Divine.**"

Here's a funny take on dictation I found. *True Christian Religion* #26: "**The angels asked me to say at their dictation that if anyone does not approach the God of heaven and earth Himself, [they] cannot enter heaven, because it is that one God who makes heaven to be heaven, and that same God is Jesus Christ, who is Jehovah the Lord, the Creator from eternity, the Redeemer in time, and the Regenerator for eternity to come. Thus He is at once Father, Son and Holy Spirit; this is the Gospel to be preached.**"

Many times spirits tried to get Swedenborg to take dictation. Can you imagine?! Some psychics claim this, but come on, what do they write down? Don't get me started.

Swedenborg wrote that he had written whole pages that were dictated and sometimes he found his hand moving without him doing it. Some spirits even "experimented" with him and wrote words down that he had not even thought of. When this happened, he said he erased what had been written!

Swedenborg wrote in *Spiritual Experiences-Word Explained* #42: "**...only the things that streamed in from God the Messiah Alone, indirectly through them, and directly**" was he permitted to record.

Because Swedenborg was such a smart man, he could discern much more than you or I could if it were us "walking around" the spiritual world. I know that I would be going, *"Look at that! Oooh! Aaah! Wow!"* The Lord prepared Emanuel Swedenborg as a scientist first before he sent him into spiritual space.

Swedenborg used this ornament in *Secrets of Heaven*

Dear Candace,

I really liked the newsletters you sent me. You faithfully present Swedenborg's Writings in a creative and approachable way. I am really impressed! You are doing a good work. Thank you for sending them. I love that they are being so well received in Africa!

I also found Swedenborg just as your grandfathers did. (In a library.) I live near Tuscumbia (2 minutes away) where Helen Keller lived. They put on a wonderful re-enactment of her discovery of language with Anne Sullivan annually outdoors at her very own house.

I went to the library just to read about Helen Keller's life. "My Religion" [by Helen Keller] was the only book that wasn't checked out about her. I really didn't want to hear about religion, confused as I was about doctrine. But, I reluctantly took it anyway.

I was sparked with a deep curiosity and hope by what she had to say about Swedenborg, and I trusted her. I got "Heaven and Hell" and "The True Christian Religion" on inter-library loan. From the first word the falsities began to dissipate and I knew. I knew from internal acknowledgment that it was true.

My first awareness of Swedenborg was 13 years ago when I saw a television commercial about his teaching. It interested me, and I wrote down the address, but I wasn't led to it until 10 years later, when I read about him again in Helen Keller's "My Religion". I recognized his name and remembered. I believe the commercial had an impact coupled with the book.

There is no Swedenborgian Church in Alabama. I found your name in the AOL (America On Line) members' profiles by searching for Swedenborg. You are very special to me already. You are one of the very first of my "sisters" I have had the opportunity to meet, and as you said, it's the Lord's Providence. Nothing happens by chance!

A.B.
Florence, Alabama
March 1998

Dear A.B.,

I love to learn how people discovered Swedenborg. It invariably is a long process of recognition and through several paths like yours. It is a shame you had to look so far and wide for Swedenborg's books. I wish more librarians and bookstore owners carried his books, but we can't dictate they stock them.

I applaud you for persevering through inter-library loans and the Internet! In recognition of your thirst for knowledge, I am sending you, by mail, ten copies of *My Religion* by Helen Keller, to donate to libraries in your area and one copy of *Poems from Swedenborg* by Leon C. Le Van for your personal library. Enjoy!

I'm glad you wrote.

March 1995

Dear *SILA* Readers,

Guideposts magazine is an upbeat philosophical publication which was founded in 1945 by Dr. and Mrs. Norman Vincent Peale and Raymond Thornburg. It is an interfaith publication with a circulation of 14 million. It was thrilling to have Emanuel Swedenborg written about in the March issue!

Yes! Helen Keller, the most famous Swedenborgian in history, wrote about her discovery of Swedenborg and it was published in *Guideposts*, June 1956. This year marks the 50th anniversary of *Guideposts* and in commemoration they are reprinting favourite articles. Helen Keller's was one! I am sending you all a copy of the March 1995 *Guideposts*.

Helen was 16-years-old when she met John Hitz, Consul-General for Switzerland in Washington, D.C. He learned Braille, so they could communicate when not visiting. Mr. Hitz gave Miss Keller a Braille copy of *Heaven and Hell*. Hitz told Helen that he knew she would not understand most of the book at first.

Miss Keller, however, did grasp what she was reading and when she became a woman, she fully understood the Writings of Swedenborg. She wrote: "I took more and more to the teachings of the New Church as my religion."

Thinking of you,
Candace

Dear Candace,

I am so glad to write you this letter. I wanted to know if you have received some letters from Ghana. This is because I have advertised SILA *here in Ghana.*

I think we need to catch more people to believe in Emanuel Swedenborg, his teachings and theories. As for me you have caught me already. I will also extend my rope to catch others. My friends are now getting to understand Emanuel Swedenborg. Expect some letters from them.

S.M.
Mamprobi, Accra, Ghana
July 1995

Dear Candace,

We are about to get a descendant of a Johnny Appleseed apple tree for the Academy of the New Church *[Bryn Athyn, Pennsylvania] copying the* Midwestern Academy of the New Church *[Glenview, Illinois]. Excitement! Did you ever profile John Chapman in* SILA*? We want to give the kids as much info as possible.*

A.F.
Bryn Athyn, Pennsylvania
December 1990

Dear A.F.,
Since both academies are Swedenborgian institutions, how fitting to have an apple tree directly from apple seeds planted by one of the greatest Swedenborgians in history, Jonathan Chapman (1774–1845), better known as Johnny Appleseed. How marvelous to have such a tree on campus! I attended the *Academy of the New Church College* in Bryn Athyn, so I'm as excited as you!

In the October 1988 issue of *SILA,* I noted that the radio personality, Paul Harvey had talked on his show, "The Rest of the Story" about Johnny Appleseed and mentioned (correctly) that he gave away Swedenborg's books for free. But, that L. M. Boyd in his column for the *Los Angeles Herald Examiner* (Sunday, 19 June 1988!) wrote (incorrectly) about Johnny Appleseed: "Long before Gideons, John Chapman, known in his tin pot hat and coffee sack shirt as Johnny Appleseed, passed out free Bibles."

Some may not know that Johnny Appleseed was a *real* person and not a folk hero. He was born as Jonathan Chapman in Leominster, Massachusetts. By middle age, he was introducing himself as "Johnny Appleseed". Twenty-six years after Chapman's death, a reporter, W. D. Haley wrote an article, "Johnny Appleseed, a Pioneer Hero" in *Harper's New Monthly* magazine, November 1871. It was the first biography of Chapman which introduced him to national attention. Because of this article, people wrote letters to their small town newspapers throughout the Midwest relating memories of him—true, false, and exaggerated. He was compared to John the Baptist and called "a voice in the wilderness heralding a new religion".

Apples were secondary to John Chapman. His inner drive—a love of all creation—came from Emanuel Swedenborg's Writings. (He was born two years after Swedenborg died.) Chapman, taken by Swedenborg's Writings, used most of his profits made from selling apple seeds (usually he gave them away) and purchased Swedenborg's books (which took months to reach the American shore from England.) He would then divide a book into two or three parts (for more extensive distribution) and gift a settler with one part.

From *History of Wayne County, Ohio; From the Days of the Pioneers and First Settlers to the Present Time* by Ben Douglass (Indianapolis, Indiana: Robert Douglass, Publisher, 1878, chapter 13, pp. 196-207):

> ...after a tiresome journey, it was [Appleseed's] custom to lie down on the rude [timber] floor, and, after inquiring if his auditors would hear "some news right fresh from heaven," would produce his few ragged books.

Chapman was a one man library. When he returned to tend an apple orchard a year or two later, he would exchange one part of a book with a settler for another!

His trade was apple man for fifty years. Carrying 300,000 apple seeds at a time in his sack, he crossed the American frontier—western Pennsylvania, Ohio, Indiana, Illinois, Iowa—on foot (he did not believe in horseback riding) planting apple seeds or selling them.

America's indigenous apple is the sour crab. One hundred years before Johnny Appleseed, the French had brought tastier apple seeds to the Great Lakes and Mississippi areas. By the time Johnny Appleseed was planting his English seeds, apple orchards were alongside Indian villages. White settlers were trading or stealing these apples. There were other apple men, but most did it as a sideline to farming. Johnny Appleseed's contribution differed for he anticipated the pattern of settlement across the Midwest and planted orchards before settlers moved in!

"As American as apple pie." This axiom is in part because of Appleseed who helped make apples an integral part of the American diet in the new world.

- apples
- dried apples—storable
- apple butter
- applesauce
- baked apple pie
- fried apple fritter
- apple vinegar—preservative
- apple cider—fresh beverage
- hard cider—storable alcohol
- apple brandy—first cash export

Johnny Appleseed was the nation's paramount orchardist of the 19th century. It is estimated he planted 17,000 apple trees.

He has been neglected by historians because they have preferred braggarts and killers. Chapman was described by Ben Douglass as a "rare force of gentle goodness". He was a barefoot New Church missionary—sincere, vegetarian, wore no furs, practiced herbal medicine. He was accepted by whites and Native Americans.

However, Hollywood put an indelible image of him in the minds of millions as a wise, eccentric folk hero because of Walt Disney's 1948 animated movie of him. There are countless novels, short stories, and poems of Johnny Appleseed's good deeds, though some are presented as fictional.

I visited my local library and found it had seven books about Johnny Appleseed in the children's section; none in the adult section. The books were listed under *Tall Tales and Legends*! He deserves more respect.

Dear Candace,
    Thanks for the Helen Keller book [My Religion]. *It was thoughtful of you to send it to me. When things die down here, I will look forward to reading it. And, no I did not know that Lincoln had read the Writings of Mr. Swedenborg. Again, thanks for thinking of us.*

Ken Burns
Producer of PBS series, "The Civil War"
Walpole, New Hampshire
January 1991

Dear Mr. Burns,
    Swedenborg (1688–1772) wrote complimentary things about Africans in his books even though it is assumed he never knew any blacks. There are no letters or diary entries about black friends or acquaintances. But, he wrote about Africans he saw in visions and about slavery being evil.
    Charles Bernard Wadström, the noted Swedish abolitionist—one of the first in Europe—was a Swedenborgian. After his trip to Africa in 1780, he published *Observations on the Slave Trade* and in 1794, *Essay on Colonisation*. These were highly regarded. Wadström tried to start a New Church (Swedenborgian) colony in Africa as well.
    Abraham Lincoln (1809–1865), the 16th president of the United States—as you know, considered to have been the greatest American president—guided his country during the gravest experience in its history, the Civil War which involved slavery. Lincoln was born in Kentucky. In 1816, when he was 7, his family moved to Indiana—partly on account of slavery in Kentucky. Johnny Appleseed (Jonathan Chapman), a Swedenborgian, gave Lincoln apple seeds. It is not known if Lincoln received any of Swedenborg's Writings from Johnny Appleseed which he gave away. However, it is known that Lincoln did own several of Swedenborg's books, later in his life, and that he read Wadström's articles.

UPDATE
    In my excitement, I wrote "Johnny Appleseed gave Lincoln apple seeds", in 1991, without giving the source. Looking for it now for this book in 2008, I can't find it! But, I know I read it somewhere. I don't make up my facts! Can any readers help me with the source? For now, I'll have to say that, "It is possible Johnny Appleseed gave Lincoln apple seeds…"

July 1997
Dear *SILA* Readers,
   I read this on the Internet and responded to it:

> My name is Susan Nordmeyer and am the Director of Interpretation at Lincoln Log Cabin State Historic Site. I am currently looking for information regarding the Swedenborg Church during the midnineteenth century, particularly in Illinois. This is due to the Swedenborg families which resided in this area and are currently being interpreted at our living history site.

Dear Ms. Frazee,
   Thank you for responding to my request on-line. I have heard from one or two others with some good leads! At this point the only information we have is current information on the Swedenborg Church which is an excellent starting point. I have assigned one of our volunteers to assist in the research process and plan on sending any new information to him as well.
   Other information on the Swedenborg Church in central Illinois came to us from historian Charles Coleman in "Abraham Lincoln in Coles County" *which talks of Abraham's visits to Stephen and Nancy Sargent and his interest in Swedenborg's writings. From this information we are also told that Stephen and Nancy held worship services in their home. Stephen and Nancy Sargent were the owners of our second living history farm. Our interpretive program at Lincoln Log Cabin is in the first person format in which staff and volunteers role-play characters from 1845. Thus any information on the Swedenborg Church in the mid-19th century would be invaluable in accurately recreating the Sargent family.*
   At this point, we have no research books on Swedenborg, only church pamphlets and oral histories from descendants of the Sargent's to guide us. I would be very interested in contacting the Swedenborg Foundation *in Pennsylvania for their assistance as well.*
   Thank you for your timely response and I look forward to reading your newsletter and working with you in the future.

Susan M. Nordmeyer
Director of Interpretation
Lincoln Log Cabin State Historic Site
Lerna, Illinois

THERE IS AN ANSWER

I couldn't believe that the *Lincoln Log Cabin Site* didn't have any research books on Swedenborg (which Lincoln definitely read!) so, I mailed Ms. Nordmeyer the huge (8lbs!) 558-page, coffee-table book on Swedenborg, published in 1988.

Dear Ms. Frazee,
I am writing to thank you for the wonderful book you sent, "Emanuel Swedenborg, A Continuing Vision", *and the newsletters. I quickly perused the book and newsletters and feel assured that there will be information useful to our program.*

As we are preparing to launch into our summer living history program, the search on the Sargents and their beliefs may subside slightly, but I hope to continue spending time on them nevertheless. Your book will undoubtedly steer us in the right direction and give us a great start on interpreting the Sargents. Thank you again for all your help and we'll be in contact soon.

Susan M. Nordmeyer

Thinking of you,
Candace

Dear Candace,
I enjoy your mailings very much and admire your staunch stand and excellent research on Swedenborgian facts. I thought knowing there was a New Church chaplain in the US Army at one time was an interesting fact. Rev. Arthur O. Brickman served in the Union in spite of being from Baltimore, Maryland. He was my grandfather. My father was the Rev. W. E. Brickman.

Vera Brickman Kitzelman
Glenview, Illinois
January 2001

Dear Mrs. Kitzelman,
How fascinating! Thanks for sharing your history.

According to research done by Judy Hyatt of the New Church Archives Office in Bryn Athyn, PA, Rev. Arthur O. Brickman was a New Church minister that travelled with the 3rd Maryland Veteran Volunteers in the American Civil War (1861–1865).

Those volunteer soldiers fought in the Civil War battles in Wilderness, Spotsylvania, Cold Harbor, and Petersburg. Apparently, your grandfather was *supposed to be* a non-sectarian minister, but nevertheless preached Swedenborgian teachings to the soldiers! He wrote several reports about his "doings" that were published in the Swedenborgian magazine, *The New Jerusalem Messenger* (published weekly in New York).

Rev. Arthur Otto Brickman wrote:

> I teach the New Church truths fearlessly, openly, and boldly, but never attack any sectarian Doctrines. My preaching is positive; I show what is true, and use the common sciences, and above all the letter of the Word, to demonstrate and illustrate the truths of the New Christian Church.

Rev. Brickman also wrote that his services were always well attended and he was asked many times for more information about what he was preaching. At the end of the Civil War, the 3rd Maryland Veteran Volunteers presented Rev. Brickman with a Gold Medal of Appreciation.

The New Jerusalem Messenger also published recollections of speeches given by Abraham Lincoln and memories of him by Swedenborgian contemporaries. Over the years, there has been extensive research done by Swedenborgian scholars tracing Swedenborg's influence on Lincoln.

In brief, the Swedenborgian couple Stephen and Nancy (Chenoweth) Sargent lived on a farm in the 1840s along the Old York-Charleston Trail in Coles County, Illinois. Their nearest neighbours, ten miles east, were Thomas and Sarah Lincoln, father and stepmother of America's 16th president. Though Abraham, at that time, was living in Springfield, he did visit his parents often, and the Sargents. Oral history and letters do tell that Lincoln did borrow books by Swedenborg from Stephen Sargent, before he was president.

The Sargent's home was an active center for Swedenborgian worship services and religious discussions because there was no Swedenborgian church building in the county. Sargent grandchildren reported that Lincoln had attended these New Church services and had been himself baptised into the New Church.

Floret Harlan Hendrickson, daughter of Burns Harlan, a son of Mrs. Sargent by her first marriage, was born in 1854 and died in California in 1946. She told her Swedenborgian pastor, the Rev. Andre Diaconoff of Los Angeles that her grandparents gave Lincoln several copies of Swedenborg's books and her great-uncle had told her that he was present at the Sargent's home for a New Church worship service when Lincoln was there.

Other oral histories collaborate Mrs. Hendrickson's. However, another Sargent granddaughter, Opal S. Hodge, of Charleston, born in 1876, disputed these claims saying that she had never heard her grandparents mention Lincoln's interest in Swedenborg or the New Church. History does record that Mrs. Hodge was 15-years-old when Grandmother Sargent died.

At the *Lincoln Log Cabin State Historic Site* in Lerna, Illinois, there are two homesteads—the two-room cabin of Thomas and Sarah Lincoln and the large timber-framed house of Stephen and Nancy Sargent.

The Sargent farm had originally more than 600 head of livestock on 400 acres of land. The house was moved closer to the Lincoln home by the *Illinois Historic Preservation Agency*. Both homes are now on an 86-acre historic site. And there are books by Swedenborg displayed in the Sargent home!

UPDATE
     Robert "Councillor" Carter III (1727–1804) found the Writings in 1787. Upon learning what Swedenborg wrote about Africans, he released his 500 African slaves from his plantation in Williamsburg, Virginia. His manumission ("to set free") is the largest release of slaves in North American history that took place *before* the American Civil War!
     It was said of New Churchman, William Rainey Marshall (1825–1896), 5th governor of Minnesota: "It was largely to his efforts, while governor, that the word "white" was stricken from the Constitution of Minnesota." (*Lives of the Governors of Minnesota* by James Heaton Baker. St. Paul, Minnesota: The Society, 1908.)

January 2006
Dear *SILA* Readers,
     Reverend George D. McCurdy is a retired Air Force Chaplain. He has a long continuous history of military service dating back to 1953. His New Church of the New Jerusalem Military Chaplaincy dates from 1968 to 1996 when he retired as a Colonel from the Massachusetts Air National Guard. Rev. McCurdy worked to get the New Church recognized by the Department of Defense. He was the first New Church minister to be endorsed by the State and Federal government. For those who like to note historical facts, put August of 1968 down as the date the Federal government accepted the New Church as an official religious member of the military chaplaincy team.
     In 1975, (New Church) Reverend Wendel Barnett was accepted into the Air Force as a chaplain and he just retired in December 2005 as a Lt. Colonel. (New Church) Reverend Martie Johnson is currently on active duty as a Seabee Chaplain. Lt. Johnson has been sent oversea to Kuwait with a possible tour of duty in Iraq.
     Rev. McCurdy continues his work with the military on behalf of the *General Church of the New Jerusalem* as its Ecclesiastical Endorsing agent. This means he works with and periodically visits the General Church chaplains and assists General Church ministers who want to join the military as chaplains.

Thinking of you,
Candace

Swedenborg used this ornament in *Secrets of Heaven*

July 1997
Dear *SILA* Readers,
   Did you know that John Pitcairn (1841-1916), the billionaire Swedenborgian patron who financed the building of the *Bryn Athyn Cathedral* in Pennsylvania met Abraham Lincoln in 1861, when he was 20? He accompanied his railroad boss and a group of security men on a secret trip—because of a rumoured assassination attempt—to transport Lincoln en route from Illinois to Washington, D.C. for his inauguration. Pitcairn brought Lincoln a cup of tea and a roll to his railroad car when Lincoln opted out of entering a restaurant. IT'S TRUE!

Thinking of you,
Candace

Dear Candace,
   Many thanks for your newsletters which I enjoy reading. You certainly have had some delightful letters; what an encouragement it is to receive such letters. I liked the way you dealt with the question of 'faith alone'. Also, the article on the teachings about the spiritual world drawn from Luke's Gospel, Chapter 16 is excellent.
   I was in a Christian bookshop and saw a new biography of George MacDonald, the 19th Century visionary author; "George MacDonald" by William Raeper. The name rang a bell because our children have several of his books, "The Princess and the Goblin" series. I looked up the index and found six references to Swedenborg. Clearly, MacDonald had read quite a bit of Swedenborg.
   He was certainly in touch with people like Thomas Carlyle (who was influenced by Swedenborg). What is also of interest is the C. S. Lewis was greatly influenced by George MacDonald! (Lewis puts forth Swedenborgian ideas and mentions Swedenborg in his "The Great Divorce".) Your efforts and energy are a positive power for us in remote Australia.

N.C.J.
Sydney, Australia
March 1989

Dear N.C.J.,
   Thank you for the news of the new biography of George MacDonald. He is my favourite children's author! How exciting to know he read Swedenborg!! I'm not surprised. I have recommended his books to many and added that they were "very Swedenborgian". Now I know why! It is wonderful to learn how people have been influenced by Swedenborg.

Dear Candace,

Did you know that Lois Wilson, the wife of Bill Wilson (one of the founders of Alcoholics Anonymous) went to the Swedenborgian church? She was a very involved member when she and Bill were stationary long enough for them to go to church. I attend a 12-step group called Al-Anon and have since 1982.

M.M.
Carmichael, California
October 1990

Dear M.M.,

Yes, I knew that Lois Wilson (1891-1988) was a Swedenborgian. Her grandfather, Nathan Clark Burnham, was a minister in the New Church.

In her autobiography, *Lois Remembers*, she wrote she "had had sound spiritual training, having been brought up in a home where love of God and of my fellowman was the guiding motive." One can only imagine her shock during World War II when she volunteered at the YWCA to be an aide to the wounded overseas and was refused on the grounds, they said, that Swedenborgians were not Christians! (This is not their policy today.) Lois, in her book, mentions what her faith is about several times. I also found many quiet references to her beliefs throughout; Swedenborgian ideas of which meanings are uncommon to the general public—"regeneration", "two as one", "love and faith", "truths", "the ancients", "spirit", "spiritual", and "Johnny Appleseed".

Lois Burnham married Bill Wilson in 1918, in the Swedenborgian Church in Brooklyn, New York. It wasn't until 1935 that Bill co-founded Alcoholics Anonymous. The Writings of Swedenborg were a major influence in the formation of this 12-step program which has been the greatest spiritual force of this century!

Swedenborg's influence on Alcoholics Anonymous is as follows:
- An alcoholic named Rowland consulted Dr. Carl Jung (a reader of Swedenborg). Jung told Rowland the only thing that could possibly free him from alcohol was an overwhelming spiritual experience and advised him to join a religious group. Rowland did. He joined the Oxford Group.
- Rowland, now a recovering alcoholic, rescued Ebby (a childhood friend of Lois's) from being committed to an institution after a bad car accident, by convincing the judge he could help Ebby turn his life around. Ebby joined Rowland's religious group.
- Ebby, now a recovering alcoholic, told Bill how he stayed sober—surrendering his life to God.
- After Bill had had a spiritual experience of seeing an indescribable white light in the hospital recovering from an alcoholic bout, he read *The Varieties of Religious Experience* by William James (a reader of Swedenborg), the psychologist/philosopher and brother of Henry (a reader of Swedenborg). This book validated Bill's experience. Bill claimed William James had been a founder of AA for the insights in his book.
- Bill wrote Dr. Jung in 1961 thanking him for his advice to Rowland and told him how that had been the start of AA.

AA and all 12-step programs are built on spiritual principles which contain religious and psychiatric truths. It was Bill's intention to make the program a universal spiritual one, not a specific religious one. This principle is a Swedenborgian concept itself—**"church specific"** is where truths are known and lived; **"church universal"** is where truths are not known, but lived. Anonymity and non-affiliation with any religion was adopted, so AA could serve the greater good for the world. Bill was influenced by his wife, Lois, and a spiritual writer, William James, both Swedenborgians. Bill Wilson's 12-steps and Swedenborg's teachings on spiritual development are similar.

Dear Candace,
How do New Church clergy handle reformed AAs when they come to the Holy Supper? Can a teetotaler even be a New Church man or woman?

A.&E.
Bayswater, Australia
March 1992

Dear A.&E.,
Yes, a woman who drinks beer and a man who drinks coffee—ANYBODY can be New Church.

As for Holy Supper, it is the most misunderstood Christian religious act. People are told the bread is Christ's flesh (they are to eat!) and that the wine is Christ's blood (they are to drink!). How can this be, let alone comprehended?!

In the 18th century, Swedenborg explained the mystery of this feast. First, he tells us Holy Supper is NOT holy. The bread and wine do NOT affect repentance. There is no magic or miracle upon partaking in it. Secondly, that one has to see the meaning of it with one's "understanding".

Swedenborg tells us again and again in his books, there is a "correspondence" of natural things with spiritual things.

Before partaking of the Holy Supper, Swedenborg suggests we:
- examine ourselves
- see and acknowledge a wrong doing
- desist from doing it
- pray for help
- begin a new life without the wrong doing
- then drink the wine and eat the bread and think about what it symbolically means—letting love and wisdom (or charity and faith) into your life

This process of self examination is when someone is controlling their own destiny and practicing things from their own reasoning. When a person is in this process, they are on their way to heaven—from being a natural person to beginning to be a spiritual person. During Holy Supper, the Lord is joined with the person (not with the bread and wine).

A.&E., I knew the answer to your question, but felt you would want as much information as possible, so I asked several New Church ministers what they do during the Holy Supper when a recovering alcoholic joins them. They told me:

Very simple: he/she is offered grape juice.

Rev. Ian Franklin
Santa Barbara, California

At least one AA member I knew would take the wine, like everyone else, not being adversely affected. That person felt a special "protection" with it being the Holy Supper. Another AA member would do no more than put the glass to her lips. You can get a de-alcoholized wine which I have felt able to offer in such circumstances.

Rev. Ian Arnold
Manchester, England

So far I haven't had to deal with it directly. An option I have considered but have not instituted is having grape juice as an option.

Rev. Nathan Gladish
San Diego, California

I feel very comfortable about having both wine and grape juice available for those who are taking the Holy Supper.

Rev. Eric Carswell
Pittsburgh, Pennsylvania

I serve both wine and grape juice. A couple of alcoholics I have talked with feel that they can take a sip of wine during Holy Supper without negative consequences. They feel that the sphere of worship is a protection against abuse. Another person would just touch the wine to her lips without drinking any. The important part is what is in a person's heart.

By the way, I have had a similar issue with the Holy Supper bread. Since I have a gluten sensitivity, I cannot eat wheat. For several years I have eaten a small amount of wheat bread during Holy Supper, simply ignoring the damage it was doing to my system. Recently, I have been making special bread for myself out of rice.

The correspondence of eating and drinking is more important than what you are eating or drinking. And, the really important part is receiving the love and wisdom to which the nourishment corresponds.

Rev. John Odhner
La Crescenta, California

Dear Candace,
I have never read Divine Providence. *What is it about? Is it somehow related to the 12 steps?*

M.M.
La Crescenta, California
August 1992

Dear M.M.,

Emanuel Swedenborg, at the age of 76, published, *Divine Providence,* in Amsterdam, Holland in 1764. This book is not a novel or an essay; it is a spiritual study book. It states the laws of Divine providence by which the Lord governs this world and the next.

Yes, *Divine Providence* does mention 12 steps "to wisdom". *Divine Providence* #36: **"I have spoken with angels at times about wisdom who said that wisdom is conjunction with the Lord because He is wisdom itself, and that [the person] who rejects hell comes into this conjunction and comes into it so far as they reject hell.**

They said that they picture wisdom to themselves as a magnificent and highly ornate palace into which one mounts by twelve steps.

No one arrives at even the first step, they said, except from the Lord by conjunction with Him; and according to the measure of conjunction one ascends; also as one ascends, one perceived that no [person] is wise from themselves, but from the Lord.

Furthermore, they said that the things in which one is wise are to those in which one is not wise as a few drops of water to a large lake. By the twelve steps into the palace of wisdom are meant goods united to truths and truths united to goods."

"The person who rejects hell" can be seen in number 1 of The Twelve Steps of Alcoholics Anonymous—"We admitted we were powerless over alcohol..."

"No person is wise from themselves, but from the Lord" can be seen in number 2 of the AA Steps—"Came to believe that a Power greater than ourselves..."

"No one arrives at even the first step, they said, except from the Lord" can be seen in number 3—"Made a decision to turn our will and our lives over to the care of God..."

Swedenborg's "palace of wisdom" is beautiful to imagine. The other twelve steps are discussed in other books of his, but not necessarily referred to as *of* the twelve steps.

Swedenborg used this ornament in *Heaven and Hell*

Dear Candace,
In yesterday's (March 7) San Francisco Chronicle, *I read a review of the new book:* My Name Is Bill: Bill Wilson—His Life and the Creation of Alcoholics Anonymous *by Susan Cheever. In the review, I was more than a little amazed to see "Swedenborgian theology" at the front of a list of influences that shaped his thought:*

[Review titled: "AA founder longed to be regular guy: Susan Cheever probes the deep issues that drove Bill Wilson, *My Name Is Bill: Bill Wilson—His Life and the Creation of Alcoholics Anonymous* by Susan Cheever. Simon & Schuster; 306 pages; Reviewed by Adam Baer". *San Francisco Chronicle*, 7 March 2004]

But the tale becomes storytelling gold when Wilson fails terribly as a husband, taking advantage of his wife's wealthy parents, and finally pulls himself out of his seemingly fatal stupor after a religious epiphany. Cheever writes that Wilson—influenced by Swedenborgian theology, the proselytizing Christian Oxford Group, William James's *Varieties of Religious Experience*, Carl Jung and the ego-stroking power of helping other alcoholics (the most famous: Dr. Robert Smith, who would co-found AA)—devised an organization (opening up his wife's Brooklyn house to drunks off the street) that might not heal an addict's unique psychological issues and personal quirks, but could well plug the void.

As I read AA books, I have often felt there must have been at least some contact with Swedenborg's books, or at least, an indirect influence. One possibility for the latter would be the writings of Emmett Fox, who, according to Martin Alfred Larson's book New Thought Religion: A Philosophy for Health, Happiness, and Prosperity *was influenced by Swedenborgian ideas. Fox's teachings definitely had an influence on Wilson and others in AA.*

I know that [New Church] Rev. Michael Cowley did some research about this many years ago. Lois Wilson [Bill Wilson's wife] told Michael in a letter that although Bill Wilson admired Swedenborg, he always credited the Oxford Group as being the source and inspiration for the Twelve Steps. (AA grew out of the Oxford Group, which promoted six steps for healing from sin and spiritual disease, including alcoholism.)

William James, who also had a profound impact on Wilson, was definitely influenced by Swedenborg. (I think that might be true of Jung, as well.)

The above notwithstanding, Michael tells me that he has never heard a statement so clearly and definitely linking Wilson with Swedenborg as the one in the Chronicle review. I'm thinking I'll have to get the book and learn what Cheever has to say about it.

Turns out, the Swedenborg/Wilson connection has been examined pretty thoroughly. It will be very interesting to see what Cheever's biography reveals. But it's hard to imagine it will go much beyond the info that's already pretty well established and corroborated.

[New Church] Rev. Jim Lawrence told me there's a Lois Burnham Wilson archive in the "Swedenborgian Library and Archives" at the Pacific School of

Religion *in Berkeley, CA. Among other things, there's a record of his correspondence with Lois on the subject.*

Seems pretty clear that the Swedenborgian influence on Bill Wilson was more of the "general influx" variety than any specific inspiration. (Probably much the same could be said about William James and Carl Jung, who both were definitely influential in shaping Bill's beliefs.)

I'm often struck by the subtlety of the Lord's leading! I'd be interested to read the results of your research.

K.P.
Cobb, California
March 2005

LETTER AFTER PURCHASING *My Name Is Bill* by Susan Cheever

Dear Candace,

I have not had time to read the book, but I did turn to the index and checked out the several references to Swedenborg that were listed. They follow below. I'm sure you'll find them interesting.

Cheever presents Swedenborg and the religion based on his teachings in a reasonably positive way, although in fact her references contain virtually nothing of the actual substance of the theology. In light of research I've obtained from Rev. Jim Lawrence, Rev. Michael Cowley, and a couple of other sources, I'm actually surprised by the amount of attention Susan Cheever gives to the role of Swedenborgian ideas/contact in shaping Bill Wilson's thinking. Maybe she knows something we don't. Anyway, here are the references to Swedenborg found in the book My Name Is Bill.

> pp. 35, 36: The spiritual awakening Bill experienced at age thirty-nine, which was a spur to the creation of Alcoholics Anonymous, was an awakening in the context of a thorough knowledge of spirituality and alcoholism. Many of the ideas put forth in the twelve steps and the twelve traditions of Alcoholics Anonymous can be traced back to the rolling hills and shady pastures of the valley where the Mad Tom Brook meets the Batten Kill. Lois Burnham and her family, who were intimately involved with Bill Wilson, were devout Swedenborgians, and educated him in the enlightened humanism of their religion...
>
> pp. 58, 59: Lois's father was a popular and wealthy man who was part of the New York community of Swedenborgians. His own father had been a minister of the Swedenborgian Church in Lancaster, Pennsylvania. The New Church, or Church of the New Jerusalem, is based on the teachings of the eighteenth-century Swedish scientist and nobleman Emanuel Swedenborg. Swedenborg, a respected philosopher, devoted the last part of his life to psychical and spiritual research and wrote interpretations of the Bible including *"Arcana Coelestia"*, a book that divides understanding into a series of steps. Although Swedenborg didn't intend to found a religion, his followers did, and American Swedenborgianism with its humanistic overtones

and its faith in an afterlife was the belief of choice for many successful professionals and wealthy businessmen at the turn of the century.

pp. 129: ... Like the Swedenborgian movement that had been such an integral part of the Burnham family, the Oxford Group aimed itself at the educated and elite, managing to recruit members like Henry Ford, Mae West, Harry Truman, and Joe DiMaggio.

pp. 209: ... of Lois's beloved mother, and her handsome father who read Swedenborg's teachings to his children in their Clinton Street living room...

pp. 238: When Bill said and wrote, as he often did, that no one person had founded Alcoholics Anonymous, and that its ideas were a synthesis of many components, from William James to Swedenborgian thought to Vermont democracy to the lessons of dozens of mistakes made in the early years of the fellowship, he was right.

I found this last a particularly interesting statement. Did Bill ever actually name Swedenborgian thought as one of the sources from which he drew and synthesized with other teachings? Cheever's statement implies this, but there is no footnote associated with it. Perhaps she was trying to emphasize the breadth and diversity of Bill's spiritual roots, but it seems odd that she would include the Swedenborgian influence and omit the Oxford Group which clearly was a progenitor of AA. Questions, questions...

K.P.

Dear K.P.,

Thanks for taking the time to send me all those references to Swedenborg in *My Name Is Bill: Bill Wilson—His Life and the Creation of Alcoholics Anonymous* by Susan Cheever.

Every few years, someone tries to explain the popularity of AA. Swedenborgians get excited by new books and articles that say Swedenborg influenced Bill Wilson—a stockbroker in New York who was one of the co-founders of Alcoholics Anonymous in 1935—because most likely they secretly want to take credit for a great spiritual growth program that works while their local Swedenborgian church is still small in numbers. I think New Church minister, Reuben P. Bell reveals a big truth about Swedenborg and AA in his short write-up below that I asked him to do. (See page 313) He says essentially, that Swedenborgians aren't responsible for the "New Church movement" as in AA, but the Lord is!!

Tony Perry wrote in the *Los Angeles Times,* 1 July 1995, article titled, "AA Quietly Marks 60 Years of Deep Impact on Society Addiction: Alcoholics Anonymous, low-profile even at its biggest convention ever, spawned the self-help industry":

> Alcoholics Anonymous is a uniquely American organization, with its underpinnings in Protestant religiosity...

I wrote Tony Perry (in part):

> This is incorrect. One of the founders of AA—Bill Wilson—married a Swedenborgian, married in a Swedenborgian church, and attended a Swedenborgian church. Bill W. was greatly influenced by his in-law's religion: Swedenborgianism, which is based on the Old and New Testaments and the Writings of Emanuel Swedenborg (1688–1772). It is a Christian religion, but not Protestant.
>
> During an alcoholic blackout Bill W. experienced seeing a white light (a near-death experience). After reading William James (influenced by Swedenborg) Bill W. felt his experience was explained and validated.
>
> Bill W. said that William James had been a founder of AA for his insights. Bill W. would not tell the press Swedenborg was a founder of AA because he wanted the program to be helpful universally and not a specific religious one. This idea alone is Swedenborgian!

K.P., you ask, *"Did Bill ever actually name Swedenborgian thought as one of the sources from which he drew and synthesized with other teachings?"* The answer is, no.

However, sometimes we aren't aware of the origin of an idea. Sometimes we are and choose not to acknowledge it, so as to leave the listener in freedom to accept the truth of that idea or not. In this case, without religious baggage. Bill, no doubt, did both those things.

In his wife's book, *Lois Remembers*, Lois Burnham Wilson wrote, not only about her upbringing as a Swedenborgian, but as a Swedenborgian would write, and possibly only another Swedenborgian would pick up on that. She wrote about "the ancients", "regeneration", "two as one", and "Mary Baker Eddy"—who took from Swedenborg.

For example, she writes, "Johnny P. of Detroit was another who traveled a lot and, like Johnny Appleseed before him, scattered seeds. Wherever he went in the Midwest, he inspired alcoholics to band together and start meetings." Few that aren't Swedenborgian know that Appleseed was a real person, Jonathan Chapman, and as a Swedenborgian passed out books by Swedenborg as well as planted apple seeds.

No doubt, some of what Lois knew and believed, she shared with Bill without saying, *"Swedenborg wrote this..."*

Susan Cheever did not omit the Oxford influence on AA in her book. Instead, she points out the Swedenborgian influence on the Oxford Group through William James. All influences on AA lead back to Swedenborg!

To learn about Rev. Cowley and Rev. Lawrence's correspondence with Lois Wilson is fascinating. In *The Messenger* (a Swedenborgian monthly), February 1991 issue, C. Corey Mills then of Ellenton, Florida, former president of the *New York Association of the New Church*, who lived close to the Wilsons, wrote, "Lois kept repeating to me that Swedenborg's 'Doctrine of Remains' added much to her understanding of her work with AA and Al-Anon."

THERE IS AN ANSWER

Swedenborgians believe that the Lord has given THE WORLD the secrets of heaven to a Swede named Emanuel Swedenborg. Some authors, having read his Writings, have in turn written about them without giving credit to Swedenborg. True Swedenborgians wouldn't care about the credit, just that the Lord's truths ARE reaching people and leading them to heaven.

Dear Candace,
Can you tell me if the following book tells anything about the Swedenborgian background? Ernest Kurtz, Not-God, A History of Alcoholics Anonymous, *Center City, MN 19791.*

A.H.
Stockholm, Sweden
May 1997

Dear A.H.,
Not once. Though this book claims to be the definitive book on the complete history of Alcoholics Anonymous, it can't be, because it does not once mention Emanuel Swedenborg's influence on Bill and Lois Wilson, Dr. Carl Jung, nor William James. The title of this book is misleading, unless you are familiar with AA philosophy or until you read the book. " 'Not-God' means first, 'You are not God,' " (page 3) which is the message of the AA program.

Not-God originally was a doctoral dissertation. Of the 436 pages, 206 are the text, the remainder is made up of Appendixes, Notes, and a Bibliography. Despite its many repetitions and scholarly slant, on the whole, it is an easy read. As for AA's origin, Ernest Kurtz stated (1979, page 33):

> The four "founding moments" in the history of the idea and the fellowship of Alcoholics Anonymous were: Dr. Carl Gustav Jung's 1931 conversation with Rowland H; Ebby's T.'s late November 1934 visit with Bill Wilson; Wilson's "spiritual experience" and discovery of William James in Towns Hospital in mid-December 1934; and the interaction between Wilson and Dr. Bob Smith through May and June 1935 which climaxed in the final and enshrined "founding moment" just recorded.

An alcoholic named Rowland consulted Dr. Carl Jung (who read Swedenborg) and was told by the doctor that the only thing that could possibly *save* Rowland from alcohol was an overwhelming spiritual experience and advised him to get *religious*, which he did. Then he *saved* Ebby (a childhood friend of Lois's brother) and then Ebby *attempted to save* Bill (who married a Swedenborgian in a Swedenborgian church). Bill had a near-death experience in a hospital (he said he saw an indescribable white light) and found *The Varieties of Religious Expereince* by William James (who read Swedenborg) helped him to understand it.

Kurtz writes on page 164:

> The Harvard philosopher-psychologist's book *The Varieties of Religious Experience* had in fact influenced Wilson at a critical moment, and early members of Alcoholics Anonymous habitually recommended this book to any who complained of difficulty with "the spiritual side" of their program.

It could be said that Swedenborgians are too willing to link up with the 12-steps because they can be found in Swedenborg's books, even though Bill W. didn't publicly talk about Swedenborg. Others felt similar links. Kurtz tells us on page 98:

> Father Edward Dowling introduced himself as a Jesuit priest from St. Louis who, as editor of a Catholic publication, was interested in the parallels he had intuited between the Twelve Steps of Alcoholics Anonymous and the Exercises of St. Ignatius, the spiritual discipline of his Jesuit order. That he showed delight rather than disappointment when Wilson wearily confessed ignorance of the Exercises at once endeared the diminutive cleric to Bill.

Swedenborgians believe that the Writings of Swedenborg are truths from the Lord received in spirit and therefore heavenly truths. Heavenly truths can be found in many religions and philosophies at the same time, even if they had never been shared, because they are from heaven and not secular.

But, Wilson did know about Swedenborg and Ernest Kurtz failed to mention him in his extensive study. I found the omission curious, until I dragged myself through the second half of the book and found these:

> page 412: Lois Wilson, *Lois Remembers* (New York: Al-Anon Family Group Headquarters, Inc., 1979), is the autobiography of Bill Wilson's wife. ... This book was completed too late to be of direct use to the present research.

> Page 417: At the time of this research, Lois was working on an autobiography, and her materials were well-arranged for reference.

Lois's grandfather was a Swedenborgian minister! Swedenborg is discussed in her autobiography many times. Kurtz just choice to ignore the theologian or was unaware of Swedenborg's influence on Alcoholics Anonymous beyond the wife's influence. This is a big omission. I plan on writing Ernest Kurtz about Emanuel Swedenborg and his influence on AA. I'll let you know, if I hear back from him. Thanks, A.H., for bringing this book to my attention.

UPDATE
Mr. Kurtz never did respond to my letter.

Dear Candace,

You asked if the 12 Steps of Alcoholics Anonymous is a Swedenborgian Program? Paragraph no. 36 of Swedenborg's "Divine Providence" *is intriguing with respect to claims about the connection between New Church doctrine and the 12 Step program of Alcoholics Anonymous:*

"I have talked with angels about wisdom on occasion, and they have told me that wisdom is union with the Lord because the Lord is wisdom itself. They have told me that they attain this union when they banish hell from themselves, and that the union is in direct proportion to the degree of banishment."

They picture wisdom, they said, as a wonderfully elegant palace with twelve steps leading up to it. No one gets to the first step except with the Lord's help and by union with Him, and for all of us, the ascent depends on that union. The higher we climb, the more clearly we realize that no one is wise on his or her own, but only from the Lord. We also realize that relative to what we do not know, what we do know is like a droplet compared to a vast lake. The twelve steps to the palace of wisdom signify whatever is good united with what is true and whatever is true united with what is good.

Many people have suggested a connection between New Church doctrine and the 12 Step AA program, but there is not much documentation to support this claim. Swedenborgian sources are essentially anecdotal, with no hard facts to go on. But rather than dismiss the possibility, or worse yet minimize the value of AA because of those claims, it might be wise to look at it with an eye on Providence, and consider it as a real possibility.

AA founder Bill Wilson did have a Swedenborgian wife. This is about the only hard fact we have, but it is a good one. And there are elements of the program that are essentially in line with what our [Swedenborgian] church would teach if we were to move beyond our institutional self-absorption and develop such a system for the world to have.

It is based on the spiritual idea of vastation. It puts reliance on a transcendent God at the root of all forward progress. It is process oriented as regeneration clearly is, and this is a major new addition to traditional Christian thinking: AA members cycle through the 12 steps, but once finished, they are not done. They just begin again, but each time from a starting point at a higher level of functioning. And this process of self-improvement never ends. Sound familiar? It should. This is the process of cyclical temptations leading to regeneration, as taught in the Writings for the New Church. And the 12 Steps are universalizing: anyone from any spiritual starting point can play, and win. There are lots of parallels here to New Church teachings on the process of spiritual perfection. So if Bill Wilson did not incorporate the Writings directly into his program, complete with references, he did come up with a plan that is remarkably similar to what they say. Coincidence?

Translating the New Church message downward to the formulaic simplicity of the AA program is not necessarily something that New Church pastors should do. Some have reportedly come close to this in the past, and some may actually be doing it now. The propriety of doing this is a discussion for another day, but it says nothing about the effectiveness of the 12 Step program itself. Applied as it normally is, outside of "religion," it can attract people who are not in states receptive to religion, and bring them into the order necessary for this to happen. And this is a *very good thing. I think we New Church people tend to look at programs like this from an elitist perspective, and find them lacking.*

So Bill Wilson's program may be a problem for our church if our ministers mimic the 12 Steps and substitute them for New Church doctrine. But that isn't Bill's fault. Have you worked closely with recovering alcoholics? It is an illuminating and humbling experience. Once in a while you get to see the Lord at work, up close. I believe that He dropped some of His New Jerusalem into that AA program, whether Bill was conscious of it or not, and I believe that's why it works so well.

<u>We worry so much about the size of our [Swedenborgian] church, so here's an encouraging little thought: If AA's 12 Step program were indeed founded on the New Church doctrine of regeneration, and if each AA meeting could then be considered a kind of New Church gathering, then the New Church would actually be the largest church in America, in terms of both numbers and activity. And better yet, it wouldn't be ours at all</u>.

Rev. Dr. Reuben P. Bell
Fryeburg, Maine
March 2005

[I added the underlining.]

Swedenborg used this ornament in *Divine Providence*

Dear Candace,

My question for the month is this: Swedenborg claimed supersensible experience of an eternal heaven and hell. The Tibetan Book of the Dead *(also supersensibly derived) corroborated much of Swedenborg's information about the life after death, but goes on to talk about an eventual reincarnation. How do you explain this?*

D.D.
Van Nuys, California
December 2001

Dear D.D.,
"In the Word, there is a spiritual sense hitherto unknown," wrote Emanuel Swedenborg in *True Christian Religion* #193. But, he tells us, it was known by the first people on earth—he called **"The Most Ancients"**. They intuitively knew and understood the spiritual and the natural worlds and of their correspondences.

Many generations later, **"The Ancients"** that inhabited the earth (descended from The Most Ancients) were still somewhat aware of those connections between the worlds. Swedenborg said that the ancient Egyptians were a part of The Ancients and their hieroglyphs (holy carvings) can only be read as correspondences, not as literal or phonetic text.

Swedenborg's doctrine of correspondences (written in the 18th century) was given to him over several years by the Lord, while his spiritual eyes were opened. The hieroglyph language was lost (not understood), until just before World War II; scholarship today collaborates Emanuel Swedenborg's Writings on the subject.

The Egyptians had their *Book of the Dead* of which they placed excerpts from with every deceased person in their burial wrappings. The Tibetans did this, too. *The Tibetan Book of the Dead* parallels *The Egyptian Book of the Dead*! Both:
- contain doctrines about heaven and hell
- describe judgment before God
- describe a jury of animal-shaped deities
  that picture manifestation of the human intellect
- tell that a dead person enters into the "full life of day" immediately after death

This demonstrates Swedenborg's claim that a common religious tradition originally covered the whole earth. Collectively, he called it, **"The Most Ancient Church"** among The Most Ancients.

The descendents, The Ancients, believing less and less in The Most Ancients' ways, began to believe in the resurrection of the physical body or in reincanation. Human and animal sacrifices and rituals of pouring oil or wine on the deceased were performed for the departed as supposed magical effects for the soul.

Daisetsu Teitaro Suzuki (1870–1966), the man who made "Zen" a household word, called Emanuel Swedenborg (in 1954), *"your Buddha of the North"*. Between 1910 and 1915, D.T. Suzuki translated four books by Swedenborg into Japanese, and wrote a book about Swedenborg's life. In 1950, Suzuki wrote that: *"Swedenborg's doctrine of correspondence holds good in Buddhism, too."*

In the book, *Swedenborg, Buddha of the North* by D.T. Suzuki, translated by Andrew Bernstein, published in 1996, Suzuki writes:

> This leads us to consider the most important difference between Swedenborg and Buddhism, and what is undoubtedly a major obstacle to any conflation. Swedenborg's Christian concepttion of the afterdeath drama is orthodox in understanding this life as a one-chance preparation for heaven or hell, since one's ruling love never changes, even to eternity (*Heaven and Hell* by Swedenborg #477, 480.) In contrast, all traditional schools of Buddhism understand the alternative to nirvana as rebirth in one of the six samsaric realms (heaven, titan, human, hungry ghost, animal, and hell), which includes the possibility of returning as a human being. However, even this difference is complicated by the fact that some Bardo Thodol passages warn the spiritual about never being able to escape from where one is inclined to go.

Suzuki describes for several pages, the parallels between the Writings of Swedenborg and *The Tibetan Book of the Dead*. He suggests that *The Book of the Dead* may be more for the living than the dead "as a way of encouraging the survivors to reform their lives—their samskaras—while they still can."

Me and Rev. Dr. Jonathan S. Rose enjoy lunch served in the courtyard of the Swedenborgian Church in San Francisco after Jonathan gave a talk about the new translations of The Writings of which he is Series Editor, 18 May 1997.
The Swedenborgian Church in San Francisco, built in 1895, is designated a National Historic Landmark by the U.S. Department of the Interior.

SILA May 1997

February 2008
Dear *SILA* Readers,

Speaking of good, Dr. Oz "America's Doctor"—as Oprah calls him—is a Swedenborgian. He wrote about it in the Nov/Dec 2007 issue of *Spirituality & Health* magazine. www.spiritualityhealth.com

According to www.Oprah.com:

"Dr. Mehmet Oz is the Professor and Vice Chairman of Surgery at Columbia University in New York City, Director of the Cardiovascular Institute, and Founder and Director for the Complementary Medicine Program at New York Presbyterian Hospital. Dr. Oz is a widely published author, including the award-winning *Healing from the Heart* and two best-selling books, *YOU: The Owner's Manual* and *YOU: The Smart Patient.* He has written numerous articles for consumer and medical publications, including *Newsweek, O, The Oprah Magazine,* and *The New England Journal of Medicine,* and has a bi-monthly column in *Esquire* magazine. He is also a regular contributor to *The Oprah Winfrey Show*."

I was watching Dr. Oz on *Oprah* on the 5th of February and almost fell off the couch when he said the word "conjugial"!

Only a Swedenborgian says "conjugial" and not "conjugal" (no "i") as in a prisoner may get conjugal visits. Dr. Oz was telling Oprah the items on his Anti-Aging Checklist and said that one thing to do is have sex. The more sex one has, the healthier one will be, he said. Dr. Oz also said:

> When you have loving conjugial love with someone and you actually have that passionate moment, you not only exchange bodily chemicals, which you do, but you stimulate chemicals within you.

It was surprising to me that Oprah did not stop him and correct him or comment in her curious way, with a, *What did you say?* Interestingly, on Oprah.com his quote above is written with "conjugal"!

"Conjugial" (Webster's Revised Unabridged Dictionary. MICRA, Dictionary.com):

\Con*ju"gi*al\, a. [L. conjugialis, fr. Conjugium. Cf. Conjugal.] Conjugal. [R.]
—Swedenborg.

It's odd that the word is not described as marriage love, the highest love of all, but only given its reference source—Swedenborg.

Thinking of you,
Candace

UPDATE

I met Oprah Winfrey, 2 September 1993. I went to a taping of her show when I was in Chicago for *The Parliament of the World's Religions* in 1993. I had requested the complimentary tickets by mail, months prior to my trip. I lined up without knowing what the show's topic was. It turned out to be about contacting the dead!! After the taping, I hurried to meet her and even though I was seated near the back, I was one of the first to reach her. I shook Oprah's hand and asked if she had ever read any books by Emanuel Swedenborg. She said, no. I told her she should, he's good!

Oprah moved my right hand from her right to her left hand and held it tightly and continued greeting other guests. After a few minutes, she smiled at me and let me go. She moved on to others.

I had the fortune to meet Raymond A. Moody, Jr., M.D. after he appeared on *Oprah*, 2 September 1993. He wrote *Life after Life: The Investigation of a Phenomenon —Survival of Bodily Death* (1975) which includes six pages about Swedenborg. Dr. Moody told me that Swedenborg is one of his favourite authors.

SILA October 1993

THERE IS AN ANSWER

Dear Candace,
Did you know that John Steinbeck mentions Swedenborg in his book The Log from the Sea of Cortez? *He writes* [Chapter 13, page 122]:

> Incidentally, there is in this connection a remarkable etiological similarity to be noted between cause in thinking and blame in feeling. One feels that one's neighbors are to be blamed for their hate or anger or fear. One thinks that poor pavements are "caused" by politics. The non-teleological picture in either case is the larger one that goes beyond blame or cause. And the non-casual or non-blaming viewpoint seems to us very often relatively to represent the "new thing", the Hegelian "Christ-child" which arises emergently from the union of two opposing viewpoints, such as those of physical and spiritual teleologies, especially if there is conflict as to causation between the two or within either. The new viewpoint very frequently sheds light over a larger picture, providing a key which may unlock levels not accessible to either of the teleological viewpoints. There are interesting parallels here to the triangle, to the Christian ideas of trinity, to Hegel's dialectic, and to Swedenborg's metaphysic of divine love (feeling) and divine wisdom (thinking).

In a way I find it very reassuring to know that many of the world's leading and foremost authors have read (rejected or not) Swedenborg. But still, my English has in some way left me in the dark here. I'm not familiar with all the philosophy terms, nor is this Hegel person known to me. So if you have any material about Hegel, I would be very glad to know.

T.H.
Himmelev, Denmark
November 1996

Dear T.H.,
No, I didn't know that John Steinbeck (1902–1968) wrote about Swedenborg in his 1941 novel! Thanks for the knowledge!

Steinbeck, a Californian, also wrote *Of Mice and Men* and *The Grapes of Wrath*. I have not read *The Log from the Sea of Cortez* (I'm going to now) but, after reading the paragraph which includes Swedenborg, all I can say is, AND PEOPLE SAY SWEDENBORG IS HARD TO UNDERSTAND?! Give me a break!

Georg Wilhelm Friedrich Hegel (1770–1831) was a German idealist philosopher. The Hegelian Dialectic is a development—one concept, the thesis, is followed by its opposite, the antithesis. He is famous for saying, "the real is rational and the rational real".

Dear Candace,

The abbreviation of your institution SILA reminded me of the exactly same Turkish word meaning "homeland". Sila in Turkish literature always brings back memories of one's homeland from which one has been separated. A bit like our journeys in this world.

I.K.
Washington, D.C.
July 2008

Dear Candace,

Thank you so much, dear Candace, for your SILA info! I don't remember if I wrote you that the word "SILA" remind me the Russian word (a power). Really, your little sheet is more capacious than some respectable big magazines.

S.L.
Kherson, Ukraine
January 2008

Dear S.L.,

So glad you enjoy *SILA*! I was delighted to look up and learn that capacious means capable of containing much; a large quantity. What a great review!

Am glad to know *SILA* is similar to the Russian word for *power*. I looked up and found it also means *power* in Slovak, *emergency* in Slovenian, and *filter* in Swedish. I think *SILA* is all those things!!

Dear Candace,

I am a humble servant of Pathway to Peace teaching yoga and meditation without any charge. I had been to Chicago to attend and participate in the Parliament of the World's Religions *at the Palmer House Hilton Hotel in September '93 as one of the co-sponsors and also as a delegate.*

I was going through a cart load of papers I had brought from Chicago and I came across Swedenborg Information of Los Angeles. I would like to have more information about heaven, hell, Satan, God, theory of reincarnation, sin, and where do we go? Is the word "devil" equivalent to "satan" in Christianity?

By the way, is there any meaning of the word "SILA"? In Buddhism sila means virtuous "conduct" or "character".

I read about the speech of [Parliament President] *Charles C. Bonney (1831–1903) delivered at the first* Parliament of the World's Religions *held in 1893. I became a co-sponsor of the 1993 Parliament because when I was in Calcutta University, 1929–1935 I got considerable inspiration by visiting Swami Vivekananada's headquarters in Calcutta, but I was very much disappointed participating in the 1993* Parliament *at the age of 83.*

Thank you for giving a patient hearing.

Dvm'Rao
Yoga Guru
Seattle, Washington
February 1994

Dear Dvm'Rao,

Your letter is well received. I am honoured you wrote.

It is pleasant to learn *SILA's* meaning in Buddhism has such integrity. Although *SILA* is an acronym (a word formed from the first letters of a series of words) from <u>S</u>wedenborg <u>I</u>nformation of <u>L</u>os <u>A</u>ngeles, a *SILA* reader from California in 1989 wrote me that "sila means in Czech, Russian, and all Slavonic languages: THE FORCE." *SILA* is proud to be a virtuous character of force for good!

Swami Vivekananada credited Mr. Bonney (a Swedenborgian) with being the man that brought Buddhism to America for the first time in 1893. Swedenborg, a writer of a new theology, wrote that all people of all religions are welcomed into heaven.

I am sorry you were disappointed with the 1993 *Parliament*. No doubt, due to the feudal antics on stage, the small conference rooms, the complicated schedules, the lack of love, and the focus on faith alone. I, too, was a frustrated participant. Unfortunately, this *Parliament* reflected the state of the world in this century. The third *Parliament* would be interesting to attend in 2093!

The questions you asked have been answered in *SILA* before. Those back issues will be sent to you and a copy of *SILA's* "*Special Report of the Parliament of the World's Religions*". Thank you for taking the time to write me your thoughts!

October 1993

Dear *SILA* Readers,

The year 1993 will be remembered for more than the Great Flood of '93 which destroyed over 10 million acres of land across 10 states of the U.S. (perilously close to Chicago) causing tens of deaths and $10 billion in damage.

The Great Flood of '93 was not God's punishment on us. It was not "an act of God", but an "act of people" — Did we drain the wetlands? Did we channel the Mississippi River with dikes and levees? Did we build cities on the flood plains? Did we habour hatred in our hearts for our neighbours? All natural disasters are reflections of things spiritual, either happening in the other world, simultaneously, or with people here on earth. Wars and misfortunes are not punishments from God, but reflections of things we allow to happen inside of us. Rescue missions, relief help, hospitals, and natural cures are acts of God, for He bends all evil towards good through people moved to charity and people moved to humility. The Lord God never does any evil or punishing for He is all love.

The year 1993 will be remembered as the centennial of a religious event that started inter-religious communication, *The Parliament of the World's Religions*. People ask: *Will there be more parliaments soon? Will we have to wait for another century to talk?*

After the 1893 *Parliament,* enthusiasm was high for another, but it waned. Now, after the 1993 *Parliament,* enthusiasm is back, but it is more than likely to wane, for the world has a long way to maturity. The first *Parliament* "appears" to have been more of a major event. Yet, back then, there weren't as many competitive arenas vying for people's time and attention. If a poll was taken on the street today, the majority of people would not know the 1993 *Parliament* had taken place. This does not and should not take away from its importance.

Our media today tends to focus, unfortunately, on the controversial and the bizarre. It reported which religions pulled out of the *Parliament* because some other religion was there they didn't approve of. Also, it was reported when the police were called to separate people from hitting each other on stage during a presentation. The *Chicago Reader* wrote this slanted commentary:

> Followers of Emanuel Swedenborg publicized him by passing out a "Ripley's Believe It or Not" item about the theft of his skull in 1816. The Royal Swedish Academy of Sciences allegedly paid £3,200 to recover it.

No word about the other pamphlets (more than 50 topics) given away at the Swedenborg Booth! We have a long way to travel inward before we will be able to hold more regular *Parliaments*.

After the 1893 *Parliament*, we on earth experienced:
- World War I
- The Great Depression
- The Holocaust
- World War II
- nuclear war threat
- assassination of President John F. Kennedy
- assassination of Rev. Dr. Martin Luther King, Jr.
- Challenger explosion
- end of the millennium

And we also witnessed:
- invention of the transistor
- man landing on the Moon
- The American Civil Rights Movement
- end of the Cold War
- eradication of small pox

But, most of all, world peace is desired. Most people believe that peace is when:
- wars cease
- security from enemies exists
- discords between people cease
- one delights from success of things
- the mind rests from cares and worries

But, this is natural peace. True heavenly peace, Swedenborg tells us, transcends that kind of peace. For there is no peace for people participating in evil. Evil people may appear as though they are peaceful and tranquil, but only when things are going their way. Internally they are burning with hatred, revenge, and ill-will. Heavenly peace is a state of mind that surpasses all other delights. It is not only an external relaxation from combat, but also an internal tranquility from untruths. True peace will be when love of self (domination) and love of the world (greed) have been removed. Eternal spiritual peace is attainable on earth by each one of us, individually.

The millennium mentioned in the book of Revelation in the Word does not refer to 1,000 years literally. It means an innumerable amount, infinite abundance, or eternity. Nothing happened to the earth in the year 1900 as nothing will happen to the earth in the year 2000. What will happen is world peace will grow, gradually, not radically, as individual spiritual peace grows.

Attending the *Parliament of the World's Religions* was a highlight in my life. It allowed me to be a tourist in an historic city, to be a sightseer of various religions, and to be an overseer of humanity in progress. I was privileged to meet many *SILA* readers in person in Chicago. What an eye opener that was for some readers. One thought I was a redhead! I am blonde. One thought I was short! I am tall. It was a delight for me to share myself with many during the *Parliament*. Writing this report for you gave me joy.

Thinking of you,
Candace

Dear Candace,
How did the Parliament all happen because of Swedenborg?

B.S.H.
Jyllinge, Denmark
July 1993

Dear B.S.H.,
Charles Carroll Bonney (1831–1903), President of the first *Parliament of the World's Religions,* was a Swedenborgian.

Swedenborg was a Swedish scientist that believed in God. He studied the sciences of his time and excelled in them. He invented an airplane—before Leonardo da Vinci!—an airtight stove, and a submarine. He discovered that the brain functions in sync with the lungs. After looking for the soul and not finding it, he turned to studying the Word of God.

Swedenborg wrote over 30 theological books. He did not start a religion. He espoused a new theology in his books. Swedenborg wrote there is a church on earth, which he calls the **"church universal"** (that transcends church organizations) which is made up of sincere people of any faith that live a spiritual moral life. This idea of the **"church universal"** is what inspired Charles C. Bonney to create the *Parliament.* Bonney was not a minister, he was a lawyer—although in his time a respected one! Being a Swedenborgian, along with being an exceptional organizer, he made the first *Parliament* happen.

It was around 1889 when Bonney got the idea about bringing all the religions together, under one roof, to talk with each other. This had never been done before. His idea came to fruition four years later. That *Parliament* was held during the Chicago *World's Fair* in 1893. Bonney thought the displays of material objects, achievements, and accomplishments, that would be viewed at the *World's Fair*, weren't enough. He wanted something nobler.

He became President of *The World's Congresses* (held at the *Fair*) and presided over the 18 Congresses: agriculture, art, commerce and finance, education, engineering, government, labor, literature, medicine, moral and social reform, music, philosophy, public press, religion, temperance, and women. Bonney wrote:

> When it pleased God to give me the idea of the World's Congresses of 1893 there came with that idea a profound conviction that their crowning glory should be a fraternal conference of the world's religions.

Swedenborg wrote in *True Christian Religion* #536: **"All who do good from religion, not only Christians, but even pagans, are accepted and after death [are] adopted by the Lord."**

August 1993
Dear *SILA* Readers,

The first *Parliament of the World's Religions* in 1893 lasted 17 days. The second in 1993 will last 9 days. The first took 3 years to prepare. The second 5 years.

The first *Parliament* had:
- ✓ 1,245 sessions
- ✓ 5,974 speakers
- ✓ 750,000 attendees

The document which stated the purpose of the 1st *Parliament* was signed by:
- ✓ a Jewish rabbi
- ✓ a Catholic archbishop
- ✓ a Protestant orthodox bishop
- ✓ a Protestant liberal bishop
- ✓ a Protestant orthodox clergyman
- ✓ a Protestant liberal clergyman
- ✓ a Quaker leader
- ✓ a Swedenborgian minister

Thinking of you,
Candace

October 1993
Dear *SILA* Readers,
   The second *Parliament* had:
   ✓ 750 sessions
   ✓ 60 exhibiters with booths
   ✓ 7,700 attendees

The Opening of the 1993 *Parliament* was attended by almost 2,000. Introductions were given by the Mayor of Chicago, Richard M. Daley and the Governor of Illinois, Jim Edgar. Leaders of the participating religions entered in procession followed by delegates of their faith. Each religion was introduced and the variously garbed representatives solemnly, yet joyously, marched down alternately two aisles to musical accompaniment by the Drepung Loseling Monks and Chicago Music of the Baroque, a 20-piece orchestra on the balcony. There were 47 dignitaries on stage.

The processional was predictably exciting, colourful, and emotional. I led the 7 Swedenborgians down the aisle. I was thrilled and honoured. We sat in the 7th row. Rev. David Roth of the *Chicago New Church* continued onto the platform as the Swedenborgian leader. *The Parliament* was opened by Dr. David Ramage, Chair of the event. Blessings from the four directions and the center were given by five Native American Elders with a peace pipe. Eight Blessings were given by:
   ✓ a Vivekananda swami
   ✓ a Evangelical minister
   ✓ a Unitarian minister
   ✓ a Fellowship minister
   ✓ a Swedenborgian minister
   ✓ a Theosophical doctor
   ✓ a Zoroaswtrian dastoor
   ✓ a Buddhist monk

Rev. Roth spoke with a strong, but gentle command. He boomed out truth and mentioned God; few did. He told me later that another religious leader on stage remarked to him that he did not know Swedenborgians were Christians and that he was delighted to learn this!

Rev. Roth's delivery of his Blessing was in great contrast to the other speakers as to clarity and pitch for his could be heard by all. I couldn't help but compare this opening ceremony to the 1893 one. It saddens me that we are too dependent upon our current technology. The art of public speaking with the exception of Rev. Roth was lacking with the 1993 speakers.

A hundred years ago, they delivered speeches at the *Parliament* without microphones to crowds of 3,000! Yet, in 1993 a third of the Opening Plenary was not heard as speakers did not stand close enough to the mike or body mikes were not used at all as with the Native American Elders during their half-hour dedication.

After the Opening Plenary of the *Parliament of the World's Religions,* I suggested we (the Swedenborgians) go for Chicago's famous deep dish pizza at *Uno Pizza* to celebrate and we did!

Thinking of you,
Candace

I'm standing next to the official banner of *The Parliament*.

SILA November 1993

Swedenborgian representatives that participated in the Grand Opening Ceremony for the 2nd *Parliament of the World's Religions*, in Chicago, 1993: Rev. David Roth of Chicago, Kay & Jim Hauck of Chicago, Me, Rev. Ted Klein of Newton, Massachusetts, Rev. George Dole of Sharon, Massachusetts, and Mary Klein of Newton, MA.

SILA November 1993

July 1993
Dear *SILA* Readers,
    Did you know that Daniel H. Burnham, a Swedenborgian, was the Head Architect of the *Columbian Exposition* in 1893 (Chicago's *World Fair*) AND also Chairman of the *Architecture Congress* held during the *Exposition*, as he and his partner, John Root (1850–1891), also a Swedenborgian, had built 224 banks, churches, offices, residences, and schools across the United States? IT'S TRUE!

Thinking of you,
Candace

Dear Candace,
    I was interested in Bonney (in June SILA*). My father was working in a booth at the 1893 fair as representative of the New Church. Perhaps my contribution will help get you to the* Parliament of the World's Religions *in Chicago. Good work!*

Richard R. Gladish
Bryn Athyn, Pennsylvania
August 1993

Dear Mr. Gladish,
    I've goose bumps. That's thrilling to know! I feel privileged you shared your family history with me. I trust I will do my part and make your Dad happy.

Dear Candace,
    I'm really excited about your trip to Chicago. I hope you have time to see the Chicago Art Institute. I went to art school there many years ago and received my BAE (art education degree).
    Also in the Art Institute is the "Burnham Library of Architecture"—donated and named for Daniel H. Burnham, the architect pictured in the last SILA. *My mother was a Burnham, daughter of Edwin Burnham, oldest brother of Uncle Dan (Burnham). What a coincidence to see his picture in* SILA. *I was born and raised in Glenview, Illinois. When you go out there, you may walk around the Park. There is a big rock with a plaque on it with my parents' names, OSCAR AND BESSIE SCALBOM. We had a nice large house there and then the property was donated to the church and there is a large playground for children on it.*
    You are the kind of person to tell interesting things about Swedenborg to the public!

Jane Scalbom Howell
Hazelhurst, Wisconsin
August 1993

SILA February 1994

This monument to Swedenborg is at Diversey Harbor in Chicago. The stone pyramid on top was not part of the original design. The bronze cast bust was stolen in the 1970s! Swedenborg was holding one of his books. I'm leaning on the Emanuel Swedenborg monument in 1993.

Plaque reads:

"IN A WORLD IN WHICH VOICE OF CONSCIENCE TOO OFTEN SEEMS STILL AND SMALL THERE IS NEED OF THAT SPIRITUAL LEADERSHIP OF WHICH SWEDENBORG WAS A PARTICULAR EXAMPLE."

FRANKLIN D. ROOSEVELT, 1938

June 1990
Dear *SILA* Readers,

In 1871, a fire almost destroyed entirely the business section of Chicago and left a third of its 300,000 citizens homeless. By 1909, a new PLAN OF CHICAGO drawn up by the city's #1 architect, Daniel H. Burnham, was approved by a group of conservative Chicago businessmen.

Burnham had previously planned the cities of Washington D.C., San Francisco, Manila, and Baguio in the Philippines. He had also planned the *Chicago World's Fair* in 1893 as a "make-believe city". It received international praise. The created "White City" emphasized convenience, safety, sanitation, sewers, pure drinking water, and beauty. (All uncommon features at that time in American cities.)

Burnham's (almost completely implemented) 1909 PLAN OF CHICAGO profoundly influenced the course of city planning in the United States. It heralded the modern city planning movement.

The designs for the *Chicago World's Fair* ("White City") and the city of Chicago, both, were based on "heaven" as described in *Heaven and Hell* by Emanuel Swedenborg! The public wasn't privy to this fact, for Burnham knew his maternal grandfather, Rev. Holland Weeks, a Congregationalist, had been tried for heresy for preaching Swedenborgianism in his congregation and was thus excommunicated from his church in Abington, Massachusetts in 1820! Daniel Burnham wasn't going to risk his career or the opportunity to build "heavenly cities" by revealing where his design ideas came from.

Thinking of you,
Candace

January 1994
Dear *SILA* Readers,
Phil Patton in the June 1993 *Smithsonian* magazine wrote:

> Nothing says more about the power of the White City than that it inspired the Emerald City. Children's writer L. Frank Baum never forgot the fair and transmuted it into Oz, there at the end of the Yellow Brick Road.

SILA readers know that the White City (the nickname for the 1893 Chicago's *World Fair*) was inspired by the cities in heaven as described by Emanuel Swedenborg in his famous books!

Thinking of you,
Candace

Drawing by Tuan Hauptmann

SILA January 1994

May 2008
Dear *SILA* Readers,
   Big news to report:

The Burnham Plan Centennial
Chicago has been making huge plans to celebrate the Centennial of:
Daniel Burnham's 1909 Plan of Chicago

SILA reader, Kay Hauck of Chicago writes: "As one of the Program Partners in this city-wide celebration, *The Swedenborg Library* of Chicago will be co-hosting appearances by Erik Larson, best-selling author of *Devil in the White City*, and Kristin Schaffer, Ph.D., author of *Daniel H. Burnham, Visionary Architect and Planner*, both of whom have been featured speakers at *Swedenborg Library* events in the past several years."

From http://ecuip.lib.uchicago.edu/burnhamplan100/about/index:

Bold Plans. Big Dreams.

This is the legacy of the Plan of Chicago. In 1909, Daniel Burnham and Edward Bennett collaborated with the Commercial Club of Chicago and others to create a new plan for the greater Chicago region. Today, their Plan still inspires us to be visionary, think regionally, recognize the value of beauty and conservation, and to plan – and implement – systematically.

The year 2009 will be a time to look back 100 years for inspiration, and appreciate the big dreams that led to Chicago's sweeping lakefront, the "emerald necklace" of County Forest Preserves, and a tradition of thinking comprehensively about the region's development.

The Centennial also is an opportunity to make and implement bold plans for the 21st Century that build on the 1909 Burnham Plan's "…steady determination to bring about the very best conditions of city life for all the people…"

Thinking of you,
Candace

UPDATE
   For an extensive explanation of Swedenborg's influence on Burnham read the article: "An Iconography of City Planning: The Chicago City Plan" by Irving D. Fisher, Ph.D. in the book, *Emanuel Swedenborg: A Continuing Vision, A Pictorial Biography & Anthology of Essays & Poetry* edited by Robin Larsen (1988).

Dear Candace,

I am in prison and was given a copy of your letter to Dr. Finney, Jr. dated 7-29-93 about the Swedenborgians and Fredrick Douglas. I myself was amazed at what was said about the Swedenborgians as I had never heard of this group in my life. Although I am Muslim and have been all my life I am very conscious of my heritage and history. You learn something every day.

One of the religious advisors here in the prison who is African-American gave me a copy of your letter, though he is a Muslim. I really want you to tell me more about the Swedenborgians and Swedenborg. This is such startling knowledge it prompted me to write you. Further, I never knew of the Parliament of the World's Religions. *Please give me more information.*

W.A.
Jefferson City, Missouri
January 1994

January 1994
Dear *SILA* Readers,

I felt it was important to put to rest the persistent non-truth that African-Americans did not participate in the 1893 *Parliament of the World's Religions* held in Chicago. This false fact came to my attention in an article published in the official *Parliament* newsletter. This jumped off the page; from June 1993 *Council of the Parliament of the World's Religion Journal:*

> "The white American Christians were still in a state of denial as to the presence or rights of African-American Christians," according to Dr. Leon D. Finney, Jr., director of the African-American Leadership Partnership of the McCormick Theological Seminary.

Even after the 2nd *Parliament* ended, which took place in Chicago last year, this historical error is still being perpetuated, and oddly enough by some Swedenborgians—verbally and in print. I wrote the following open letter to Dr. Finney in Chicago and handed it out as a flyer at the 2nd *Parliament of the World's Religions:*

29 July 1993
Dear Dr. Finney,

I read the article about you in the June 1993 issue of the *CPWR Journal*. I was surprised to read that "Frederick Douglass was barred from being a formal presenter at the World Parliament" in 1893, and that you are taking a leadership role, this time, at the 1993 *Parliament* to ensure "that African-American Christians share center stage with people of other spiritual beliefs and nationalities."

The impression this article left me with was that no blacks were allowed at the *Parliament* in 1893 and I knew before researching the matter that this could not have been true as Charles C. Bonney, the President of the *Parliament* in 1893 was a Swedenborgian and Swedenborgians historically have always known what Swedenborg thought of Africans.

"Africans surpass all other Gentiles in interior judgment." That's from the 2-volume *True Christian Religion* (#837) by Emanuel Swedenborg, published in 1771. Swedenborg never had any black friends or acquaintances, but he "met" many Africans in the next world and wrote favourably about them. Followers of Swedenborg were instrumental in the abolition of slavery and I am enclosing an old issue of *SILA* which refers to this subject.

I am also gifting you with Swedenborg's bestselling book, *Heaven and Hell*. I have marked the pages that he talks about Africans. In almost all his books, he mentions Africans, and that was over 200 years ago!

I obtained an original copy of the official program of the 1893 *Parliament* and was pleased to find many blacks represented on stage, including Frederick Douglass. The fact that he was, as you say, barred from being a formal presenter—I have seen no reference to him being barred in the 100 year old books I have read—I can only imagine it was done for political reasons, not spiritual.

I am enclosing two pages from the book, *The New Jerusalem in The World's Religions Congresses of 1893* edited by Rev. L. P. Mercer (1894) to show you that the Swedenborgians' platform was shared by blacks.

And am also sending you a photocopy of part of the pamphlet: *The African and the True Christian Religion. A Review by Rev. L. P. Mercer, With Extracts from an Address of Dr. Edward W. Blyden* (1893) which was handed out at the *Parliament* in 1893.

I am writing you as a Swedenborgian to publicly apologize for any mistreatment of African-Americans in 1893 in regards to the *Parliament of the World's Religions* held during the Chicago *World's Fair* at the *Palace of Fine Arts*. I humbly tell you and all African-Americans that Charles C. Bonney did not intend this event to be marred with slander or hatred towards blacks, and I likewise carry the Swedenborgian flame of honour towards blacks as potential angels in Heaven along with everyone else into this century at the *Parliament of the World's Religions* in 1993.

I look forward to meeting you at the *Parliament*.

Thinking of you,
Candace

UPDATE

Rev. Dr. Leon D. Finney, Jr. (1938–) did not respond to my letter. He is currently pastor at the *Metropolitan Apostolic Community Church* in Chicago and Chairman and CEO of *The Woodlawn Organization*. Woodlawn is an area in the southside of Chicago. It became run-down, slum infested, and predominately black in the 1960s when whites fled as blacks moved in.

The Council for a *Parliament of the World's Religions* (CPWR) decided to hold a parliament every 5 years. 1999: 1–8 December, Cape Town, South Africa. 2004: 7–13 July, Barcelona, Spain. 2009: 3–9 December, Melbourne, Australia. Los Angeles wants it in 2014! (www.parliamentofreligions.org)

Dear Candace,
I have been to the Wayfarers Chapel several times when I lived in the Los Angeles area. It's so beautiful!

M.M.
Carmichael, California
October 1992

Dear M.M.,
Wayfarers Chapel—affectionately called "the Glass Chapel" as its walls are glass! or "the Wedding Chapel" as it has held over 700 weddings annually since it opened!—was designed in the 50s by the American architect Lloyd Wright (1890–1978), eldest son of the renowned architect, Frank Lloyd Wright. The *Wayfarers Chapel* is artistically situated on the shore of the Palos Verdes peninsula, over-looking the Pacific Ocean, about an hour's drive from Los Angeles. Its contemporary architecture features not only glass walls, but also triangular glass roof panels, a stone altar, a stone bell-tower, and live greenery that grows around the circumference of the chapel, inside!

Swedenborg described a chapel he "saw" in *Secrets of Heaven* #10514: **"The light of their sun is let in through the openings between branches and everywhere transmitted through crystals."** Also that: **"The art of architecture comes from heaven."** (See *Conjugial Love* #12)

UPDATE
Eric Lloyd Wright, son of Lloyd Wright, designed the Visitors Center. It was dedicated in 2001—the year *Wayfarers Chapel* celebrated its 50th anniversary.

I'm standing next to the National Memorial to Swedenborg plaque (1994)

Sally (my sister) and her husband, Ken Tait visiting *Wayfarers Chapel* (2007)

Dear Candace,
   Good luck in your mission. You might want to reproduce "Ripley's Believe It or Not!" re: Swedenborg.

                                                              P.B.
                                                      Elmhurst, Illinois
                                                        October 1990

Dear P.B.,
   Were you aware that there have been THREE *Ripley's Believe It or Not!*® comics featuring Emanuel Swedenborg? Yes!!!
   The most recent was published, 2 August 1988, to commemorate his 300th birthday. I asked *Ripley's* (headquartered in Toronto) to print a new comic to mark this momentous Tricentenary and they did! (Not an easy feat. It took many letters and phone calls.) *Ripley's Believe It Or Not!*® used to have a newspaper comic strip.

   Text from the first two comics about Swedenborg reads:

Emanuel Swedenborg
The Man Who Was Master of Many Trades
by Robert L. Ripley (1934)

   No single individual in the world's history ever encompassed in himself so great a variety of useful knowledge. He was a psychologist, philosopher, mathematician, geologist, inventor, metallurgist, mineralogist, botanist, chemist, aurist, physicist, zoologist, aeronautical engineer, assayer, musician, author, traveler, crystallographer, instrument maker, machinist, cabinet maker, legislator, mining engineer, economist, editor, poet, linguist, biographer, reformer, astronomer, bookbinder, physiologist, hydrographer. He made the first sketch of a glider-type airplane. Invented a submarine, machine gun, ear trumpet and airtight hot air stove. Discovered function of the ductless glands and that the brain animates synchronously with the lungs. Wrote and published first Swedish algebra.

UPDATE
   Steve and I were featured on the *Ripley's Believe It Or Not!*® TV show in 2002 and in *Ripley's Believe It Or Not!*®: *Expect the Unexpected* book (2006) on page 133 under the heading "Bunny Heaven". We like that!
   Ripley Entertainment, Inc. were most gracious in permitting their original Swedenborg comics to be included in this book. To my knowledge, these have never been printed in a non-Ripley book before! Edward Meyer—Vice President of Exhibits & Archives—responded to my request: *"I don't know if you will remember me, but I have been with* Ripley's *for 30 years and remember your first and subsequent requests well... I'm very impressed that you are still so passionate about Swedenborg."* I did remember, and thank Mr. Meyer!
   In 1993, *Ripley Entertainment, Inc.* moved its headquarters to Orlando, FL.

THERE IS AN ANSWER

Emanuel Swedenborg #19340916 © 2008 Ripley Entertainment, Inc.

Originally the first two comics of Swedenborg were in colour.
(above) Sunday, 16 September 1934
(next page) Sunday, 25 January 1948

Emanuel Swedenborg #19480125 © 2008 Ripley Entertainment, Inc.

Emanuel Swedenborg #19880802 © 2008 Ripley Entertainment, Inc.

Originally this comic was in black & white.
Tuesday, 2 August 1988

Dear Candace,

Thank you for sending me an incredible tribute to Swedenborg by an amazing lady, Helen Keller, in her book, My Religion. *(I still have to re-read the book to soak in its sweetness proper.)*

However, I would like to comment on one or two issues that have had an instant effect on me. In My Religion, *Keller gave me a very close look and indeed a soulful touch of the Writings and the man behind them, Swedenborg.*

I entirely agree with her about his beyond-the-natural-genius-insight of the natural, spiritual and celestial worlds. He was indeed a chosen servant of God. This lady herself is a true manifestation of God's love. And that God is Love.

Every morning and evening, when I spend quality time with the Lord who sees our souls and hearts, I rejoice. I'm never ashamed. I stand in His presence with my head up. Not because I conquered all my temptations, but because I tried to overcome them, sometimes with tears rolling down my cheeks, enlisting His help through constant prayer and renewed my steps whenever I stumbled.

I'm struck with the Writings and I'm sure it is one meal nobody should miss in a lifetime.

I tell you what, the Writings are the greatest thing that ever happened in my life! If Swedenborg arose today and told me, "Oops the Writings are wrong," I'll spend the rest of my life convincing him otherwise!!!

Anonymous
Nairobi, Kenya
June 2003

The Swedenborg Society was founded in 1810, incorporated in 1925. It's in the heart of Bloomsbury in Central London, just a short walk from the *British Museum*.

The Swedenborg Society
20-21 Bloomsbury Way
London
WC1A 2TH
United Kingdom

www.swedenborg.org.uk

No, Swedenborg did not live here! It's a Swedenborg *publishing* house. *"The house in Clerkenwell in which Swedenborg died was demolished many years ago,"* Richard Lines of *The Swedenborg Society* wrote me. Clerkenwell is an area in the borough, Islington, which is part of London.

Dear Candace,

I am in debt for your thoughtfulness and generosity in sending the Swedenborg 1989 Date Book and Helen Keller's My Religion. *My thanks for your kind comments. It would please me to be able to reciprocate in some way.*

Every good wish.

Norman Cousins, Ph.D.
UCLA School of Medicine
Los Angeles, California
July 1989

UPDATE
Norman Cousins (1915–1990)

Dear Candace,

Thanks for Helen Keller's book. I hope I can find time to read it.

Jack Smith
Columnist, Los Angeles Times
Los Angeles, California
September 1989

UPDATE
Jack Clifford Smith (1916–1996)

Dear Candace,

Just a note to thank you for My Religion *by Helen Keller. I look forward to reading it!*

John Bradshaw
(author of Healing the Shame that Binds You*)*
Houston, Texas
July 1990

November 1989
Dear *SILA* Readers,

 I wrote M. Scott Peck, M.D., author of *The Road Less Traveled* and gifted him with Helen Keller's biography, *My Religion*. I told Dr. Peck how a friend of mine had attended a lecture of his and rose to speak during the question and answer period. She had commented to him how much of what he had just said, reminded her of Swedenborg. Dr. Peck's reply to her was that when he retires, Swedenborg was on the top of his list to study. I received the following letter in reply:

> *Dear Candace,*
> *Dr. Peck has asked me to thank you and the anonymous person who attended his lecture! Thank you for Helen Keller's book on Swedenborg and Dr. Peck looks forward to reading it as soon as he has the time. He was correctly quoted and is, indeed, interested in learning much more about Swedenborg.*
>
> Kathleen Fitzpatrick
Executive Director
The Foundation for Community Encouragement
New Preston, Connecticut

Dear Ms. Fitzpatrick,
 Thank you for corresponding on behalf of Dr. Peck. Please convey to Dr. Peck my excitement in realizing that Swedenborg was indeed the *first psychologist*. Amidst many ideas, he explained the concept of "hereditary evil"—a tendency to evil that is passed on through just a few generations. This concept was directly opposed to the prevailing concept of his time of "original sin"—being born guilty of all evils back to Adam.
 Psychology today is at the forefront of understanding hereditary evil as it studies the regeneration or degeneration of a family. And Swedenborg's Writings are textbooks being cracked open for research in this field.
 How exciting!

Thinking of you,
Candace

UPDATE
 Morgan Scott Peck (1936–2005)

January 1990
Dear *SILA* Readers,

I sent Maya Angelou Helen Keller's *My Religion*, the *Swedenborg Foundation's* date book, and a note on a (Swedenborgian) *Wayfarer's Chapel* postcard, saying that I thought she may be interested in learning about Swedenborg. I received the following letter:

> *Dear Candace,*
> *Thank you very much for your gifts. I shall enjoy them. Please accept my best wishes for your own work and your life.*
>
> *Joy!*
> *Maya Angelou*
> *Winston-Salem, North Carolina*

Dear Maya Angelou,
To receive a thank you note from such a renowned writer as yourself attests to your greatness. I was moved by a truth you wrote in *I Know Why The Caged Bird Sings* (New York, NY: Random House, 1969, page 23):

> Of all the needs (there are none imaginary) a lonely child has, the one that must be satisfied, if there is going to be hope and a hope of wholeness, is the unshakable need for an unshakable God. My pretty Black brother was my Kingdom Come.

Swedenborg wrote, over 200 years ago, that people can worship what they have some idea of, but not what they have no idea of.

Miss Angelou, you put your faith in your only, older brother as your parental figurehead and therefore could transfer that trust in a human being to God in a healthy way. Some children have difficulty later, as adults, in accepting God. They, having experienced misguided faith in an alcoholic or verbally or physically abusive parental figurehead feel unsafe to transfer their learned distrust in a human being to God.

We only know what we learn. As we can learn, we can unlearn.

I trust Helen Keller's book will be a good introduction to Swedenborg for you and you will discover anew your unshakable God through the truths revealed to Emanuel Swedenborg.

Thinking of you,
Candace

Dear Candace,
Somewhere I read that Eddie Albert is a Swedenborgian. As was Lillian Gish. Do you know anything about this?

P.R.
San Francisco, California
June 1992

Dear P.R.,
The *Swedenborg Foundation* — a nonprofit publisher of Emanuel Swedenborg's books, founded in 1849, headquartered in ~~New York~~ (see page 57) — made a 30-minute dramatic documentary of Swedenborg's life story, titled, *Swedenborg: The Man Who Had to Know.*

Eddie Albert narrates this award winning film and Lillian Gish has a cameo in it. She plays Mrs. William Castel, the woman who gave the dinner party in Gothenburg, Sweden at which Emanuel revealed his clairvoyance by detailing to his friends a fire happening 300 miles away in Stockholm. (Lillian Gish also was in the *Swedenborg Foundation* film, *John Appleseed and the Frontier Within.*)

It is more than likely you saw these two actors names on a brochure put out by the *Swedenborg Foundation* advertising these films.

Lillian Gish is a member of the *Swedenborg Foundation*. Eddie Albert is not a member of the *Foundation*.

In Toronto, about seven or eight years ago, I was asked to replace a stand-in that wasn't working out on a film already in production titled, *Head Office,* starring Judge Reinhold, Jane Seymour, Rick Moranis, Danny DeVito, and Eddie Albert. On my first day, I approached Mr. Albert nervously, and said, "Mr. Albert, I enjoyed your work on *Swedenborg: The Man Who Had to Know.*" I will never forget his surprised look and the pregnant pause before he said, "Thank you!" He was called back to the set. The opportunity did not rise again for us to talk.

UPDATE
Lillian Gish (1893–1993)
Eddie Albert (1906–2005)

Dear Candace,
I've been studying the Word and Swedenborg for three years now, but I still feel like an infant amongst this vast knowledge.

J.K.
Lancaster, California
October 2002

Dear J.K.,
I can identify with that. And the angels in heaven feel the same, too!

Dear Candace,

I have a new bit of info. When Rev. Jonathan Rose was in Copenhagen in '91 he discovered that in Søren Kierkegaard's (the Danish philosopher and existential writer) private library, in the Royal Library were two of Swedenborg's books. No one had known that this very famous work was influenced by Emanuel Swedenborg. He is often seen as the first existentialist, about 100 years after Swedenborg. Jonathan Rose is a marvelous person.

Bridget Swinton-Hauptmann
Tyllinge, Denmark
September 1992

Dear Bridget,

What exciting news! What a find! I know Jonathan well. A year older (I think) than me. He grew up in a Swedenborgian community called Caryndale (Kitchener, Ontario, Canada), an hour's drive from where I grew up in Mississauga. The Toronto and Caryndale Swedenborgian churches socialize together regularly. I agree with you, Jonathan is a great guy.

Søren Kierkegaard (1813–1855), the Danish philosopher and theologian is considered one of the founders of existentialism—a philosophical attitude which is the opposite of rationalism. Existentialism says a person is responsible for their own choices. Kierkegaard, in articles, tackled the problem of what it means to be a true Christian. I wrote Jonathan and asked him what he had found. He replied:

Dear Candace,

Boy did I ever love getting together with the Hauptmann's last year! It was great.

As for Kierkegaard, I was looking through the card catalog in the Royal Library in Copenhagen under Swedenborg. They had an enormous collection of cards. As I leafed through it, I found two which had Kierkegaard's personal library written on them. One was a first edition of Heaven and Hell *(i.e. De Coelho et Inferno) and the other was a handwritten card which I could not decipher to save me life! But still the author was Swedenborg, and the location was Kierkegaard's personal library.*

I wish I could tell you more, but there it is. It was the first I had ever heard of any kind of relationship between Swedenborg and Kierkegaard.

Thanks for your interest.

Rev. Dr. Jonathan S. Rose
Swedenborgiana Library Archivist
Bryn Athyn, Pennsylvania

Dear Jonathan,

What a spine-tingling disclosure. I'm tantalized. Thanks for sharing your discovery. Good work!

UPDATE

Rev. Dr. Jonathan S. Rose is now President of the *Swedenborg Foundation* and Series Editor of "The New Century Edition of the Works of Emanuel Swedenborg" for the *Swedenborg Foundation*.

Dear Candace,

I've just been on the phone to the Royal Library. They say that there are 3 of Swedenborg's Writings in Søren Kierkegaard's private library. Heaven and Hell *in Latin, published in 1758, and* The Doctrine of the Lord *in Latin published in 1763, and* The Doctrine of the New Church *in German, published in 1795.*

Bridget Swinton-Hauptmann
Jyllinge, Denmark
April 1993

Dear Bridget,

Oh, that's great to know! Thanks for making the phone call! (*The Royal Library of Denmark* has been standing since 1657.)

SILA Readers may recall in September '92 you had brought to our attention that Rev. Jonathan Rose had discovered Kierkegaard owned two books by Swedenborg. Now you have sleuthed that Kierkegaard owned <u>3-books</u> of the Writings.

Kierkegaard was the youngest of seven children. It is sad that his mother, his sisters, and two of his brothers all died before he was 21. At the end of his academic life, he started to criticize the Christianity of his fervent father. He wrote many of his essays under the pen name, Johannes de Silentio.

He died unheralded, but during the early 20th century his work enjoyed acclaim and inspired modern theology and existentialism.

Emanuel Swedenborg influenced August Strindberg (1849–1912) the Swedish author and dramatist. This is known from his own letters, personal diaries, and literary works. It was Swedenborg who saved Strindberg from madness.

Strindberg wrote the play, *To Damascus,* in 1898. A famous adaptation of Parts I and II was done by another Swede, Ingmar Bergman (who read Swedenborg) in 1974, at the *Royal Dramatic Theatre*, in Stockholm. Strindberg made this intriguing connection, talking about *Damascus* in a letter to Gustaf af Geijerstam—Swedish novelist (1858-1909), 13 March 1898 (*Brev* vol. 12. pp. 279–280):

> Yes, it is no doubt a poem with a terrifying half-reality behind it. The art lies in the composition, which symbolizes the Repetition Kierkegaard speaks about; the action unfolds toward the Asylum; there it strikes the point and kicks back, the pilgrimage, the repeated lessons, the repeated swallowing.

Swedenborg used this ornament in *Secrets of Heaven*

Dear Candace,
I didn't know about that link between Blake and Swedenborg. Are there specific works by Blake that are more obviously influenced by Swedenborg?

J.Z.
New York, New York
April 1993

Dear Candace,
I used to read William Blake a lot, and doubtless saw footnotes and commentary relating Blake's thought to Swedenborg's.

J.M.
Stockton, California
April 1993

Dear J.Z. and J.M.,
William Blake (1757–1827) went from being a believer in Swedenborg to being a critic to being appreciative of him. Most everything Blake drew and wrote was influenced by Swedenborg. I recommend the book, *Blake and Swedenborg: Opposition is True Friendship,* Edited by Harvey F. Bellin and Darrell Ruhl (1985). Some Blake books obviously influenced by Swedenborg are:

- *Songs of Innocence* (1789)
- *The Marriage of Heaven and Hell* (1793)
- *Songs of Innocence and of Experience* (1794)
- *The (First) Book of Urizen* (1794)

At first, Blake—poet and artist—was enthusiastic about the idea that a New Church as described by Swedenborg would abolish the errors of the old churches. But, he soon became disillusioned with the organization in its infancy in London, England. However, while publicly rejecting Swedenborgianism, he freely used Swedenborg's concept of correspondences (e.g. plant symbolism) throughout his poems and engravings. *The Marriage of Heaven and Hell* is a satire of Swedenborg's book, *Heaven and Hell*. Blake wrote this AFTER *The Marriage of Heaven and Hell* was published:

> The works of this visionary are well worth the attention of Painters and Poets; they are foundations for grand things.

Dear Candace,
Just a note to tell you how much my wife and I enjoy your publication. I am sorry I had to miss the Blake Symposium, because I also do illuminated poetry. (What an artist and poet!)

B.O.
Woodland Hills, California
February 1995

Dear Candace,
You sent me that nice invitation about William Blake and even though I was not able to attend, it was still a very sweet gesture.

Anonymous
Denmark
February 1995

Dear B.O. and Anonymous,
    I knew that most of my readers would be unable to attend the *William Blake Symposium* held Saturday, 29 October 1994 at *The Huntington* in San Marino, CA (which is a 10-minute drive from my house) but, invited you all the same to keep you informed of an event that relates to Swedenborg. I will continue to let *SILA* readers know about events that may be of interest to them because of a Swedenborg tie-in. I will always try to give a sense of history to my readers and a sense of vision.
    I attended the all-day *William Blake: Images and Texts Symposium* with nine other Swedenborgians. I was the only one, however, that endured to the end. (Emphasis on *e n d u r e d*.) Although it was wonderful to see 150 people dedicate their Saturday to a series of lectures, it was tedious to listen to a lot of drivel.
    "Blake is very difficult to understand," one lecturer told us.
    "And people think Swedenborg is hard to understand!" said (New Church) Rev. John Odhner. "I wonder what Blake would think if he was here?"
    "Not much," I replied.
    The Huntington Library, Art Collection, and Botanical Gardens is a gorgeous institution serving scholars. It was founded by Henry Edwards Huntington (1850–1927) and his wife, Arabella Duval. Mostly influenced by his wife, they amassed one of the greatest research libraries in the world. On 207-acres, their residence, built by 1914, now houses the art collection.
    Mr. Huntington, in purchasing original edition works of William Blake, accumulated one of the largest collections of his books and letters, and the largest number of pages from Blake's illuminated books.
    After registration, coffee, and pastries, the attendees were welcomed to the symposium by Shelley Bennett from *The Huntington* and Robert Essick from the *University of California*.
    First up was Joseph Viscomi from *University of North Carolina*. His lecture was titled, "In the Caves of Heaven and Hell". Within the first minute, he mentioned Emanuel Swedenborg! The Swedenborgians in the front row were thrilled. Viscomi said that Blake's illustrated book, *The Marriage of Heaven and Hell,* was written as a reaction to Swedenborg's book, *Heaven and Hell.* It was a satire of Swedenborg. Viscomi said that Swedenborg greatly influenced Blake. Illuminated printing was a technique used by Blake. To save money, Viscomi told us, Blake used both sides of his copper. Viscomi did not stand at the podium or on the platform when he spoke and showed a colourful slide show. Wearing a body mike, he moved around the carpeted floor oozing enthusiasm for his subject. It was a joy to experience his zeal. Little did we know, at that early hour, that the first speaker up would prove to be the best of the symposium.
    Tilottama Rajan from *University of Western Ontario*, Canada was second up and her lecture was titled, "Dis-Figuring the System: Narrative Process in Blake's

Early Prophecies". Rajan stayed at the podium and read her speech to us, alternating her arms folded in front, held behind her back, or on her hips. Her scholarly approach was boring and confusing. She told us: "Blake is not to be read or looked at, *but felt.*" ....Huh?

Jerome McGann from *University of Virginia,* Charlottesville gave a humourous 10-minute "Response" to Viscomi and Rajan's lectures. He demonstrated that Viscomi gave an interpretive presentation and Rajan a critical one.

David Bindman from *University College of London*, Canada was next with "Blake and the Abolition of Slavery". He showed a gloomy slide show about slavery. It was a weary presentation showing little relevance to Blake.

Ann Mellor from *University of California* followed with "Sex, Violence, and Slavery: Blake and Wollstonecraft". She showed a gloomy slide show about sex and slavery. Mellor said Blake declared that wives are no different than blacks. She claims that Blake did not want to end slavery, but to liberate women. She gave an irksome report on female bondage.

Morris Eaves from *University of Rochester* gave a humourous 10-minute "Response" to Bindman and Mellor's lectures. He demonstrated that both used historical evidence for their arguments. He said that it is urgent that there be a contemporary understanding of Blake. ....Why?

The keynote address was given by W.J.T. Mitchell from *University of Chicago* titled, "Form and Chaos in Blake's Art". His extemporaneous speech was humourous and casual. He told us that Blake was first perceived as incompetent and mad, although a major artist. Mitchell proceeded to demonstrate with slides 10-feet tall that Blake was similar to excrement. He used the word "excrement" so many times that people were snickering and talking and rolling their eyes throughout! I can't truly tell you what he was going on about because it was nonsensical.

During a fancy box-lunch, a wine and cheese reception after the keynote address, followed by a three-course dinner, I talked with several attendees. Most were aware of Swedenborg. Mr. Viscomi enthusiastically admitted to me that he admired Swedenborg and was intrigued to learn that Czeslaw Milosz had written about Swedenborg in his book, *The Land of Ulro,* after I showed the book to him. Mr. Viscomi said he had seen Milosz the week before! Mr. Eaves told me about the recently published 5-volume series titled, *William Blake: The Illuminated Books,* Edited with Introductions and Notes by Morris Eaves, Robert N. Essick, and Joseph Viscomi. Mr. Eaves said he wanted a Swedenborgian critique of Volume 3 and asked me to review it. Its cover's fly-leaf states (*Princeton University Press*, 1993):

> The introduction and notes to *The Marriage of Heaven and Hell* offer a wealth of new information on how Blake used (and abused) the writings of Emanuel Swedenborg to stake his own claims to political and prophetic truth.

Each volume costs $75. I only bought one. I will review Volume 3, *The Early Illuminated Books,* in the future.

UPDATE

The future is now. I slogged through *William Blake: The Early Illuminated Books*. I want to scream from a rooftop: WHY DO PEOPLE SAY SWEDENBORG IS HARD TO UNDERSTAND WHEN THEY WILL READ THROUGH THIS STUFF?! Or did anyone? No doubt, one can enjoy this book's reproductions of Blake's art, but the scholarly articles are, well, scholarly.

This 5-volume series was commissioned by the *William Blake Trust*. You don't learn these facts from the book: *William Blake Trust* is an educational charity founded in England in 1948 by Sir Geoffrey Keynes and endowed by the estate of Walford Graham Robertson. The *Blake Trust* calls William Blake a "poet, printer, prophet." ....What? Prophet??

I call Blake a good artist that wanted an audience. An audience he didn't get when he published his works himself. Who was his audience for *The Marriage of Heaven and Hell*? People that knew about Emanuel Swedenborg's book, *Heaven and Hell*, that's who! Who else would have got the satire of his book? It took Morris Eaves, Robert N. Essick, and Joseph Viscomi 28-pages to explain what Blake was making fun of! Apparently, Blake had made fun ("satire") of others before. Was Blake not just mocking a popular book for his benefit?

From this book, I learned that Blake was born in 1757, the year of the Last Judgment as recorded by Swedenborg. Blake drew and wrote *The Marriage of Heaven and Hell* in 1790, a play on 33 years since the Last Judgment and Jesus Christ dying at 33. He includes "Memorable Fancies" in parody of Swedenborg's "Memorable Relations"—anecdotes of things he saw in the spiritual world.

The authors write: "Nonetheless, the extent to which the *Marriage* is saturated with Swedenborg has never been properly estimated or understood. Unfortunately, we have only enough space to provide suggestive traces of documenttation." Many references are given to Swedenborg's numbered paragraphs attempting to show where Blake got his info. I can envision Blake laughing at making the scholars work at this. It's ridiculous. I'm not impressed. Scholars scouring through the Writings looking for Blake comparisons is a futile use of the Writings. Did this exercise open up the hearts of these men? No, I don't think so. It was a treasure hunt for words. Read this (pp. 118):

> As intellectual satire, the *Marriage* fits reasonably well into the category called Menippean or Varronian satire, or sometimes anatomy, and fits best, perhaps, into the subcategory identified with the Greek prose satirist Lucian of Samosata (A D c. 125–200), whose works such as *Dialogues of the Dead, Voyage to the Lower World,* and *The True History* (3rd ed. in English, 1781) exemplify the Lucianic 'News from Hell' type (Tannenbaum).

Get that? I didn't. A writer reveals self as well as their subject matter. William Blake was jealous of Swedenborg and mocked him. Blake wanted to be the prophet. The authors of *William Blake: The Early Illuminated Books* want others to take Blake seriously and by throwing around terms and names the average person is not aware of tells the reader they aren't as educated as the writers.

After reading this book, I am not surprised now when people tell me that they've heard of Swedenborg through Blake, but know next to nothing about him. They're not going to learn about Swedenborg from Blake.

January 2006
Dear *SILA* Readers,

I absolutely cannot contain my excitement that Swedenborg's Theological Writings and all his other manuscripts—scientific, political, letters, diaries—are designated as so precious to the world, that they are now listed with the United Nations as something to be preserved and protected for centuries to come!! What an honour and forethinking on UNESCO's part that the world is not even truly aware of yet.

I think it's great and appropriate that the Program announcing Swedenborg's works being registered with UNESCO had the "wrong title" on it because the "wrong title" is absolutely correct as Rev. Ragnar Boyesen pointed out in an article in *New Church Life* magazine. Swedenborg's Writings ARE *The Memory of the Word!* He did give us the internal meaning of God's Word! Program was meant to read: "World" — *The Memory of the World.*

Remember, Swedenborg told us that there is no such thing as an accident. This "error" reminded me of the "error" that *LIFE* magazine made when they picked *The 100 Most Important Events and People of the Past 1000 Years* (1998). They picked Swedish botanist, Carl Linnaeus as #100, but printed Swedenborg's photo instead of Linnaeus's "in error"!

There are no accidents! Swedenborg is one of the most influential persons in history and what he wrote is and will be studied for thousands of years to come.

If you are one of the few that have discovered Swedenborg's Writings and because of them are consciously thinking and living as a new Christian, it is your duty to preserve and protect his books, and to share them with others because someone did that before you... *for you!*

Thinking of you,
Candace

From http://unesco.org:

> UNESCO—the United Nations Educational, Scientific, and Cultural Organization was founded on 16 November 1945. UNESCO has launched the Memory of the World Programme to guard against collective amnesia calling upon the preservation of the valuable archive holdings and library collections all over the world ensuring their wide dissemination. Documentary heritage reflects the diversity of languages, peoples, and cultures. It is the mirror of the world and its memory. But this memory is fragile. Every day, irreplaceable parts of this memory disappear for ever.

From *New Church Life*, January 2006; emphases added by me:

SWEDENBORG'S WRITINGS ELECTED TO UNESCO'S *MEMORY OF THE WORLD*

by Rev. Ragnar Boyesen

Two Swedish writers who have influenced the world's culture, Emanuel Swedenborg and Astrid Lindgren, were honored at a special seminar on November 8th, 2005, in Stockholm, Sweden.

The seminar was arranged by the Swedish UNESCO Council to inform the public of the two unique libraries selected by UNESCO for its Memory of the World International Register. As a cultural arm of the United Nations, UNESCO strives to document and preserve cultural treasures throughout the world.

This seminar marked the recognition of the importance of Emanuel Swedenborg's archives and that of the renowned author of children's books, Astrid Lindgren.

On behalf of the Swedish Royal Academy of Sciences, Professor Dr. Inge Jonsson, who originally proposed the Swedenborg archive for nomination, received a framed UNESCO memorial of acceptance. A brass plaque having The Memory of the World designation will be placed at the Royal Academy of Sciences, which cares for the more than twenty thousand pages of Swedenborg's original manuscripts.

Eva Hermansson, representing the Swedish UNESCO Council, explained that the international effort to create *The Memory of the World Register* started in 1997 as the prominent part of the familiar UNESCO World Heritage List. To date the register consists of 121 international collections of material of value to humanity from 57 countries on all continents. Selection of each library or museum is considered a unique honor to its parent country. Sweden's national archivist, Jan Dahlin, described the selecting process.

At first, the committee supposed that Swedenborg's influence was important only in northern Europe!

When the advertising for this seminar was being prepared, he explained, **an error was discovered in the heading of the program. It had UNESCO's unique register down as**

"Memory of the Word."

(Perhaps in more ways than one this mistake indicates an underlying dignity which is gently nudging the world to realize its importance.)

To explain the shifting fortunes of the collection of Swedenborg's manuscripts, Dr. Jonsson gave an inspiring account of its history. He outlined Swedenborg's development and described the document collection donated by the family after his death. A whole chest of documents was carted to the Royal Academy of Sciences where Swedenborg had been a member.

Efforts to have all the manuscripts collected and photo lithographed were begun. This was first undertaken by the Rev. Dr. Rudolf Tafel who was employed 1869−1870 to investigate, coordinate, and see the manuscript collection through this process. Production of 110 sets of 40 separate volumes, 500 pages each, was underwritten from America at a total cost of $45,000. The copying and binding were done in Tubingen, Germany and the volumes were later donated to major libraries in Europe. Funds for this noble effort ran out after one-fourth of the collection was completed.

Late in the 1880's, however, the final reproduction in 18 handsome volumes by a new photo-type process took place in Stockholm. It was financed by friends of the New Church in America and completed under the able direction of the Rev. Alfred Stroh.

Dr. Jonsson concluded his talk by remarking that no one becomes a prophet in his own country. Obtaining all the information relating to this manuscript collection was seen as a project for the future.

Some readers may wish to view the information about Swedenborg on the UNESCO web page: http//portal.unesco.org.

(http://www.newchurch.org/news/publications/NewChurchLife)

From http://unesco.org:

Emanuel Swedenborg Collection

Emanuel Swedenborg (1688−1772) is one of the internationally best known of Swedish writers. After a successful career as a scientist and a technician he went through a religious crisis in the 1740's, which ended in a revelation commanding him to devote the rest of his life to interpreting the Holy Scripture and reporting what he had seen and heard in the world of spirits and angels.

In obedience to this divine task, he spent his last twenty-five years writing a great number of books, in which he attempted restoring the internal sense of the Biblical Word, as he understood it. After his death in 1772, his manuscripts, some 20,000 pages, were donated by his heirs to the Royal Academy of Sciences in Stockholm, of which Swedenborg was a member.

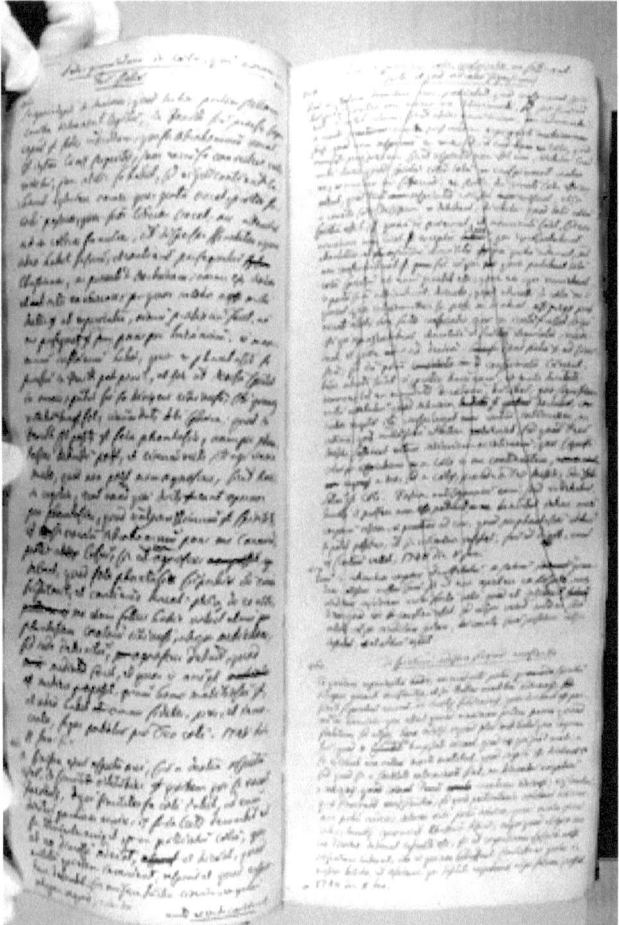
Pages of Emanuel Swedenborg's original dream notes

It is one of the biggest existing collections of manuscripts from the 18th century, and besides one of the very few in modern times that has served as the basis for a new Christian church. Swedenborg's message has found many receivers all over the world, and at least some of them look upon his manuscripts as relics. Because of their holy status many of the papers were also reproduced in a photo-lithographic edition as early as around 1870 by American and British Swedenborg congregations, and the technique was then used for the first time on a large scale. There are still quite a few Swedenborg societies and churches extant, particularly in the United States and the United Kingdom. Some of these are translating and publishing his writings in new editions.

http://portal.unesco.org/ci/en/ev.php-URL_ID=23259&URL_DO=DO_TOPIC&URL_SECTION=201.html

Dear Candace,

Did you know that at The Huntington *there was also a large shield (I do not know whether it was the original or a copy) of another Swedenborgian, a contemporary of William Blake, the sculptor Flaxman? This very elaborate shield is regarded as Flaxman's masterwork. I enjoyed the Blake pictures at* The Huntington *a number of years ago, while the largest exhibit is at the* Tate Gallery *in London.*

H.G.
Berkeley, California
June 1995

Dear H.G.,

John Flaxman (1755–1826) was the most influential representative of Neoclassicism in British sculpture. He even designed for Wedgwood pottery. Blake and Flaxman were good friends, by the way. I called up *The Huntington* and they do indeed have Flaxman's 36½ inch, round, silver gilded shield titled, "The Shield of Achilles" (1821). There were five originals and *The Huntington* in San Marino, CA acquired one in 1973. Thanks for sharing.

Dear Candace,

Bravo to you for all the work you've done. I am enclosing another bit of info about George Inness. His work is in the Art Institute Collection (Chicago) and for a long time they had an Inness Room—now turned into a gallery for contemporary decorative art.

Another well known New Church (Swedenborgian) artist of that era was Charles Francis Browne. There were more, less well known—all following in the scenic landscaped painting tradition.

K.H.
Chicago, Illinois
June 1995

Dear K.H.,

Thank you for sending *SILA* 20 photocopied pages from *The Eccentrics and other American Visionary Painters* by Abraham A. Davidson (1978). Thanks for highlighting all the Swedenborgian references! I'd like to share the following:

- "George Inness (1825–1894) was a devoted adherent of the precepts of the Swedish mystic Emanuel Swedenborg."
- "William Page (1811–1885) introduced Inness, around 1866, to the teachings of Swedenborg, according to which there exists a spiritual, invisible world, fundamentally different from, yet resembling, the world perceived by the senses."

- "Inness's funeral was presided over by the Reverend J.C. Ager, a Swedenborgian minister."
- "Without more elaboration, the writer of Inness's obituary in the *New York Evening Post* ventured that 'with more mental balance…he would have been the greatest landscape painter of any time or people.'"
- "In August 1851, in Florence, Page was living immediately below Inness, but the two men did not then have much to do with each other. The year before, Page had been introduced to Swedenborgianism by the expatriate American sculptor Hiram Powers."
- "William Page's Cupid and Psyche (1843) is in the Collection of John D. Rockefeller III, New York."
- "Page's portrait of his third wife, Sophie Candace Stevens Hitchcock, was begun in Rome in 1860 and finished in New York the next year. Page convinced her of the validity of the teachings of Swedenborg. Her ambition for Page led her to write President Ulysses S. Grant in 1877 to get him to pose for a portrait."

Dear Candace,

I can't remember the exact title of the Le Fanu novel, but he was fascinated by Swedenborg and read his work extensively, although nobody seems to have ever heard him express those beliefs. A large amount of his work utilizes ideas he got from Swedenborg. I think the book was Uncle Silas. *All of Swedenborg's works are terrific. I did read* Heaven and Hell *and about half of volume one of the commentary [*Secrets of Heaven*] on Genesis.*

S.H.
Los Angeles, California
July 1995

Dear Candace,

I am somewhat familiar with Swedenborg and Swedenborgianism. The only references I have run across being the influence of Swedenborg on the libretto for Berlioz's THE DAMNATION OF FAUST *and the use of Swedenborgianism as a plot element in Sheridan Le Fanu's* UNCLE SILAS. *I would, however, be interested in finding out more about the man and his works. What can you tell me?*

R.M.
Atlanta, Georgia
July 1995

Dear S.H. & R.M.,

Louis Hector Berlioz (1802–1869), the French composer, conductor, writer, and critic did write the music (1846) for the story, "The Damnation of Faust" by Johann Wolfgang von Goethe (1749–1832). Goethe, the German poet, novelist, and playwright was one of the most influential writers of modern European literature. Faust is considered his masterpiece.

"Faust" is described in *The World Book Encyclopedia* (1995) as follows:

> Faust is a man who desires complete knowledge, unlimited experience of life, and self-perfection. Guided by Mephistopheles, the devil, he moves from one realm of human experience to another without ever attaining full satisfaction. At the end of part II, Faust is saved by God's grace in spite of his guilt and pride. The devil loses a wager for Faust's soul because Faust continually sought perfection.

Both Berlioz and Goethe read Swedenborg and were influenced by him. In *Berlioz and the Romantic Century* by Jacques Barzun (1950, pp. 489), the author states:

> ...Berlioz made up mysterious syllables which he ascribed to the "unknown tongue" that Swedenborg speaks of as that of the damned...In the later version of the melologue, Berlioz substituted French verses in his own in order to keep for the Damnation of Faust the tongue he had invented. Hasty readers have thought that these vocables were given in Swedenborg's works but this is not so, nor does Berlioz imply it. The work of Swedenborg's that Berlioz read must have been The Spiritual Diary, also called Memorabilia.

I thank you, *SILA* readers, for bringing *Uncle Silas* (1864) by Sheridan le Fanu (1814–1873) to my attention as I was not aware of this novel. (I've read it now.) *Uncle Silas* is not to be confused with *Silas Marner* (1861) by George Eliot (another Swedenborg reader) nor with its current movie adaptation, *A Simple Twist of Fate,* starring Steve Martin (1995).

I found *Uncle Silas*—which is considered one of the first psychological thrillers—one of the most boring novels I have ever read. All the characters, including the main character of Maud Ruthyn, are gloomy, sullen, and grotesque. Cousin Monica is the kindest, in an odd gossipy way. This novel is a long drawn out mystery that circles around the suspicion of insanity, the catastrophe of suicide, and the suspicion of murder. And Uncle Silas is rarely seen!

Swedenborg is, indeed, throughout the novel. Sheridan le Fanu did read Swedenborg and was influenced by him. But, his Swedenborgians are portrayed as secretive, suspicious, and uncaring. Read this from Chapter 24:

> "Odd-looking person—one of the Swedenborg people, is not he?" continued the Rector. "So I am told."
> Who were these Swedenborgians who had got about him—no one could tell how—and held him so fast to the close of his life? Who was this bilious, bewigged, black-eyed Doctor Bryerly, whom none of us quite liked and all a little feared.

Dear Candace,

John W. Goethe was recently mentioned in SILA in connection with Belioz's opera. Goethe is "*universally acknowledged to be one of the giants of world literature*", as declared by the Encyclopedia Britannica. He was outstanding in poetry, dramatics, science and many other fields. It is not so well known that he called Swedenborg "*the most graced seer of all times, to who the angels spoke through all senses.*" His great drama "Faust" is generally regarded as the crowning masterwork that highlights the entire human condition.

The story begins in heaven, where the Lord gives the devil, called Mephistopheles (light-hater), the permission to tempt Doctor Faust by all available means. Mephisto confesses that he always wants to do harm and is confident that he will ruin Faust, yet he admits that in the end he accomplishes what is good. "*But this one you will lose,*" Mephisto says to God.

On Earth, the professor Faust, close to despair and suicide, promises his soul to the devil, if he will bring him real fulfillment, signing the contract with his blood. Mephisto promises "*You will be like God*" and introduces him to an unbelievable range of adventures and entertainments. In the end, however, Faust finds the fulfillment of his life in a gigantic project that will be useful for generations to come, thus saving his soul and bringing him close to his beloved Gretchen in the realms of the blessed.

In the last highly dramatic scenes, a number of Swedenborg's descriptions of events from the Other World (memorabilia) are woven in: A choir of angels strew roses, but over the devil and his associates, the flowers are perceived as some disgusting sticky burning substance like pitch and sulfur (Act 5). When the angels draw nearer, Mephisto draws back, although he feels attracted, for the atmosphere of love takes his breath away. He feels burnt out and he disappears, giving up his prey. Among the angels appear saints and novitiates to heaven, who desire to see the Earth through the eyes of someone on Earth. They turn away because everything seems so dark as compared with the bright spheres of heavenly love.

Gretchen, who had gone to heaven earlier, though condemned to death on Earth, welcomes Faust. She is surrounded by heavenly singing choirs. Among them are angelic famous figures from all ages, who have repented and are redeemed. Faust is invited to teach the newcomers about his experience on Earth, and the conclusion contains "*All things corruptible are but a parable*", reminding of what Swedenborg wrote **"The whole natural world corresponds to the spiritual world... also every particular of it..."** *from his* Heaven and Heaven #89.

Rev. Horand K. Gutfeldt, Ph.D.
New Church minister
Berkeley, California
February 1996

Dear Rev. Gutfeldt,

Thank you for a fine *Faust* synopsis.

I was privileged to have had an opportunity to see a Faust play performed shortly after writing the July *SILA!* *Randy Newman's Faust* was performed at the *Mandel Weiss Theatre* in La Jolla, CA, Saturday, 28 October, $37.00. Randy

THERE IS AN ANSWER

Newman is an American pop artist (*Short People*) and a movie music scorer (*The Natural, Maverick, Toy Story*). Faust is his first musical comedy play.

Newman read Goethe and thought *Faust* was a great story and that he's "always been fascinated by anything with heaven in it" (*People* magazine, October 1996). Yet, Newman is a self-labeled atheist. This is evident in his updated loosely adapted version of Goethe's 1788 play. Newman's God admits He doesn't really know the answers to many of life's mysteries. He is an egotistical, all too human-flawed God. He is a CEO out of touch with his flock. He smokes and swears. His heaven is a stereotypical heaven—for the remorse. Yet, the angels are wingless! Newman's devil is called Lucifer, nicknamed Luke. He is charismatic and profane. Newman's Faust is a *Dumb and Dumber* (1994 movie) character. To Luke, he asks, "Let me get this straight. I can have anything I want and you get my soul? What's the catch?"

This *Faust* has some catchy music tunes, but sparse stage sets, weak costuming, and a loss of the original story which is based on a real person, a Dr. Georg from the 15th century. This morality tale has been told in books, plays, and movies numerous times. It speaks to the price we pay for fame and fortune. Goethe's *Faust* is a cornerstone of German literature. *Randy Newman's Faust* is a statement on the lack of morality in the 1990s.

Swedenborg used this ornament in *The New Jerusalem and its Heavenly Doctrine*

Dear Candace,
You know, it is quite possible that more people have been exposed to Swedenborgian ideas than know about Swedenborg.

J.M.
Toronto, Ontario, Canada
July 1992

Dear J.M.,
I agree with you. Some are not aware that their beliefs came from Emanuel Swedenborg's pen...uh, quill! Here are some reasons why not:

- Swedenborg chose to publish most of his books anonymously or not at all. He was not on a personal quest for recognition, but on one to disseminate truth.
- Swedenborg wrote more than most people have time to read which left the door open for plagiarism by writers and religious leaders to claim as their own. The result was credit was given to others first, when truly it belonged to Swedenborg. This is not entirely impossible to prove.
- Swedenborg did not publish his scientific 4-volume work titled, *Brain,* which contained the first recorded discoveries of:
  a. the functions of the cerebellum
  b. the pituitary gland and spinal fluid
  c. the location of thinking and memory in the cerebral cortex
  d. the complete action of the nervous system
  Swedenborg wasn't looking for scientific praise; he was looking for the human soul! *Brain* was published 110 years after his death!
- Swedenborg did not publish his book, *Rational Psychology* (published 114 years after his death!), which espouses:
  a. the distinction between the conscious and the unconscious
  b. the correspondence between the natural world and the spiritual world
  c. the marriage of perception and reason
  d. the correlation of motives and ruling love
  e. the altered states of mental life
- Swedenborg did not name his philosophy or psychology, though his theology was named by his contemporaries as Swedenborgianism, much to his chagrin.
- Rev. Walter R. Martin, a Baptist minister, labeled Swedenborgianism a "cult" in his 1965 book, *The Kingdom of the Cults.* Martin praised Swedenborg the man, but designated his theology non-Christian. He wrote: "Swedenborg was a rationalist, and paradoxically, a mystic." The result was people believed Martin, for it appeared he had thoroughly analyzed Swedenborg in ten pages as he started with plaudits for his scientific achievements.
- Some people preferred spreading Swedenborg's ideas without mentioning where they came from, for the betterment of society in general, without threat of criticism.

Some of Swedenborg's "ideas" familiar to us are:

- the hypothesis for the formation of matter out of energy (a primitive atomic theory)
- the nebular hypothesis theory (how the solar system was formed from cloud)
- finding longitude by means of the moon
- slavery as deplorable
- kindergarten
- the airplane
- life on other planets
- dream study
- 12-step recovery programs
- the near-death experience

Swedenborg's doctrines can be glimpsed in Carl Jung's works, deciphered in Robert and Elizabeth Browning's poems, and seen as inspirational to the Chicago *World's Fair* in 1893. They breathed life into George Inness's art and changed death-art in the form of the deceased depicted as wingless angels.

Yet, the most striking feature of Swedenborg's contributions and the most controversial is that he tells us heaven is not closed. It is not as some graveyards are —for one faith only—leaving suicides, executed criminals, and unbaptised babies with unmarked graves in unconsecrated ground as the "unsaved".

Heaven is for anyone, no matter what religion. Anyone can enter heaven, if they have lived in faith and charity according to their chosen religion.

Swedenborg used this ornament in *The New Jerusalem and its Heavenly Doctrine*

Dear Candace,

Of all the reading I've done about Carl Jung I was not aware of Swedenborg's influence, although I see the similarities in their explanations of the Spiritual. I am most aware of Jung's relationship with and being influenced by Sigmund Freud. Even after their split, their theories remained basically similar (except in the areas of sex and religion). I have not read any of Swedenborg's books.

E.J.L.
Covina, California
June 1997

Dear E.J.L.,

The Swiss psychiatrist, Dr. Carl G. Jung (1875–1961) said of Swedenborg:

> I admire Swedenborg as a great scientist and a great mystic at the same time. His life and work has always been of great interest to me, and I read seven fat volumes of his writings when I was a medical student.

If you pick up a book by Swedenborg and can't make heads nor tails of it, please don't be discouraged. Try something <u>about</u> Swedenborg instead. I suggest:

The Swedenborg Epic by Cyriel O. Sigstedt
A Swedenborg Scrapbook by Brian Kingslake
The Presence of Other Worlds by Wilson Van Dusen
The Natural Depth in Man by Wilson Van Dusen
Poems from Swedenborg by Leon C. Le Van
Murder Among the Angels by Stefanie Matteson

April 2008
Dear *SILA* Readers,

Rev. Dr. Martin Luther King, Jr. (1929–1968) read Swedenborg! I learned that from the Swedenborgian Church of North America newsletter, *The Messenger*, February 2008, "MLK Connection to Swedenborg Revealed" by (New Church) Rev. Dr. James Lawrence:

> Morehouse College in Atlanta acquired the Martin Luther King Collection last year and recently provided a tantalizing preview of King's interest in the Writings of Emanuel Swedenborg.

I contacted my friend, Jim. He told me that our friend, Ted Bosley had made the discovery.

Thinking of you,
Candace

Dear Candace,
There's no more to be gleaned until they open up the new collection. They're guarding it like a pit bull at Morehouse College, which is probably what they should do. They have at least four to five curators working full time trying to catalog everything before they open the floodgates, which will be sometime around Christmas. So.... it will be interesting to see how substantial his "essay" is, but just from the snippet I've seen, I was impressed, because he doesn't make a generalized positive statement, but offers specific insights about Swedenborg's theology that indicates he really had engaged it to some extent. It will be so interesting to read what else he had to say! All the best.

Rev. Dr. James Lawrence
Dean, Swedenborgian House of Studies, Pacific School of Religion
Berkeley, California
www.psr.edu

I contacted Ted Bosley.

Dear Candace,
On the MLK Jr. connection, it could only have been Divine Providence that led me to see that written comment about Swedenborg in King's own hand.
I was at Sotheby's auction house in New York two years ago this June to meet with one of the specialists there who had handled a number of Greene & Greene objects in recent years and there happened to be the exhibit of King's

personal papers, which had already been sold privately to Morehouse College (see link to a New York Times article: http://www.atlantaga.gov/client_resources/media/mlk%20papers.pdf).

I had some time on my hands (rare) and so began to wander around the exhibit, captivated by the inspiring sermons I was reading in King's own handwriting. I could suddenly feel how his genius worked, the ideas apparently flowing directly from his mind to the page with few cross-outs or erasures.

I came to a small glass display case containing books from King's shelf and I noticed one book, Emerson: A Modern Anthology *edited by Alfred Kazin and Daniel Aaron (New York 1958). On the opening (blank) pages of his paperback copy MLK had written something. The name Swedenborg literally jumped at me from the page. Heart pounding, I searched for a piece of paper and pencil to record what I had just read, about the afterlife and how Swedenborg "enables us" to contemplate what it means to be present in life, and in the afterlife.*

> Swedenborg enables us to understand why we were created, why we are alive and what happens to us after our bodies die. Swedenborg enables us to have the best possible understanding of God's message as it exists in those Bible Books which constitute God's Word.
>
> Martin Luther King, Jr.

My mother had entered the spiritual world only two weeks earlier, so I was feeling the force of this message very personally. I was fairly certain, too, that no one in the sphere of Swedenborg studies had known about this heretofore obscure item.

Since the book was in a glass case I could not turn the page to see if there was more. I think there may be. I wrote in an email to Jim Lawrence about this back in September. (Why I waited so long to be in touch with Jim about this probably has more to do with my pretty full life, and regularly losing track of slips of paper, than my enthusiasm for the subject.) It seems to me that it may be worth a visit to the King archives at Morehouse College in Atlanta to determine if there is more of King's thoughts on Swedenborg.

Edward R. Bosley
Director, The Gamble House
Pasadena, California
www.gamblehouse.org

Dear Candace,
   Re: The quote by Martin Luther King, Jr. [April]. It gives me great hope, as evidence that the Lord's New Church is much, much bigger than the General Church and other [Swedenborgian] organizations that I know about, with all our failings.

Rev. Lawson Smith
Kempton, Pennsylvania
June 2008

THERE IS AN ANSWER 365

Dear Candace,
Being a woman of colour with no racism intended I find that a lot of your people tend to be atheist. Would you dispute what I have just written? Do you celebrate Xmas? Are you too of the opinion that the white race is superior to any other race?

B.B.
St. Andrew, Barbados, West Indies
February 1995

Dear B.B.,
I can't dispute you saying that a lot of white people tend to be atheist. There are some white Christian people that think nothing of committing adultery, robbery, or blasphemies. In fact, the Swedish author, Emanuel Swedenborg wrote that those people are really atheists in their hearts. Swedenborg said that a person cannot be a Christian, more than in name only, unless they acknowledge and follow the Lord God Jesus Christ which means living according to the Ten Commandments.

I, as a Swedenborgian, do celebrate Christmas. And, no, the white race is not superior to any other race of people. I am pleased you felt safe enough with me to ask such a hard hitting question.

The month of February is Black History Month in North America. A month to celebrate and tell the stories of African-Americans in lectures, exhibits, parades, and community activities.

The mass migration of Africans—"black gold"—to North America started in 1619. The first Africans landed at Jamestown, Virginia. In fact, there were exactly 20 blacks. The human cargo in a Spanish frigate was destined for the West Indies. But, the Spanish ship met up with another ship (unknown origin) and Captain Jope of the Spanish ship pretended that his crew was in need of food and he traded 20 humans for food. Those humans landed in ~~Jamestown~~.*

Carter G. Woodson (1875–1950) an educator, created the idea of Negro History Week in 1926. By the 60s, it had become a month long study. The month of February was chosen because Abraham Lincoln was born 12 February and George Washington, 22 February. *SILA* celebrates Black History Month because, for one thing, there are more black Swedenborgians than white around the globe!

Seven years after Swedenborg died, Charles B. Wadström, a Swede, organized a society of Swedenborgian readers for the purpose of abolishing the African slave trade. This group preceded all other efforts. Wadström wrote (*The Intellectual Repository and New Jerusalem Magazine*, 1866, volume 12, pp. 486):

> In the year 1779 a society of affectionate admirers of the writings of that extraordinary man, Emanuel Swedenborg, assembled at Norkjoping in Sweden, in consequence of reflecting on the favorable account this eminent author gives, both in his printed works and manuscripts of the African nations.

Wadström was sent by the King of Sweden on a scientific expedition to explore the west coast of Africa for a good location to put a Swedish colony to operate against the slave trade. Sadly, the new colony of Swedish and English settlers was destroyed in 1795 by French privateers, killing most. But, Wadström's two small books on abolishing the slave trade found their way into the hands of leading abolitionists around the world.

Rev. John R. Hibbard, a Swedenborgian minister, in his autobiographical article, "Reminiscences of a Pioneer" for the Swedenborgian magazine, *New Jerusalem Messenger* (1884), wrote about Abraham Lincoln, who he had met. Rev. Hibbard said that Lincoln's principles of religion and government had been largely formed from the Writings of Emanuel Swedenborg. It was common knowledge among Swedenborgians that Lincoln read Swedenborg's books. Some were given to him by his friend, the Honorable Isaac S. Britton, State Superintendent of Common Schools in Springfield, Illinois in 1842 or 1843.

White Swedenborgians have been organized as a religion in South Africa since 1850. In 1919, Rev. Theodore Pitcairn (a millionaire by birth) went to South Africa to become Superintendent of the Basuto (now Lesotho) New Church. My paternal grandfather, Fred Cavendish Frazee (1882–1966) went with his wife, Olive (Bostock, 1880–1972) to South Africa in 1920 to work at the Swedenborgian missions. Fred was Supervisor of the Missions for ten years and had organized a brass band there. Much of the missions' history is oral history as there was a fire in the 1930s and all documents were destroyed.

The white and black Swedenborgians worshipped together until the 1960s when they became victims of apartheid. The Swedenborgian missions were declared a white zone and black Swedenborgians had to leave. Now, with apartheid abolished, blacks and whites worship together again.

Besides the white Swedenborgians' missionary efforts, two black men, unknown to each other, in the early 1900s discovered Swedenborg for themselves in Africa. Each man converted thousands of Africans to Swedenborgianism. From their efforts, there are today tens of thousands of black Swedenborgians. Even though there are more black Swedenborgians in the world than white (I belong to a black church!), African-Americans have not embraced Swedenborg in as great a number. But, it is known that there are some African-American ministers (of different Christian faiths) preaching in their pulpits from Swedenborg's books!

UPDATE

*It was a Dutch ship, the *White Lion*, with an English Captain, John Colyn Jope that brought the first "20 and odd Negroes" to America, that arrived at Old Point Comfort (Fort Monroe), Hampton, Virginia, not Jamestown, in 1619. The Africans were captured from the Portuguese ship, *São João Bautista,* by Jope. He traded some of them for food on U.S. soil. Some scholarship says Africans were brought to Florida and Texas as early as the 1500s by Spanish explorers.

David Mooki (1876–1927), a Catholic minister, bought a second-hand copy of *True Christian Religion* in a furniture store in 1909 in Krugersdorp, South Africa. He was convinced of the authenticity of Swedenborg's words.

His son, Rev. Obed Mooki was "From his early friendship with Nelson Mandela and continuing throughout his lifetime..." (*A History of the New Church in Southern Africa* by Jean Evans, pp. 5). "In 1944 the ANC Youth League was founded by a group of people....Nelson Mandela...were among them. Obed was also one of the early members, and preliminary meetings were, in fact, held in one of the classrooms at the *Mooki Memorial School*." (Ibid. pp. 68)

Africanus Mensah (1875–1942), a Methodist missionary, discovered Swedenborg in Ghana in 1915 through an ad in an American journal. He started a New Church in Nigeria after he was tried and expelled from the Methodist Church.

"Portrait of a Swedish Gentleman Instructing a Negro Prince" (1789)
That title was changed in 1792 to:
"The Benevolent Effects of Abolishing Slavery"
or
"The Planter Instructing his Negro"

It is by Swedish painter Carl Frederik von Breda (1759–1818). (Pictured above reading a book by Swedenborg) Carl Bernhard Wadström (1746–1799) purchased Prince of Mezurado (Monrovia, Liberia), Peter Panah (c.1771–1790) in order to free him. Wadström paid for Peter's board and schooling and taught him about the Writings. He told him that blacks are equal to whites and can go to heaven! Shocking at the time!

February 1995
Dear *SILA* Readers,

Researching the African-Swedenborgian story was extremely fascinating to me since my family history is connected to Africa. Not only did my paternal grandparents work in South Africa, my father, Keith, was born in Durban, South Africa.

Fred and Olive Frazee adopted two infant white boys, not related to each other, two years apart. My father, Keith (born 7 May 1923, adopted December 1924) has memories of his father shooting snakes out of trees in South Africa. Once his father shot a snake that was under his childhood wagon! Keith was 7-years-old when his family returned to Victoria, British Columbia, Canada.

I never knew my grandfather, but I was told by my father that he was a chiropractor, an accountant, and a Royal Canadian Mounted Police Officer on the prairies. All these professions qualified him to work on the New Church missions in South Africa. Fred Frazee also assisted Rev. Theodore Pitcairn on his treasure hunt expedition looking for gold bullion aboard the Dutch Ship *Grosvenor* that sunk on return voyage from the East Indies in the 1760s. The *Grosvenor* treasure hunt is famous for its recovery attempts which have never been successful to this day.

My grandmother (who I knew) was a teacher at the *Academy of the New Church* in Bryn Athyn, PA (having graduated from *Columbia University*) when she met Fred while he was visiting Bryn Athyn. They married. She moved with him to Portland, Oregon, then Victoria, British Columbia, and then Zululand, South Africa.

I enjoyed calling (the white, New Church) Rev. Andrew Dibb (who I know personally) in South Africa, twice, to check facts for this February *SILA*. He laughed when I told him that we celebrate Black History Month. "It's black history month here," Andy said, "every day!"

Thinking of you,
Candace

UPDATE
Grosvenor found off the Transkei Coast, South Africa, 1999!
www.dispatch.co.za/2000/07/20/features/GROSVENO.HTM

Photo, circa 1930, *New Church Life* magazine (1930)   *SILA,* July 1995

Photo, circa 1930, *New Church Life* magazine (1930)   *SILA,* July 1995

Dear Candace,

As you might know, this week has seen the 200th anniversary of the passing of an act of Parliament in London on 25 March 1807, abolishing slavery. During the course of some research on the Internet, I came across an interesting item entitled *"William Blake and the Radical Swedenborgians"* by Robert Rix.

Rix discusses the many spin-offs of early Swedenborgianism into various social and political matters, such as human rights and the French revolution, as well as the effect of Swedenborgianism on intellectuals such as Goethe and Lavater. Rix notes [http://www.esoteric.msu.edu/VolumeV/Blake.htm]:

> Swedenborg had said nothing on the institution of slavery, but his mystical notion of the high spiritual status of the African race provided intellectual fuel for the abolitionist cause, which we otherwise mostly think of as couched in the Evangelical idiom of William Wilberforce or Hannah More. The link between Swedenborg and abolitionism goes back to 1779 when Wadström, in Norköpping, had established a society, which was probably the first organised abolitionist movement in the world. He writes in an account that this was "a society of affectionate admirers of the Writings of that extraordinary man, Emanuel Swedenborg ... in consequence of reflection on the favourable account this eminent author gives, both in his printed works and manuscripts of the African Nations."

On contacting a friend, Rev. Risto Rundo of the Lord's New Church, over Rix's article, he responded (in part):

> I read somewhere that Goethe said about Swedenborg (in a letter to Lavater?) that he agreed with Swedenborg that the next life is an EXTERIORISATION OF MAN'S MENTAL LIFE. That is the best definition of the after life that I know. Also I read that Goethe wrote again to Lavater? about Swedenborg: "That old man in whose bosom the Angels lived."

So far I have failed to track down these two quotes of Goethe; Candace, can you throw any light on them please?

H.R.
Colchester, England
April 2007

Dear H.R.,

No, I wasn't aware of the Bicentenary of the 1807 Abolition of the Slave Trade Act in England. Thank you for bringing such a wonderful moment in history to my attention!

Americans celebrate Juneteenth (June 19th) as Emancipation Day for freed African-Americans. Texas was the last state to free its slaves, 19 June 1865. (www.juneteenth.com) This day represents a special day of freedom in all parts of the United States. Swedenborgians celebrate June 19th, 1770 as the birthday of their religion. So, FREEDOM DAY is an appropriate celebration for the world!

I am aware of Carl Bernhard Wadström (1746–1799) and his passion for abolishing slavery because of what Swedenborg wrote about seeing Africans in heaven! What a radical thought in the 18th century! Wadström was born in Stockholm, lived in England, and died in France. He was one of the leaders who started the French abolitionist movement. In 1788, Wadström was baptised into the Swedenborgian faith in London. William Blake read Swedenborg and attended the same London New Church church as Wadström. In agreement with the New Church abolitionism, Blake wrote "The Little Black Boy" from *Songs of Innocence*, 1789.

OF NOTE
1) Lydia Maria Child (1802–1880), who read Swedenborg, wrote the first anti-slavery novel, *Hobomok: A Tale of Early Times* (1824) — a love story between a white female and a Native American male. She wrote *An Appeal in Favor of that Class of Americans Called Africans* (1833).
2) Abraham Lincoln (1809–1865), the 16th President of the United States (1861–1865), started reading Swedenborg around 1842.
3) Harriet Beecher Stowe (1811–1896), author of *Uncle Tom's Cabin* (1852), read Swedenborg.

I differ with Robert William Rix (Professor at the *University of Copenhagen*, Denmark). Swedenborg DID write about slavery! Slavery is not exclusive to Africans. I'll share a few (of many) quotes.

True Christianity #710: **"Does anyone fail to remember and love someone, who out of zealous love for his country fights an enemy to the death, so as to free his country from the yoke of slavery?"**

Apocalypse Explained #182: **"...that in the moral life of such a [person] there lurks nothing else but the desire of obtaining all things in preference to others, thus a desire that all others may serve one, or that one may possess their goods: it is evident from this that one's moral life is not moral in itself; for if one obtained what one aimed at, one would enslave others and deprive them of their goods. And because all means savour of the end, and are, in their essence, such as are their ends, on which account they are also called intermediate ends, therefore such a life, regarded in itself, is nothing but craftiness and fraud."**

Conjugial Love #499: **"[A deceiver in hell] will admit that these are fantasies and deceptions, invented to enslave souls, so that they can catch and shackle both great and small, rich and poor, and keep them under the yoke of their control."**

As for those Goethe quotes, I found this one by Dr. Marguerite Block of *Columbia University* who wrote in her speech, "Swedenborg and the Romantic Movement" (Invitation to the Commemoration Dinner, New York City, 1918); www.soc.hawaii.edu/LEONJ/LEONJ/leonpsy/instructor/gloss/block.html:

> In a letter to Lavater, he [Goethe] says: "No one is more inclined than I am to believe in another world besides the visible one; and I have imagination and vitality enough to feel that even my own limited ego can embrace a Swedenborgian conception of the spirit-sphere."
> ...Goethe, who at the age of nineteen, while ill at Frankfort, began the

study of magic, alchemy, Pietism, Herrnhutism and Swedenborgianism—an event apparently trivial in itself, but fraught with tremendous consequences for subsequent literary history.

Johann Kaspar Lavater (1741-1801), born in Switzerland, was a Protestant theologian, poet, and physiognomist—one who practices the art of judging human character from facial features.

From "Schoenberg and the Occult: Some Reflections on the 'Musical Idea'" by John Covach (*Theory and Practice:* Journal of the Music Theory Society of New York State 17 (1992) pp. 103-118):

> According to Max Morris (1899, 503; cited in Benz 1938, 156), Goethe's enthusiasm for Swedenborg's writings can be found in his review of a book by J. C. Lavater (Goethe [1772]), in which he recommends Swedenborg to Lavater as the "worthiest seer of our age" ("gewürdigsten Seher unsrer Zeiten"); and in a letter to Lavater dated 14 November 1781 (Goethe [1781], 371-74) in which Goethe voices his admiration for Swedenborg.

And in a letter dated 9 April 1781, Goethe wrote: "...From thinkers such as Swedenborg he learned of the intensity of the inner intellectual mystic experience."

THANKS to Rev. Erik E. Sandstrom in Bryn Athyn, for when asked, he produced this gem from Lavater's book, *Insights into Eternity [Aussichten in die Ewigkeit* (4 vols. 1768-1778)]:

> We [Goethe] wish him [Lavater] success in his enterprise, and if he will accept our advice he has pondered quite enough, nay already too much, on these things. Let him now lift his soul and gaze upon all this thought produce, like so much earthly stuff and feel more deeply the Spirit-Whole and only the Other in the self. To do this we wish him the inmost fellowship with the honored Seer [Swedenborg] of our times around whom was the bliss of heaven, to whom the spirits spake through every sense and member, in whose bosom angels dwelt. May their glory enlighten him and if possible so shine through him that he may know what happiness is and have an idea what is the speech of prophets when the unspeakable things fill the spirit.

The "Exteriorisation" quote was not found. Possibly, it is an incorrect memory. But, if any *SILA* readers know of it, please write and tell us.

Dear Candace,
Believe me the Feb issue of SILA *is probably the best issue, but you always out do yourself as time goes on. You have taught a lot about kindness and Swedenborgians. Rev. Andrew Dibb said it's black history month there (South Africa) every day. Well it should be that way here every day. I can count the white people on one hand that have truly been a friend to me in my life. You showed spirituality without a tincture of racism. Thank you.*

Anonymous African-American
U.S.A.
July 1995

April 2007
Dear *SILA* Readers,
As for Swedenborgian spin-offs, here's a doozy of a list written by Canon William Barry in "The Religion of America" in the *Atlantic Monthly* magazine (Volume 11, pp. 468–479) in 1913:

> Swedenborg was the father of Mormons, Spiritualists, Second Adventists; the direct guide of Thomas Lake Harris; the ancestor, several times removed, of Mrs. Eddy and her Christian Science. Swedenborg occupies in the development of these modern religions a place corresponding to that of Bacon as regards the Inductive Method. I am not speaking figuratively;—you may trace the amazing doctrine and its consequences along the path of Latter Day Saints, in the life and writings of Harris or Lawrence Oliphant, etc.

The other day, an acquaintance was telling me about her church and not knowing, I asked her what religion it was. Mormon, she said. I asked her what she believed. She told me that anyone can go to heaven, there are three levels of heaven, and marriage is for eternity. I delighted that she knew these things and didn't tell her they were from Swedenborg. I was just glad that the Lord had led her to these truths in a way best suited for her reception.

Thinking of you,
Candace

Dear Candace,

Let the fact you know you contributed be your main reward. If we wait on the world or the opinions of others we can wait forever. God notices. Best wishes.

Van
Wilson Van Dusen, Ph.D.
[author of The Natural Depth in Man *(1979);*
The Presence of Other Worlds: The Findings of Emanuel Swedenborg *(1974)]*
Ukiah, California
May 1988

Me and Wilson Van Dusen stand beside a marble bust of Swedenborg at the *Swedenborgian House of Studies* at *Pacific School of Religion* in Berkeley, CA, 9 November 2002. I went there to hear him lecture. Since Van's passing in 2005, his library and manuscripts were given to *Swedenborgian Library and Archives* at *SHS*.

Two of Swedenborg's small oil lamps are in the *Swedenborgian House of Studies*!! When I held Swedenborg's lamps in my hands, I cried with joyous awe. I was touching something a great man had touched! This is not worship of a man, but admiration of a servant of the Lord. I am so thankful for Swedenborg, the man. By the earthly dim light from his small lamps, Swedenborg wrote brilliant words which will ignite us up.

May 2006
Dear *SILA* Readers,

I found this eye-opening comment by the actor/writer John Intini which was in *Maclean's* (Canadian magazine), 7 November 2005: "I wonder what God thinks about Jesus. For real. We never get his take. You know, just normal father-son stuff." Oh my, I had never thought about that before. I guess millions of people have thought about such a scenario. The reason there wasn't one, however, is because they are the same person!

I agonized over how to answer Z.M.'s question. Z.M's acceptance of the Writings as true, yet thinking that only "New" Christians will be allowed in heaven, is to me another reason why Swedenborgianism has not grown rapidly! It's not fully understood. Too many people want to close heaven to only those of their chosen faith. Elitism. (I-know-the-truth-and-you-don't!) That's what's unique about Swedenborgianism. It's a belief that anyone can become an angel. What's so horrible about that?

I like that Z.M. thinks that *"the acceptance of the Writings of Swedenborg will spread like wildfire and grow exceedingly fast electrifying the world"*. But, I say, not until the Writings are understood!

Yes, to be in heaven one must know, believe, and love that the Lord is God (One Divine Person) and in loving Him you live by His Ten Commandments. But, in His mercy, if you don't know or understand that concept on earth (even after being told!), you will have a decade or two to grasp it after your natural death.

The beginnings of the New Church religion as described by Swedenborg, first began in heaven and then trickled down to earth. (Swedenborg said he saw the Lord gather His twelve disciples together, June 19th 1770 and told them to evangelize once again, but this time around the spiritual world.) The first earth-converts to Swedenborgianism debated whether there should be a distinct religion called "New Church" or a melding of current religions with the Writings—extra theological curricula. (You know, like Tom Cruise says, one can be a Catholic-Scientologist or a Jewish-Scientologist. Is that true? Can it work? I doubt it.)

Though the teachings of the Writings were "new" to the first church-building-converts in the 18th century, the first male receivers of the Second Coming were from the "old" Christian churches with their notions of how church should be—somber, stoic, plain-spoken, with little emotion. Swedenborgianism remained that way, secluded and scholarly, until the 1960s, when its church summer camps fostered a new openly emotional movement. But, it must evolve more!

The Writings are too big, too important, and too thrilling to be for just another Protestant church. No need to protest anymore. True spiritual freedom was restored during Swedenborg's lifetime. He witnessed the new age's birth—the Last Judgment took place in the spiritual world in 1757.

Have I given too much information? Not to my thinking. It just may take some people decades to grasp the new truths. While a few "get it" upon first discovering the Writings, most don't. Swedenborgianism actually won't spread like wildfire, for then it would be burning a path threatening destruction instead of healing. Swedenborgianism will spread like sunshine for then it will warm with love and shed light with understanding, spiritually into hearts and minds.

Thinking of you,
Candace

Dear Candace,

Your letters are great! I like the way you talk to people and enlighten them. You are much better than the reverends of the New Church. They preach like other Christian priests.

A long time ago I wondered why Swedenborg stopped with the Arcana *[Secrets of Heaven] after the two Moses books. But when I tried to explain "Israel" and "Egypt" in a little essay, I found out, that he had said it all in Moses I and II. After leading the children of Israel out of Egypt, they had been lead out from hell. And the highest level to reach was reached by the Lord, because He alone fulfilled the true Sabbath. It's all described there.*

So it wasn't really necessary to give a "verse-by-verse" exposition for the four Gospels. It would have been too long anyhow. But it's not easy to find out. You really have to study Swedenborg quite well. No wonder your reader K.P. asked this question in the April issue. Whole Mankind are children of Israel, and that's why the Bible explains it all, even for all other religions. Swedenborg was the seer who really saw! You know all that. I always get excited when I start reading Swedenborg.

I think there already is a lot of Swedenborgianism in the world, although people are not aware of it. But the ideas are there. I can see it among YOUNG people. They get the truth directly into their hearts without books and preachers. It is like you wrote in your May SILA: *"Swedenborgianism will spread like sunshine for then it will warm with love and shed light with understanding, spiritually into hearts and minds". Thank you for your wonderful engagement for Swedenborg!*

U.G.
Darmstadtl, Germany
July 2006

Dear Candace,
    More strength to your arm!

B.H.
Jyllinge, Denmark
August 2004
(never published)

I was interviewed on NBC news in Atlanta where I directed *The 3rd Angel Festival* during the time of the 1996 *Summer Olympics*. Mayor of Atlanta, Bill Campbell, gave a PROCLAMATION that 2–6 July 1996 were *ANGEL FESTIVAL DAYS!*

Dear Candace,

I was really impressed with the staff while visiting the Bryn Athyn Cathedral, they couldn't have been more helpful, informative and pleasant. I sense that you and your organization are the same. It's rather ironic that the one Christian religion that makes the most sense is the one that is least known or understood. I'm really not a religious person myself but have quite a profound interest in religion.

R.W.
Lindenwold, New Jersey
June 2008

Dear Candace,

    Hey, you sign off on just about everything "Thinking of you". What exactly are you thinking of me?

Anonymous
Jefferson City, Missouri
September 2000

Dear Anonymous,

    I chose that "sign off" on purpose to help me focus on a spiritual love for my neighbour. The love that is essential of the church is charity. (The other essential is faith.) I am referring to "church" in the Swedenborgian context as being where the Lord is acknowledged. He is acknowledged in people's minds and hearts and not in brick buildings. Swedenborg says the church can be in one person!

Thinking of you,

Candace

Readers of the Writings

Drawing by Bridget Swinton   *SILA* Feburary 1993

BIBLIOGRAPHY

Bellin, Harvey F. and Ruhl, Darrell. Editors. Blake and Swedenborg: Opposition is True Friendship. New York, NY: Swedenborg Foundation, 1985.

Benz, Ernst. Emanuel Swedenborg: Visionary Savant in the Age of Reason. Translator: Nicholas Goodrick-Clarke. West Chester, PA: Swedenborg Foundation, 2002.

Benz, Ernst. Zeitschrift fuer Kirchengeschichte: Swedenborg und Lavater, pp. 153-216, 1938.

Bergquist, Lars. Swedenborg's Secret. London, England: Swedenborg Society, 2005.

Block, Marguerite Beck. The New Church in the New World: A Study of Swedenborgianism in America. New York, NY: Henry Holt and Company, 1932.

Bradley, Don. Freemasonry in the 21st Century. Burbank, CA: Native Planet Publishing, 1997.

Brock, Erland J. Editor. The New Philosophy: The Journal of the Swedenborg Scientific Association. Bryn Athyn, PA: Swedenborg Scientific Association, January–June, 2003; July-December, 2006.

Brock, Erland J. et al, Editors. Swedenborg and His Influence. Bryn Athyn, PA: The Academy of the New Church, 1988.

Corbin, Henry. Swedenborg and Esoteric Islam. Translator: Leonard Fox. West Chester, PA: Swedenborg Foundation, 1999.

Davidson, Abraham A. The Eccentrics and Other American Visionary Painters. New York, NY: E. P. Dutton, 1978.

Dexter, Henry Martyn. The Congregationalism of the Last Three Hundred Years, as Seen in Its literature: With special reference to certain recondite, neglected, or disputed passages 1876–1879. Harper & Brothers, 1880.

Diamond, Jared. Guns, Germs, and Steel: The Fates of Human Societies. New York, NY: W. W. Norton & Company, 1999.

Dole, George F. A Scientist Explores Spirit: a compact biography of Emanuel Swedenborg with key concepts of Swedenborg's theology. West Chester, PA: Swedenborg Foundation, 1992.

Eaves, Morris. et al, Editors. William Blake: The Early Illuminated Books. Princeton, NJ: Princeton University Press, 1993.

Evans, Jean. A History of the New Church in Southern Africa 1909–1991 and A Tribute to the late Reverend Obed S. D. Mooki. Cardiff, Wales: Self-published, c.1993.

Haley, W. D. Johnny Appleseed: A Pioneer Hero. (1871) Sandwich, MA: Chapman Billies, 1994.

Hallengren, Anders. Gallery of Mirrors: Reflections on Swedenborgian Thought. West Chester, PA: Swedenborg Foundation, 1998.

Henderson, W. Cairns. Selected Editorials. Editor, New Church Life, 1950–1974. Bryn Athyn, PA: The Academy of the New Church Press, 1978.

Hines, Thomas S. Burnham of Chicago: Architect and Planner. Chicago, IL: Phoenix, 1979.

Hyde, James. A Bibliography of the Works of Emanuel Swedenborg. London, England: Swedenborg Society, 2002.

James, William. The Varieties of Religious Experience. (1902) Touchstone, 1997.

Jones, William Ellery. Editor. Johnny Appleseed: A Voice in the Wilderness. West Chester, PA: Swedenborg Foundation, 2000.

Keller, Helen. My Religion. New York, NY: Swedenborg Foundation, 1986.

Kingslake, Brian. Swedenborg Scrapbook. London, England: Seminar Books, 1986.

Larsen, Robin. Editor. Emanuel Swedenborg: A Continuing Vision. A Pictorial Biography and Anthology of Essays and Poetry. New York, NY: Swedenborg Foundation, 1988.

Lawrence, James F. Testimony to the Invisible: Essays on Swedenborg. West Chester, PA: Swedenborg Foundation, 1995.

Le Van, Leon C. Poems from Swedenborg. New York, NY: Swedenborg Foundation, 1987.

Martin, Walter. The Kingdom of the Cults. Minneapolis, MN: Bethany House, 1965.

Mercer, L. P. Editor. The New Jerusalem in The World's Congresses of 1893. Chicago, IL: Western New-Church Union, 1894.

Moody, Jr., Raymond A. Life After Life: The Investigation of a Phenomenon—Survival of Bodily Death. New York, NY: Bantam, 1988.

Odhner, Carl Theophilus. Annals of the New Church. Bryn Athyn, PA: Academy of the New Church, 1904.

Raeper, William. George MacDonald. Herts, England: Lion Publishing, 1987.

Randi, James. An Encyclopedia of Claims, Frauds, and Hoaxes of the Occult and Supernatural. New York, NY: St. Martin's Press, 1997.

Rhodes, Leon. Tunnel to Eternity: Swedenborgians Look Beyond the Near Death Experience. Bryn Athyn, PA: Leon Rhodes, 1996.

Rose, Jonathan S. et al, Editors. Scribe of Heaven: Swedenborg's Life, Work, and Impact. West Chester, PA: Swedenborg Foundation, 2005.

Sigstedt, Cyriel Odhner. The Swedenborg Epic: The Life and Works of Emanuel Swedenborg. New York: Bookman Associates, 1952.

Silverman, Ray. Editor. Helen Keller: Light in My Darkness. West Chester, PA: Swedenborg Foundation, 1994.

Silverman, Ray and Star. Rise Above It: Spiritual Development through the Ten Commandments. Philadelphia and Phoenix: Touchstone Seminars, 2000.

Sluiter, Engel. "New Light on the "20. and Odd Negroes" Arriving in Virginia, August 1619". The William and Mary Quarterly, Third Series, Vol. 54, No. 2 (April 1997), pp. 395-398. Williamsburg, VA: Omohundro Institute of Early American History and Culture.

Söderberg, Henry. Swedenborg's 1714 Airplane: A Machine to Fly in the Air. New York, NY: Swedenborg Foundation, 1988.

Suzuki, D. T. Swedenborg: The Buddha of the North. Translator: Andrew Bernstein. West Chester, PA: Swedenborg Foundation, 1996.

Swedenborg, Emanuel. Letters and Memorials of Emanuel Swedenborg. Translated and edited by Alfred Acton. Volume 1 (1709–1748) Volume 2 (1748–1772) Bryn Athyn, PA: Swedenborg Scientific Association, 1955.

Swedenborg, Emanuel. Swedenborg's Journal of Dreams (1743–1744) Editor: William Ross Woofenden. Bryn Athyn, PA: Swedenborg Scientific Association, 1989.

Swedenborg, Emanuel. Arcana Coelestia 12-volumes (1747–1756) New York, NY: Swedenborg Foundation, 1905–1910. Arcana Caelestia, London, England: Swedenborg Society, 1983. Secrets of Heaven Vol. 1, The New Century Edition. West Chester, PA: Swedenborg Foundation, 2008.

Swedenborg, Emanuel. Spiritual Diary (Spiritual Experiences) 5-volumes (1747–1763) London, England: James Speirs, 1883.

Swedenborg, Emanuel. Heaven and Hell (1758) New York, NY: Swedenborg Foundation, 1979. The New Century Edition. West Chester, PA: Swedenborg Foundation, 2000.

Swedenborg, Emanuel. Miscellaneous Theological Works: The New Jerusalem and Its Heavenly Doctrine; The White Horse; The Earths in the Universe; The Last Judgment; and others. New York, NY: Swedenborg Foundation, 1988.

Swedenborg, Emanuel. The Four Doctrines: The Doctrine of the Lord, The Doctrine of the Sacred Scripture, The Doctrine of Life, The Doctrine of Faith (1763) New York, NY: Swedenborg Foundation, 1984.

Swedenborg, Emanuel. Divine Love and Wisdom (1763) London, England: Swedenborg Society, 1963. The New Century Edition. West Chester, PA: Swedenborg Foundation, 2003.

Swedenborg, Emanuel. Divine Providence (1764) West Chester, PA: Swedenborg Foundation, 1996. The New Century Edition. West Chester, PA: Swedenborg Foundation, 2003.

Swedenborg, Emanuel. Apocalypse Revealed 2-volumes (1766) West Chester, PA: Swedenborg Foundation, 1997.

Swedenborg, Emanuel. Conjugial Love (Marital/Marriage Love) (1768) West Chester, PA: Swedenborg Foundation, 1998.

Swedenborg, Emanuel. Posthumous Theological Works of Emanuel Swedenborg: Autobiographical Letters; Invitation to the New Church; The Canons of the New Church; The Doctrine of Charity; and more. New York, NY: Swedenborg Foundation, 1978.

Swedenborg, Emanuel. True Christian Religion. 2-volumes (1771) London: Swedenborg Society, 1950. New York, NY: Swedenborg Foundation, 1981. True Christianity. The New Century Edition, West Chester, PA: Swedenborg Foundation, 2006.

Swedenborg, Emanuel. The Apocalypse Explained 6-volumes (1785–1789) New York, NY: Swedenborg Foundation, 1997.

Synnestvedt, Sig. Editor. The Essential Swedenborg: Basic Religious Teachings of Emanuel Swedenborg. New York, NY: Swedenborg Foundation, 1970.

Tafel, Rudolph L., Editor. Documents concerning the Life and Character of Emanuel Swedenborg. 3-volumes (1875–1877) London, England: Swedenborg Society, 1877.

Taylor, Douglas. Spirituality That Makes Sense. West Chester, PA: Swedenborg Foundation, 2000.

Toksvig, Signe. Emanuel Swedenborg, Scientist and Mystic. New York, NY: Swedenborg Foundation, 1983.

Trobridge, George. <u>Swedenborg: Life and Teaching</u>. New York, NY: Swedenborg Foundation, 1970.

Van Dusen, Wilson. <u>The Natural Depth in Man</u>. New York, NY: Swedenborg Foundation, 1979.

Van Dusen, Wilson. <u>The Presence of Other Worlds: The Findings of Emanuel Swedenborg</u>. New York, NY: Swedenborg Foundation, 1974.

Waite, Arthur Edward. <u>A New Encyclopaedia of Freemasonry</u>. Avenel, New Jersey: Wings Books, 1996.

White, William. <u>Emanuel Swedenborg: His Life and Writings</u>. 2-volumes. London, England: Simpkin, Marshall & Co., 1856.

Wilson, Lois. <u>Lois Remembers</u>. New York, NY: Al-Anon Family Group Headquarters, Inc., 1979.

Woofenden, William Ross. <u>Swedenborg Researcher's Manual: A Research Reference Manual for Writers of Academic Dissertations, and for Other Scholars</u>. Bryn Athyn, PA: Swedenborg Scientific Association, 1988.

Dear Reader,

Creating my Bibliography was fascinating to me. The number of people that helped in my spiritual education is astounding. It's glaring to me. And to think that Swedenborg has no Bibliography for his books! His work was original. Anyone that writes an angel or spirituality book after Swedenborg's death, owes thanks to Emanuel Swedenborg. We are all just students of his. But, he'd say, *Don't thank me, thank the Lord.*

INDEX

A

abortion, 103–104, 249
abstinence, 45, 237
alcohol, 145, 197, 237, 239, 296, 303–304, 306–312, 314, 343
anger, 159, 197, 208, 255
apocalypse, 68, 76, 158

B

burden, 205

C

charity, 76, 103, 124, 146, 158, 159, 160, 193, 235, 246, 271, 275, 304, 321, 350, 361, 377
children, 62, 119, 125, 126, 147, 156, 183, 185, 214, 235, 343
corpse, 117, 122, 263

D

déjà vu, 45, 96, 97
devil, 29, 96, 117, 119, 129, 153, 155, 158–159, 164, 172, 192, 194, 320, 356, 358
dreams, 31–32, 60, 94, 108–109, 119, 173, 185, 256–257

E

emotion, 32, 91, 111, 215, 254
enlightenment, 36, 152, 164
eternity, 20, 30, 47, 51, 76, 95, 105, 124, 130, 143–144, 156, 172, 174, 195–196, 204–205, 213–214, 217–218, 221, 234, 243, 270–271, 273, 315–316, 323, 372
evil, 13, 30, 32, 45, 65, 71, 81, 94, 96, 100, 108–110, 116–118, 120, 124–127, 129–130, 140, 144, 145–146, 148, 153, 160–162, 164, 168, 183–184, 196, 198, 199, 206, 208–209, 211, 214, 226, 237–239, 251–252, 254–255, 257, 276, 297, 321–322, 342

F

faith, 23, 56, 61, 66, 76, 81, 96, 103, 119, 137, 146–147, 160, 180, 181, 186, 189, 192–193, 199, 202, 205, 229, 235, 246, 249, 257–258, 264–265, 270–271, 275, 276, 278, 302–304, 309, 321, 323, 325, 343, 361, 370, 374, 377
fear, 29, 118, 122, 124, 144, 192, 204, 244, 273, 319
food, 14, 123, 162
freedom, 36, 45, 51, 60, 68, 71, 77, 78, 96, 103, 118, 124, 144, 160, 161, 166, 172, 177, 179, 183, 199, 205, 206, 234, 236, 239, 247, 310, 370, 374
future, 32, 50–51, 76, 77–78, 82, 118–120, 123, 168, 171

H

happiness, 65, 76, 111, 118, 200, 202, 213–214, 218, 220, 372
hatred, 126, 192, 202, 205, 218, 255, 319, 358
hell, 55, 58, 65, 97, 104, 110, 116, 125–126, 129, 134–135, 159, 196, 214, 276, 320

I

infancy, 71, 129, 166, 199, 344
intelligent design, 132
intuition, 129, 315

K

kill, 104–105, 196, 205, 237, 239, 296

L

last judgment, 29, 71, 76, 203, 205, 243–244, 248, 263, 350, 374

M

millennium, 231–232, 322–323
miracles, 66, 77–78, 94, 120, 134, 173, 234
morality, 238, 359
murder, 129, 196
mysteries, 84, 95, 138–139, 189, 199, 202, 206, 236, 262, 265, 304, 358

N

new earth, 137, 243

P

pain, 129, 139
peace, 92, 134, 322–323
perception, 217, 257–258, 360
prayer, 45, 65, 120, 135, 138, 162, 202, 208–209, 229, 246–247, 269, 304
psychic, 49–51, 119
psychology, 2, 21, 24, 228, 231, 360

R

reincarnation, 31–32, 96, 97, 119, 315, 320
repent, 45, 147, 197, 208, 250, 304, 358

S

sad, 84, 93, 111, 211
second coming, 13, 23, 32, 70, 88–90, 129, 134, 137, 194, 205, 213, 245, 247, 374
secret, 21, 65–66, 90, 129, 167, 189, 217, 230, 273, 311
self examination, 45, 172, 198, 279, 304
sex, 20, 56, 62, 103, 118, 131, 145, 214, 253, 317, 362
sin, 13, 45, 119, 147, 164, 193, 205, 270, 307, 320, 342
smoking, 45
suffering, 128, 139, 270
suicide, 9, 82, 196, 357, 358

T

temptation, 128, 134, 139, 152, 313, 340
Ten Commandments, 104, 126, 135, 143–144, 146, 196, 208–209, 217, 248, 258, 365, 379
theology, 129, 271, 276, 307, 321, 323, 346, 360, 363
time and space, 95, 123, 132, 215

V

vegetarianism, 237–240, 296

W

wings, 92, 149–150, 166, 169–171, 180–181
wisdom, 20, 32, 46, 56, 65, 82, 90, 101–102, 111–112, 118–119, 127, 129, 139–141, 143, 145, 152, 155–156, 158–159, 164, 171, 177, 180–181, 202, 206–207, 216–217, 227, 229–230, 241, 247, 263, 278, 291, 304–306, 313, 319

©Sweden Post Stamps

Dear Reader,

It was very difficult for me to end this book. There is soooo much more I want to share. Oh, well, I can tell you more in next month's *SILA*! Write me. To receive a reply, please send a self-addressed stamped envelope.

Thinking of you,

Candace

Drawing by Bridget Swinton   *SILA* August 1992

www.ingramcontent.com/pod-product-compliance
Lightning Source LLC
Chambersburg PA
CBHW020634230426
43665CB00008B/163